THE
UNSPOKEN
MOTIVE

A Guide to Pyschoanalytic Literary Criticism

MORTON KAPLAN

ROBERT KLOSS

Fp *The Free Press*
New York

Library of Congress Catalog Card Number: 79–163609

printing number
1 2 3 4 5 6 7 8 9 10

Copyright
Acknowledgments

The authors and publisher have made every effort to determine and credit the
holders of copyright of the selections in this book. Acknowledgment is gratefully
made to the following authors and publishers who have granted permission to use
selections from copyrighted publications.

Alfred Adler. From *The Science of Living* is reprinted by permission of Dr. Kurt
A. Adler. Copyright © 1929, by Kurt A. Adler. Renewed 1957.

Franz Alexander and Sheldon T. Selesnick. From *The History of Psychiatry*
reprinted by permission of Harper and Row, Inc.

Maud Bodkin. From *Archetypal Patterns in Poetry* is reprinted by permission of
Oxford University Press, London.

A. C. Bradley. From *Shakespearean Tragedy* is reprinted by permission of St.
Martin's Press, Inc. and Macmillan, London and Basingstoke.

Joseph Campbell. From *The Hero with a Thousand Faces,* Bollingen Series XVII
(copyright © 1949 by Bollingen Foundation), is reprinted by permission of
Princeton University Press. From *Creative Mythology,* Volume IV of *The Masks
of God* is reprinted by permission of The Viking Press, Inc. Copyright © 1968 by
Joseph Campbell.

Frederick C. Crews. From "Anesthetic Criticism," Chapter One of *Psychoanalysis
and Literary Process* is reprinted by permission of Winthrop Publishers, Inc.
Copyright © 1970 by Winthrop Publishers, Inc. From *The Sins of the Fathers:*

THE
UNSPOKEN
MOTIVE

Hawthorne's Psychological Themes is reprinted by permission of Oxford University Press, New York.

M. D. Faber. From "Oedipal Pattern in *Henry IV*," in *The Design Within: Psychoanalytic Approaches to Shakespeare* is reprinted by permission of Science House Publishers. From *Suicide and Greek Tragedy* is reprinted by permission of Sphinx Press, Inc.

Leslie Fiedler. From "Archetype and Signature". First published in *The Sewanee Review* LX,2 (Spring, 1952). Copyright © 1952 by The University of the South. Used by permission. From "Come Back to the Raft Ag'in, Huck Honey!" from the book *Psychoanalysis and American Fiction* edited by Irving Malin. Copyright © 1965 by Irving Malin. Published by E. P. Dutton and Co. Inc. in paperback and reprinted with their permission. From *Love and Death in the American Novel* is used by permission of Stein and Day/Publishers. Copyright © 1960, 1966 by Leslie A. Fiedler.

Louis Fraiberg. From *Psychoanalysis and American Literary Criticism* is reprinted by permission of Wayne State University Press and Louis Fraiberg.

Sigmund Freud. From *The Standard Edition of the Complete Psychological Works of Sigmund Freud (passim)* is reprinted by permission of Basic Books, Inc. from *The Collected Papers of Sigmund Freud,* edited by Ernest Jones, M.D., Basic Books, Inc., Publishers, New York, 1959.

Wilfred L. Guerin *et al.* From *A Handbook of Critical Approaches to Literature* is reprinted by permission of Harper and Row, Inc.

Frederick J. Hoffman. From *Freudianism and the Literary Mind* is reprinted by permission of Louisiana State University Press.

Norman N. Holland. From "Romeo's Dream and the Paradox of Literary Realism," *Literature and Psychology,* 13 No. 4(1963) is reprinted by permission of Leonard Manheim. From *Psychoanalysis and Shakespeare* is reprinted by permission of McGraw-Hill Publishers. From *The Dynamics of Literary Response* is reprinted by permission of Oxford University Press, New York.

Aldous Huxley. From *Tomorrow and Tomorrow and Tomorrow and Other Essays* is reprinted by permission of Harper and Row, Inc.

Stanley Edgar Hyman. From *The Armed Vision* is reprinted by permission of Alfred A. Knopf Inc. and Mrs. Stanley Edgar Hyman.

Jolande Jacobi. From *The Psychology of C. G. Jung* is reprinted by permission of Yale University Press and Routledge and Kegan Paul Ltd., London.

Ernest Jones. From *The Life and Work of Sigmund Freud,* Volume II by Ernest Jones, M.D., Basic Books, Inc., Publishers, New York, 1955. Used by permission. From *Hamlet and Oedipus* is reprinted by permission of W. W. Norton & Co., Inc. and Victor Gollancz Ltd., London.

C. G. Jung. From *The Collected Works of C. G. Jung,* ed. by G. Adler, M. Fordham, H. Read, trans. by R. F. C. Hull, Bollingen Series XX, volume 6, *Psychological Types* (copyright © 1971 Princeton University Press), vol. 7, *Two Essays on Analytical Psychology* (copyright © 1953 and 1966 by Bollingen Foundation), vol. 9i, *The Archetypes and the Collective Unconscious* (copyright

Contents

Preface   ix

Acknowledgments   xi

Psychoanalysis and Literary Criticism   1

Fantasy in Fiction   45

Fantasy of Immortality:
Conrad's *The Nigger of the
Narcissus*   47

Fantasy of Passivity:
Melville's *Bartleby the Scrivener*   63

Fantasy of the Devouring Killer:
Kafka's *A Hunger Artist*   80

Fantasy of the Family Romance:
Shakespeare's *The Tempest*   88

Fantasy of Innocence:
Sophocles' *Oedipus the King*   105

Fantasy of Paternity and the
Doppelgänger:
Mary Shelley's *Frankenstein*   119

The Development of Psychoanalytic Criticism   147

Appendix: The Dissenting Schools   287

Index   315

Preface

In 1906, with psychoanalysis in its earliest years, Jung brought to Freud's attention a little-known novel by a German writer of the nineteenth century, *Gradiva* by Wilhelm Jensen. Freud found in this work a dramatization of his major discoveries: the repression of infantile sexuality, its disguised "return" in the form of a neurosis, and the dispelling of that neurosis by the equivalent of a psychoanalytic treatment. He published his analysis of the novel the following year, and so began the alliance of depth psychology and literary criticism.

Freud was more concerned with demonstrating the validity of his theories than with interpreting literature for its own sake. If artists commonly depict the unconscious, he declared, then artist and analyst are "both right or both wrong." Having already found the oedipus complex in works of Sophocles, Shakespeare, and Dostoyevsky, artists acknowledged to have held the mirror to nature, Freud had indeed found striking support for psychoanalysis in spheres removed from his private practice, from the Viennese middle class, and from the century in which he lived.

In the decades that followed, and with this new means of probing the motives of fictional characters, psychoanalysts and critics alike were able to demonstrate how pervasive in fiction are the irrational, the infantile, the unconscious. Notable examples are Marie Bonaparte's *Life and Works of Edgar Allan Poe*; Ernest Jones' *Hamlet and Oedipus*; studies by such men as Ernst Kris, Hanns Sachs, Lawrence S. Kubie, Simon Lesser, Norman Holland, Phyllis Greenacre, and Frederick C. Crews; and many shorter analyses in the psychoanalytic and literary journals.

The Unspoken Motive is an attempt to bring together the various components of this discipline in a single text. Part I offers the basics of psychoanalytic theory in the context of illustrations from fiction, and the criteria which justify and make fruitful the application of this theory to literature in general. Part II offers examples of psychoanalytic criticism, with emphasis given to the ways in which fiction exemplifies how characters are moved by unconscious fantasies far more than by any preoccupation with the world in which they live. Part III offers an historical and critical review of the leading psychoanalytic critics from Freud to the present, with emphasis on a methodology for their evaluation. At the conclusion there is a brief account of some dissident psychological theories and a bibliography of basic works. Parts I and II have been written by Dr. Kaplan; Part III and the section on the dissidents by Dr. Kloss.

Acknowledgments

I wish to express my indebtedness to Dr. Jacob A. Arlow, who in so many ways helped me to understand the power of the unconscious, and to Leonard F. Manheim, who first drew me into the field of psychoanalytic criticism, and with whom the idea for this book was first conceived.

M.N.K.

In gratitude to my parents, who first gave me life; to Dr. Ira Mintz, who has helped me see it steadily and see it whole; and to Jackie, who renews it daily.

R.J.K.

Psychoanalysis and Literary Criticism

Psychoanalysis has been a beleaguered science since its inception, understandably so, in view of the established beliefs it has opposed. Freud found a parallel in the discoveries of Copernicus and Darwin, which met with fierce rejection for "outraging man's naive self-love": the earth taken from the center of the heavens, man made kin to the ape, and finally consciousness reduced to no more than a piece of our mental life. A belief in the unconscious is indeed the cornerstone of Freud's psychology; the shibboleth, he called it, of the psychoanalyst. But vanity is only part of the reason that even today many deny its existence, since men will, in fact, readily acknowledge appetites, passions, fears, and irrational goals whose source within themselves they do not understand. A fuller explanation of this denial has to do with the infantile character of the motives themselves which psychoanalysis attributes to unconsciousness.

The concepts that infantile behavior is sexual and holds the model for perversions, that the young harbor incestuous and homicidal feelings which they may never outgrow, that even healthy adult behavior may have roots in the unconscious and infantile, are all provocative in the extreme and difficult for many to accept. We do not wish to think that we have failed in any respect to outgrow our childhood. We take pride in the status of adulthood, achieved only after many years of longing for the power, pleasure, and responsibilities which it brings. Acceptance into society has required that the passions of infancy be given up. And when psychoanalysis constrains us to see that we have been less successful in that regard, our whole identity, our sense of security in the world, and our self-esteem are all challenged. Such jeopardy is powerful reason for being disposed to deny the validity of Freud's doctrines. It is, ironically, in our very desire to be mature that we may resist recognition of how much in us has remained immature.

There is a further reason for this opposition to psychoanalytic theory. It is generally felt that the Freudian insists on abolishing man's virtues and viewing them as merely a screen which covers baser motivation—finding, for instance, perverted sexual desires where nothing sexual is intended, and ferocious hostility at the heart of generosity and self-sacrifice. And never (so the protest goes) will the Freudian accept the assertion that such emotions are far from one's mind, since the analyst comes armed with the "Unconscious" and can always say, "You think it but don't know it."

In fact, however, the reverse is true. The Freudian conception of neurosis affirms the lengths to which men will go, the sacrifices they will make, to be moral. It takes no analyst to tell the world that men harbor sexual and aggressive passions. The uniqueness of the Freudian view is precisely that it predicates so much on the wish to be good and virtuous. Psychoanalysis points specifically to the need for expiation born of guilt and to defenses against unbridled passions as the root of neurosis. And it views viciousness and corruption as a traumatic inheritance from childhood—from a time when one's nature is as yet unformed, when one is necessarily uncivilized. Freedom from neurosis, in the Freudian sense, is not a liberation from restrictive morality, but a more successful severance from childhood, which ends the need for expiation and defense.

Many traditional literary critics object fervently to the use of psychoanalysis in criticism for reasons quite apart from the question of its scientific validity. All too often, however, their objections demolish straw men. They rightly repudiate some works of psychoanalytic criticism, but fail to attribute their defects to plain critical ineptness or an amateurish grasp of theory. The justification which critics offer for a theoretical opposition to this criticism, however, is more complex and one which we must examine in some detail. In the first place, it is asserted that characters in fiction can have no unconscious thoughts; and that if we attribute these thoughts to them, it is entirely an invention of our own. Strictly speaking, this is true. But, also strictly speaking, neither can it be said that characters in fiction have conscious thoughts. They have no thoughts whatever. They are, it has been pointed out, no more than ink on paper.

Fictional characters are representations of life and, as such, can only be understood if we assume they are real. And this assumption allows us to find unconscious motivation by the same procedure that the traditional critic uses to assign conscious ones. For instance, if a male character announces to a young lady that he loves her, we are disposed to think that he is telling the truth. If he then proposes marriage, we conclude that his intentions are genuine. But if he subsequently does not show on the day of the ceremony and later claims that he overslept, we begin to view him differently. If he misses the ceremony a second time with another questionable excuse (a business emergency called him away), we cannot help but question his protestations of love. Whatever may be the motives he acknowledges to himself, we must infer, in light of his behavior, motives of a very contrary character. And if he seems unaware of negative feelings about the marriage, we can only conclude that he does not wish to face them. They are painful to him, and so he denies them by ignoring their existence. He may, for instance, unconsciously feel guilt, or fear of sexual inadequacy, or violent anger.

Needless to say, as critics first and psychologists second we must look again to the text before a choice of motive can be made. But in looking to the text for an unacknowledged (that is, unconscious) motive, we still do no more than we did when we first believed in the completeness of his love. The text itself directs us to the unconscious as much as to the conscious.

This inferential procedure is evident in the essays in the next chapter of this guide. For instance, the analysis of Melville's *Bartleby the Scrivener* is predicated upon the disparity between the expressed wish of an employer to rid himself of an employee, and his endless procrastination in bringing the dismissal. The analysis of Kafka's *A Hunger Artist* is similarly based upon the contradiction between the ostensible and the genuine motives of a man who starves himself in order, he claims, to set a record and to astound the world, but who then fails to keep count of the days he goes without food. The analysis of Conrad's *Nigger of the Narcissus* deals with the fact that the crew of the *Narcissus* wish to vent their anger against a sailor who malingers, but nevertheless continue to wait on him in servitude.

The psychoanalytic view of Mary Shelley's *Frankenstein* is based on a scientist's inappropriate horror when he achieves a hard-earned success in a humanitarian endeavor to reproduce life. Insight into the psychology of Prospero, in Shakespeare's *The Tempest,* is gained through an analysis of the magician's fear of the very events over which he has omnipotent control. And in Sophocles' *Oedipus Rex,* the keynote of the psychoanalytic interpretation is the contradiction between Oedipus' confessed ignorance of the identity of his parents (as well as his wish to avoid parricide and incest) and his unhesitating murder of a man and marriage to a woman, both of whom are old enough to be his parents. In every case there is manifest in the text a contradiction between motive and behavior, so that unconscious motivation, objections notwithstanding, must be inferred.

Another objection to the use of psychoanalysis in criticism is that the author knew nothing of Freudian theories and may, indeed, have died long before such theories were first propounded. In this connection, one is reminded of the cartoon which shows a number of Greek physicians bent over their ailing patient. "We know what the problem is, Oedipus," they say, "but we don't have a word for it." Creative writers have never needed Freud to tell them that men lust for their mothers, rage murderously against their fathers, suffer guilts whose source they will not face; that they project anger to discredit others and so preserve good conscience, and turn to perversions out of an inability to establish normal sexuality; that they often deceive themselves about their own intentions more than they can ever deceive the world. Freud has given us a model and a vocabulary by which to understand how such things come to be, but he was the first to confess how well artists have always known intuitively the substance of his discoveries. In any case, the artist offers a dramatic description of life, not a formal interpretation of it.

Yet another objection is that in most works of fiction the literary character does not have a childhood. He begins life, so to speak, with the first page of the story or with his entrance upon the stage. And an analysis of his character which is based upon inferred circumstances, having to do with a childhood he never had, is almost sure to prove baseless speculation, a begging of the question.

This lattermost objection is often based upon a confusion between analysis of the text and more theoretical considerations which are not offered as an interpretation of the work. For instance, in our analysis of the hunger artist (Part II) there is a discussion of the childhood experiences which *might* produce the kind of self-imposed starvation that kills the protagonist. But the psychoanalytic interpretation of the story was the prior determination of how self-imposed his starvation was and how the unconscious motives for it were manifest in the story. If the psychoanalytic critic himself confuses the distinction between the two procedures, offering as criticism of text what is only psycho-analytic theory, he must then, of course, be taken to task. But a theo-retical consideration of how literary characters have their counterparts in life is in itself hardly extraneous to an understanding of the text.

Still another objection, and by far the most crucial, would have it that psychoanalytic interpretation is far-fetched and offers motives contrary to those which move men in life. To put it somewhat differ-ently, it is said that the analytic critic attributes an unrealistic degree of irrationality to fictional characters. For instance, in Part II we attribute to the crew of the *Narcissus* an unconscious wish to escape death forever. We view the hunger artist as a man who defends himself against his own inpulses to murder with his teeth and devour his enemies. The narrator of *Bartleby the Scrivener,* in the analytic view, adopts a delusion of grandeur in order to justify the passivity which rules his life. And Oedipus, it is maintained, pursues his questioning of others not only to obtain the truth, but also to obscure it for as long as he can.

In each case the objection of traditional critics might be not so much that we assign unconscious motives, as the nature of the motives themselves. They are, it might be said, too bizarre, too deranged, too illogical for sane and rational men. And since there is no alternative psychology to apply to these characters, the traditional critic frequently foregoes any analysis of them as individuals. The characters are viewed as prototypes, semi-allegorical figures who exemplify themes. The hunger artist, a man who starves himself to death in a cage, becomes every artist unappreciated by a bourgeois society. The narrator of *Bartleby,* who all but destroys his life and who escapes through no doing of his own, is simply representative Man who cannot disown his fellow man. Oedipus, we are to believe, is destroyed by pride, while fate and the gods are the instruments of destruction—as though the play were no more than pagan allegory and Oedipus the personification of Pride.

Such traditional interpretations, ironically, are more loosely tied to the text than the seemingly more speculative psychoanalytic view. The Freudian method accepts the starving man as precisely that, as one who chooses to die in a very real cage. Both the narrator of *Bartleby* and Oedipus (the solver of riddles *par excellence*) are taken to task for their failure to understand what others know without difficulty. Characters are interpreted in light of the premise that they possess all the complexity of people in life. If the Freudian points to the bizarre, irrational, or deranged motives for explanation, at least it can be said that this method makes itself answerable for every detail in the story—something often beyond the reach of a traditional approach which deals in conscious and rational motives only. Ultimately, this traditional objection to the Freudian method is based, not on its playing loose with the text, but on a repudiation of Freudian theory as such.

This repudiation returns us to the point at which we began. Psychoanalysis is not widely accepted as a valid and scientific psychology of man's behavior. It is the judgment of this writer, however, that the greater part of those who take exception to it do so out of a relative unfamiliarity with its theoretical depth and scope. Nothing, perhaps, could better describe how widespread is this unfamiliarity than the fact that even some psychiatrists who attend psychoanalytic training clinics to become psychoanalysts do not have, when they begin training, more than a superficial knowledge of psychoanalysis. Many of them then face for the first time as professional doctors the question of whether there is such a thing as unconscious motivation. And how widespread is a familiarity with Freudian theory among the far greater number of psychiatrists who do *not* choose to receive such training?

The situation on university campuses is no better. As a student in an introductory course in psychology at the City College of New York, I was once told on the first day of lectures to beware of "pseudo-psychologies, such as astrology, phrenology, and psychoanalysis." I have not forgotten the dialogue which ensued when I objected on the grounds that psychoanalysis was a valid psychology. "Why is it," the teacher asked, "that patients choose to see an analyst, and pay such large fees?" "To get well," I replied. "Why is it, then, that such patients are invariably reproached by the analyst for resisting the treatment?" he continued. "Because they do not want to get well," I answered. "Just so," he went on, "how can an explanation of behavior which contradicts itself be scientific?" On the simplest level, the teacher did not, perhaps, make allowance for the patient's ambivalence by which one rejects the very thing he seeks. But the objection had to do also with a facet of psychoanalysis not quite so easy to defend.

I recall that as a patient in treatment I had the feeling, lying on the couch with the analyst classically out of sight, that I was damned if I did, and damned if I didn't. If I spoke out, my problems were manifest. If I remained silent, that too was a symptom. If I spoke of my mother as I remembered her from childhood, I was told that I was steadfastly ignoring vital events of the present. If I concentrated on the present, it turned out that I sought to bury the analyst under the tedium of irrelevant information. If I expressed the anger felt during the day, that anger was judged a cover-up for other hostilities. And if I controlled anger, it was to run from myself. How could health be a thing separate and distinct from neurosis, I thought at the time, if there was nothing I did or said which would not supply grist for the Freudian mill?

I overlooked that that was the point of being neurotic. One can be neurotic in a variety of ways. It seemed to me for a time, as it did to this university psychologist, that the psychoanalytic method was a foolproof way of explaining behavior after the fact, without reference to controlled testing or other means to validate that explanation. This question of controlled testing is commonly raised by teachers in university departments of psychology. It is, indeed, the issue with which many decline to accept psychoanalysis as the dominant psychology of our day. And if such is the case with departments of psychology, it is not beyond expectation that departments of literature equally hesitate to stress the use of psychoanalysis in literary criticism.

It is true that psychoanalysis has a way of explaining events after the fact: describing, for instance, the forces which motivate the paranoid, without offering the means to predict who will become paranoid, or why one individual becomes a paranoid and another adopts a second disorder or manages to remain healthy. But Freudian psychology has not invented paranoia, or sado-masochism, impotence, frigidity, phobias, addictions, perversions, delusions, obsessions, compulsions, hysterical afflictions, or any of the other mental disorders which burden mankind. Yet it offers a single descriptive model, based on the facts of childhood development, which makes comprehensible not only these derangements but also endless phenomena besides—including dreams, slips of the tongue, forgetting, accident-prone behavior, jokes and laughter, reader and audience absorption in fiction and drama, the superstitions of savages, and the dynamics of mob behavior. And these facts are observable in all children.

The Freudian view of the child's nature—his fears, desires, misconceptions, the psychological "defenses" adopted for security, his strengths and weaknesses at every stage of development—is, in fact, the focus of psychoanalytic theory. The derangements of later life eloquently describe how completely the child is father of the man. Many people today are familiar with the oedipus complex, one's first, momentous exposure to a love-triangle. But even that complex is partly the inheritance of much that has gone before. In this respect, the growth of the human personality would resemble the development of the modern computer if we were to make one crucial change: If the first computer designed, as primitive and inefficient as it is, were not replaced by the next more successful model, but rather joined to it. And as succeeding models up to the most advanced and complex are made, each is merely fused to all that has gone before.

In this fashion, thoughts of the most realistic and complex run together with others primitive and unreal. Such a view opposes the

notion that personality is a monolith. Rather, it is full of disparate
pieces in even the sanest of men. In the adult, wishes from childhood
contend with mature aspirations, and for many men the gratification of
childhood desires may continue to give almost the only happiness they
know. The past fears of childhood, having no relation to the actual
threats confronting the adult, may nevertheless control behavior. And
the same may be said for the effects of undiminished infantile anger.
Guilt born of the turbulent thinking of early years may drown out the
innocence of adulthood desires—rather than the commonly assumed
reverse.

This momentous discovery of Freud's, the survival of unconscious
childhood feelings, has won slow acceptance in such small measure
because we cannot verify it on the basis of our own self-awareness. It is
difficult in the extreme to acknowledge that a desire, anger, guilt, or
fear is an alien intruder into our thinking from another time and other
circumstances. Rather than abolish these feelings, when we perceive
them, we look to the present to conceal them or to justify their existence. In *Bartleby,* for example, the narrator is for no external reason
afraid of conflict. But he does not let himself perceive that this fear
arises from within. Rather, he yields to it by "choosing" a profession
which avoids conflict. And we see only later how dominated he is by
this fear, past all reason and conscious awareness, when he is unable to
deal with a deranged employee who will do no work nor leave the
office.

Infantile anger may be concealed in the businessman who tells
himself it is a dog-eat-dog world and that one must murder the competi-
tion to survive. If he has chosen a highly competitive field, the facts will
seem to bear him out. But such a man may then find himself emotionally unable to distinguish his competitors from friends or his own
children. If they, in turn, abandon him in anger, it becomes harder than
ever to see that his own anger came first and that it rules his life like a
self-fulfilling prophecy. In this way, Kafka's hunger artist enacts an
infantile, phobic avoidance of food to control murderous anger. When
he is able to sublimate this behavior into an "artistic performance,"
winning fame and money by starving, he loses sight of the phobia. It is
only with the approach of death, when fame and money are no longer
to be won, that he is able to see otherwise and to recognize that he
starves because he must, out of inner necessity.

It is an invariable feature of the neurotic that he confuses choice and necessity. So long as he finds advantages in his behavior and so long as he can adjust his identity, find self-respect and a measure of fulfillment with his behavior, he will not know how forced his actions are. Indeed, given the fact that he prospers, there will be little to suggest that he *is* forced, and little to be gained from pointing it out. Neurosis, as a psychological condition, has meaning not in terms of what one should or should not do and not even in some hypothetical ability to change one's life at will. Rather it has to do with a pervasive rigidity of thought, in which inner necessity determines patterns of action even when they are clearly damaging to one's self. Neurosis is simply the inability both to learn from mistakes and to make a profitable choice of action based on what one has learned.

In this light, many things must be determined before the presence of neurosis is indicated. One obviously cannot make arbitrary judgments about what constitutes profitable behavior for other people. In a varied society such as ours, the most extreme of life-styles can have their meaningful place. We have the choice to seek wealth or freedom from possessions, the fidelity of marriage or the variety of a single life, the gregariousness of a social world or the withdrawal into music or books, political activism or raising orchids in the living room. If we seek danger or security, pleasure or responsibility, factual knowledge or the light of mysticism, no designation of neurosis for such goals is possible, save in the context of their forced continuance in the face of prohibitive cost and a helpless wish to change.

It would be impossible to calculate how extensively writers have made use of this distinction between choice and necessity. Frequently the dramatic point of an entire story is the gradual disclosure that what is taken by the fictional character and reader alike to be matters of choice are, in fact, fixed forces of inner motivation. For instance, the climax of *A Hunger Artist* is the artist's final recognition that he starves because he must. And Oedipus seems, for much of Sophocles' play, bent on obtaining the truth. But we find at last that he persists in his questions in a mechanical and meaningless way, long after the truth has been obtained. (Sophocles has Jocasta kill herself on fewer facts than Oedipus has gained, as unmistakable evidence of how irrational and forced his questioning has become.) The narrator of *Bartleby* seems anything but a man in the chains of neurosis. For the longest time we might take him to be somewhat irresolute, perhaps compassionate to a fault. We might judge him eccentric for choosing to relocate his business simply to get away from an employee who will not leave his office. But, again, the culmination of the story brings to the reader the insight that there is no limit, however costly, to the accommodations he will make to avoid conflict; and on this basis his protestations of conscious control are no longer credible.

It is both astonishing and tragic that men go to such lengths to conceal from themselves their own loss of autonomy. One thinks of Edgar Allen Poe's dictum that it had yet to be determined whether madness is or is not the loftiest of intelligence. If by madness is meant the inspiration by which we achieve creativity or the courage of mind and heart to find original solutions to the problems of life, such "madness" is no doubt sublime. But the world is full of lunatics who will claim as much for their lives. Every alcoholic corrupting on the streets of the Bowery, the killer in prison, the fanatic who burns himself to death with gasoline on the steps of the United Nations, the emaciated eater of grains and other "purified" foods, the crusader against the Communist-Jewish-Homosexual conspiracy who finally hangs himself as the last tribute to his cause—these men all make claims to the courage of their solutions and the worthiness of their cause. They persist in an unquestioned conviction that they rationally determine their lives, even when they "choose" to die. And if some, in a moment of anguish and truth, confess they cannot explain their motives, they are no less tragic and no less mad—so long as they cannot act to change matters.

These examples, no doubt, are extreme. But in a lesser fashion, many seemingly adjusted men in society exercise as little freedom of choice. They adopt professions, contract marriages, have children, vote, travel, live regulated lives and seem undistinguishable from their fellows; and yet through it all, they violate their lives with equal force, and without awareness that it is their own doing. The profession may bring endless anxiety; the marriage may be consumed with hostility; the children may be alienated by harsh discipline; the voting may voice the rancor of fixed prejudice; and travel may bring the boredom of a mind without interest in anything outside of itself. Such men are often eloquent in their disclaimer of responsibility. They are not "neurotic." Life is at best difficult. Wives are unreasonable, children ungrateful, and society corrupt. Nothing could be less credible to them than that they unknowingly conspire to keep their world precisely as it is.

Occasionally men glimpse the truth. A man who marries many times, but always the same kind of woman and with the same results, or the man "betrayed" by every child and every friend he has, may suddenly see that life cannot be fixed that way and that the fault must lie in him. He will, in all likelihood, however, be unable to change. It is difficult to disown unconscious motives, precisely because they are hidden; it is like trying to throw away a possession one cannot find. And we see this situation in fiction, too. The crew of the *Narcissus* realize in time that they are in the "spell" of a "weird servitude," but never why. The hunger artist sees that he starves of necessity but, not conscious of the true explanation, he offers us the untenable idea that he starves because he has "never found the food he likes." The narrator of *Bartleby* perceives that he "obeys a wondrous ascendency" which his clerk has over him, but never perceives the reason. And so, without knowledge of why they act as they do, they never change.

The dynamics by which unconscious motives direct behavior, and conscious ones are rationalized in order to make such behavior comprehensible and acceptable, can be seen with the technique which directed Freud to his earliest discoveries: hypnotism. It is possible to put in the mind of a hypnotized subject post-hypnotic suggestion which the subject will not remember when he awakens. He will then, for instance, remove his shoe in public in response to the suggestion that he do so whenever the hypnotist scratches his nose. The motive force is the suggestion, yet the subject is unconscious of it. And most to the point, he will automatically supply himself with an acceptable reason for his action—that his shoe suddenly hurt him or that his sock needed pulling up. The unconscious motive is manifest, the spuriousness of rationalization unmistakable.

This situation differs from a neurosis, however, on a number of counts. First, and most obvious, the action is neither costly to the individual nor continued habitually over a period of time. More important, the "suggestion" is received from the hypnotist; but the neurotic is as accountable for the motives which remain unconscious fully as much as for any conscious motive. They express only his own desires and fears. Finally, the hypnotic subject remains ignorant of the suggestion for no personal reason; he has been instructed to forget while in a suggestible state, and so he does. But the neurotic opposes acknowledgment of unconscious motives with all the repressive force which caused them to be disowned in the first place. The neurotic resists facing, with a force that can be greater than the will to live, desires which are liable to elicit disgust, shame, guilt, self-reproach, as well as fears too painful to tolerate. He would rather give them their sway in ways which permit him to remain ignorant of their true nature and then rationalize in order to justify and accept their influence over his life. He will look for every means to find "secondary gains," advantages and benefits which can be drawn from the very behavior he has no choice but to enact. If he must starve, he may become a "hunger artist" who wins renown. If, like the narrator of *Bartleby,* he must tolerate outrageous behavior in others, he may believe it is his divine mission from the inception of the universe to do so. And such secondary, compensatory gains then make it even more difficult for the neurotic to confront the true forces which direct his life. Even if he should cease to be satisfied with such gains, finding the cost too great; even if, in his inability to alter his behavior, he sees he is controlled by unconscious motivation; and even if he seeks help in psychoanalytic treatment—so great is this force of resistance to the painful truth that he will then struggle against the enlightenment which the analyst offers.

There is no more profound question to be asked, regarding neurotic behavior, than how it is the neurotic comes to possess motives so disruptive that they cannot even be faced in the interests of giving them up. How can the mind be so divided against itself? How is it, to put the question in the strictest terms, that passions should come into such internecine conflict with conscience, so that a part of both thereafter remain unconscious and unchangeable? As previously mentioned, the psychoanalytic answer has to do with the character of infantile thought and its continuance into adult life. And a grasp of this theory is the *sine qua non* for psychoanalytic criticism. For this reason a description of the dynamics is given here in some detail. It is not meant to be technical nor complete, but rather to focus on such theory as is most relevant and usable for the literary critic.[1]

The Dual Instinct Theory

The psychoanalytic concept that the most basic of human drives are those of libido and aggression should surprise no one. Love and hate, the creative and destructive principles, were judged even by Plato to be the "innate pattern of the soul," our desires and temper which need to be controlled by reason. The control of these drives in the psychoanalytic view is, however, more complex than anything envisioned by Plato. To begin with, society must enforce instinctual renunciation for its own survival. The child's free pursuit of pleasure and unrestrained aggression must be opposed by taboo, custom and law. As Freud observes in *Civilization and Its Discontents,* renunciation is the price we must pay to live in society. But, as with the demands of society, the drives are themselves a means to survival: aggression preserving the individual, and sexuality the species. This opposition between human drives and the demands of society creates a dilemma which may never be resolved. Although the child may inhibit his murderous aggression and repress even the knowledge of a wish to kill parents or siblings, the drives must be given their due. The child's whole character may turn to generalized aggression, seeking thereafter persons and occasions on which that transferred anger may be spent. In addition, the very efforts of the child to withhold aggression from his family may result in his conscience turning the drive against himself. Conscience is normally derived from the commandments, attitudes and values of the parents which are internalized by the child in the interests of adaptation. If the parent voices his thou-shalt-nots in a kindly, patient and rational way, in like manner can the child deal with himself. But with a punitive parent, the child must fear not only the loss of love and security, but the imagined consequences of disclosing his own anger. If he wishes death to a parent, he can easily imagine death will be his punishment. In such a situation the child's usual identification with the parent becomes an identification with the aggressor. He may wield against himself a punitive aggression which combines the anger of the parent he fears, and his own anger that he dare not express.

· Similarly the drive to pleasure, particularly oedipal desires, once blocked, may thereafter be transferred to parental surrogates and substitute situations. And, like aggression, the drive may be turned toward the self. The primary narcissism of the child, normally relinquished in large measure through the love he learns to feel toward others, may be reinforced. Self-love, for all that it is childish, is better than not being loved at all. His character may, with self-indulgence, self-glorification, indifference to others and a general solipsism, turn to so inflexible a narcissism that affection given and taken may be forever relinquished.

The Ego

It is important to note that the drives are flexible in the extreme. They require enactment, but the ways and means are for the ego to determine. As with the drives, the ego functions in the interests of survival, but in its discerning way it seeks survival on the highest level, adaptation in society. Consequently normal and neurotic behavior cannot be differentiated simply on the basis of how the drives are blocked or find suitable expression. The reality principle, a function of the ego, involves the process of learning, evaluating and adopting goals for the purpose of finding in society the eventual implementation of drives that cannot be immediately enacted. The child's immature experiences have a crucial effect in determining how rewarding will be these ways and means. The pleasures and angers in nursing, in bowel training, and in perceiving the separateness of parents from oneself and vying for their love, constitute the ego's actual involvement in a world it is slow to understand. Hopefully the ego finds formulas in action which reconcile the drives and the demands of society. But when the child judges them irreconcilable, for real or imagined reasons, the ego undertakes measures which make the best of a bad situation, one which entails thereafter neurosis and character disorder. Hence we must consider in some detail the vicissitudes of the ego in the infant's primary modes of thought, and in the child's early experiences in the world.

The Primary Process

A first and momentous feature of the infant psyche is its inability to conceive of negation. It cannot think "no." This might not seem as fundamental a limitation as in fact it is. The infant cannot distinguish between himself and the external world—that is, between what is self and what is not-self. A sense of chronology is impossible, since that calls for a separation between "now," and "not-now." It can make no separation between one object or idea and all others which resemble it, so that they become interchangeable in thought. This feature of the infantile mind bears witness to what an abstraction, what a sophisticated idea, the concept of negation really is. The ability to affirm the importance of what does not exist, to see as a positive thing the non-existence of something, enables us not only to distinguish one thing from another, but to organize their relationships, according to *but, if, however, yet, almost, merely, partially,* and so on. The infant not only cannot *think* "no," he cannot think whatever *implies* "no." The consequences of such an archaic mode of thought, as will be seen and as can readily be imagined, are enormous. The mother who gravely pronounces "no!" to her child asks for more from him than she may imagine.

Another feature of this earliest thought is the absence of a verbal language. Since the infant has almost no experience of the world beyond what it sees and has no language to categorize experience, the visual images themselves, as they are seen and remembered, function as a language. Our own dreams at night, for instance, illustrate (as dreams illustrate all other aspects of this "primary process" of infantile thought) how a multitude of feelings and ideas may be expressed in images alone. And taken together, these two ingredients of infantile thinking determine other important features. Thought predicated on perceiving similarities but not distinctions, and on having visual images for its archaic language, must necessarily be highly figurative in operation. Symbolism, allusion, analogy, and metaphor become basic to the representation of anything.

It would be difficult to exaggerate the consequences in adult life of this symbolic character of infantile thought. It affects our love of imagery in poetry, our response to symbolism in fiction, the figurative character of so much of our verbal language, the way we learn about the world based on the assumption that things shaped in the same way have similar functions and derive from similar forces, and our desire for things because of their symbolic value. For instance, cars become phallic, strength becomes masculinity, a woman's height or large breasts make her equatable with the cherished mother remembered from childhood, the "fatherland" may be given the uncritical devotion we gave our own fathers. Such consequences of figurative thinking as these are fairly complex and sophisticated. But in more naive fashion, figurative thought is equally common in children. For instance, the child imagines that infants are born anally, since he already knows that things are expelled from the body in that way. He imagines that sexual intercourse is an act of violence (should he observe it) because of its obvious resemblance to a struggle. He may think that females have penises, simply because males have them. Since animals kill and devour, the child may fear his parents may punish him by killing and eating him in just that way. Dreams, of course, exemplify this kind of thought. Any object, in dreams, may be represented by anything else analogous to it.

Representation of the penis by a gun, spear, pencil, faucet, or snake; and of the vagina by a bottle, room, house, cave, or mouth are well-known and are symbolically used in this way as much in fiction as in dreams. The peculiarities of neurotic thinking fully exemplify this kind of figurative thinking. This writer recalls an incident which involved a friend awakened by a phone call from his mother in the middle of the first night after his honeymoon. His mother had dreamed that his left leg was paralyzed. Assuring her in an almost patronizing tone that her dream meant nothing and that he was quite well, he then awoke in the morning only to find that the leg was indeed for the moment paralyzed. It is not difficult to see at work here the kind of symbolism which produces so many psychically determined "conversion" symptoms. His mother's equation of blocked sexuality with a paralyzed leg found equal acceptance in the unconscious thoughts of her son. Similarly, obsessional ideas that seem to have no meaning often constitute the figurative expression of other, more emotion-laden ideas, and the same can be said for compulsive acts. Lady Macbeth's compulsive hand-washing is the classical literary example of such thinking, in which spots on a white hand express not only the thought of blood, but the guilt of murder on her conscience. Similarly, a phobic avoidance of some apparently harmless situation, or counter-phobic activity (such as climbing mountains or racing cars) typically represent no more than a figurative translation of the fear which the individual is trying psychologically to avoid or overcome. The obsessive doubting of the crew of the *Narcissus*, as to whether one sailor is or is not dying, is similarly based on that sailor's predicament figuratively expressing their own fears of mortality.

Perversions, too, may be adopted for what such sexuality figuratively suggests. The homosexual who enacts the role of the woman— "getting" the man's penis—may unconsciously (and irrationally) be seeking not femininity, but a masculinity which he believes he can obtain only from another man. And the "moral masochist," the neurotic who unconsciously seeks failure, punishment, or defeat may derive a kind of feminine sexual gratification based on the resemblance between the sexual act and a violent struggle. Even psychotic thought retains this quality. There was a psychotic woman who had once sought to legally change her name to "Angel America." One has only to consider the desirable attributes of angels or what it means to be called "Miss America" to perceive the figurative logic of this madness.

A third momentous feature of infantile thought is the primacy of what Freud calls the pleasure principle. Thought is directed by needs, wants, appetites, without qualification or compromise. A mind already without a sense of past and future can know nothing of the anticipation or postponement of pleasure. Without a sense of reality, it can know nothing of the reasons pleasure cannot be immediately obtained. Without the concept of negation, all pleasure is sought and thought to be obtainable. Without an understanding of the boundary between self and the external world, all objects which produce pleasure are felt to belong to the self for the sole purpose of affording pleasure. Such thought is of course pure narcissism. And when one considers that this early system of thinking remains "intact" and urges its boundless appetite upon all later "systems," one can readily see not only how radically different mature thought is, but what efforts must be made to contain so uncompromising a primary narcissism.

The Nursing Child

The child begins to develop a more realistic understanding of the world almost immediately. Life impinges, and interaction affects the child profoundly from the beginning. Since the infant relates pleasurably to the external world and derives the nourishment necessary to survive, both at his mother's breast, the use of his mouth is inevitably the first focus of learning. Nursing is an uncomplicated action for the infant, but he is affected greatly by the way the breast is given, withdrawn, and withheld. And once the importance of his mouth is learned, it becomes a way of relating to the world which never lessens in psychological importance. Obesity, self-imposed starvation, the desire to destroy by biting and devouring, fear of being devoured, alcoholism, kissing and other oral foreplay, the use of the mouth in homosexuality, ulcers—all may express attitudes toward the mouth which have their origin in sucking at the breast, just as do thumbsucking and the sucked security blanket.

This is not to say that nursing as an infant is alone sufficient to produce later and more complex behavior, but rather that a highly efficient way to pleasure is learned and forever offers itself as a solution to those who experience difficulty in obtaining pleasure in more complicated ways. And sucking at the breast inevitably has meaning well beyond the pleasure obtained. Biting and refusing nourishment become a focus for aggressive drives. And, too, the infant begins to acquire a sense of reality. The breast is not there when it is wanted. And it vanishes before satiety. It is a terrible lesson for the infant, that the breast is not part of himself and that he is dependent upon something which is outside of himself, something he cannot control.

There comes at this time a first recognition that pleasure depends upon not only the satisfaction of his wants, but upon a certain disposition of what is outside himself. His identity has its bounds; he is dependent upon what is not himself. What is *not* himself, the breast which is *not* there, the pleasure which *was* there but now is gone, the anticipation of pleasure to come: the first year of life brings concepts of negation and time, as well as the concept of self. But, again it must be stressed, his first responses are never abandoned. Part of his thinking will be forever disposed to ignore such abstract distinctions.

The best example in fiction of the infantile importance of the mouth derived from nursing is the sucking-stones episode in Beckett's *Molloy*. Molloy is obsessively determined to suck stones he picks up from the beach (sixteen in number) in a fixed sequence, although he finally throws away all but one which, as he tells us, he then either loses, swallows, or throws away. We have in this funny, seemingly incomprehensible situation a figurative portrait of the child seeking to control the mother's breast on demand and then venting his anger against her by treating the breast as a thing of no importance.

Anal Discipline

What follows next in the infant's development is equally momentous and far more complex. Although the pursuit of the pleasures of the mouth bring a dependence upon the world, the infant's appetite is not seriously challenged. We must eat to live. But after a year of life, the child is expected to grasp something completely alien to the instincts of his body and the perceptions of his mind. His defecation suddenly incurs the wrath of parents. Now he must come to understand that the impulses of his body are a threat to his own security. There could hardly be imagined a more difficult lesson. To keep the love and protection of his parents he must withhold defecation for the right time and the right place. The lesson is difficult, not merely because he must exercise the concept of negation (something is *not* to be done), nor because he must grasp a sense of time (not now but *later*), nor even because he must make concessions to forces outside himself. Henceforth he must be divided against himself with the need to defecate and the drive to pleasure, both in conflict with his need of the approval of the adults who are themselves a source of pleasure and a means to his survival. It is the tripartite conflict of the forces Freud characterized as id, ego, and superego: needs of the body, consideration of reality, and conscience derived from the discipline of parents.

With control of the needs and pleasures of the anal sphincter, the child begins to be civilized—not only because such control is demanded by society, but because self-regulation is the criterion for all civilized behavior. Renunciation of needs, drives, instincts, is the price we pay for the benefit of social life and culture which this renunciation makes possible. It is equally true that this requirement imposed on the child gives him a strong motive—and instrument—for antisocial behavior. One must defecate, as well as eat, to live; and the anger which rises up in the child during toilet training is born not only of the frustration of his primary drive to pleasure, but out of this drive to live. And the child at this age has all the means to richly express his anger by defecating at the wrong time and place, to the acute disappointment and discomfort of his parents. But his anger is also a danger, since it risks their withdrawal of love and security, and risks their retributive anger. It is a predicament unique to the human species and allows for that malady equally peculiar to mankind, the neurosis. When one's own impulses become a threat to survival—when, in other words, the struggle for survival must be waged against oneself as much as against the world—we can win one battle only at the expense of the other.

Some of the more obvious consequences of toilet training, as psychoanalytic theory has shown, are the extremes of obedience and disobedience in whatever has symbolic reference to feces: on the one hand, the determination to frustrate the world by dirtiness, unpunctuality, stinginess, obstinacy; and, on the other, by a scrupulous adherence to the reverse traits. We have in our language in the expletive "shit!"—in the notion of how one person craps all over another, in the designation of anything worthless as shit, anyone wrong who thinks himself completely right as full of shit, and lies in general as bullshit—the same rebellious expression of feelings born of toilet training. The best examples in fiction are, again, in the novels of Beckett. Molloy, for instance, recognizes in himself an ungovernable tendency to incontinence, so that he breaks wind three hundred and fifteen times in a space of nineteen hours, having counted them on this occasion. But then he reasons that this amounts to an average of sixteen farts an hour, or "not even one fart every four minutes." "Damn it," he concludes, "I hardly fart at all."

The humor of this situation has to do with the infantile victory, inflicting endless farts on the world and yet at the same time, in a child's magical way of denial, the dangers of disobedience are removed so that the is as incontinent as he likes, yet he "hardly farts at all." When, in the inspiration of his crazy thinking, he half-recalls that he was born through his mother's anus, and terms this experience his "first taste of shit," he finds a primitive and powerful language for telling the reader how sordid his life really is.[2]

Another metaphor by which to describe the child's mind at this age is the medieval palimpsest, a parchment on which reality writes new thoughts without ever erasing the script from earlier ages. Lawrence Kubie gives the following clear description of the process:

... cravings arise in body tensions, with the consequence that the symbolic thought world of the child starts with his own percepts of parts of his own body, of his own body products, of his apertures, and of the sensations associated with his body needs. No new percept can be perceived apart from the residue of previous percepts and the resultant pre-existing concepts. As experiences multiply, therefore, there can be no new percepts apart from older concepts, and vice versa, although in different experiences the two can be intermixed in different proportions. Consequently, the growth of the symbolic process starts with what the infant needs, the parts of the body which become involved in these needs, how these needs become wants, and how they are represented in feeling, in thought, in speech, and in act. All of this is focused internally at first, every new external stimulus making its initial impact on our psychic life only by relating itself to that which was already present. Thus in the initial stages of development every external percept must be apperceived in relation to some prior internal experience.[3]

This developmental model, or more accurately, fusion of models, which characterizes the progressive complexity of the child's mind has one further feature of incalculable importance. The child's thoughts, interests, and actions cannot be considered as something separate from his sexual development. Freud's theory of the sexuality of the infant and child—one of his most astounding and important discoveries—and his theory of the unconscious are his two most difficult ones to accept. They are the basis of his psychology, and an acceptance of psychoanalytic ideas which precludes either one of these ruptures the coherence of his ideas, aside from ignoring the wealth of data from which they are derived. Resistance to the idea of infantile sexuality is partly the result of a confusion between sexuality and the narrower form of its expression, genital sexuality. Fenichel has given us the briefest and most persuasive description of the reasons so much of childhood behavior must be viewed as sexual:

Why does Freud call these infantile phenomena sexual? First, because they constitute the native soil from which the sexuality of the adult subsequently develops; second, because every adult who is in any way blocked in his sexuality falls back to infantile sexuality as a substitute; third, because the child experiences his sexuality with the same emotions the adult feels toward his; fourth, because the aims of these strivings are identical with the aims observable in adult perversions, and no one has ever doubted that the perversions are anything but sexual.[4]

This is not to say that children are perverted. They derive a good deal of pleasure from the bodily stimulation of the mouth during the time of nursing, and later of the anus as well as genitals. They perpetuate these pleasures by thumbsucking, withholding of the bowels for pleasurable release, and autoerotic stimulation of the genitals. And since all children routinely pursue any activity which is pleasurable to the body, these activities are no more than their automatic response to the world. In time, the disapproval of the world induces feelings in them of shame and disgust, so that they are disposed to find new, and adult, means of bodily gratification. Children have no fixed sexual identity as male and female beyond the non-sexual aspects of the roles they are encouraged to adopt, in terms of dress, games, deportment, and so on. Only the adoption of adult heterosexual activity, or at least the desire for such, constitutes such an identity. And this desire must be acquired—in effect, it must be learned with the help of environmental forces—and the world is full of those who fail in this achievement or who succeed with only partial success. Should the adoption of one's sexual identity be blocked, no innate "instinct" will hinder the assumption of the opposite sexual role. We are bisexual by nature. We seek adjustment in the world by active efforts, or by passively seeking help, whichever seems to work best. And on the basis of what the environment makes possible and rewarding, learned active and passive traits extend into sexual behavior. The choice is not in any simple fashion made between one sexual identity or the other.

The Oedipus Complex

The Oedipus complex, the love triangle of the child's early years, is the most widely misunderstood aspect of psychoanalytic theory. To put it briefly, that complex depends entirely on what the particular child has become in association with particular parents in a particular society. It has few fixed features. In this regard contemporary psycho-analytic thought departs somewhat from Freud's attempt to formulate an instinctual explanation for the vicissitudes of these childhood years. But Freud is explicit enough about the importance of environment in the determination of this complex. For instance, he writes:

I do not assert that the Oedipus complex exhausts all the possible relations which may exist between parents and children; these relations may well be a great deal more complicated. Again, this complex may be more or less strongly developed, or it may even become inverted, but it is a regular and very important factor in the mental life of the child; we are more in danger of underestimating than of overestimating its influence . . . . Moreover, the parents themselves frequently stimulate the children to react with an Oedipus complex, for parents are often guided in their preferences by the difference in sex of their children, so that the father favours the daughter and the mother the son; or else, where conjugal love has grown cold, the child may be taken as a substitute for the love-object which has ceased to attract.[5]

The question remains, as a problem in dispute, whether the childhood attachments formed are "sexual" in content. Everything, of course, depends upon how one chooses to define the word. If it is argued that "sexuality" necessarily implies the knowledge of, and physical desire for, sexual intercourse with another person, then children of three or four are not sexual. The mature desire for genital union is absent. The non-Freudian judgment that therefore the child is not sexual in his emotional attachments is succinctly put by Clara Thompson:

When the child shows more than a passing interest in the erotic relations with the parents one must seek its source in erotic attitudes of the parent toward the child. In our western culture where families are small and the parent has the chief care of the child, the relation to the parents constitutes the child's first experience in living with his fellow man. Here rivalries, jealousies and hostilities about all sorts of things first come to life. We would question whether sex as such is the invariable cause of the rivalry and hostility. The child plays the parents off against each other as a method of dividing and ruling, as well as feeling hostile to them whenever they obstruct the development of his interests. Only when the parent has an erotic interest in the child is the child's sexual interest stimulated to the point of becoming a problem.[6]

Freud's own reply to this argument is based, as psychoanalytic theory must invariably be based if it is to have validity, on the testimony of obtainable experience. For instance, his definitive analysis of this complex was based upon the report of a physician regarding the behavior of his five-year-old son (*Analysis of a Phobia in a Five-year-old Boy*). I recall the occasion when my five-year-old nephew was, in a grand sweep, romantically kissed by his mother. When his father humorously said, "Wow, that was quite a kiss," the child in all seriousness replied, "Now you know how I feel when you kiss Mommy." How is one to draw the line here, over the question of sexuality? The ardent affection the child felt, the desire to give that affection expression by physical means, as well as the jealous competitiveness toward his father, all bore the unmistakable stamp of a lover's psychology. Since attitudes the child develops toward his mother at this age profoundly affect his future sexual relationships toward women as an adult, the case for childhood "sexuality" all but argues itself. The best description of the child's sexual behavior, I think, is still the one given by Freud:

One might try to object that the little boy's behavior is due to egoistic motives and does not justify the conception of an erotic complex . . . . [But] when the little boy shows the most open sexual curiosity about his mother, wants to sleep with her at night, insists on being in the room while she is dressing, or even attempts a physical act of seduction, as the mother so often observes and laughingly relates, the erotic nature of this attachment to her is established without a doubt. Moreover, it should not be forgotten that a mother looks after a little daughter's needs in the same way without producing this effect; and that often enough a father eagerly vies with her in trouble for the boy without succeeding in winning the same importance in his eyes as the mother. In short, the factor of sex preference is not to be eliminated from the situation by any criticisms.[7]

This is not to deny that the Oedipus complex affects the development of the child for many reasons other than the strictly sexual. The child needs tenderness from both parents, their continued attention, and assurance of affection. Without it, his life can be as desolate as it is for any lonely adult. He is dependent upon his parents for his identity as a person and for his very life. He will, with a strength equal to that of any adult, develop hatred and jealousies for innumerable reasons, depending upon the character of his family.

This is the world he must deal with, not with the world at large. His parents may be seductive, punitive, inconsistent in their feelings, weak, unloving, envious, competitive, even—to say the worst—deranged. And the child cannot understand that his life· is not eternally fixed to those conditions. Indeed, he may imagine, in his immaturity, that his life is worse than it is. For instance, he may attribute the hurtful behavior of his parents to his own "wrongdoing," and suffer over a groundless guilt. He may feel murderous anger, but fail to understand that such anger is human, conceivably justified given his suffering, and yet something quite different from translating that anger into violent action. Since he has no way to know the contrary, he may imagine that parents are possessed of murderous feelings toward him (if *he* can have them, it is logical to think that they do too). He may think he will, in fact, be destroyed in the way he childishly imagines he might destroy them; by tearing them to pieces with his teeth. (Children are practical, if not more primitive. They have no access to poisons and pistols. But biting siblings, as almost all children do, gets results; and so they continue to think in those terms, in fear as much as in anger.) Jacob Arlow has pointed out to me how this childhood fear of being eaten finds constant expression in children's cartoons, as well as in fairy tales.

Since, in addition to such fears and frustrations, the child loves his parents stubbornly and deeply, his problems of adjustment can be beyond calculation or remedy. Children are incapable, to use a well-known example from Shakespeare, of loving Caesar for one reason and destroying him for another. Loving and hating the same person is intolerable for them. And so, if the external situation cannot be changed, they must find means to change themselves psychologically. And the means they choose in changing themselves produces the inflexible, unprofitable, and unconscious motives which constitute a "neurosis" in later life.

There is no limit to the lengths to which a child will go to adapt to his world, to adjust to the requirements imposed by his parents and to gain an identity as an integrated person. His brain is an adaptive mechanism without parallel in the world. Whatever serves those adaptive purposes will rule his thinking. Insofar as dangers are imposed from *without,* he will respond to the "reality principle"; with objectivity, practicality, far-sightedness, inventiveness, discretion, rationality—with courage and patience beyond measure. Dangers imposed from without are *real,* and must be clearly seen and assessed. Survival depends upon avoidance of wishful, prejudicial, superstitious, contradictory, inflexible thought. Infantile "primary process" thought must be relinquished, and concepts of time, negation, the limitations of one's self, and the separate identity of other things recognized. The child must, as Freud put it, partly forego the "pleasure principle," or else pleasures and life itself will come to an end.

But, tragically, that is only half the problem. The child must alter himself to such an extent that anything *within himself* which blocks his development is itself a threat to survival. When one considers how much a child can achieve in his first years of life—language, social values, abstract thought—what difficulties of adjustment imposed by the world are beyond his powers? The far greater problem is the unsocial force of his own passions. And in the means he uses to deal with this problem lies much of the psychoanalytic explanation of neurosis.

The Inner Defenses

One thinks, in this connection, of Sophocles' *Oedipus Rex.* Oedipus is warned by the Oracle at Delphi that he is destined to murder his father and marry his mother. He is not sure of the true identity of his parents, but he runs from the city where those who might be his parents live, in the hopes, he tells himself, of evading his "destiny." He meets, soon after, a company of men with whom he disputes possession of the road, is struck on the head, and promptly slaughters all but one of them, including a white-haired old man. When he reaches Thebes, he wins the right to wed the widowed queen, a woman a generation older than himself. Years later, when he learns that he has destroyed both his parents, he blinds himself and is driven from the city.

It is easy to see, on a moment's reflection, that Oedipus' "destiny" was easy to avoid; he need only have foregone the pleasures of killing older men and marrying older women. That he does not do so tells us clearly enough that his heart is not in such an avoidance. The extent to which the play as a whole supports this view is indicated in our analysis of the play in Part II.

But even the passions of parricidal and incestuous wishes, assuming he has them, are not his problem. Ironically, as contradictory as it sounds, Oedipus' tragic destiny is the result of the efforts made to *oppose* his own passions. The explanation of how this can be involves most of the fundamental tenets of psychoanalytic theory. We have already seen the first; Oedipus is not the victim of circumstance or the gods; the pain of his life, blinded and driven from the city for his crimes, is the outcome of crimes he chose to risk committing. In this regard he is like every neurotic, whose cure can only begin with the insight that the pain of his life is the consequence of his own unconscious doing. The second tenet has previously been discussed—that parricidal and incestuous motives are the passions of childhood. To put it briefly, the child rightly understands these passions are a threat to his existence. The situation is no different from the problem he faces at the time of toilet training, when the drives of his own body bring him into conflict with the demands of his family and when a failure to comply incurs their wrath. The danger of a murderous wish against his father is a comparable problem of self-control. The father is too big and strong to fight against. The mother would be horrified if she knew that he even wished to commit the murder. If the father knew, he might retaliate with his own murderous anger—and not be deterred from destroying his "dirty, immoral, ungrateful son."

Oedipus Rex gives the clearest indication of how this retaliation can be rightly feared, since Oedipus' first parents, knowing of the possibility that their son will commit such crimes, have him cruelly bound, exposed to the elements and (they think) to certain death. Such are, moreover, not the only reasons the child must deter his own passions. Just as the infant takes into himself, "incorporates," the attitudes of his parents regarding defecation in order to be secure against a dangerous lapse of control at any time, the child permanently adopts as his own the general morality of his parents. Depending upon how seductive his mother is, and how punitive his father, the conscience he acquires may inflict upon him the most painful sense of guilt and warnings of the direst punishment. Under the weight of all this pain and fear, the child could not endure life. And since nothing in the external situation can be changed, short of winning his mother and destroying his father, he must find new means to change himself.

The means he chooses is the third of these psychoanalytic tenets: repression. The passions which are so dangerous are thrust from conscious thought. Such a strategy has a two-fold purpose. There is the hope that a motive which is not thought about will, therefore, not be enacted; and in this way the child will be "defended" against the dangers of angering parents. And, too, there is the hope that the refusal to acknowledge such motives to himself will alleviate his own intolerable guilt. In this light, repression is a defense against a variety of ills, both within and without.

Repression is successful in that impulses which are taboo can be controlled. Life will go on, and a measure of peace be maintained in the family. But to vary an adage, what is out of mind is not out of sight. When impulses are warded from consciousness, they nevertheless maintain an existence separate from the realistic, and maturing, conscious personality of the child. New opportunities for pleasure come with attachments to new people; a truer understanding of how "natural" are erotic and hostile wishes, and how exaggerated one's fears of punishment, comes with time. But the old system is locked into place: infantile guilt and fear opposed to infantile passion are repressed from consciousness but active still.

That is the predicament of Oedipus at the time the oracles reveal his "destiny." He has no knowledge that he wishes the fulfillment of their prophesies. Indeed, he thinks that he runs from them. And in a sense he does, in that he leaves forever his step-parents. But he murders and marries individuals who might be, as he very well knows, his true parents. Since in reality he has little to gain, and much to lose, in terms of guilt and disgrace, we can only understand his actions in light of the wishes which belong to infancy. To put it differently, his erotic and murderous passions are "displaced" onto people who by virtue of age can represent his parents. From the point of view of mental stability, this is an ingenious solution. Repressed passions find satisfaction after all. The old guilt and fear of punishment is avoided, since the meaning of what he does is hidden from him.

The play contends that, by an extraordinary coincidence, they are in fact his long-lost parents; a dramatic *dénouement* not very true to life. But the consequences of this kind of displacement of unconscious passions from parents to substitutes is one of the most common, easily observable features of neurotic behavior. And the costly consequences are unavoidable for the neurotic, just as they have become for the blinded, deposed Oedipus. The hostility which is displaced from the father to teachers, police, and employers, or anyone else equatable with the father on any basis, can spoil chances for adjustment and success; yet this anger cannot be combated since the achievement of its original repression puts it now out of conscious reach. And as the individual looks for justification of this displacement, finding fault with authority figures, he cannot even detect the fact that his anger is unrealistic and forced. Oedipus, for instance, never troubles himself about killing not only the two men who force him off the road and strike him, but almost their whole company. He is no doubt justified in anger, even perhaps in striking back. But the savagery of his response, excessive out of all cause, is the perfect dramatic formula for communicating how anger feeds unconsciously on a source greater than the provocation given. Nor could we expect to find in Oedipus an awareness of displacement as the underlying reason for his marriage. He presumably finds Jocasta a desirable person in her own right, and he has, after all, earned the right to rule Thebes as her husband.

Since repression so often fails to inactivate oedipal passions, and since, as a result, all manner of symbolically equivalent means of expression are sought, new defenses may have to be found. For instance, if teachers, employers, and officials in power become the object of anger originally felt against the father, any anger—even when it is justified—may seem taboo, and provoke guilty feelings appropriate only to the murder of one's father. In this way it becomes necessary for the neurotic to further restrict his freedom of action, avoiding even necessary and profitable conflicts in life, in order to allay unconscious and infantile guilt. There is, in fact, more than one defense mechanism at work in this situation. The anxiety, which the neurotic feels, is "defensive" since it keeps him from conflict; and in the irrational, non-literal terms of unconscious thinking, this means an avoidance of the anger with which he might murder his father. But, in addition, non-assertive personality traits are also acquired, to further insure avoidance of all conflict; a defensive measure referred to as "reaction formation." One thinks immediately of Melville's lawyer in *Bartleby,* a man who chooses a conflict-free profession and remains peaceable, passive, and unprovokable, throughout his life, even under outrageous conditions.

Defenses against incestuous, as well as parricidal, wishes bring about the same restriction of action. The neurotic who feels anxiety with women and who, in consequence, avoids sexual relations, spoils opportunities for such relations. By rendering himself impotent or suffering a general deadening of sexual appetite, he may be defending himself against his own dangerous, infantile desire to transgress with his mother. A reaction formation against this desire can involve extreme and rigid attitudes of propriety, decorum, and morality, all of which can effectively blunt his sexual appetites. Freud has pointed out how certain neurotics may be unable to desire women they also respect, since that recapitulates the combination of feelings they felt for their mothers. Such men are destined to bring to their relations with women one feeling or the other, but never both—and in consequence they are able to enjoy sex with prostitutes or "immoral" women; but unable to enjoy relations with their own wives. Paul Morel's inhibitions with Miriam, and sexuality with Clara, in Lawrence's *Sons and Lovers* is one of the clearest expressions in literature of this process.

In the absence of such a reaction formation, oedipally driven men may spend their whole lives unconsciously pursuing equivalents of their mother. For instance, the Don Juan is attracted to women he has never possessed, since the fact of their unavailability is the link to his mother. Hence, in such men the desire for the woman vanishes at precisely the point it becomes strongest in other men: with sexual consummation. Men who feel impelled to "rescue" women, to solve their problems, lift them up out of all difficulties and despair, to heal their suffering at whatever cost to themselves, have a similar oedipal motive, since the child thinks (for good reason or in wishful fantasy) that his mother needs him in order to escape the undesired and tyrannical father. Marriage between races and religions may similarly symbolize sexuality with the mother, since any socially established sexual taboo may symbolize the incest taboo (the Southern abhorrence of miscegenation may, for some Southerners, derive its virulence from an unconscious equation of this kind).

Maurice Valency's analysis of the medieval courtly love tradition, in his *In Praise of Love,* describes the same dynamics in literature. The love poetry of that genre was dominated by the theme of a young man's attraction to the high-born wife of a powerful nobleman. As this literary tradition developed, the young lover aspired to, and received, less and less physical reward—ultimately accepting no more than a "spiritual union" with his desired, but idealized lady.[8] We can see in this poetic tradition, on the one hand, the oedipal attraction to the woman who most resembles the mother—that is, the woman who is married, unobtainable, more mature than the young lover. On the other hand, there is an evident reaction formation, in which he becomes idealistic and spiritual to the point of renouncing the sexual desire which initiates the whole procedure. The inability of Hamlet to avenge his father, as Ernest Jones has shown, involves the same ambivalent dynamics. The prince, wishing parricide and incest, must identify with the uncle who murders Hamlet's father and marries his mother. In consequence, Hamlet is unable to ally with his father in effecting retribution. And neither can he control his sexual rivalry for his mother. Although his father commands him to "leave her to heaven," he continues to torment her for giving her sexual favors as she does. He defends against his impulse to compete by remaining passive; but he exacts a lover's revenge.

Oedipal situations in fiction are, of course, ubiquitous. But little is generally gained for critical purposes in pouncing on every suggestion of this complex. To put it differently, men pursue conscious and adult goals, however much they may also respond to unrelinquished wishes from childhood. And for most men, the contribution made by mature motives greatly outweighs the infantile. If a measure of immature thinking is present in so many of us, nevertheless men can be more meaningfully differentiated on the basis of their differing conscious aspirations. For instance, the man who marries a virtuous woman partly because her virtue reminds him of the best qualities of his mother is a very different man from the one driven inappropriately to rescue a prostitute by marrying her, solely because an infantile rescue fantasy dominates his thinking. Oedipal elements in fiction are critically important only when such elements govern the story. Oedipus should not take the risks he knowingly takes in tempting the fates. Hamlet, as he acknowledges himself, cannot explain why he remains inactive. This is when it is profitable to talk in terms of an Oedipus complex. The work, to put it briefly, must in itself be puzzling, and an oedipal explanation must be the resolution of that puzzle before the psychoanalytic approach becomes viable or informative.

In spite of these defenses, one never relinquishes the pleasure principle; one can turn in endless directions, in reality or phantasy, for the satisfactions that cannot be directly obtained. In a certain sense, substitute pleasures may themselves be considered a defense since they strengthen a rejection of the original, dangerous oedipal wishes. The situation is particularly clear when these gratifications are pursued in a forced way, or when the degree of satisfaction obtained is hardly worth the effort to secure them, or when mature pleasures of a non-oedipal character must also be abandoned. Defenses are unconscious and rigidly adopted, so that their presence is manifested specifically by an inability to relinquish them for something better. A common defensive tactic of this type is that of "regression." One reverts to pleasures which were safely enjoyed prior to the desires and fears of the oedipal situation. One returns to earlier physical pleasures, which now constitute "perversions" (that is, a turning from the mature for the immature). If the adolescent fears to use his penis because he unconsciously equates heterosexuality with breaking the incest taboo, he may adopt sexual uses for his mouth and anus, the earliest organs of pleasure for the child. His behavior, in effect, declares to his father and the world, "you need not castrate me; I do not use the offending organ."

Ironically, the mature desire for heterosexuality may still be retained in a variety of subtle ways (no pleasure is entirely given up, except at death). For instance, the homosexual may have the fantasy that taking the phallus into his mouth will magically give him the greater masculinity which belongs to his sexual partner (not unlike the savage who devours the lion for its strength). And the homosexual who takes the active role similarly expresses a determination to retain heterosexuality. He enacts a homosexual sexual role as close to the heterosexual one as possible—save that his defensive needs will not allow a woman as sexual object. (If such sexual preferences are cultivated in the child by an overtly sexual adult, such sexuality will, of course, not have the same defensive character.) Exhibitionism, voyeurism, and fetishism are also perversions in which heterosexuality is renounced—although, once again, the desire for mature sexuality may be also, if indirectly, evident: The pervert chooses a woman to watch, or to witness his own exposure; or an article of her clothing may become a fetish.

Masochism can also constitute a perverted defense against the dangers of heterosexuality. The man who visits a brothel which specializes in whipping its clients has clearly renounced the pleasures of heterosexuality, although the substitutive pleasures may not seem to be in evidence. It is important to recognize that pain is not in some mysterious fashion taken *as* pleasure by the masochist. Rather, pain allays the guilt which accompanies the desire for sexuality—it is, it has been said, the price of admission. Where, then, is the pleasure? In simpler situa-

tions, heterosexuality may become possible for the masochist after his
suffering. But where no such evident pleasure is obtained as an end-
result, one will find that it exists not in reality but in fantasy.

As Freud has shown, in his *Contribution to the Study of the Origin
of Sexual Perversions* (1919), fantasies of a heterosexual kind can
accompany the masochistic experience. Given the infantile equation
between a violent and a sexual act, the female can phantasize a
prohibited and guilt-laden sexual union with her father quite easily in
such a masochistic situation. The French film *Belle de Jour* vividly
depicted the indifference of a grown woman to the normal embraces of
her husband. The woman then offered herself, in a brothel, to the
abuses of unloving men in order to experience the only possible sexual
pleasures she could obtain. Her fantasies of being degraded and humili-
ated gave an equally clear picture of how masochism may find expression in varieties of pain other than merely the physical.

Similarly, the masochist may unconsciously seek failure in business
or professional life, or elicit scorn, rejection, or other behavior from
others which pains and humiliates him, as equivalents of masochistic
punishments. Such behavior may still represent attempts to alleviate
guilt, and this form of masochism is appropriately termed moral masochism. This behavior, for the man, may be even more "overdetermined"
(that is, caused by a combination of motives). The experience of pain
or failure in itself alleviates guilt, since it is a voluntary acceptance of
punishment. But in keeping with the infantile idea that the sexual act is
violent, suffering can unconsciously signify the adoption of a feminine
sexual role—in effect, a disguised form of homosexuality. Whether the
stronger motive in masochism is expiation to placate a dangerous
father, or a feminine sexual pleasure in fantasy, varies with the individual. But in every case this voluntary suffering is sought as a defensive
gain against both the imagined threats from without and the remorse of
conscience from within. Such is engendered by the crucible we term the
Oedipus complex; a cause of neurosis it assuredly is.

An excellent example in fiction of the sexual meaning of masochism,
and its alliance with sadism, is Kafka's *In a Penal Colony*. In this story
an officer is dominated by ambivalence toward two "commandants."
He feels an unswerving devotion to the first, and a raging anger against
the second. There is in such a split the suggestion of a child's ambivalent feelings toward his father, in which the loved and hated parent
is characterized in fantasy by separate people. And the commandant's

absolute power to punish is similarly part of an infantile conception of an omnipotent father. As the "climax" of the story, the officer throws himself into a deadly machine and destroys himself in a most painful fashion. Since the story provides no convincing motivation for suicide, the reader is compelled to look to symbolism for the motives. The instrument of punishment is a device shaped like a human figure, with liquid-injecting needles. The victim must strip and lie face down on a "bed," as it is called. As the machine vibrates downward, the victim is made to vibrate upward against it, and the needles penetrate his body, killing him.

It takes little ingenuity to see a consistent and vivid metaphor for the sexual act. In the language of symbolism, the officer submits sexually to the commandant. But his pain is real, too, as it is for any suffering masochist. It is understandable he should seek such pain. The officer has himself already destroyed many men with the machine. And he shows no conscious guilt about it. But if such killing has represented to him an acting out of a wish to unman and destroy his father, that wish must be atoned for. The infantile conscience, harsh in the extreme, requires the talionic punishment; and the guiding injunction behind the machine's operation is appropriately, "guilt is never to be doubted." In brief, his destruction dramatizes an overdetermination of motives: feminine sexual masochism as well as expiatory seeking of punishment.

In the neurotic, there is another defense which adds to this fusion of infantile passions, fear, substitute pleasures and anger, and expiation. The adoption of a defense may *itself* be unacceptable to the mature personality, so that a *defense against the defense* becomes necessary. Such a predicament is, of course, grotesque and tragic. But it is not uncommon. For instance, if homosexuality, as a defense against conflict with the father, is unacceptable; then homosexuality too must now be defended against. This particular inner conflict may be represented by the individual who protests too much; who displays constant, excessive, and violent anger against homosexuals; who habitually seeks to "outman" every other male; and who in subtle ways perpetuates the problem (as by developing an uncanny talent for spotting homosexuals). His attraction to homosexuality is indicated by the vigor of his avoidance.

This defense against another defense frequently takes the form of "projection." A homosexual attraction to other men may be partially denied by the belief that other men are attracted to oneself. Such a defense is less effective than repression since the idea of homosexuality is not kept from consciousness. But at least one's own desires are denied by attributing them to others. This projective mechanism may find expression not only in the idea that one is sexually sought by others, but in the idea that one's wife is open to the sexual advances of other men. When such suspicions are unfounded, and obsessively held against all contrary evidence, such jealousy is pathological; this is a defensive need to deny the danger of homosexual, not heterosexual, infidelity. The individual thinks: "Other men are jeopardizing my marriage, but they are attracted to my wife, not to me."[9] Needless to say, such pathology can destroy an otherwise successful marriage since it cannot be allayed by anything the wife does or says in her defense.

Murderous anger and guilt may also be projected outward (anything painful, in fact, may be projected). The paranoid characteristically attributes to forces outside himself a variety of destructive intentions which are his own. *Oedipus Rex* illustrates this well enough. Oedipus adopts the conviction, without any evidence, that the most respected men in the city, a celebrated seer and his brother-in-law, are engineering a plot to discredit him and take his crown. Events have made him consider the possibility that he is himself guilty of parricide—and so he twists from guilt by angrily accusing the most unlikely men in the kingdom of just such a crime.[10] But the horror he feels and the assumption of certitude about a plot he has only imagined signify his own need to avoid the pain of guilt. He screams at the seer, "Are these taunts to be indeed borne from *him*?—Hence, ruin take thee! Hence, this instant! Back!—Away!—Avaunt thee from these doors!" And to Creon: "Hast thou a front so bold that thou hast come to my house, who art the proved assassin of its master—the palpable robber of my crown?" Even his wife is not exempt from this forced projection of guilt. These projections, carried to an extreme, bring psychosis. Eventually the paranoid loses his sense of reality altogether. Such can be the constraints of inner necessity. Frankenstein, to use another example from our analyses in Part II, similarly projects murderous rage and guilt onto the monster of his creation.

There are a number of other defenses the neurotic can adopt against his own dangerous passions, and against awareness of guilt. There is the defense of "isolation," in which an idea is admitted into consciousness provided the feelings attached to it are kept repressed. The reverse may

also obtain; one may experience painful feelings, but without knowledge of the causes which gave rise to them. In psychoanalytic treatment, particularly in our society familiar with Freudian tenets, a
patient may readily confess an attraction to his mother or quite easily
see that she is seductive toward him. But the shame, guilt, fear which
belong to his complex will be denied. The patient will discuss these
matters readily, even volunteering interpretations based on the oedipal
association. But it is all an intellectual exercise, not personally felt. In
effect, his very objectivity serves to defend against the feelings too
painful to face. Or the patient may come into treatment overcome with
guilt, anxieties, particularly in his sexual life. Yet the suggestion that
such problems are appropriate to, and derived from, his childhood love
for his mother meets with such revulsion that the patient may termi-
nate treatment. Ideas or feelings can be tolerated; but not both.

Another defense is that of simple denial. One can adopt an idea at
variance with reality and hold to it tenaciously. The condemned man
awaiting execution comes to believe that the walls of his prison may
crumble, setting him free. The terminal patient may anticipate a
medical breakthrough that will save him. The helpless child will imagine
he is tremendously strong. The coward makes a show of bravado in a
frightening predicament. Our analysis of *The Nigger of the Narcissus*
suggests that the crew of a ship hold steadfast to the idea that a fatally
stricken crewman may even yet not die, solely in order to deny the
truth of their own mortality. Most men, indeed, live with the sense of
having a vast expanse of time left them, emotionally discounting how
quickly life goes. Such denial is healthy and desirable, to say the least.
But in denial, unpleasant facts are magically transformed by the omnipotence of thought. What is, can be what we choose to believe. And, if
we are lucky, life may take its time in correcting the delusion. These
various defenses (repression, displacement, sublimation, regression,
reaction formation, projection, transference, isolation, denial, and
others as well) are never acknowledged by the fictional character to
himself or to the reader. They must be inferred, as with the neurotic in
life, on the basis of behavior in the text which leaves us no other choice
if we are to understand him.

The single, overriding fact about the psychoanalytic view of neurosis
is that feelings, once acquired, outlive the conditions in which they first
arise. They possess a psychological autonomy with which the mature
individual must somehow deal, just as he must deal with the problems

of the external world. In effect, he lives on two fronts, one relating to the present and the other to his past. This cannot be said of some characters in fiction, whose only motives are conscious and whose goals are sought by appropriate means. When they fail, it is at least not because they wished to fail. And since in all but the most surrealistic fiction (as Kafka's *A Country Doctor,* or Coleridge's "Christabel") conscious motives are given prominence, one must take the utmost precaution before setting those motives aside and adopting others by which to understand the character. We must give the literary figure the benefit of the doubt and take him at his word as long as his actions support his acknowledged motivation.

Only when we find the most dramatic inconsistency between intentions and actions can we begin to infer that the character is engaged in a hidden conflict within himself. But even then, the varieties of possible inner conflict are endless. They may have to do with infantile preoccupations regarding orality and anality, with incestuous and parricidal passions, with any number of possible defenses against those passions, with—at the extreme—defenses against defenses. In addition, the character is still possessed with a greater or lesser compliance in his conscious self with those hidden motives. He may, on the one hand, confess that he is possessed by moods, spells, feelings which he does not understand; or, on the other, he may energetically deny they are forced from within himself and seek to relate them to the external world. A mere detection of the fact of neurosis still leaves the greater problem of analysis unresolved.

This is the point at which there is the greatest danger of faulty analysis. The psychoanalytic critic has so many possible explanations for neurotic behavior that he may impose an interpretation with only minimum support from the text itself. He may, indeed, project *his own* motives onto the literary character. Hence the hallmark of good psychoanalytic criticism is the extent to which interpretation is supported by all the details of the story. To be sure, the psychoanalytic critic will make various assumptions—that is, that there can be such things as unconscious motivation, unthinking rationalization of those motives, and the survival of infantile thought. One cannot hope to demonstrate the whole validity of psychoanalytic theory through the analysis of a single story. Fiction, at best, dramatizes a slice of a man's psychological life. And whatever else is not given can never be directly known. But the psychoanalytic critic who solves problems of motivation which cannot be explained by any other means, and who relates those motives to all parts of the story, cannot be faulted for "over-ingeniousness" except by those who reject psychoanalysis altogether.

The good psychoanalytic critic approaches a story with an open mind about what may be directing the thoughts and actions of the character. Such a critic is prepared to find, if there is evidence for it, that contradictory motives are simultaneously at work; that reality is the least of the character's problems, and that the conditions in which he lives and strives are not so much a challenge to him as the outward manifestation of unacknowledged inner problems. This critic is prepared to find the character in literature far more responsible for everything that happens to him than appearances would ever suggest. In the analyses which follow, we deal with characters who are victimized, deceived, spellbound, overcome by coincidental circumstances, manipulated by deranged people, deprived of life, love, and good fortune—and yet who seek and foster the very conditions they abhor. They are victorious in defeat. They are in most cases men who—to use Freud's revealing metaphor—snatch defeat from the jaws of success, because for them an outward defeat is an inner triumph.

The only generalization that can be made regarding neurotic patterns dramatized in fiction is that there is an overriding tension between psychological forces of desire and anger, on the one hand, and fear of punishment and guilt on the other. In most works of fiction in which neurosis is manifest, one half of that opposition is given fuller dramatization and the other is implied. *The Hunger Artist, Bartleby the Scrivener,* and *Oedipus Rex* give the fullest description of the consequences of fear and guilt, while the passions at work are represented by subtler means. In *The Tempest* and *Frankenstein,* the gratification of desires and angers is clearly obtained, while the effects of conscience are not clear and can be seen only when they are looked for. In effect, one finds represented in fiction not only conscious and unconscious thinking but also the division between passions, fears, and considerations of reality.

There are, in this light, six modes of thinking possible. Orthodox criticism easily identifies the first three: conscious passions, fears, and considerations of reality—all openly expressed, and related to the external action of the story. But there may be a simultaneous interaction, on an unconscious level, without reference to external events; and these will be characterized by infantile passions, fears, and naive ego percep-

tions. The relative weight given each of these six features varies widely
from one work to the next. The story itself, in every case, must
determine what importance we are to assign to any single element. We
need only be prepared for the possibility that all are simultaneously
present. We can expect that tales of monsters will dramatize infantile
passions; and nightmarish tales of imprisonment and inexorable agents
of punishment will depict the oppressive infantile conscience. But in
most fiction analysis of literary characters is complex, yielding the same
variety of psychological motives as found in life. An analysis that finds
only phallic symbols everywhere, or minor elements of the oedipus
complex, is as simplistic and untrue in life as it is in fiction.

The question of whether or not the artist can be psychoanalytically
understood through his work is considered in Part III. Our objection to
this question is founded upon two considerations. First, there is no
validated reason to think that what an artist puts on paper he enacts in
his life. We are what we do, not what we might wish to do in some
repressed, or creative, corner of our heads. No wish is ever given up, and
if it survives from infancy to inspire a creative work of fiction, on what
possible basis can that be called a neurosis? In addition, what are we to
do with the fact that different works by a single artist lead to contrary
conclusions about that artist's psyche? How many Shakespeare's are
possible if we approach his many plays for biographical facts? The
fiction of Beckett is a particularly good case in point. His novels offer
the most sophisticated, tragic, and comic view of the world. Yet, one
can find in his characters every variety of disorder imaginable. In
Molloy alone we can find elements of anality, orality, obsessive doubting, homosexuality, conversion symptoms, masochism, psychosis, isolation, incest, psychopathy, paranoia, anorexia, loss of identity, and
sadism—to mention them in random order. Yet, one also finds humor,
compassion, even a philosophic description of the human condition.
The novel ranks with anything written in the twentieth century. Is
Beckett psychotic because elements of psychosis prevail in his fiction?
If so, he is like no other psychotic who has ever lived. And on that basis
he cannot, so far as the reader can know, be psychotic at all.

There is another consideration which, rightly or wrongly, has never
been of particular interest to this writer: the question of how the
prevalence of psychoanalytic ideas in our society has influenced the
subject matter and style of modern writers. Creative writing, as Laur-
ence Kubie points out,[11] depends upon the free association of ideas in

the preconscious mind of the artist and is adversely affected by unconscious material of obsessional force. Such creativity is diminished, too, by conscious ideas which the artist is determined to implement propagandistically into his fiction. In our judgment, a deliberate effort to dramatize a formal knowledge of psychoanalytic theory in fiction will, for this reason, have a disastrous effect on the creative process. Among the best examples of this consequence is the fiction of Iris Murdoch and Lawrence Durrell. In Miss Murdoch's *The Unicorn,* for instance, one of the protagonists is enamored of another man's wife. At the end of the novel he reaches the following insight into his own attraction to this woman, an insight which parodies psychoanalytic theory:

He understood it now, he saw exactly how it had been. Hannah had been to him the chaste mother-goddess, the Virgin mother. The sin which Hannah was, through her own sinless suffering, redeeming for him had been the sin of his own mother's betrayal of him with his own father. Hannah was the mother who was sequestered, immaculate, chaste, the unmoved mover. Because of his unconscious resentment of his own mother's sin of sex, he had been, he explained, unable to establish any satisfactory relations with women other than those of Courtly Love. He would identify the woman he loved with his mother and then make her unapproachable and holy.[12]

Such dynamics might conceivably exist in a literary character. But they would be dramatically acceptable only as something acted out, as something repressed and not available to consciousness. The sudden illumination of text-book formulas seems factitiously imposed. And the artist's knowledge seems to have been merely put into the character's mouth. Oedipal dynamics of a formulaic variety are also to be found in Miss Murdoch's *The Italian Girl, The Time of the Angels,* and *A Severed Head.* In each novel there is imposed a mechanical rendering of how fascinating and repellent oedipal love and its taboo equivalents can be. But the characters are rarely allowed to speak for themselves. They seem to serve only the requirements of the oedipal motif. Similarly, in Durrell's *Alexandria Quartet* there are more than twenty overt or disguised sexual relationships. Incestuous ties figure in almost all of them. In some there is a struggle for dominance. Most of the lovers are deceived, broken psychologically, crippled or brought to death or suicide. They may deceive themselves about their own wishes, but here too the reader is confronted at every turn with the most obvious uncovering of this complex of emotions. There is lacking the constant diversity in the resistance to, and compliance with, incestuous wishes that is found in life. Because of the number of such involvements and their resemblance to one another, the reader loses the oblique and intuitive exposure to incestuous motives that he experiences in himself or others. It all seems cut to measure. For instance, in *Mountolive*, Leila gives this description of seeing Nessim, her grown son, naked:

It was a shock, I mean to suddenly see Nessim's naked body floating in the mirror, the slender white back . . . . I sat down and to my own surprise, burst into tears, because I wondered suddenly whether my attachment for you [Mountolive] wasn't lodged here somehow among the feeble incestuous desires of the inner heart. I know so little about the penetralia of sex which they are exploring so laboriously, the doctors. Their findings fill me with misgivings.[13]

Leila may not know much about psychoanalysis, but Durrell assuredly does. (He himself, in his critical work, *A Key to Modern British Poetry*, speculated about the influence Freudian psychology would have on contemporary writing.) When a conscious knowledge of this psychology leads the artist to offer elements of the oedipus complex as a prevailing feature of his work and supplies to the characters themselves such knowledge, it begins to lose verisimilitude to life. Even with resistance on the part of the mature personality, unconscious motivation has its own ways of finding gratification against a variety of hidden defenses. The dynamics are subtle, complex, and unique with each individual. The artist who gives up an intuitive understanding of his characters for a schematic formula of human behavior cannot create characters complex enough to seem real and true-to-life.

Notes

1. For a complete introduction to psychoanalytic theory, see Freud, *A General Introduction to Psychoanalysis*, and Otto Fenichel, *The Psychoanalytic Theory of Neurosis*. For a briefer survey, see Ives Hendrick, *Facts and Theories of Psychoanalysis*.
2. For a perceptive analysis of anal imagery in the fiction of Norman Mailer, see "*The Naked and the Dead*: The Triumph of Omnipotence," in Andrew Gordon, *Literature and Psychology*, XIX, 3-4 (1969), pp. 3-13.

3. "Problems and Techniques of Psychoanalytic Validation and Progress," in E. Pumpian-Mindlin, ed., *Psychoanalysis as Science* (Stanford, Calif.: Stanford University Press, 1952).
4. Otto Fenichel, *The Psychoanalytic Theory of Neurosis* (New York: Norton & Co., 1945). p. 56.
5. *A General Introduction to Psychoanalysis,* trans. by Joan Riviere (New York: Pocket Books, 1969), pp. 217-18.
6. Clara Thompson, *Psychoanalysis: Evolution and Development* (New York: Hermitage House, 1950), p. 39.
7. Riviere, *General Introduction,* p. 342.
8. Maurice Valency, *In Praise of Love* (New York: The Macmillan Co., 1961). Valency (p. 115) writes:

> We hardly need to be reminded, in this psychological age, that the dynamic experience of the poet is imbedded in the unconscious and constitutes his artistic predisposition. Poets are doubtless made, not born; but they are made early in life. The love which teaches the poet how to sing is very likely not the result of an adult experience, nevertheless it is indispensable to his calling. Consequently, it is always out of a deep and sincere feeling that the poet sings, though he himself may not be aware of its nature or its proper object.

For an analysis of the psychoanalytic implications of Valency's study, see the third section of this book.
9. For a detailed analysis of such dynamics, see Chapter 16 of Freud's *General Introduction,* particularly pp. 264-65.
10. See also the character of Creon in Sophocles' *Antigone.*
11. Lawrence S. Kubie, *Neurotic Distortion of the Creative Process* (New York: Noonday Press, 1961).
12. Iris Murdoch, *The Unicorn* (New York: Viking Press, 1963), p. 267.
13. Lawrence Durrell, *Mountolive* (New York: E. P. Dutton, 1961), pp. 53-54.

Fantasy in Fiction

Fantasy of Immortality: Conrad's
The Nigger of the Narcissus

i Defenses Against Death

The Nigger of the Narcissus[1] is the story of a ship's homebound voyage from the East, and of an ailing Negro, James Wait, who dies before the journey ends. The Negro captures the imagination of the crew, so that in time they identify with him in his illness. They suffer his approaching death in the belief that their own lives are somehow in jeopardy; and feel a complexity of moods, anger, fear, rebelliousness, courage, and doubt about whether the man is in fact dying, all of which are related to that merging of identity. The Negro makes himself "master of every moment of their existence," so that they "serve him in his bed with rage and humility." As the narrator puts it, "the secret and ardent desire of our hearts was the desire to beat him viciously with our fists about the head; and we handled him as tenderly as though he had been made of glass. . . ."[2] This ambivalence which the men feel toward James is so complex in its origin that the narrator can explain it only in the vaguest terms, as an "infernal spell," a "weird servitude," and a "colossal enigma."

In his 1914 Preface, Conrad gives us no specific explanation of the crew's behavior. He tells us only that James is "the center of the ship's

psychology and the pivot of the action."[3] Critics of the novel are
generally agreed that Wait's preoccupation with death, and a fear of
death among the crew, combine in some fashion to produce the spell.
For instance Albert Guerard finds Wait "a Death, and a test of responses to death."[4] And Ian Watt writes that he is "a symbol, not of
death, but of the fear of death, and therefore more widely of the
universal human reluctance to face . . . facts."[5] But these interpretations describe the situation without explaining it. Why, after all, *should*
the crew identify with Wait? Why should they serve him if they wish to
destroy him? Why can they never make up their minds about whether
or not he is a dying man? Why does the crew find no better explanation
of events than that they are caught in a colossal enigma?

The descriptive terms which the narrator uses, such as *spell, weird,
enigma, nightmare, supernatural, infamous mysteries,* are often selected
by artists to dramatize unconscious motivation in characters, since such
words convey the sense that events are determined by secret and hidden
causes. This is where an explanation can be found, in motivation the
men themselves do not recognize, and which in consequence they
characterize as a "weird servitude." The best way to uncover this
motivation is to see what confronts them in the character of James
Wait. This dying, tubercular Negro aboard the *Narcissus* has a genius for
denying the fact that his death is near. His fear of death is so overwhelming that he adopts a variety of defenses against it, defenses which
are then unconsciously taken up by the crew. In this way the spell is
cast, and, to repeat Conrad's phrase, James becomes the center of the
ship's psychology. An understanding of his defenses, then, will give us
the key.

The simplest of James' defenses is that of outright denial: in utter
disregard of the facts, he denies that he is dying. Such a defense is
comparable to the child's magical belief in the omnipotence of thought;
as though, in Hamlet's words, there is nothing either good or bad, but
thinking makes it so. It is the defense adopted by adults who, suspect-
ing they may have an illness, convince themselves they are well simply
by not seeing a doctor. Chapter I gives us a subtle example. Wait has
one of his first fits of coughing, a "roaring, rattling cough that shook
him, tossed him like a hurricane, and flung him panting with staring
eyes headlong on his sea chest." Nevertheless he gasps, "I have a cold
on my chest." One sailor wisely replies, "Cold! you call it . . . should
think 'twas something more." Soon to die, and plainly sounding it,

Wait's reply, in its tone of ironic ambiguity, denies that it is anything more: " 'Oh! you think so,' said the nigger upright and loftily scornful again."[6]

As James grows progressively worse he refuses all medicine, takes to his bed, and wastes away. He continues to assert that there is nothing really wrong with him. "Been out of sorts now and again this year," he wheezes.[7] Coughing violently, he adds, "I am as well as ever." Not long before his death, he can still exclaim to the captain, "I've been better this last week . . . I am well. . . . I was going back to duty . . . tomorrow—now if you like."[8] Had such blunt denials been his only defense against the fear of death, there would have been no story. The crew would merely have disbelieved him and given him scant sympathy. The journey home would have been, save for the great storm, indistinguishable from a thousand others. But James adopts a more complex form of denial as well, one which powerfully affects the crew. He hides his sickness behind the mask of a malingerer, frequently contradicts his own denials of illness during the voyage, declaims insistently his approaching death, and in consequence receives favors, comforts, and privileges from the crew. He deludes himself with the pretense that his illness is no more than a deliberately chosen sham and that, therefore, it need not be feared.

In keeping with this pretense of illness, James taunts the shipmates who keep him awake at night with: "Much you care for a dying man!" When scolded by Mr. Baker for being slack at his work, James replies that his lungs are "Going—or gone. Can't you see I'm a dying man? I know it!" And the narrator tells us that "he would talk of that coming death as though it had been already there, as if it had been walking the deck outside, as if it would presently come in to sleep in the only empty bunk; as if it had sat by his side at every meal."[9] When brought before the captain for not working, James—so it is rumored—coughs all over the captain's meteorological charts, and gets, in consequence, a dry, comfortable cabin sick bay. It is, in fact, all a dodge he has used before! In a highly revealing conversation with the sailor Donkin, James reveals how successfully he has fooled himself in this way and denied his fears:

"Ye 'ave done this afore 'aven'tchee?" Jimmy smiled—then as if unable to hold back he let himself go: "Last ship—yes. I was out of sorts on the passage. See? It was easy. They paid me off in Calcutta, and the

skipper made no bones about it either .... I got my money all right.
Laid up fifty-eight days! The fools! O Lord! The Fools! Paid right off."
He laughed spasmodically. . . . Then Jimmy coughed violently. "I am as
well as ever," he said, as soon as he could draw breath.[10]

How perfectly Conrad blends the two motifs. James laughs at the fools
who treat him as though he were ill and, asserting he is as well as ever,
coughs so violently he cannot breathe. Such a denial of illness, so
contrary to reality, is the measure of the fear which occasions it.

One notes how such a role suits the psychological requirements of
defense. As Fenichel points out, one can deny fear and anxiety either
"by denying the existence of a dangerous situation, or by denying the
fact that one feels afraid."[11] Wait's outright denial that he is sick is an
example of the former. The problem with such a simple defense is that,
as Anna Freud writes, "it can be employed only so long as it can exist
side by side with the capacity for reality testing . . . ."[12] In other
words, short of a psychosis, Wait cannot, in the face of realistically
observable symptoms, simply deny his illness. By playing the role of
malingerer, by affecting symptoms, he creates an external situation
which makes denial possible. Since the presence of real affliction is
obscured by his pretense of symptoms, he can fearlessly assert to
himself and the crew that he is dying—but think to himself that in
reality it is all an act, and that therefore he need not be afraid.

He makes himself an extraordinary phenomenon, a dying malingerer
whose shamming achieves other defensive purposes as well. Wait is able
to *actively* associate himself with death, rather than *passively* be its
victim. Like the condemned man who hangs himself, the mere fact of
exercising choice allays the fear of death, perhaps because the child first
associates his fears with the fact of his own helpless passivity. It is a
primitive defense, akin to magical thinking, one which Fenichel describes in his discussion of denial:

Sometimes the original anxiety situations are not avoided but are
sought, at least under certain conditions; the person shows a preference
for the very situation of which he is apparently afraid. . . . The active
repetition of what has been experienced passively . . . remains the principal mechanisms in fighting anxiety. Frequently the search for situations formerly feared becomes pleasurable precisely because they are
actively sought.[13]

Accordingly, as a last defense, Wait is able to displace his fears onto the crew. The intimidation of others, as with the proverbial cowardice of the bully, denies that one is himself afraid. This, also, is a primitive mode of defense, based on an identification with the aggressor. Since James is afraid of death, he enacts the role of Death himself come to frighten the crew. The narrator describes how it works:

. . . a black mist emanated from him, a subtle and dismal influence, a something cold and gloomy that floated out and settled on all the faces like a mourning veil. The circle broke up. The joy of laughter died on stiffened lips. There was not a smile left among all the ship's company.

Men stood around very still and with exasperated eyes. It was just what they had expected, and hated to hear, that idea of a stalking death, thrust at them many times a day like a boast and like a menace by this obnoxious nigger.[14]

The various defenses used by Wait during the voyage are, however, never psychologically successful. The principal reason has to do with their contradicting one another. On the one hand, he asserts he is perfectly well and, on the other, declares he is dying. The problem with such contradictions is not that it is irrational. The mere insistence in the face of illness that he is well is irrational enough. When painful thought and feeling must be dealt with, rationality is dispensable. Rather, the problem has to do with the difference between deliberately play-acting an illness and having the fact thrust at him by the crew. His posture as a malingerer sustains in his own mind so fragile a denial that he cannot endure to hear from the crew the very idea he has implanted in their minds. Time and again Wait reverts from assertions of illness to denial, precisely when the facts of his condition are expressed by someone else. When one sailor, Singleton, merely puts it to him as a question ("Are you dying?"), James is "horribly startled and confused." Such a situation graphically illustrates Fenichel's point about the distinction between an active and passive involvement with a feared situation. It is a predicament laden with dramatic irony, since eventually James suffers in the company of those taken in by his malingering, and befriends Donkin, the one man who consistently accuses him of playacting. Poor James: as with neurosis in general, the very defenses adopted beget the need for more defenses.

So fundamental to the action are James' defenses against death that Conrad has even provided a symbolic prefiguring of the motif. The first notable event in the story is the sudden appearance of James Wait aboard ship, after the crew has been assembled for the roll-call. Preparations for the morning departure are underway, but then momentarily stopped by the sudden cry "Wait!" The chief mate is confused, thinking his orders have been countermanded and not perceiving that James has merely shouted his own name. Apart from the fact that the event is exactly what it purports to be—that is, the arrival of a late-comer with a confusing name—there is also a level of narration which is subtly and symbolically communicated. We know from dream analysis that departure on a trip is a frequent representation of dying, just as it is a common metaphor for death in poetry. Hence to delay, however briefly, this journey from which no traveler returns, is to resist death. Freud writes that "dreams of missing a train . . . are dreams of consolation for another kind of anxiety felt in sleep—the fear of dying. 'Departing' on a journey is one of the commonest and best authenticated symbols of death. These dreams say in a consoling way: 'Don't worry, you won't die' (depart) . . . ."[15]

One is reminded of that superb moment in Bergman's *The Seventh Seal* when Death himself reaches out to touch a knight returned from the Crusades. "Wait!" the knight cries. "They always say that," Death replies. In Conrad's story, the first mate's confusion specifically draws our attention to James' last name as a command to wait, so that James becomes in this subtle fashion like the Crusader. The cry of "Wait," at the start of a voyage which brings death, duplicates in symbolism what *The Seventh Seal* expresses in allegory. And the first mate's confusion, thinking the shouted name a directive, is, in this light, a correct perception—an example of dramatic irony in keeping with the symbolic meaning of the episode.

ii Obsessional Doubt

We see, then, that James is engaged in a complex defense against the fear of death. It is a formula for defense which has an extraordinary effect on the crew. By alternatively asserting and denying the fact that he is dying, James throws the men into endless doubt. They might easily have caught a malingerer, or sympathized in moderation with a dying man. But something happens to them when they have to deal with a man who is both at the same time. They can never decide if he is dying or not. Doubt—seemingly so simple a state of mind—corrupts them in a fashion they do not themselves understand until they are, in the narrator's phrase, cast into an infernal spell.

Realistically, there should be no doubt. James is, after all, plainly dying. His sickness is apparent to a number of men almost from the beginning. Singleton, Podmore, and the captain all see it easily enough. The crew is plagued by a doubt which is obsessive, since it has an involuntary life of its own so tenacious that it persists even after James has died. Habitual doubting is a familiar form of obsessional thought and, as such, expresses unconscious purpose. The unconscious purpose is, in this case, the "colossal enigma."

When we first meet James, after the *Narcissus* has gone to sea, almost all the elements of this enigma are manifest. We find that James immediately succeeds in his defensive determination to transfer his fear of death to the crew. By talking of death as though it were a personified figure come to live with the entire crew, James instills in them an anxiety they cannot identify, but which can be nothing other than his own ever-present fear of dying. As previously quoted, the narrator, very much one of the crew himself, describes how this subjugation of the crew is experienced as an ineffable dread: "He seemed to hasten the retreat of departing light by his very presence; the setting sun dipped sharply, as though fleeing before our nigger; a black mist emanated from him, a subtle and dismal influence, a something cold and gloomy that floated out and settled on all the faces like a mourning veil". Death could not be better described than as a black, cold, and gloomy mist that settles on the face like a mourning veil. It is perfectly true that the crew have no rational reason to fear death. They are not themselves ill. But it is understandable how the "idea of a stalking death, thrust at them many times a day" might stir latent fear which all men have, in the knowledge that death is always certain, even if it is not soon to come.

And so with their own fears of death now greatly aggravated, they seek an extraordinary defense against fear, through obsessive doubting. If they can cast doubt on the certainty of death in the case of a man almost dead already, they can indulge (however irrationally and unconsciously) the fantasy that the inevitability of their own death is no longer certain. If one man can resist an illness which is assuredly fatal, the laws of death are overturned, and to what can they not all aspire? If

James proves invulnerable to death, so might they all prove invulnerable. In consequence, they question throughout the story whether James is dying, although the fact is always plain to see.

The narrator writes that James' intimacy with death is "paraded" by him with such "affectionate persistence" that they find death's presence "indubitable, and at the same time incredible." "No man," he reasons, "could be suspected of such monstrous friendship." This situation is a Gordian knot which they can easily cut through simply by recognizing that James is a deliberate sham in many of his actions, but that, ironically, he is also fatally ill. The narrator asks, "Was he a reality—or was he a sham—this ever-expected visitor of Jimmy's?" The simplest answer, one which forever eludes both narrator and crew, is that James is both. And it is their own fantasy which keeps them from that truth.

The narrator describes the effect James has on them in terms which do imply their shared fantasy of immortality although he never makes it explicit. He tells us that James was the "fit emblem of their aspirations"; that James' intimate accomplice "seemed to have blown with his impure breath undreamt-of subtleties into our hearts." He never tells us what their aspirations or undreamt-of subtleties are. But later passages describing their reaction make it clearer. For instance, the narrator writes:

Jimmy's steadfastness to his untruthful attitude in the face of the inevitable truth had the proportions of a colossal enigma . . . . His obstinate nonrecognition of the only certitude whose approach we could watch from day to day was as disquieting as *the failure of some law of nature.* He was so utterly wrong about himself that *one could not but suspect him of having access to some source of supernatural knowledge.* He was absurd to the point of inspiration.[16]

The best description the narrator gives us of this process of fear spreading to the crew, and their adoption of James' fantasy of invulnerability to death, is the following:

We understood the subtlety of his fear, sympathized with all his repulsions, shrinkings, evasions, *delusions*—as though . . . *without any knowledge of the meaning of life.* We had the air of being initiated in some infamous mysteries. . . . We lied to him with gravity, with emotion, with unction, as if performing some moral trick *with a view to an eternal reward.* We made a chorus of affirmation to his wildest assertions. . . . [17]

It is clear that the crew are at times conscious of the fact that James must die; they know they are lying to him. And they tell themselves often enough that they lie for James' sake. But at such times they forget their sense of having been cast into a detestable spell—a spell which the following passage clearly describes:

He would never let doubt die. He overshadowed the ship. Invulnerable in his promise of speedy corruption he trampled on our self-respect, he demonstrated to us daily our want of moral courage; he tainted our lives. Had we been a miserable gang of wretched immortals, unhallowed alike by hope and fear, he could not have lorded it over us with a more pitiless assertion of his sublime privilege.[18]

This is a perfect example of why the literary critic is constrained to infer unconscious motivation. They have no conscious desire to serve James, yet they do it. And one need only listen to the suggestiveness of the language used to perceive again their implicit desire. The "sublime privilege" of James *is* his "invulnerability." And they serve him to share it. The narrator puts their desire hypothetically: . . . *"had we been a miserable gang of immortals."* But why, after all, should immortals be miserable for being immortal? The narrator is defining their condition more accurately than he knows. They *are* a miserable gang of immortals. They accept consciously the misery of servitude to James, to share the unconscious fantasy of being immortal. Until his very death, James continues "perfectly invulnerable in his apparent ignorance" of death; and so long as he does, they serve him, renewing "the assurance of life—the indestructible thing!"

Needless to say, the whole thing is illogical in the extreme, so illogical they will not fully acknowledge the fantasy to themselves. But their actions show plainly enough how they share in it. Only when James dies at last do they come to a somewhat clearer understanding of what has happened: "We did not know till then how much faith we had put in his delusions. We had taken his chances of life so much as his own valuation that his death, like the death of an old belief, shook the foundations of our society."[19] Theirs is a society founded on a shared delusion and, like youth itself, it cannot endure.

iii

We have concentrated thus far on James and the majority of the crew, and suggested that they are in an unspoken conspiracy to deny the inevitability of death. There are exceptions, notably the cook Podmore, old Singleton, and the captain. Each recognizes that James is dying; each remains impervious to the doubts which infect the crew. However, they are not foils, for each in his own way illustrates a formula peculiar to himself for achieving what James and the crew achieve by obsessive doubting.

Podmore, for instance, is ready at all times for his death. When one of the sailors, Belfast, warns him that his habit of falling asleep with his pipe in his mouth will kill him one day, we read:

"Ah! sonny, I am ready for my Maker's call . . . wish you all were." Podmore would answer with a benign serenity that was altogether imbecile and touching. Belfast outside the gallery door danced with vexation. "You holy fool! I don't want you to die," he howled, looking up with furious, quivering face and tender eyes. "What's the hurry? . . . the divyle will have you soon enough. Think of Us . . . of Us . . . of Us!" And he would go away, stamping, spitting aside, disgusted and worried. . . . "[20]

It would be difficult to imagine that Belfast is disturbed merely at the possibility of losing a friend and their only cook, particularly since the likelihood of such an accidental death is unlikely. The violence of Belfast's reaction—*vexation, howled, furious, quivering, stamping, spitting, disgusted*—tells us plainly enough how wide is the gulf between the cook ready for his maker, and the crew who are not. But we note that Podmore's "benign serenity" is not fearlessness at death's finality, but rather the Christian assurance that heaven waits for him and that death itself will die. He contemplates, the narrator tells us, the secret of the hereafter. He enjoys the "pride of possessed eternity." Why, after all, *should* he fear death? In one poignant scene, he attempts to reconcile James to his imminent death by readying him for salvation. Had the cook succeeded, James would have been spared his merciless terrors. As it is, nothing shakes James from his denials, and he howls out, humorously consistent with his defenses, that he is being "murdered."

Singleton has another formula. He is, we are told, "a child of time."

The epithet is well chosen, since for most of the story his attitude toward death is like that of a child. Time has no meaning for him, and he grasps the fact of death so abstractly that he feels no fear. He is "ever unthinking," with a "vast empty past and with no future, with his childish impulses." He knows "how to exist beyond the pale of life and within sight of enternity," and knows "neither doubts nor hopes . . . [nor] fear."

This is a serenity equal to Podmore's, and it permits him to confront James with a matter-of-fact acceptance of James's death that startles the crew, sets their hearts thumping, and their mouths agape: "We'll get on with your dying . . . don't raise a blamed fuss with us over that job. We can't help you." When one sailor, tormented by their usual doubts, then asks Singleton if James will die, the oracular reply, "Of course he will die," gives some of them a moment's relief from doubt. But nothing could better dramatize how that doubt has served their own purposes than what follows. They are told, and it comes to them with a force of revelation, how the remark might equally mean that eventually all of them must die. This is the very idea they have been resisting all along, and so they are "appalled." Singleton has given them a certitude they do not want, an obvious one which they yet would not have perceived for themselves. And so they hate him for the remark, and return to their doubts.

Singleton's childlike indifference to the facts of time and death, unlike the secure faith of Podmore, is, however, not invulnerable. During the great storm, he keeps himself lashed to the wheel for more than thirty hours. He is the oldest man aboard, and to do such a thing, for all his great strength, in itself bespeaks a denial of age. But when it is over, the childish innocence is gone. The narrator gives us a vivid description of the defense which has served him so well, and the pathos of its inevitable loss:

He had never given a thought to his mortal self. He lived unscathed, as though he had been indestructible . . . . Old! It seemed to him he was broken at last. And like a man bound treacherously while he sleeps, he woke up fettered by the long chain of disregarded years. He had to take up at once the burden of all his existence, and found it almost too heavy for his strength.[21]

No one, not even he, escapes the mourning veil.

The captain is another who has no doubts about Jimmy. On the occasion that Podmore attempts to ready Jimmy for his death, Jimmy breaks down in screeching and sobs, his defenses momentarily rent. After the crew has gathered round, Captain Allistoun enters and learns what has occurred. He is immediately enlisted into the ranks of those who support James's delusion. The captain tells us:

When I saw him standing there, three parts dead and so scared . . . no grit to face what's coming to us all—the notion came to me all at once, before I could think. Sorry for him . . . . If ever creature was in a mortal funk to die! . . . I thought I would let him go out in his own way. Kind of impulse. . . . I fancied he asked me for something.[22]

And so he tells James there is nothing the matter with him but that, for shamming sick, he must remain confined to his bed, until the end of the voyage. At this moment James is, in reality, far too ill to return to work although he insists he is well enough to get up. And so the captain chooses the one action which permits the delusion, in James and the crew, to continue.

This portrayal of the captain is Conrad's most ingenious handling of his theme in a minor character. Like Podmore and Singleton, he sees that James is three parts dead. But unlike them, he takes no refuge in a faith in the hereafter or in a childlike obliviousness of his own mortality. His refuge and defense is far subtler and involves his compassion for James, an empathy so unusual that the mates are "more impressed than if they had seen a stone image shedding a miraculous tear of compassion over the incertitudes of life and death." How perfect the narrator's example is. In the context of this story, death is an incertitude only in the minds of men who will not face the certitude when it confronts them. Although we cannot doubt the sincerity of the captain's desire to have Jimmy "die in peace," we cannot overlook the fact that, in consequence, he joins the conspiracy with so many others aboard ship. Conrad implies the presence of additional and unconscious motivation in the emphasis given to the seemingly unbidden character of the captain's impulse to lie to Jimmy, and to tell him he is perfectly well: "The notion came to me all at once, before I could think . . . . I thought I would let him go out in his own way. Kind of impulse."

The situation is, in this way, comparable to adults who lie to children about death. We say to children that the dead have "gone away," that they live in heaven and watch over us, or have gone into a long sleep. We profess to believe none of this, but as Jacob Arlow has pointed out, we lie more for our own sakes. Children do not require lies; they cannot conceive of death even when it is explained to them. Ironically, it may be that our explanations, based on what they have experience with, are more frightening to them than the truth—making them fear, for instance, a trip to be taken by a parent, or even their own going to sleep. We tell children what we ourselves would like to believe. The captain put it very well when he said that James had "no grit to face what's coming to us all." James' death is an emblem of what awaits them all; and although the captain knows the truth, he plays in his own way the same magical game of denial.

The crew's reaction to the captain's insistence that James is sham-ming, and that he not be permitted to leave his bed, surprises the captain, but is explicable in light of our analysis. The crew revolts, complaining to the captain's face, threatening that they will not work, growling, hissing, and cursing. On the following day the captain asks them what it is they want, but they cannot tell him. As the narrator indicates in his suggestive way, they want the ineffable: "They wanted great things. And suddenly all the simple words they knew seemed to be lost forever in the immensity of their vague and burning desire. The knew what they wanted, but they could not find anything worth saying."[23] Incapable of explaining, one sailor in wavering voice offers the obvious rationalization that they did not want to go shorthanded— as though the loss of one hand, one who had never done much work at his best, mattered at all to them.

What matters is the "immensity of their vague and burning desire," for "great things." The captain has given them assurance that James is fit to work. And the spell, in which they have made "a chorus of affirmation to his wildest assertions," seems at the last moment capable of fulfillment. The dying man has only to get up and go back to work, for death to be defeated as a victory for them all. But the captain will not let him up, and they understandably cannot find the words for the frustration of so irrational and unconscious an aspiration as the wish to escape mortality.

The two most dramatic events in the story are the overturning of the ship during a gale, and the burial of James at the end. Both events underscore aspects of this immortality motif. The gale is of such immensity that the narrator tells us that most seamen see in their lives only one or two of such nights. With the ship fallen on its side and the men lashed to the deck for survival, the crew suddenly remembers that James is caught below in his cabin. Their rescue attempt, under conditions almost hopelessly hazardous, attests to the courage and solidarity of men who sail ships, a breed Conrad so often celebrates. But in this case, ironically, they freely face death before the storm, wildly scrambling over the half-submerged deck of an overturned ship, not merely to save a man, but to insure the survival of that man whose uncrushable will to live they vicariously share. One can find, in their action, again that element of denial so constantly present in this story. It is not they who are afraid, not they who are faced with death. The mortal danger belongs to James, and they will save him. And so, even as they increase the risk of their own deaths, their fear of death is removed. Conrad signals this inward victory in the midst of jeopardy by their grotesquely inappropriate mirth, which the narrator rightly equates with mania. When one of them is caught half-overboard, they laugh: " ... as if hysterically injected with screaming merriment, all those haggard men went off laughing, wild-eyed, like a lot of maniacs ... ." This manic merriment can only express a release from fear, another release conjured in the imagination against obvious realities.

The symbolic scene which follows is another rendering, more vivid and concrete perhaps than anything that has gone before, of the immortality theme. James is imprisoned in a room below. Wondering if he is dead or alive, they knock on the bulkhead and then hear him "screaming and knocking below ... with the hurry of a man prematurely shut up in his coffin." His predicament epitomizes what has been his stance throughout the story—three parts dead in his coffin and still shouting wait! As always, his fear so cuts through them that they cannot tolerate it: "The agony of his fear wrung our hearts so terribly that we longed to abandon him, to get out of that place deep as a well ... back on the poop where we could wait passively for death in incomparable respose." Instead, as the sea threatens to drown them at every moment, they work fiercely, cutting their hands and "speaking brutally" to one another. It is the "weird servitude" all over again. They might accept death for themselves, but James' fear overcomes them. And now they all but succeed in their "wildest aspirations," pulling James up and out of his coffin, making death wait in the very place where he most reigns victorious. Appropriately enough, the ship itself soon struggles to stand up, and then rises "as though she had torn herself out from a deadly grasp." It is as though the destiny of the ship, as well as of the men, has depended on James' survival.

The culmination of the story is the uncanny refusal of James, even dead and wrapped in the Union Jack on a burial plank over the sea, to go. Incredibly, even now, he waits:

James did not move.—"Higher," muttered the boatswain angrily. All the heads were raised; every man stirred uneasily, but James Wait gave no sign of going. In death and swathed up for all eternity, he yet seemed to cling to the ship with the grip of an undying fear. "Higher! Lift!" whispered the boatswain, fiercely. "He won't go," stammered one of the men. . . . [24]

The scene is uncanny because for one magic moment he seems to have achieved the ultimate, impossible victory. The moment is, perhaps, as poignant as any in fiction. The reader himself, who has wavered back and forth with his doubts about James, who has felt the same spell in his wish that death might be cheated, wonders for an instant if James has, after all, found "access to some source of supernatural knowledge" to bring about "the failure of some law of nature."

The spell is broken when one of the sailors cries out to him to be a man. There is a *double entendre* here, as there was in James' name. "Be a man" means not only have the courage to face death, but accept the death which is natural to men. This is a truth they have unconsciously resisted and helped James to resist; but as though accepting it now, James finally goes, sliding off the planks with the "suddenness of a flash of lightning." The crew breathes a sigh "like one man"—and they are joined by their shared fantasy no more.

The ship, too, rolls as if "relieved of an unfair burden." The breeze springs up, and the ship is becalmed no more. As Singleton foretold, they can reach land only after James dies. We have come full circle to the symbolism which began the story. The journey which symbolizes death cannot be completed until death is consummated. And when it is completed, the narrator writes that the ship in her berth "had ceased to live." He never sees any of the crew again, and sadly tells us that "a gone shipmate, like any other man, is gone forever." They are all men, like James, and all must die. In memory he sees the forlorn ship adrift in Hades, manned by a crew of Shades. The tale, in its fullest sense, expresses the tragedy of human mortality and the futility of any efforts to escape. Only the sea, the narrator writes, is immortal. Such a mood of tragedy may have invaded Conrad himself. After writing *The Nigger of the Narcissus*, he felt a revulsion for the story and left the sea forever.[25]

62   Fantasy in Fiction

Notes

1. Joseph Conrad, *Three Great Tales* (New York: Vintage Books, 1900). Future references are to this edition.
2. Conrad, *Tales,* p. 57.
3. See Joseph Conrad, *The Nigger of the Narcissus* (New York: Doubleday, Page & Co., 1924), p. ix.
4. Albert J. Geurard, *Conrad the Novelist* (Cambridge: Harvard University Press, 1958), p. 109.
5. Ian Watt, "Conrad Criticism and *The Nigger of the Narcissus,*" *Nineteenth-Century Fiction*, 12 (1958), 275.
6. Conrad, *Tales,* p. 20.
7. Conrad, *Tales,* p. 82.
8. Conrad, *Tales,* p. 92.
9. Conrad, *Tales,* p. 29.
10. Conrad, *Tales,* p. 86.
11. Otto Fenichel, *The Psychoanalytic Theory of Neurosis* (New York: Norton & Co., 1945), p. 480. Future references will be to this edition.
12. Fenichel, *Neurosis,* p. 90.
13. Fenichel, *Neurosis,* pp. 480-81.
14. Fenichel, *Neurosis,* pp. 28-29.
15. Sigmund Freud, *The Standard Edition of the Complete Psychological Works, The Interpretation of Dreams* (London: Hogarth Press, 1962). V, p. 384.
16. Conrad, *Tales,* p. 107. Emphasis added.
17. Conrad, *Tales,* pp. 107-9. Emphasis added.
18. Conrad, *Tales,* p. 37
19. Conrad, *Tales,* p. 120.
20. Conrad, *Tales,* p. 16.
21. Conrad, *Tales,* p. 76-77.
22. Conrad, *Tales,* p. 98.
23. Conrad, *Tales,* pp. 103-4.
24. Conrad, *Tales,* p. 124.
25. See Conrad's 1914 Preface to *Tales,* p. xi.

Fantasy of Passivity: Melville's
Bartleby the Scrivener

i

Melville's *Bartleby the Scrivener*[1] is a work of comic irony comparable to such novels as Ford's *The Good Soldier* or Durrell's *Justine,* both of which use the device of fallible narrator. In *The Good Soldier,* for instance, Dowell is an unperceptive, sentimental, sexually impotent man, married to an immoral sensualist. The focus of the novel is not the inevitable failure of the marriage, but the very efforts of this man—who has never felt toward his wife "the beginnings of a trace of what is called the sex instinct"—to comprehend and describe that failure. So long as he cannot acknowledge the importance of sexuality in human relationships his narrative vision is corrupted, and that is the whole point of the story. In a superb analysis of *The Good Soldier,* one which we can apply to *Bartleby* as well, Mark Shorer writes:

The fracture between the character of the event as we feel it to be and the character of the narrator as he reports the event to us is the essential irony . . . . Perhaps the most astonishing achievement in this astonishing novel is the manner in which the author, while speaking through his simple, infatuated character, lets us know how to take his simplicity and his infatuation.[2]

Melville's narrator is no less enmeshed in an effort to explain events beyond his comprehension. And the manner in which the author enables us to understand both the causes and the extent of that limitation rivals the full artistry of Ford's achievement.

"I am," this narrator writes, "a man who, from his youth upwards, has been filled with a profound conviction that the easiest way of life is the best." This belief, he tells us, has made him a certain kind of unambitious lawyer, one who can "in the cool tranquility of a snug retreat, do a snug business among rich men's bonds." And for thirty years he allows nothing to invade this peace—until he hires the scrivener Bartleby. The conflict which follows seems on the surface no more than an obscure antagonism in a Wall Street office, between the narrator and an employee who will not work. But in fact they collide with a force as intense as any which may bedevil two men. With precise accuracy, Bartleby undermines the tenuous code by which this lawyer has lived. The narrator's passivity, prudence, and life-long obsession with safety are all challenged with uncanny success. And as he continues to describe these events, he never suspects the nature of the role he himself has played.

The main character of the story (or so the narrator believes) is Bartleby, a pale, silent scrivener who comes into his employ. At first Bartleby does an extraordinary amount of writing, but he refuses to do any other work, objecting each time with the incongruous remark that he "would prefer not to." Angry and astonished at this challenge to his authority, the narrator nevertheless allows Bartleby to remain, because of his ceaseless industry as copyist. But as the days follow, the complete oddity of the man becomes apparent. He lives at night in the office, associates with no one, never speaks except to answer (and not always then), never leaves the office, eats nothing but ginger nuts, and with increasing frequency stands unmoving, either in the center of the room or looking out the window at a "dead brick wall." At last the scrivener declares he will do no further work of any kind. When the narrator concludes that Bartleby is the victim of an incurable disorder and fires him at last, he finds that Bartleby would prefer not to be dismissed and would prefer not to leave the office.

Even under these conditions, the narrator allows Bartleby to remain, thinking that to do so is an act of charity and a service to God. But when his clients and colleagues all begin to talk about the strange, immobile apparition in his office, the narrator can tolerate Bartleby no longer. Unable to simply put him out, the lawyer himself moves, locating his office elsewhere. For a time Bartleby is still successful in refusing to change his life. Turned out of the office by the landlord and the new tenant, he haunts the building, "sitting upon the banisters of the stairs by day, and sleeping in the entry by night." In order to avoid any publicity, the narrator now tries to persuade the scrivener to find a new job, and even to come home with him until a job can be found. But Bartleby refuses in his usual manner, and at last is taken to prison as a vagrant. There, emaciated by his refusal to eat, he stares at a dead-wall in the yard, and finally dies in a foetal position at its base.

The narrator ends his story with what he calls a "suggestive rumor," that Bartleby once worked in a dead-letter office. "Conceive a man by nature and misfortune prone to a pallid hopelessness," he concludes, "can any business seem more fitted to heighten it than that of continually handling these dead letters, and assorting them for the flames?" But this is a maudlin view of Bartleby's character. The thought that there is a faulty communication among men may cause distress, but not madness. The world is full of grave-diggers, hangmen, and asylum attendants, who do not become Bartlebys. The narrator errs, and ascribes a factitious cause to Bartleby's derangement, because he fails to see the motivation behind such bizarre and self-destructive behavior. We can well understand why it is difficult enough to perceive the motivation implicit in *neurotic* behavior; and Bartleby's derangement, by almost any standards a psychosis, all the more completely masks the underlying motivation which directs him to his dead-wall reveries. The narrator has, in addition, his own reasons for misconstruing Bartleby's purposes. But if we take our cue from the psychoanalytic view, specifically of a manic-depressive psychosis, much in the text will support this understanding of the man.

Bartleby's disorder may be termed a psychosis because his surrender to symptoms is so complete that he breaks with reality. He makes no effort whatever to communicate with others, to end his depression, or break out of his immobile stupor—in short, no effort to comply with basic needs, including the need to eat. So complete is his submission that we have no reason to believe he is aware that anything is wrong. His comment, that he would prefer not to work, is like a later remark, when he is emaciated to the point of death, that he would prefer not to eat dinners. The language is rationally put, but the sense is bizarre and alien to rational goals. He speaks of "preferences," but no alternatives seem possible to him. Such behavior conforms with that of the manic-depressive. Silvano Arieti's description of the depressive stupor of this disorder seems almost to have been written as a portrait of Bartleby:

Depressive stupor is the most pronounced form of depression. Here there is more than retardation: the movements are definitely inhibited or suppressed. The patients are so absorbed in their own pervading feeling of depression that they cannot focus their attention on their surroundings. They do not seem to hear; they do not respond. They are mute, with the exception of some occasional utterances. Since they cannot focus on anything, they give the impression of being apathetic, whereas they are actually the prey of a deep, disturbing emotion. These patients cannot take care of themselves. Generally, they lie in bed mute, and have to be spoon-fed.

Unless they are successfully treated during the attack, physical health may suffer severely. They lose up to a hundred pounds in certain cases . . . .[3]

This description accords well with Bartleby's immobility, apathy, and helplessness. But the only clue it offers to the inner motivation of the man is the comment that beneath the depression is disturbing emotion. But, we may ask, what is the nature of an emotion so uncompromising that it renders him incapable of both sanity and life? The basis for an answer is given in various ways by the story itself. Bartleby, after all, has an extraordinary effect on the small world in which he lives. If we dismiss his passivity as simply a crazed negation of life, we miss the fact that in his own bizarre fashion he achieves a great deal. If we look, in fact, with a disinterested eye at the towering strength with which he refuses to comply with the demands of his world, and at the shattering effect he has on the man who represents that world to him, we will find he achieves an absolute "adjustment" on his own terms. Like a fallen Satan, Bartleby gives up one world to reign in another. The choice may be an insane one, but it is not without its own motivation.

The keynote to Bartleby's psychology is given in a superb description of the underlying dynamics of depressive behavior, by Walter Bonime. Dr. Bonime writes out of a psychoanalytic practice with depressives and with a theoretical orientation well-defined and fruitful. He points out that the psychotic person exhibits crucial attributes also found in the neurotic—specifically, that both are engaged in purposive behavior and that those purposes are best understood in the context of their social action. He offers a description of the depressive individual that brings us directly to the motives of the scrivener:

> ... the depressive is an extremely manipulative individual who, by helplessness, sadness, seductiveness, and other means, maneuvers people toward the fulfillment of demands for various forms of emotionally comforting response. The emotional and behavioral corollary to this extreme manipulativeness is an almost allergic sensitivity to being influenced; this engenders forms of elusiveness manifested in helplessness, withdrawal, physical and mental retardation, manic behavior, stubbornness, irresponsibility, unproductive preoccupying activities, and various types of failure and self-destruction.[4]

The manipulativeness of the depressive is the most significant fact of this description. Behind apparent apathy there is purposive action. The man who "would prefer" to do nothing, on the contrary, indulges in the power to frustrate. It is a grim battle in which the depressive spares himself least of all. Dr. Bonime vividly describes this tenacity in terms which again bring Bartleby directly to mind:

The depressive is determined to prevail, to win in every interpersonal encounter. For him life is a battle—with individuals and with fate. He is going to get what he wants, and he is not going to be forced to exert himself responsibly in pursuit of a more realistic goal. ... He will sacrifice some or all of his potentials for living, but in his subjective, distorted, competitive emotional orientation he will nevertheless be victorious.

In the competitive world of the depressive, this rebellion is a living declaration that "Nobody's going to make me do anything, nobody can force me to respond." The depressive even carries this out by escape into psychosis or suicide, in which extreme instances the process may be a charade of "You can't make me live on your terms," or "at all."[5]

This description of the uncompromising depressive is the criterion by which to judge Bartleby. To understand how successful he is in these terms, however, we must look again at the narrator. It is in the interaction between them that Bartleby's victory is enacted. And behind the self-deceptions of the narrator's story, the force of that victory is unmistakable.

ii

Bartleby enacts his depression in the company of an antagonist exquisitely picked. There could hardly be imagined an interlocking of disorders greater than that which exists between the narrator and his scrivener. They are as intricately joined by nature and temperament as Othello to Iago, or Mario to the magician Cipolla. The narrator has lived all his life out of the reach of conflict, evidently with amazing success. He is now confronted in Bartleby with a man who must not only be fired, but forcibly taken from his office—if not directly by him, then by the police at his command. This would seem to be a not very difficult task, even for a peaceable man. He has, after all, no other rational choice, and morality and the law are on his side. But the difficulty of the task should not be judged solely on the basis of external obstacles. One is reminded of Hamlet, the man with no compunctions about killing and with all the motivation and opportunity he needs to kill, who yet delays so long he must at last exclaim:

> I do not know
> Why yet I live to say "This thing's to do,"
> Sith I have cause, and will, and strength, and means
> To do 't.[6]

As the story gradually makes clear, the difficulty for Melville's narrator, as much as for Hamlet, is within the mind.

The first confrontation takes place shortly after Bartleby is hired. The scrivener has already indicated manic-depressive behavior, in the unnatural intensity of his diligence: the narrator tells us that "he did an extraordinary quantity of writing. As if long famishing for something to copy, he seemed to gorge himself on my documents. There was no pause for digestion. He ran a day and night line, copying by sun-light and by candle-light."[7] And we see something of the melancholia which underlies the mania, in the narrator's observation that Bartleby "wrote on silently, palely, mechanically." But when Bartleby is asked to proofread documents—a standard part of any clerk's duties—he replies, as he invariably will, that he would prefer not to. His employer sits for a time in "perfect silence, rallying [his] stunned faculties." Understandably, and almost the last time his response to Bartleby will be so rational, he decides that either Bartleby misheard him or he misheard the reply.

He repeats his request, but Bartleby, in his unvarying way, states that he "would prefer not to." "Are you moon-struck?" the narrator asks in high excitement, striding across the room. "Moon-struck" is a fair enough appraisal of the scrivener, but the narrator has merely put the question rhetorically. It will be a considerable time, a revealingly long time, before he considers again the question of Bartleby's sanity. On this occasion, when the scrivener voices again his refusal, the lawyer returns to his desk. Now he tells himself that he would have "violently dismissed" Bartleby from the premises, were it not for his peaceable manner. He writes that he would have "as soon thought of turning my pale plaster-of-paris bust of Cicero out of doors," and concludes that he is too hurried by business to take any corrective action.

There is something odd in all of this. The refusal of an employee to do his job should be equally objectionable in any tone of voice. And when the narrator concludes that he is hurried by business, he has in fact already retreated from Bartleby across the room to his desk. Equating his clerk with a plaster-of-paris bust of Cicero is perhaps understandable, given the scrivener's pale, inexpressive face. But to justify inaction on the basis of this resemblance seems far-fetched, even bizarre. Most curious is his comment that he would have *violently* dismissed Bartleby if the scrivener had been an ordinary man. An ordinary man can be simply told to go. If he wishes to save face because of his own passivity, we would expect him to refer to an *immediate*, not violent, dismissal.

On the second occasion that the scrivener is asked, and refuses, to proofread, the narrator responds in much the same way. He writes that he is "momentarily turned into a pillar of salt," and that with "any other man I should have flown outright into a dreadful passion, scorned all further words, and thrust him ignominiously from my presence. But there was something about Bartleby that not only strangely disarmed me, but in a wonderful manner, touched and disconcerted me."[8] We note that he still imagines violence, which he refers to now as a "dreadful passion," as his only alternative to inaction. There is, in this repeated association to violence, the suggestion that he is passive with Bartleby because, for him, *any* action implies getting violent. We may recall that he has carefully shunned conflict all his life, made himself an eminently safe and prudent man and, as he puts it, suffered nothing ever to invade his peace. One wonders why such a design for living has been necessary. Perhaps, we can begin to infer, the overriding motive of his life has been a struggle to contain violence latent within him, violence needing only the smallest conflict to set it off.

If this is the case, if the "cool tranquility" of his "snug retreat" is a defense against his own murderous aggression, it becomes clear why he should so weakly suffer a clerk's challenge to his authority and why he works so hard to sustain his passivity with rationalizations. He must have the idea, however unconsciously, that were he to act in anger, he might kill the scrivener. There is a subtle measure of support for this view in his allusion to Lot's wife. He may choose the metaphor with the thought that he is himself as inert as a pillar of salt. But there is the suggestion, too, that he is paralyzed by the sight of destructive rage— not God's, but his own. He seems to sense the presence of this unconscious motivation with his comment that he is "strangely disarmed" in a "wonderful manner." "Strange" and "wonderful" often imply, as we have seen elsewhere, a sense of unconscious motivation. And the term "disarmed" itself suggests the prevention of violence.

The theme of passivity as a defense is underscored by what follows. He turns to his other employees for support, which they readily give. One of them thinks it perfectly right that Bartleby should be asked to proofread, another declares the scrivener should be "kicked" from the office, and a third thinks the scrivener is a "luny." Theirs is the realistic and normal response, reached without effort. We see how simply the problem can be solved when no unconscious inhibition intervenes. It is revealing enough that the narrator should need their guidance in the first place, and even more so that he now ignores it, concluding once again that he is too busy to face the problem.

And so, in the following scenes, we have the picture of a man who only partially suspects the extent of his ambivalence and who alternates between extremes of anger and abject surrender. Each time he surrenders, he offers himself new grounds to justify doing so. He decides that Bartleby "means no mischief" and "intends no insolence"; that his "eccentricities are involuntary"; that with a less indulgent employer Bartleby might be "driven forth miserably to starve"; and that in consequence he can get along with Bartleby notwithstanding his behavior. Finally, and by this time not surprisingly, Bartleby is permanently excused from anything he would prefer not to do—which is to say, everything but the work of copying. As the narrator tells us:

His steadiness, his freedom from all dissipation, his incessant industry (except when he chose to throw himself into a standing revery behind his screen), his great stillness, his unalterableness of demeanor under all circumstances, make him a valuable acquisition.[9]

In short, he converts a depressed and recalcitrant clerk with tendencies to catatonic stupor into a fortunate gain for the office; a piece
of legerdemain designed solely to persuade himself. His argument leaves
conveniently out of account what a painful experience for him surrender has been. For instance, he writes that he "could not, for the very
soul of me, avoid falling into sudden spasmodic passions with him. For
it was difficult to bear in mind all the time those strange peculiarities,
privileges, and unheard of exemptions . . . ".[10] And, although he cannot let himself get angry, his repressed anger forces him back again and
again to new confrontation. We read that "the passiveness of Bartleby
sometimes irritated me. I felt strangely goaded on to encounter him in
new opposition—to elicit some angry spark from him answerable to my
own."[11] He is caught between an anger he can neither effectively
repress nor translate into action, so that each time he must be humili-
ated by the very encounter he has brought about. As he writes on one
such occasion:

I staggered to my desk, and sat there in a deep study. My blind
inveteracy returned. Was there any other thing in which I could procure
myself to be ignominiously repulsed by this lean, penniless wight?—my
hired clerk? What added thing is there, perfectly reasonable, that he will
be sure to refuse to do?[12]

That "added thing" is Bartleby's refusal, one Sunday morning, even
to admit his employer into the office (Bartleby has been living there
and is not yet ready to open the door). It is the ultimate degradation
for the narrator, who "slinks away," in spite of "sundry twinges of
impotent rebellion." He keeps repeating to himself, as he goes, that his
inaction is the result of Bartleby's "wonderful mildness," but this
explanation, as usual, begs the question. He never examines *why* this
mildness should have such an effect on him. Even the language he uses
beclouds the issue. For instance, he writes that he is "awed into a tame
compliance" by the "austere reserve," of his clerk's "eccentricities."
Were he to describe Bartleby's behavior more accurately as crazed and
now criminal, his own situation would become intolerable. He would
have to end his passivity, something he cannot do, or begin to question
his own sanity, something he does not wish to do.

The insistence that it is Bartleby's mildness which is the narrator's
undoing is not, however, without an element of truth. Walter Bonime's
central point about the psychodynamics of depression is worth recalling

in this connection: that it is a passive means to defy, manipulate, and defeat the world. The virtue of passivity is that it masks aggression under the guise of helpless suffering—a mask useful not only to prevent retaliation by the world, but to conceal from oneself, in order to allay guilt, the nature of this aggression. Bartleby's verbal formula for refusing to work is, in this light, a perfect extension of such a strategy. He uses the conciliatory word for the obstinate action.

It is one of the ironies of the story that such a transparent formula, so unlikely of success, should in fact so often succeed. Of course, this is so only because the narrator is the perfect victim, one whose inhibitions prevent him from identifying the aggression behind the mask of his clerk's passivity. He does, on one occasion, struggle with Bartleby to make him say "will not," rather than "prefer not," as though that change alone would end the ascendancy the clerk has over him. But Bartleby wins that struggle, too, as he wins all the others. Eventually, the narrator even tries to identify with his victorious clerk, as though that might erase his own ignominy. In perhaps the only comic scene in the story, however grim it may also be, the narrator catches himself using the same expression. He tells us that "somehow, of late, I had got into the way of involuntarily using this word 'prefer' upon all sorts of not exactly suitable occasions." Bartleby's formula for domination has not been lost on the other employees, either; and the lawyer finds that they too are, quite unconsciously, using the expression themselves. For instance, with the employee named "Turkey":

"Oh, *prefer?* oh yes—queer word. I never use it myself. But, sir, as I was saying, if he would but prefer—"
"Turkey," interrupted I, "you will please withdraw."
"Oh certainly, sir, if you prefer that I should."[13]

They identify with Bartleby, not for his depressions, the emptiness of his life, or his isolation from the world, but because of their intuitive sense that it is all a purposeful struggle for power, a struggle they see Bartleby win each day in the office. They rightly understand he is the aggressor who seems never to get caught.

iii

Up to now, Melville has preserved a certain dramatic ambiguity. His narrator, for all the transparency of his rationalizations, has not been

without at least some measure of justification for his inaction. His clerk
has done good work in copying. And we can almost sympathize with
the lawyer's continued sense that so mild a man can be tolerated and,
perhaps in time, even reasoned with. (Bartleby's passive suffering has its
demoralizing effect on the reader, too.) In addition, the narrator often
takes his submission with a light heart. There is almost something comic
about the way thoughts of decisive action (by "intimating the unalter-
able purpose of some terrible retribution very close at hand"), are
immediately reversed ("I half intended something of the kind. But
upon the whole, as it was drawing towards my dinner-hour, I thought it
best to put on my hat and walk home for the day"). We might almost
think that some comic resolution of the conflict is also at hand.

What does happen, however, is not in the least bit comic. The
narrator recognizes, however slowly, how deranged his clerk is, with his
catatonic depressions, his emaciation, his unending obstinacy. Concluding that Bartleby is the "victim of innate and incurable disorder," he
decides at last to tell him that his "services were no longer required."
On his first attempt, he makes the mistake of trying to reason with
Bartleby, forgetting that one cannot reason with an incurable disorder.
But when he has failed to voice the dismissal, he achieves his clearest
sense that the problem is within himself. He tells us that "I strangely
felt something superstitious knocking at my heart, and forbidding me
to carry out my purpose, and denouncing me for a villain if I dared to
breathe one bitter word. . . . "[14] The old inhibition is still in force, not
permitting a word in anger. Bartleby, however, as though sensing the
imminence of dismissal, fights back with his own peculiar weapons. He
declares that, henceforth, he will do no further work of any kind. It
would appear that this is too much, even for the narrator. As politely as
possible, he tells him at last to go. True, he gives the clerk six days'
notice, not the usual thing with employees who will do no work
whatever. But the termination, he says, is "unconditional." The struggle, for these men, may be more against inner forces than against each
other, but it is as grim and ruthless, in its way, as the shedding of blood.

When the time is up, Bartleby is, of course, still there, standing in his
corner motionless. Surely something now must give, we think. There is
nothing more for the clerk to refuse to do, no more threats left for the
lawyer to make. Something does give, and it is that which has been
increasingly compromised from the beginning—the narrator's sanity. He
was able to persuade himself, once before, that Bartleby was a valuable

acquisition. Now he takes one further step out of reality. He gives
Bartleby severance pay, gives him instructions for locking the office and
leaving the key, bids him goodby and farewell, and walks home "plum-
ing" himself on his "masterly management in getting rid of Bartleby."
In short, he concludes the clerk will go because he, the narrator,
assumes it. As he tells us, "I *assumed* the ground that depart he must;
and upon that assumption built all I had to say." This is infantile belief
in the omnipotence of thought, to think something will happen because
one has assumed it will. But at least it is madness with a method, since
he has controlled his violence—that is, the greater problem, for him,
than even Bartleby. This he has achieved, and he takes consolation in it:
"The beauty of my procedure," he writes, "seemed to consist in its
perfect quietness. There was no vulgar bullying, no bravado of any sort,
no choleric hectoring, and striding to and fro across the apartment,
jerking out vehement commands. . . . "[15]

The next morning, however, having "slept off the fumes of vanity,"
he is realistic enough to wonder if his clerk has really gone. When he
finds Bartleby still in the office, he is reluctant to give up his "doctrine
of assumptions," as he calls it. He momentarily imagines acting as
though Bartleby has really gone, pretending not to see him, and walking
"straight against him as if he were air." It is crazy thinking, and he
recoils from it. As if to recover his sanity, his freedom of action, and his
rightful authority all at one stroke, he finally gives expression to his
anger and advances on Bartleby "in a sudden passion." When Bartleby
replies, as dispassionately as ever, that he would prefer not to leave, the
violence which has begun to leak out can no longer be kept from
consciousness, although the lawyer is still not without his defenses. He
thinks of a murder committed in a business office, one which involved
others, not Bartleby and himself: "I remembered the tragedy of the
unfortunate Adams and the still more unfortunate Colt in the solitary
office of the latter; and how poor Colt, being dreadfully incensed by
Adams, and imprudently permitted himself to get wildly excited, was at
unawares hurried into the fatal act. . . . "[16] The idea of killing is there,
but the names have been changed. It is a good example of how "free"
association, like dreams, reveals more than one knows.

Nothing, however, has changed. Bartleby is still there, and the
narrator tries to "fancy, that in the course of the morning, at such time
as might prove agreeable to him, Bartleby, of his own free accord,
would emerge from his hermitage, and take up some decided line of

march in the direction of the door." As usual, the narrator's language is the rhetoric of the lawyer, blurring the outlines of his own thinking. He is, to put it bluntly, reduced to the point of merely wishing that his clerk would prefer to go. The situation is as intolerable as ever; another defense against his own anger must now be found and another step taken out of the real world. He adopts a fantasy, less rational even than the magical thinking of his "doctrine of assumptions." He decides that he has a mission, predestined from eternity, to keep and care for Bartleby! Thus he converts the ignominy of defeat into the exalted idea of a divine purpose. The humiliation of defeat, which he cannot erase at the risk of murderous violence, he dispels with a delusion of grandeur.

Such a retreat from reality is shocking and gives the full measure of how costly his inhibition has become. He writes that "gradually I slid into the persuasion that these troubles of mine, touching the scrivener, had been all predestined from eternity, and Bartleby was billeted upon me for some mysterious purpose of an allwise Providence . . . . At last I see it. I feel it; I penetrated to the predestinated purpose of my life. I am content."[17] This is the contentment of an all-but psychotic delusion. We have a vivid illustration of the premise that the line between neurosis and psychosis can often not be clearly drawn. The narrator is not psychotic, but this delusion is. And we have, too, an example of how the bizarre elements of psychosis may be themselves part of the individual's efforts to save himself and his integration in the world. With this delusion, the narrator at least escapes from a hell in which he can no longer live. And he is able to conclude, with no sense of humiliation or despair: "Yes, Bartleby, stay there behind your screen. . . . I shall persecute you no more. . . . "[18]

The narrator has not run from the world altogether, and his sense of reality helps to determine his next move. He becomes worried by the fact that his professional colleagues and acquaintances begin talking about the strange creature, the apparition, standing immovable in the middle of his office. The narrator's divine purpose has not been revealed to *them,* and the lawyer's reputation and practice is threatened. The narrator also has the queer idea that Bartleby will outlive him and so gain final possession of the office! This idea we can perhaps ascribe to his inveterate equating of conflict with murderous violence. Children often have murderous thoughts against their parents with the gratifying, and seemingly innocent, thought that they will "one day" outlive them. There is no reason for the narrator to care who possesses the premises when he is dead and gone. But the fear makes sense as another defense against his own murderous wishes. We can presume that, on the point of losing his profession, his violent wishes must be at their most intense. And so he projects them onto Bartleby, and imagines the clerk will outlive him (that is, might kill him). In any case, the narrator, as is the case with any neurotic, must decide how sick he is going to be. To put it differently, he must decide how much loss of adjustment in the external world he will tolerate in the interests of resolving inner problems. The choice is not always a conscious one, but it must always be made. Deciding he will not give up his profession, he does the only thing left to do. Unable to force Bartleby to go, he packs his own bags and moves his office elsewhere.

There is an utterly poignant moment when everything is moved, and Bartleby is left motionless in the middle of the naked room. Although their lives are highly disparate, each is pursuing the dictates of inner necessity. Bartleby remains uncompromising, although now he is left with nothing, while the narrator runs from conflict, but hangs on to his profession. Bartleby, of course, is the more forlorn figure, and the lawyer, even now, feels sympathy and self-reproach for leaving. The reader, too, is likely to feel more compassion for the scrivener. But one must beware the tactics of depression. The lawyer seems to have learned the lesson, and he goes.

The remainder of the story illustrates one last fact about the neurotic. Reality sometimes protects them from realizing the full proportions of their own malady. When the new tenants find Bartleby "haunting the building generally, sitting upon the banisters of the stairs by day, and sleeping in the entry at night," the narrator is appealed to as the person responsible for having left him there. He agrees to speak to Bartleby because, as he tells himself, he might otherwise be "exposed" in the newspapers. What it is that he might be exposed for, he does not go into. It is, presumably, the old guilt born of latent violence which makes him vulnerable to intimidation. Back he goes to the old office and to more "reasoning" with Bartleby. At this point a most extraordinary thing happens, more bizarre and incomprehensible than anything that has gone before. After failing to persuade Bartleby to leave the office (as though that were ever possible) and failing to persuade him to take up some other profession (as though that were ever the problem), the narrator invites Bartleby to come home with him: " 'Bartleby,' said I, in the kindest tone I could assume under such exciting circumstances, 'will you go home with me now—not to my office, but my dwelling—and remain there till we can conclude upon some convenient arrangement for you at our leisure? Come, let us start now, right away.' "[19]

Nothing is more certain than that, once lodged with the narrator, Bartleby will prefer to remain. And in light of his failures with the scrivener to date, he could hardly expect to have the strength to then force him to leave. Yet he tells us that this invitation is one "which had not been wholly unindulged before." One hardly knows at first what to make of this folly. It is comprehensible only as the last and most extreme gesture of defense. His leaving the office has not worked; he is back and responsible for the clerk all over again. Trapped by an unconscious guilt which makes him fear "exposure," there is nothing else to do except take up the association; but at least in the privacy of his home, away from the prying eyes of the world. And the scrivener's demented strategy of passive and depressed suffering has always had its effect on the narrator. Fortunately for the narrator, Bartleby replies: " 'No: at present I would prefer not to make any change at all.' "

This obstinacy has its measure of grandeur, too. One finds such uncompromising stubbornness in the rages of the infant, where Bartleby's malady may indeed have had its orgin. In any case, we shall never know the full extent of the narrator's capacity for neurotic accommodation, since, through no doing of his (he would say through no fault of his,) Bartleby is led unprotesting to the tombs. The lawyer visits him there, and finds him "standing all alone in the quietest of the yards, his face towards a high wall." The narrator has another one of his revealing free-associations, imagining that "all around, from the narrow slits of the jail windows, I thought I saw peering out upon him the eyes of murderers and thieves." It takes little analysis, at this point, to perceive that he has projected again his own guilt. It is the guilt which prevented him from sending the scrivener to prison in the first place, and which now makes him feel responsible for his being there.

Bartleby, now that he is in prison, declares that he "prefers not to dine today." He always has new measures of obstinacy to refute the world. And so, when the narrator finds him later at his wall, he is "strangely huddled at the base . . . , his knees drawn up, and lying on his side, his head touching the stones." In death, his foetal position links him again to the infant. This equation between depressed obstinacy and the infant is an explanation for the sympathy and compliance such men can extort from the world. All suffering children are victims, since they have not yet the freedom to create their own problems. And so it is difficult for the reader to break the spell with the thought that Bartleby has killed himself, and with as much freedom to do otherwise as any of us possesses.

The narrator seeks at the end to explain the scrivener as the victim of his previous work in a dead letter office, which occupation fatally intensified an already "pallid hopelessness." The irony of the story is sharpest at its conclusion. At the beginning, the narrator had said that a description of himself was necessary for "an adequate understanding of the chief character about to be presented." But he has never understood the scrivener, beyond the dim sense that he is a "bit deranged." And attributing derangement to the effects of a dead-letter office is sentimental, and simplistic. But, above all, he does not understand that for the greater dramatization of his own inner conflicts, for his own perilous touch of madness, he himself has been the chief character. He can live in the world only as long as a passive avoidance of conflict is allowed him, and as long as anything which in the least disturbs the violence within him is kept away. Such neurotics are not often spared through an entire lifetime all conflict except the passivity of an obstinate clerk.

Notes

1. Richard Chase, ed., *Selected Tales and Poems* (New York: Holt, Rinehart and Winston, 1964).
2. Ford Madox Ford, *The Good Soldier* (New York: Vintage Books, 1955), with an Interpretation by Mark Shorer, pp. vii, xiii.
3. Silvano Arieti, "Manic-depressive Psychosis," *American Handbook of Psychiatry* (New York: Basic Books, 1969), I, p. 427.
4. Walter Bonime, "The Psychodynamics of Neurotic Depression," *American Handbook of Psychiatry* (New York: Basic Books, 1966), III, p. 245.
5. Bonime, pp. 245, 247.
6. Chase, IV, pp. iv, 45-48.

7. Chase, p. 100.
8. Chase, p. 102.
9. Chase, p. 107.
10. Chase, p. 107.
11. Chase, p. 105.
12. Chase, p. 106.
13. Chase, p. 114.
14. Chase, p. 113.
15. Chase, p. 117.
16. Chase, p. 120.
17. Chase, p. 121.
18. Chase, p. 121.
19. Chase, p. 127.

Fantasy of the Devouring Killer:
Kafka's *A Hunger Artist*

Kafka's *A Hunger Artist*[1] is perhaps one of the most powerful, perfectly told tales ever written. It conveys the essential Kafka formula, the depiction of a world which is at once convincingly real and yet nightmarish. There is a succession of events determined by the rational judgment of the protagonist, but this rationality in time seems no more than a cover for madness. The subject matter is both fascinating and repellent; and at the end, one is at a loss to know whether there has been enacted a triumph or a defeat.

The story itself seems simple enough. A professional faster wins renown and financial rewards by giving performances in one city after the next. Under the management of an impressario, he places himself in a small cage, and fasts for forty days and nights. Experience has proven that popular interest can be sustained for no longer; and so, on the fortieth day, each time, the artist is released from his cage amidst much celebration, and the fast is ended.

The dramatic focus of the story at first has to do with the artist's dissatisfaction both with his audience and with his own performance. In spite of his strict adherence to the honor of his profession, onlookers cynically believe he secretly obtains food. Since the hunger artist is continuously watched by no one, he alone is certain of the integrity of his performance. In addition, he is not allowed to fast beyond forty days, and so is prevented from establishing a record.

In the story thus far there is not much to suggest that he is mad. We do not know the circumstances that have led him to fasting. And such a profession seems uncommonly painful. But we must credit him with having successfully earned fame and fortune, and might almost envy him for that reason. His wish to set new records is understandable and might correspond to the heroic desire and dedication of men who first scale mountains, cross deserts, or reach the poles of the earth. Or so we can imagine.

Less comprehensible is his disclosure that fasting is not the test of endurance we feel it must be, but rather something effortless to do. We read that "he alone knew, what no other initiate knew, how easy it was to fast. It was the easiest thing in the world. He made no secret of this, yet people did not believe him."[2] We can well understand that people do not believe him. It cannot be that living confined to a cage without food for forty days is the easiest thing in the world. Such a statement is not only false, but absurd in its extreme exaggeration. Nor is that all of such absurdities. We read that he wishes to extend his fast, not for another five, ten, or twenty days, but "beyond human reason." Indeed, he feels that there are "no limits to his capacity for fasting,"[3] a conviction manifestly false. He is flesh and blood, and in time must inevitably die of starvation. Children may dream of saving the world, winning wars single-handed, or writing plays to put Shakespeare to shame. Their ambition knows no limits, because they ignore the realities which always and inevitably compromise achievement. But the hunger artist is a grown man, and the delusion that he is, in effect, exempt from the laws of life is a first indication that his "artistry" is a form of madness.

This ambiguous balance between ambition and derangement is now progressively altered by events. Public interest in fasting turns to revulsion, and the "pampered" hunger artist is suddenly deserted by amusement seekers. We read that, because he is too fanatically devoted to fasting to choose another profession, he hires himself to a circus as merely one of the many attractions. The narrator tells us that the artist has not lost his sense of the real situation, and in some respects that is true. He chooses not to look at his contract, knowing he must accept the terms since fasting is no longer in demand. He accepts the placement of his cage far from the main attraction, near the animal cages. And, reluctantly perhaps, he recognizes that the people streaming past his cage are not there to see him, but the menagerie of carnivorous cats.

But why, after all, should we still accept uncritically his fanatic devotion to fasting? His profession was comprehensible when it brought him fame and fortune, but these rewards are no longer attainable. Given the renunciation necessary, denied food and caged like an animal, his continued fanaticism is not an explanation of his actions, but rather irrational behavior which in itself needs explaining. Equally curious is the artist's avowal that with permission to fast as long as he likes (a permission which is granted), he now will "astound the world by establishing a record never yet achieved." His fellow professionals at the circus smile, aware that no amount of fasting will astonish a world that has revolted against his art. We see in such boasting the loss of his former "sense of the real situation."

The climax of the story, as so often in the fiction of Kafka, is the sudden, unmistakable disclosure of derangement. The artist has his wish and is allowed to fast without interruption. But we learn that the notice board that tells the number of fast days, which at first changed every day, "had long stayed at the same figure." Such a cruel indifference to the artist's fate was, perhaps, foretold by the unpopularity of his art. But, with the force of revelation, we learn that not even the artist himself keeps count of the interminable days that now pass! We suddenly see that the elaborate reasons he has given us for his torturous life were rationalizations. He does not simply fast for money or fame; and now it is clear his wish to set new records is equally factitious. The artist himself recognizes this truth. When his existence in the filthy, unattended cage is at last remembered by the overseer, he is released and asked why he has fasted for so long. On the point of death from starvation, the artist replies, "Because I have to, I can't help it." Voicing our own puzzlement, the overseer asks him the final question, "and why can't you help it?" With no rationalizations left which might seem to answer the question, and unable to find within himself the motive which has brought him to death, the artist gives us a crazed and absurd reply:

Because I couldn't find the food I liked. If I had found it, believe me, I should have made no fuss and stuffed myself like you or anyone else.[4]

The absurdity of this answer is the point at which a psychoanalytic interpretation must begin if we are to understand the hunger artist. So long as conscious motivation supplied by the protagonist is consistent with his behavior, and sufficient to explain it, psychoanalysis has little to contribute. But when, as we have it here, nothing in his consciousness explains his behavior, we must look again to the text for evidence of unconscious motivation. But it is in symbols that we shall find its expression, rather than in direct disclosure, since the drama of this story is precisely the artful concealment of just this motivation.

The most revealing evidence is given, appropriately enough in this puzzling story, at the end. Into the cage of the artist, now dead and buried, they put a young panther, whose "noble body, furnished almost to the bursting point with all that it needed, seemed to carry freedom around with it, too; *somewhere in his jaws* it seemed to lurk; and the joy of life streamed with such ardent passion from his throat . . . ."[5] The artist and the panther seem, on the one hand, curiously connected. One replaces the other. Both live in cages. And both are caged to restrict what they eat. But, on the other hand, the panther retains his freedom—or the only kind of freedom that matters in this story, the freedom to eat without compunction. The hunger artist goes to the other extreme and allows himself no food at all.

If we surmise that they are alike and yet different in one further respect, we can find an explanation of his derangement. The panther is caged because the "ardent passion of his throat" is that of the murderous carnivore. Caging him will restrain, but never change, the character of this desire. If we make the assumption, as improbable as it first seems, that the hunger artist feels the same ardent passion to kill with his teeth and jaws and to devour what he has destroyed, we can begin to understand why, unlike the panther, he chooses to live in the cage and starves himself to death. He is a man, and men feel guilt; he is not a beast with freedom in his jaws and license by nature to eat whatever he wishes. But just as the cage does not affect this freedom of the panther, it does not diminish the artist's murderous appetite. And so he must fast without end until he is dead.

Psychoanalysis has familiarized us with how the murderous passions of childhood are often expressed in fantasies of devouring a hated sibling or parent. And since the child also loves his parents, these passions must be repressed. The grownup who says to the shy little boy or girl, "Come here, I won't eat you," gives unconscious recognition to the child's fear that his punishment will fit the same crime which he harbors in fantasy. Jacob Arlow has pointed out to me how the films which children take such delight in are so frequently cartoons which depict the dangers of being eaten. The mouse fears the cat, the cat the dog, the lamb the wolf, and the little boy the giant. These cartoons affirm the invulnerability of all helpless creatures to the danger of being eaten. Nothing is so certain, for instance, as the triumph of the mouse over the cat. However often it is repeated, and however predictable, the escape of the weak from the jaws of the strong never loses its appeal. Such an unvarying formula gives us a true picture of how profound is the child's fear that he himself may be devoured. And, as surprising as it may seem, their popularity with adults shows how such fears can be unconsciously retained into maturity.

These fears, of course, are irrational. But they are based, in their own way, on a kind of logic. The child's wish to devour a hated parent or sibling is based on the fact that he has already experienced mastery of the world in his ability to take food and eat it. Nor has it escaped him that biting others with his teeth inflicts pain and damage. And as parents well know, it is by no means rare to see children bite when they are angry. Since the child can only conceive of death, in any case, as an absence, the disappearance of the food he eats is a powerful suggestion as to how he can kill. The child, in turn, attributes to the adult the same impulses which he himself experiences, since he has no reason to know otherwise. In this way, he may come to fear for his life, not merely because the parent is angry for one reason or another, but because he expects retaliation for his own murderous wish to devour. Neurosis is born of the need to control such infantile impulses which are felt to be dangerous. As the child represses them, he may succeed in preventing their being acted out. But in many unpredictable ways this defensive measure restricts his freedom of action to adjust in the world, and this maladjustment becomes his neurosis.

Neurotic behavior, then, has a twofold aspect. It manifests both impulses which are never perfectly repressed, as well as the continued efforts to control them, an aspect of human behavior psychoanalysis terms compromise formation. In fiction, we frequently find greater dramatic emphasis given to defensive behavior, with the original impulses against which they are instituted merely implied in symbol and suggestion. For instance, our analysis of Melville's *Bartleby the Scrivener* (p. 63) attributes to the narrator a passivity adopted in order to contain a prior, and unconscious, impulse to violence. Similarly, the hunger artist chooses to fast for reasons the story never directly gives in a convincing fashion. And they are certainly not reasons consciously recognized by him. He only knows that he fasts because he must. His behavior is made comprehensible as an appropriate, but neurotically harsh, defense only if we attribute to him the prior impulse to murder by devouring.

In support of this analysis there is, first of all, the seemingly simple fact that the artist's performance has its greatest impact on children. As the narrator tells us: "It was the children's special treat to see the hunger artist; for their elders he was often just a joke that happened to be in fashion, but the children stood open-mouthed, holding each other's hands for greater security, marveling at him as he sat there. . . ."[6] Such a passage supports the premise that the artist's performance has meaning primarily to the infantile, be it in the child or, unconsciously, in the adult. The normal adult is not afraid, since a starving man in a cage is a threat to no one. But the children react to the *meaning* of the event. Just as they fear that a cage will fail to contain the devouring panther, they fear the artist's self-imposed fast may fail to contain the murderous impulses against which they are instituted. And so the children hold hands for "greater security."

On a second occasion, Kafka links the artist's performance to the child's psychology and signifies that it is children who best understand. During the time the artist is fasting to his death for a world grown indifferent, he has "all too rarely" a "stroke of luck." We read that "when some father of a family fetched up before him with his children . . . the children, still rather uncomprehending, since neither inside nor outside school had they been sufficiently prepared for this lesson—what did they care about fasting?—still showed by the brightness of their intent eyes that new and better times might be coming."[7] There are a number of revealing touches here. The intentness of the children's eyes expresses the "lesson" they are learning. It is this lesson which instills the fascination for fasting which then perpetuates the popularity of the art. And the lesson must be learned in childhood or not at all. For the crime of wishing to devour forbidden food—brothers, sisters, and parents—the renunciation and defense must be starvation. The *lex talionis* is the only morality they know. And the spectacle of a caged and starving man implies the character of his crime well enough. (That the children make no distinction between criminal *wishes* and criminal behavior is, of course, characteristic of their psychology.) In this regard, the protagonist's "artistry" is no different from that of other art forms, such as fiction, films, and the drama, in which we vicariously participate in the conflict between gratification and punishment.

Another kind of support for this thesis is given by the relays of permanent watchers who supervise the artist's fast and see to it that he eats no food. They are, the narrator tells us, "usually butchers, strangely enough." A butcher slaughters the living for food, and he kills brutally. Having such men guard the artist against prohibited eating unites perfectly the antinomy central to the story. To put it differently, the butchers, like the panther, dramatize the activity against which the artist's fasting is a defense and atonement. When Kafka writes that it is "strange" that butchers should be chosen, he draws our attention to the hidden dynamics of that choice. "Strange," "weird," "uncanny," "dream-like," "inexplicable," "nightmarish," are (p. 48) the terms writers use to suggest that the explanation of events is to be found in symbols, rather than in the protagonist's consciousness.

Another striking instance of support is the artist's reaction, during a long fast, when onlookers sympathize with his melancholy and tell him it is the result of his fasting. At such times he reacts, we are told, "with an outburst of fury," and shakes the bars of his cage "like a wild animal."[8] With the economy of a dream episode, all the elements of the story are here. In the manner of dream disguise, cause and effect are brought together—but, as so often in dream symbolism, in reverse. It is precisely to contain the fury of a wild animal that he puts himself in a cage. We see this equation between animal and artist at the time the artist is hired by the circus, and his cage is placed alongside the menagerie. We read that "when the public came thronging out in the intervals to see the animals, they could hardly avoid passing the hunger artist's cage." In the language of symbolism, he is part of the menagerie, and caged for the same reason as the other animals. As critics have asserted, the artist is an alien in society. However, his alienation is based not on a bourgeois indifference to art, as has been suggested, but on the desire of most people to avoid guilt and renunciation for their passions and desires. The cats are magnificent because of the "freedom which lurks in their jaws," a freedom from guilt which the world cannot diminish. And an artist who starves himself out of guilt is a sorry spectacle by comparison. Only those who feel the same guilt can appreciate the "artistry" of such an achievement of renunciation.

His predicament is that of every neurotic who is the victim of an uncompromising conflict between passion and conscience. As a neurotic, his "solution" merely perpetuates, rather than resolves, the opposition. Kafka dramatizes the pathos of this sickness when he describes how the artist suffers "from the stench of the menagerie, the animal's restlessness by night, the carrying past of raw lumps of flesh for the beasts of prey, the roaring at feeding times, which depressed him continually."[9] He must witness every day the act which he seeks to prevent and which cripples his whole life. It is easy to understand his depression. Caged, emaciated, dying, still he must endure the sight of raw flesh carried to beasts of prey—as though to mock the twisted purpose of his existence.

We can note, in conclusion, that the fame, fortune, and records established by the hunger artist illustrate the strategy of sublimation. That is to say, the quest for money and recognition through starving is itself genuine. It expresses the determination of the mature personality to make the best of a bad situation. Given the necessity to starve, the artist accomplishes as much with his life as such a terrible inhibition allows. But the strength of his "appetite" still requires the harshest measures of defense: a cage, starvation, emaciation, ultimately death; so that his derangement is always manifest, fame and fortune notwithstanding. It is one of the tragic ironies of the human condition that the measures we use to contain the savagery within us, and which we sustain with so much effort, may imprison and kill us in spite of all our pains. And the world, as in Kafka's story, too often neither understands nor cares.

Notes

1. Franz Kafka, *The Penal Colony: Stories and Short Pieces* (New York: Schocken Books, 1969).
2. Kafka, *Penal Colony,* p. 246.
3. Kafka, *Penal Colony,* p. 247.
4. Kafka, *Penal Colony,* p. 255.
5. Kafka, *Penal Colony,* 255. Emphasis added.
6. Kafka, *Penal Colony,* p. 244.
7. Kafka, *Penal Colony,* p. 253.
8. Kafka, *Penal Colony,* p. 249.
9. Kafka, *Penal Colony,* p. 253.

Fantasy of the Family Romance:
Shakespeare's *The Tempest*

i

One of the least analyzed aspects of Shakespeare's *The Tempest*, but a highly intriguing one to the psychoanalytic critic, is the resemblance of this play to a fairy tale. In his Introduction to the Arden *Tempest*, Frank Kermode has pointed out that "ultimately the source of *The Tempest* is an ancient *motif*, of almost universal occurrence, in saga, ballad, fairy tale and folk tale."[1] His own analysis, however, describes the more immediate forces which affect the play: Pastoral drama, discoveries in the New World, and current ideas about primitive man, supernatural arts, and the effects of "nature" and "nurture" on the noble or corrupt. He lists no more than a few of the fairy tale resemblances, and, judging as he does that such elements are normally present in Shakespeare's plays, he carries this analysis no further. Primitive elements are, however, considerably more than an original source surviving in a few details. Typical fairy tale symbolism, characterization, and wish fulfillment fill the play and give it much of its meaning and strange beauty. Below is a list, in the most general terms, of resemblances in the play to fairy tales. On the left are quotations from Macleod Yearsley's *The Folklore of Fairy-tale*,[2] and on the right the correspondences we can find in *The Tempest*:

1. "Benevolent or malevolent spirits." (6)

Ariel, Juno, Ceres, Iris, Sycorax, etc.

2. "They are actuated strongly by the human passions of resentment and gratitude." (13)

Sycorax's rage against the disobedient Ariel, and Ariel's gratitude to Prospero.

3. "They are not necessarily immortal." (13)

Sycorax dies.

4. "In many tales . . . [Fairyland] is a realm of surpassing beauty." (15)

The island is likened to a paradise.

5. "The monarch may live in all the pomp and splendour of barbaric royalty, and may yet have to earn his living." (30)

Prospero has the splendour of his magical powers, yet is constrained to live in a "full poor cell."

6. "The heroine is carried off by some ogre, dwarf, or monster, and rescued later by the hero." (35)

The monster Caliban attempts to rape Miranda, but the noble Ferdinand wins her.

7. "It is a wide-spread savage belief that the souls of the dead animate trees . . . natural phenomena make the idea of an animal turning into a man, a tree, or a stone, or *vice versa*, easy to understand. Every savage believes he has the power to effect such a transformation, although he generally leaves such matters to the medicine-man." (58)

Sycorax confines Ariel to a cloven pine for a dozen years, from whence he is released to life by the magic of Prospero.

8. "The magic sleep occurs in many folk-tales, but usually as an accessory incident only." (68)

Prospero puts almost everyone on the island into a magic sleep at one time or another, for various purposes.

9. "The magic wands of fairytale." (74)

Prospero has a magic robe and staff.

10. "The dead or apparently dead are restored to life by [various means including] magic." (76)

Prospero boasts of how "graves at my command / Have wak'd their sleepers, op'd, and let 'em forth."

11. "Usually the hero performs certain tasks, in which he is helped by his oppressor's daughter." (80)

Prospero commands Ferdinand to bear logs to the cell, and his daughter offers her assistance.

12. "There is scarcely a fairytale to be found which does not contain some item of wizardry and magic."

Prospero performs all manner of magic, as did Sycorax before the play begins.

13. "To the domain of contagious magic belongs also the belief that a man's name is an essential part of himself." (84)

According to their names, Miranda is a wonder, Prospero prospers, *Caliban* may be an anagram for *canibal* (that is, savage man). Miranda is instructed to withhold herself from Ferdinand by not revealing to him her name.

14. "There are such magic incidents in fairy-tales as . . . the Miraculous banquet . . . Cap of invisibility, Transportation by Magic . . . and 'levitation.' " (88, 90)

Prospero provides a magic banquet for the nobility. Ariel is invisible, and at the banquet Prospero is also invisible. Ariel, if not Prospero as well, levitates at the banquet. Ariel magically disperses the ship's crew to various parts of the island.

The Tempest belongs more particularly to a class of fairy tales which includes *Cinderella, or the Little Glass Slipper,* and *Beauty and the Beast,* stories in which a young girl magically achieves marriage to a prince. The resemblance to *Beauty and the Beast* is in fact unusually close. Prospero's loss of his dukedom and retreat to his cell, his isolation with Miranda, the bestiality of Caliban, and other features of the play, have a striking duplication in this folk story. *Beauty and the Beast,* of course, is far simpler in design. But its simplicity conveys in easily analyzed fashion the same dynamics which can be found—in a more complex and covert dramatization—in *The Tempest.* For this reason, we begin our analysis of Shakespeare's play with a close examination of the *Beauty* tale.

In one popular version, a rich father loses his money and withdraws to a small forest cottage with his three daughters. Beauty, the youngest, is mistress of the house, since the mother is dead. Although her sisters suffer the hardships of their life, Beauty is content and grows more beautiful. When the father leaves home in the hopes of regaining a portion of his lost wealth, the sisters ask for rich gifts, while Beauty asks only for a rose. Returning without money or gifts, the father attempts to pluck a rose for Beauty in the garden of Beast's castle. For this crime, Beast threatens the father with death and offers to relent only if Beauty is given to him. Beauty saves her father's life by going to live with Beast. She retains her chastity and in time falls in love with Beast; at which point he is transformed into a prince and they are happily married.

It is not difficult to see in this symbolic story the fantasies common to young girls who, in guarded fashion, first feel romantic love toward their fathers and who then transfer that feeling to more acceptable, although no less idealized, young men. For instance, the father's loss of wealth is part of the "family romance," which Freud has described so well.[3] As part of that formula, the young girl's affectionate attachment to her father leads her to exalt him and imagine that if his station in life is less than glorious, it is only because accident has robbed him of the grandeur formerly and rightfully his. The initial absence of one parent is another time-honored device, found in the literature of many cultures, for the dramatization of a child's wishes both to be rid of one parent and to have the other all to himself. We do not mean that Beauty, or any fairy tale heroine, could ever kill her mother. Conscience sticks tenaciously to gratification no less in fiction than in life. The value of having the mother already dead is precisely that Beauty remains innocent of responsibility and becomes mistress of her father's house simply out of necessity. But we will miss the point of the story if we do not see how perfectly necessity conforms to the wish. The whole tale is designed to gratify Beauty's desires, and what happens before the story begins is no less a part.

In this light we can well understand why it is that Beauty should be so content with her life and grow more beautiful under conditions which her father and sisters find cruelly harsh. Her status as mistress of the house, as symbolic replacement of her mother, more than compensates for her humble station. Her sisters ask for rich gifts because they wish their former life might be restored, while Beauty's humble request expresses in part her desire that their life remain unchanged. Her request should not be taken as a virtuous scorning of the goods of this world, in contrast to the materialism of her sisters. Her father is ambitious enough to seek and obtain wealth in the first place, and to strive to recover as much of it as he can. And the sisters ask for rich gifts only on the assumption that some of that wealth can be regained. Never does the tale romanticize poverty. Beauty simply wishes love from her father infinitely more than material goods, and the romantic gift of a rose from him is prized beyond all else. One hesitates to ascribe to this affection of daughter for father a specifically sexual basis, as is suggested by the traditional equation between a flower and a woman's sexuality. Certainly Beauty at no time oversteps the bounds of perfect chastity. And the gift of a rose from one's father is of course innocent of wrongdoing. An insistence upon a sexual interpretation would seem to epitomize the excesses of which psychoanalysis has been accused. Our reply, however, is that the story leaves us no other choice. In a forest where roses can be obtained elsewhere, why should the father steal from the garden of Beast? Why should the crime be punishable by death? Any why can the father be absolved of guilt only by giving up his daughter to another man? These events can be explained only by inferring that the gift of a rose, however much it is an outwardly innocent gesture, implies in symbolic form the fantasy of unsanctioned love. It is indeed a crime for the father to take the sexuality of his daughter. Her sexuality does belong by rights to another man. And so the harshest of penalties must be imposed, and absolution can be obtained only by instituting a proper sexual union: Beauty must be given to her prince-in-disguise. We can see that morality is as much a part of the story as a wish for unsanctioned love. The crime is not only kept within the confines of symbol, but represented as a transgression of the father, not the daughter. It was Beauty, however, who set him the task in the first place. And so her father's seeming responsibility is only part of an ongoing formula for the disguise which morality requires when forbidden wishes are gratified.

Morality is responsible for another, and perhaps the most puzzling, feature of the tale. In a story which answers to wish fulfillment, why is it necessary for the prince to be at first so ugly? The easiest explanation would be that his misshapen appearance symbolizes the bestiality of his sexual appetites. But such an idea is immediately contradicted by the story, in which the beast is a model of courtesy and decorum. He makes no advances, loves Beauty tenderly, repeatedly proposes marriage, and takes her many rejections of him with a patient heart. He is very much the prince from the beginning, his ugly appearance notwithstanding. If this bestiality belongs not to the prince, can we infer that, in the language of symbolism, it "belongs" to Beauty herself? There might appear to be no reason for Beauty to project bestiality onto the prince, since he is the appropriate man for her to accept and marry. But feelings obey inner logic more than the facts of reality. A young girl whose first sexual love is directed toward her father will not easily turn to another man free of the guilt born of her first incestuous tie. All sexuality may come to seem unsanctioned, hence "monstrous."[4] This attitude will be particularly pronounced if the father has still not in fact been given up. Such is indeed the case. In support of this interpretation we do find that Beauty has great difficulty giving up her father, and that only when she does can the prince shed his bestial form.

When Beauty leaves her father for the prince, we see in a number of ways how incomplete is the break. First, the fairy tale tells us that she leaves him solely in order to save his life. The idea of saving a parent's life is a standard feature of fantasy in which the child wins love through this most heroic of actions.[5] As a second indication of this tie to her father, Beauty retains her chastity in the castle of the prince. It cannot be said that she does so because of the prince's bestial appearance; at the end of the story she wishes to give herself to him completely, before his bestiality has been shed. Considering how tenderly the beast-prince courts her throughout the story, her sustained virginity suggests that her heart belongs elsewhere. More revealing is the manner in which at one point she leaves the prince. Beauty learns that her father, now that she is gone from him, is dying. And so she saves his life all over again by leaving the castle and returning to him (how unmistakably she is master of all events, going where she wills, and doing what she wishes!). Finally, as the clearest expression of this rescue motif, the beast-prince, missing Beauty more than he can bear, begins to die. Now she must choose between them, and she makes the moral choice at last. She returns to the castle. Such a sequence of events, living first with one, then another, then going back and forth again, and always to save the life of a heart-broken man, gives the perfect representation of a young girl's divided heart and tangled fantasies.

And so we come to the moment when she gives up her father forever. To save her beast-prince she throws herself "in an agony of grief . . . down over his body, without any sense of horror." She cries out, "no my dear Beast, you shall not die . . . . You must live to become my husband. From this moment I am yours. I imagined I had no stronger feeling for you than friendship, but now I know that I cannot live without you." Her love for him is complete and does not in the least require his magical transformation. His shedding of ugliness expresses the one fact of their union which has changed: her father has been given up. Beauty can lie with Beast (that is, enter into sexuality) without any sense of horror that her love is tainted. And with that horror gone, the prince's bestiality vanishes. Earlier in the story, Beauty had said: "there are many men far worse monsters than you are [including] many men I have met who, behind a handsome face, hide a false, bad heart." She herself perceives that a bad heart makes the monster. We have only to recognize that, in this symbolic fairy tale, the bad heart as well as the good has been hers.

ii

Aside from the many resemblances between *The Tempest* and fairy tales in general which were previously listed, there are many striking resemblances to *Beauty and the Beast*. As in the Beauty tale, we find also in *The Tempest* the following details. The heroine has a name which implies her beauty. Her mother is dead from the outset of the play. She lives with her father in a humble cell since he has lost his former station in life. She is by default mistress of her father's home. She saves his life (when they are cast adrift on their "rotten carcass of a butt," as her father tells the story). She retains her chastity against the sexual advances of a beast. She falls in love with a prince and wins him in marriage. She is helped by magic, and at the end blessed by spirits.

Critics have not conceded to Miranda the central role through wish-fulfillment possessed by heroines in fairy tales. Even Sachs, in his psychoanalysis of the play, finds (as critics generally do) Prospero to be the protagonist. And, it it true, Prospero is the one who draws his enemies to the island and takes vengeance upon them; it is he who arranges the suitable marriage for his daughter, and retakes his stolen dukedom; it is his magic which rouses the spirits, orders the elements, and manipulates the characters. But these accomplishments, which might have been made into a dramatization of wish-fulfillment, are not so handled by Shakespeare. Prospero's enemies are merely chastised and immediately forgiven. The noblemen are killers who have shown only the most perfunctory and enforced repentance; yet Prospero has no wish to punish or take pleasure in his triumph over them; nor does recapturing his lost city seem to give him pleasure. It is, he tells us, a place to which he will retire and where he will give every third thought to his death. One senses that, as a great magus, his life on the island has been satisfactory. Giving up his powers, magic robe, staff, and occult books hardly seems a fulfillment. He had, we may recall, retired from public life when he ruled in the first place, and recovering this lost office does not bring the purified pleasure usually characterized as

wish-fulfillment. True, arranging his daughter's marriage gives him pleasure. But with her beauty and his ability to arrange matters, that issue
was never in doubt. Prospero himself tells us that he cannot be as
"glad" of the marriage as are the lovers themselves, since he saw their
marriage coming from the beginning.

Conceding that *The Tempest* has its resemblances to fairy tales, and
in some respects to *Beauty and the Beast,* it still remains to be shown
that these resemblances are more than the ".primitive origins" Kermode
described. To put it differently, is the basic substance of *The Tempest*
as explicable in terms of a young girl's fantasies, as is *Beauty and the
Beast?* If we make allowances for the facts that *The Tempest* is drama,
and far more beautiful and believable than a fairy tale, we can still
answer affirmatively. Recall that the *Beauty* tale, in accordance with
the family romance, contrasts the reality of the father's humble station
in life with a "time when he possessed greatness." And this magnifica-
tion of the father is part of the wish fulfillment in which the daughter
becomes mistress in her father's house and only afterward leaves him
for another man. *The Tempest* has this same two-fold structure. Not
only does Miranda first enjoy exclusive possession of her father, but the
text makes it clear that Prospero's magic is more for his daughter's sake
than for revenge. The sequence in which Prospero's enemies suffer
"flam'd amazement" and a "fever of the mad," in which they are
transported, put to sleep, enticed with chimerical banquets, have de-
nunciations hurled at them by spirits, and are brought to contrition is
all part of that romantic vision.

Support for this perspective on Prospero is given by many additional
details. First, Prospero gives a perfunctory forgiveness to men who are
killers and whose repentance has been forced by circumstance only.
The point of Prospero's manipulation of these men is, in this dramatic
context, not revenge, but the romantic display of his powers. One has
only to consider that, with Prospero's powers given up at the end, he
cannot be said to have used them to safeguard his future. But that was
never the point of his behavior. Why, after all, should he give up his
magic powers at all? He admits to a coming retirement as Duke, and
nothing now prevents him from pursuing this vocation as he had when
first he ruled. The answer is that Miranda has no longer the desire to
romanticize him. She is engaged at the end to a prince. She now sees
her prince as a thing divine; and the glorification of a father by a young
girl succeeds to the more mature interests of a woman. With the charm

Miranda has thrown over him dispelled, he becomes a human figure at
the end, who can say:

Now my charms are all o'erthrown
And what strength I have's mine own,
Which is most faint . . . . [6]

His superhuman powers, more than anything else in the play, were the
baseless fabric of a vision, the stuff dreams are made on. In this sense,
as in the *Beauty* fable, the father's destiny accords with the changing
wishes of his daughter.

Fenichel has pointed out how "the fairytale makes it possible for the
child to manage the contradictory feelings it has for its mother" by the
device of "an entirely good mother, and an entirely wicked stepmother,
so that the love and hate felt against the same person is divided between
two people. . . ."[7] In both *Beauty* and *The Tempest* this splitting
occurs, and in connection with a second feature. The child's conception
of death is faulty at best. The dead are imagined to have "gone away,"
so that conceivably they may yet return. The child imagines her hated
mother as a wicked witch, partly to justify her death and replacement.
But the mother is also loved—hence the frequent appearance of the
fairy godmother, really the good mother not dead at all. In the *Beauty*
tale, the mother is dead at the outset. But a lady appears to Beauty in a
dream, when she is first at Beast's castle, assuring her all will be well.
And when the spell over Beast has been broken, this beautiful lady
again appears. Like Prospero with his art, she promises that Beauty will
be a queen, and then transports them all to the kingdom where Beauty
will reign. This spirit is as much the loved mother, as the mother dead
at the beginning was hated.

The Tempest has no benevolent fairy lady, although the spirits who
consecrate the coming marriage are a suggestion of this. But it has its
unloved mother, Sycorax, the foul, blue-eyed witch. Many details
identify her symbolically as Miranda's mother, and much of the play is
illuminated if we work with such an equation. To begin with, many
details link Prospero and Sycorax as husband and wife. Both Prospero
and Sycorax are banished, and their lives just barely saved. Both come
to this island wielding their arts and controlling spirits. Both bring a
child (although hers is not yet born). And Prospero threatens Ariel with
the same punishment Sycorax executes against him. In addition, Prospero's wife is as conspicuous by her absence as is Sycorax's husband. It

is hard to miss, in all of this, the suggestion that, on the level of fantasy, they belong to each other, Miranda's loved father and hated mother. A further resemblance in history, and in keeping with the family romance, is the fact that both Miranda's acknowledged mother and the witch are dead when the play begins. Since the fantasy-possession of the father typically has the mother disposed of as a witch, we can view Sycorax symbolically as the mal-prospering mother of Miranda. To be sure, Sycorax does not function as Miranda's mother in any simple or obvious way. Nor is such an identity an integral part of the plot. That is the point of symbolism in general: meaning is communicated in ways quite apart from the literal situation.

The equation of Miranda's mother and Sycorax brings us to the question of Caliban's identity. Kermode points out a curious linking of identity between Caliban and Miranda. One must of course feel a certain repugnance to equating him with Miranda as the single child of a magus and a witch. Caliban is male, ugly, evil, sexual. Miranda is female, beautiful, virtuous, and chaste. And assuredly they deal with one another in the play as independent people. One has only to think of Caliban's attempt to rape Miranda, or of Caliban's comic worship of Stephano, to see the absurdity of simply forcing them into a single identity. We must keep in mind the two-fold structure of a *Doppelgänger* motif. Are the two William Wilsons in Poe's short story one man or two? And Stevenson's Dr. Jekyl and Mr. Hyde, or Wilde's Dorian Gray and his portrait, or Conrad's Captain and secret sharer: are they two, or one and the same? The answer can only be that they are both. The situation is, in this respect, no different from the splitting of the mother into the two aspects viewed by the child. On the narrative level, witch and fairy go their very separate ways, but only to represent in the terms of a child's fantasy the single mother who fills both roles in life. Why can we not intuitively perceive, as reader, that one character, independent enough on his own terms, also dramatizes aspects which belong to another character. We are greatly helped to this intuition when each half of the equation displays half of a human personality, as with the benign fairy and malignant witch. Miranda and Caliban at least fit this requirement, since one displays the heights to which virtue may attain, while the other is entirely wicked.

The situation is not unlike what prevailed in the *Beauty* tale. The prince was an independent character who became Beauty's husband. But, in addition, he was invested with attributes which had their origin

in the wishes and guilt of Beauty. Similarly, there are aspects of
Caliban, however much he exists in his own right, which relate directly
to Miranda and duplicate the dynamics of projection as in the Beauty
fable. For instance, in one of the most moving and revealing passages in
the play, Caliban reports the circumstances of his childhood. He tells
Prospero:

> When thou cam'st first,
> Thou strok'st me, and made much of me; wouldst give me
> Water with berries in't; and teach me how
> To name the bigger light, and how the less,
> That burn by day and night: and then I lov'd thee . . . .[8]

We see that there is no suggestion here of the Caliban whom critics have
called the evil touchstone of the play. He is, on the contrary, just like
every child: born, fed, caressed, taught language, loved, and taught to
love. And what is his crime, for which Prospero calls him *abhorred* and
filth, and condemns him to painful slavery? It is similarly the crime of
every child: he wishes to be sexual and a parent himself. As in the
Beauty tale, the ugliness of the monster is an emblem of the child's
unsanctioned sexuality. If it is true that this play has at its core the
daughter's initial possessiveness toward her father, as well as subsequent
choice of a prince, the guilt of a wish to unsanctioned sexuality belongs
to Miranda at least as much as to poor Caliban. If this play relegates the
mother to the status of a dead witch, to whom does the monstrousness,
the "bad heart," belong? It must belong to the heroine, whose wishes
are gratified throughout the play. A most delicate monster she is, under
the gabardine of disguise.

As previously mentioned, Kermode does call our attention to how
Shakespeare has linked the identities of Miranda and Caliban at a number of points—specifically, the accounts given of their education; their
first sight of men; and seeing the assembled nobility. Prospero tells us
he was schoolmaster to Miranda, as he was to Caliban. When Miranda
first sees Ferdinand, she finds him "a thing divine," and Caliban finds
Stephano a "wondrous man." Miranda says, "This/ Is the third man
that e'er I saw . . . "; and Caliban tells us, "I never saw a woman,/ But
only Sycorax my dam and she." Finally, Miranda's "O brave new
world,/ That has such people in't!" is echoed by Caliban's "O Setebos,
these be brave spirits indeed!" These are minor but noticeable connec-

tions and support the *Dopplegänger*, even if they could not alone establish it.

There are a number of additional incidents in the play which lend some measure of support for this view of the play, as a sophisticated rendering of the family romance. They are incidents which otherwise pose unresolvable problems of explication in the text. The first is a curious scene early in the play. Prospero determines to tell Miranda all the facts of their former life. One would think she would be eager to know of the outside world, of the royalty they lost and of the forces which caused the loss. But as the story is told, Miranda is singularly inattentive about this "dark backward and abysm of time." As Kermode observes, Prospero is giving Miranda "the remarkable facts for the first time."[9] Yet Prospero must persistently call for her attention with such admonitions as:

I pray thee, mark me . . .[10]
Dost thou attend me?[11]
Thou attend'st not?[12]
I pray thee, mark me.[13]
Dost thou hear?[14]

In her protestations that she is listening "most heedfully," she tells him, "Your tale, sir, would cure deafness".[16] But Prospero is no fool, and her denial has an ironic edge. An explanation of this strange inattention is given by her sudden shift to the most responsive interest when she herself becomes the subject of the tale. Then she is tearful, hearing how she and her father were sent together from the city. She wants to know why the two of them were not destroyed, and thinks sorrowfully of the trouble she may have been to Prospero, adrift on the sea. Miranda, in short, is interested only in whatever has brought and kept her father and her alone together. She expresses not a word of regret for what he has lost, and we can infer she has been as content on the island they share as was Beauty, who grew, we are told, more beautiful when mistress of another full poor cell. Miranda, like Beauty, is interested no doubt in some noble creature, but without having quite given up her father. She makes the point well enough when Prospero tells her how ignorant she has been of their life prior to the island. She replies, "More to know/ Did never meddle with my thoughts."

Another and more considerable problem of explication has to do with Prospero's immense perturbation over the conspiracy of Caliban and his confederates. He abruptly breaks off the masque presented to Miranda and her prince, more "distemper'd," Miranda says, than she has ever seen him. It is not an anger feigned for effect since he tells the probably frightened Ferdinand:

> Sir, I am vex'd;
> Bear with my weakness; my old brain is troubled:
> Be not disturb'd with my infirmity:
>   . . . a turn or two I'll walk,
> To still my beating mind. [16]

It is, of course, true, that Caliban and his men are on the way—Caliban hopes—to both knock a nail into Prospero's head and wed Miranda to Stephano. Such is abundant reason for perturbation, except the play itself is at odds with such an explanation. Prospero's powers on the island are for all purposes omnipotent, fully adequate to deal with the would-be murderers Sebastian and (Prospero's own usurping brother) Antonio. So are they more than adequate for a slavish monster and two drunken sailors. Kermode himself makes the point when he writes:

Having wondered that Prospero should so excite himself over an easily controlled insurrection, we are now puzzled by his turning to console Ferdinand in a distress which is far less apparent . . . . [17]

Even at the moment Prospero loses his temper, his agent Ariel has left these foolish conspirators "dancing up to th' chins," in a foul lake, which "O'erstunk their feet." And when they finally reach the cell, they are driven by Prospero, and his spirits in the shapes of dogs, to goblins who will "grind their joints/ With dry convulsions . . . ."

Kermode offers two explanations for this "apparently unnecessary perturbation of Prospero at the thought of Caliban." He suggests that Prospero is disturbed because Caliban's plot is reminiscent of the past usurpation and ingratitude of his own brother. But Prospero's brother is himself present on the island, and *still* plotting murder. Yet Prospero falls into no vexation, foiling that plot, or when confronting his brother at the end. Kermode also suggests that Shakespeare is following "neo-Terentian regulations" in his construction of the play. Accordingly, the action at this point requires an *epitasis,* an increase in dramatic tension. Since Kermode finds Prospero's anger dramatically unconvincing, he concludes that it "may be a point at which an oddly pedantic concern for classical structure causes it to force its way through the surface of the play."[18] Kermode seems himself reluctant to conclude that Shakespeare would mar his play out of concern for a classical structure which he freely and frequently ignored.

There is, however, another explanation for Prospero's vexation, based on the more curious fact that he is *frequently* moved to apparently needless anger. In the first act, Prospero harshly upbraids the wondrous Ariel, who wishes only his freedom to live (air that he is) in a cowslip's bell and under the blossom that hangs on the bough. When Ariel denies forgetting all Prospero has done for him, the magician replies, "Thou liest, malignant thing!" and threatens Ariel with imprisonment all over again:

If thou more murmur'st, I will rend an oak,
And peg thee in his knotty entrails, till
Thou hast howl'd away twelve winters.[19]

Prospero's intimidation is not only unjustified, given Ariel's compassionate nature and his natural desire for freedom, but mystifying in light of Prospero's powers to command. Why should we not pick the most logical explanation of all, that Prospero is angry precisely because he does not wish to give Ariel his freedom. He has agreed to do so, of course. But he might be distressed at the thought that the hour to do it has almost come. This does not quite clear up the mystery, however, since we now have to account for his reluctance.

We can obtain a better insight into the reasons for his anger on the next occasion it breaks out. Prospero sets a task for Ferdinand so that, as he puts it, winning Miranda will not seem too easily accomplished. And ostensibly with this end in mind, he also charges Ferdinand with desiring his own defeat on the island. He says:

thou dost here usurp
The name thou ow'st not; and hast put thyself
Upon this island as a spy, to win it
From me, the lord on 't.[20]

And he now threatens to manacle his neck and feet together and give him only sea-water to drink; so that in effect he threatens to kill the young prince. When Miranda beseeches her father to have pity, his reply is again unusually harsh:

Silence! one word more
Shall make me chide thee, if not hate thee, What!
An advocate for an imposter![21]

One notes that with so many accusations to throw at Ferdinand, he
picks the one which makes them competitors for the island and everything on it. He might have, for instance, charged Ferdinand with being
unworthy of his daughter. Or he might have insisted that Miranda
would be foolish to marry this first man she has seen from the outside
world. In either case he would successfully make Ferdinand's winning
of Miranda more difficult, as is Prospero's professed motive. Although
the accusation he chooses is a pretense, we can, as with things said in
jest, take it as partly in earnest. Prospero picks the one charge which
alludes to that most primitive of all fantasy motifs in which the suitor
must destroy the father to win the daughter, a motif similarly expressed
in the *Beauty* tale. Setting an actual task for Ferdinand, that of
collecting logs, is widespread in fairy tales, and understandably so. It
expresses in symbol the father's opposition to giving up his daughter,
even though, as in this play, he may also help to bring it about.

Another occasion when Prospero is angered seems to support this
primitive motif. Prospero has agreed to their marriage, and confessed
that Ferdinand has wonderfully proved his worthiness. Now he adjures
Ferdinand to chastity until the actual marriage, which is understandable
enough. But he does so in language which, if such adjuration is required, speaks ill of Ferdinand.

If thou dost break her virgin-knot before
All sanctimonious ceremonies may
With full and holy rite be minister'd,
No sweet aspersion shall the heavens let fall
To make this contract grow; but barren hate,
Sour-ey'd disdain and discord shall bestrew
The union of your bed with weeds so loathly
That you shall hate it both . . . .[22]

It is not difficult to catch the sound of a father unconsciously angered
at the advent of his daughter's sexuality. We may best ascribe this
feeling simply to an ambivalence. He loves her and wishes to see her
happily married to Ferdinand. And so he does not acknowledge a
sexual possessiveness toward her. He keeps it attenuated and hidden.
But it is there, and it subtly finds expression.

We have come full circle from *Beauty and the Beast.* In that fairy tale, the father sought unsanctioned sexual possession of his daughter and came into mortal conflict with her suitor. The morality of the tale required that such a motif be carefully couched in symbol. Prospero is infinitely above the sexual possession of his daughter. But he is not above anger at giving her up. The rivalry may be disguised, but it is still sexual rivalry. One imagines that had the prince been anything less than perfection, he might not have fared so well. One is reminded of poor Caliban, who first sought sexual possession of Miranda. He was assuredly the least eligible of creatures. But one wonders how justified, even there, Prospero is in calling him "filth" ever after. If Caliban can say, at the end of the play,

> I'll be wise hereafter,
> And seek for grace. What a thrice-double ass
> Was I, to take this drunkard for a god,
> And worship this dull fool![23]

he cannot be entirely, as Prospero says, an "Abhorred slave,/ Which any print of goodness wilt not take. . . ." Caliban is forever shut out from the love of Prospero, not for being intractably wicked, but for the extent of Prospero's anger over the sexual character of Caliban's crime.

The series of episodes in which Prospero vents excessive anger are, in this light, all related. His anger at Ariel is connected with giving him his freedom. Such freedom signifies the end of Prospero's power and with it the loss of his daughter. At the time of the masque, when Miranda is formally given up, Prospero vents his anger, not at the rival who cannot be denied, but at the creature who already stands in his mind for the unacceptable sexual possession of his daughter. We see, in this regard, how more complex this drama is than the most intricate fairy tale. Events are not entirely organized around the wishes and guilts of the heroine. Prospero, too, has his wishes, kept carefully in check by his own conscience. And, of course, there is much else in the play beyond these "primitive" elements. But the primitive is no less part of its meaning and power.

Notes

1. Frank Kermode, ed., *The Arden Edition of the Works of William Shakespeare* (Cambridge: Harvard University Press, 1958), p. lxiii. Future references will be to this edition.
2. London: Watts and Co., 1924. Reissured by Singing Tree Press, 1968. Future references are given in the text.

3. Sigmund Freud, *Moses and Monotheism, The Standard Edition of the Complete Psychological Works of Sigmund Freud* (London: Hogarth Press, 1964), pp. 12-13. Future references are to this edition.
4. For an excellent example of this kind of projection, see Theodor Reik's analysis of *The Tales of Hoffmann* entitled "The Three Women in a Man's Life," in William Phillips, ed., *Art and Psychoanalysis* (New York: Criterion Books, 1957), pp. 151-64.
5. See Freud, "A Special Type of Choice of Object Made by Men" *Standard Edition,* XI, p. 172.
6. Kermode, *Shakespeare,* Epilogue.
7. See also Otto Fenichel, *The Psychoanalytic Theory of Neurosis* (New York: Norton & Co., 1945), p. 157.
8. Kermode, *Shakespeare,* I, ii, 334-38.
9. Kermode, *Shakespeare,* Comment to I, ii, 59.
10. Kermode, *Shakespeare,* I, ii, 67.
11. Kermode, *Shakespeare,* I, ii, 78.
12. Kermode, *Shakespeare,* I, ii, 87.
13. Kermode, *Shakespeare,* I, ii, 88.
14. Kermode, *Shakespeare,* I, ii, 106.
15. Kermode, *Shakespeare,* I, ii, 106.
16. Kermode, *Shakespeare,* I, lv, 158-63.
17. Kermode, *Shakespeare,* fn 146, p. 103.
18. Kermode, *Shakespeare,* Introduction, p. lxxv.
19. Kermode, *Shakespeare,* I, ii, 294-96.
20. Kermode, *Shakespeare,* I, ii, 456-59.
21. Kermode, *Shakespeare,* I, ii, 478-80.
22. Kermode, *Shakespeare,* IV, i, 15-23.
23. Kermode, *Shakespeare,* V, i, 294-97.

Fantasy of Innocence: Sophocles' *Oedipus the King*

As Lord Raglan has shown in his comparative study of myths, the life of Oedipus shares salient details with innumerable ancient heroes, including Theseus, Romulus, Heracles, Perseus, Jason, Apollo, Zeus, Joseph, and Moses.[1] Otto Rank has indicated how a number of mythic details accord with an unconscious wish of childhood to vanquish a hostile father or a representative of him and to achieve marriage to a woman symbolically, if not literally, the mother.[2] Freud had himself viewed the Oedipus legend as a dramatization of infantile wishes, and so termed those wishes the "Oedipus complex."[3] The extent to which this complex is common to childhood and underlies the neurosis was, of course, one of his principal discoveries. The importance which psychoanalytic theory attributes to this complex receives a measure of support from the prevalence of these variant myths in so many cultures and illustrates, as Freud so often pointed out, the agreement which exists between the artist's vision of human conflict and the psychoanalytic description. But, ironically, Freud exculpated Oedipus from the complex; he maintained that the presence of parricidal and incestuous crimes in the play by Sophocles appealed to an *audience* fascinated by the breaking of taboos they had themselves wished to break in childhood. He seems to have attributed the crimes themselves, within the context of the play, to the consequences of fate introduced as a secondary elaboration by Sophocles. For instance, he writes that "the hero of the Oedipus legend too felt guilty for his deeds and submitted himself to self-punishment, although the coercive power of the oracle should have acquitted him of guilt in our judgement and his own."[4] And again he writes:

> . . . it is still the hero himself who commits the crime. But poetic treatment is impossible without softening and disguise. The naked admission of an intention to commit parricide, as we arrive at it in analysis, seems intolerable without analytic preparation. The Greek drama, while retaining the crime, introduces the indispensable toning-down in a masterly fashion by projecting the hero's unconscious motive into reality in the form of a compulsion by a destiny which is alien to him. The hero commits the deed unintentionally and apparently uninfluenced by the woman. . . . After his guilt has been revealed and made conscious, the hero makes ηo attempt to exculpate himself by appealing to the artificial expedient of the compulsion of destiny. His crime is acknowledged and punished as though it were a full and conscious one—which is bound to appear unjust to our reason, but which psychologically is perfectly right.[5]

Although innocent, Oedipus must suffer for the unconscious guilt of the audience. The tragic effect of the play, Freud reasons, results from that involvement, since the play itself "is an amoral work: it absolves men from moral responsibility, exhibits the gods as promoters of crime and shows the impotence of the moral impulses of men which struggle against crime."[6]

Subsequent critics and psychoanalysts have similarly not held Oedipus accountable for his crimes and have generally maintained he is a victim of destiny. Moses Hadas puts the view succinctly when he writes, "Only a proud and impatient man—one who would kill in a traffic dispute—would also have the fortitude to pursue the truth as Oedipus did. His sins were committed unwittingly; by human calculations he had behaved well as a man."[7] Thomas Gould, in his introduction to an excellent new translation of the play, similarly writes:

> [Oedipus] is not presented . . . as a man who can never choose one course of action instead of another when he perceives that one fits his vision of how he would like things to be and the other does not. But his

existence has been so used by divinity for its own purposes that in two instances at least, he is drawn into doing things that are not only contrary to his own character but contrary to the character of all but the most depraved human beings.[8]

Perhaps Sophocles would have agreed with them. It is not to be imagined that Sophocles possessed a theoretical understanding of an Oedipus complex. But an artist dramatizes men, not theories. The man Oedipus, as we have him in this play, is as much possessed of oedipal wishes as any character we can find in fiction. We need not fasten on a few details and then shift to psychoanalytic theory for support. The play itself consistently supports such a view. We need only make one assumption, and it is an assumption made by traditional critics as well: that Oedipus is motivated, and that his motives are to be understood by his actions. No other assumption is needed to infer an Oedipus complex, quite apart from theoretical disputes about whether men commonly harbor the wishes of this complex, whether it is, in fact, the "nucleus" of every neurosis—or, indeed, whether neurosis itself exists. It is not simply that psychoanalytic theory informs the play; the play itself offers support for the theory.

There is no question but that Oedipus does not, and cannot, know that the white-haired man he kills at the crossroads is his father and that the widowed queen he marries is his mother. If we assume, however, that this ends the question of his *responsibility* for the crimes of parricide and incest, it becomes easy to overlook how much in the play contributes to a contrary view. Technically he is innocent, but one can be guilty according to the spirit while innocent according to the letter of responsibility. His guilt may be best seen if we examine the play not in the dramatic chronology by which it unfolds, but as events are lived by Oedipus. We do best to begin, in classical psychoanalytic fashion, with the earliest facts we can obtain about the protagonist. Oedipus himself describes the central events of his early life. He tells us that in his youth he was told by a drunken reveller that he was not the true son of his supposed parents Polybus and Merope. At that time Oedipus was disturbed by the imputation, but was comforted by his foster parents' anger. According to his recollection of this scene, we do not know whether they explicitly denied the imputation. But in any case, when the taunt thrown at Oedipus persisted, Oedipus was now

sufficiently in doubt to journey secretly from his foster parents' city in
order to learn the truth at Delphi. He gives this description of the
Delphic prophecy and his reaction to it:

I went to Pytho. But Phoebus sent me away dishonoring my demand.
Instead, other wretched horrors he flashed forth in his speech. He said
that I would be my mother's lover, show offspring to mankind they
could not look at, and be his murderer whose seed I am. When I heard
this, and ever since, I gauged the way to Corinth by the stars alone,
running to a place *where I would never see the disgrace in the oracle's
words come true.*[9]

   Indeed having heard the prophecy, Oedipus possesses much greater
reason to settle the question of his parentage, the need to avoid
parricide and incest. Yet Oedipus flees from Corinth, the one place
where some part of the truth might have been learned. It might be
argued that he cannot afford to return since that alone would be to risk
the predicted crimes. But how can we understand that he now runs
from Polybus and Merope *as though he had no doubt* of their being his
true parents? He assumes for no apparent reason that separation from
them must ensure avoidance of the predicted crimes. Yet doubt had
sent Oedipus to Delphi in the first place, and that doubt had not been
allayed. This play will later demonstrate that Oedipus never forgets that
the identity of his parents is in question. Long after he is married, and
has children, he will respond to the merest allusion of Teiresias, with
the reply: "Who? Wait! Who is the one who gave me birth?" There is no
rational explanation for his assurance that separation from Polybus and
Merope guarantees that he will "never see the disgrace in the oracle's
words come true." Quite the contrary, he journeys from the one place
where the truth could be found. The illogicality of his action is a first
indication that something is at work within him of which he is not
conscious. His unfounded assurance, that the prophecies are obstructed
by his flight, itself allows for their eventual fulfillment, and we may
begin to suspect that he unconsciously wishes it.
   The means to resist the prophecies are, after all, not difficult to
achieve. He need only refrain from killing a man and marrying a
woman, both a generation older than himself. On this basis, the question of his parentage need never be resolved. Whether he learns the
truth or not, he can never be guilty. Yet Oedipus not only puts from his
mind his doubts about his parentage, he soon thereafter kills a white-

haired older man and weds a widowed queen old enough to be his mother. It is true that he does not know they are his parents. But he knows, if he would but think about it, that they very well might be his parents. It is true that he is dealt with harshly on the way to Thebes. He is pushed from the road and struck on the head by Laius. But men have suffered worse without recourse to killing. And Oedipus has good reason for self-control in the company of white-haired older men. It may be, too, that having earned the right to rule at Thebes, he might choose to wed the respected queen of that land. But, again, he has better reasons for hesitating. If he is clever enough to solve a Sphinxian riddle beyond the calculations of other men, he can also consider the risks of what he does. Yet he marries as though he remembers nothing of his predicted fate or of his doubts about his parentage. Since we know that this knowledge and doubt were consciously in his mind, we must conclude he has repressed them for his own reasons.

Obviously one cannot say he commits these crimes in the hope that Laius and Jocasta *are* in fact his parents. The oedipally driven neurotic who weds a much older woman, or who rages unjustifiably against authority figures, relates to such people for their *resemblance* to his own parents. Such a neurotic displaces his feelings. And although he is not conscious of the motives which underlie his actions, the inappropriateness of anger or sexual choice will suggest that a displacement has occurred. The murder of Laius and marriage to Jocasta are inappropriate enough, given Oedipus' wish to avoid his predicted fate. And so we have further reason to believe he murders the one, and weds the other, in part because they are parental figures to him.

The years pass, and a plague descends upon Thebes. In order to find a remedy, Oedipus sends Creon to Phoebus. Returning, Creon states that the city cannot be healed until the murder of Laius is avenged. Creon refers to the "men who killed him with their hands," and Oedipus wonders where the men can be found. Creon then reinforces the idea of guilt shared by many men, with the report of the one eyewitness, that "bandits chanced on them and killed him—with the force of many hands, not one alone." But at this point a curious thing happens. As though he has not heard Creon, Oedipus refers to the guilt of a single man. He cries out: "How could a bandit dare so great an act . . . " And he continues: "Whoever murdered him may also wish to punish me—and with the selfsame hand." And again: "Whoever has clear knowledge of the man who murdered Laius, son of Labdacus, I command him to reveal it all to me." Although he has heard the plural reference (indeed, he will later assert his innocence on the basis that he had understood that many were said to have committed the crime), he persists in referring to a single murderer.[10] Gould, in his commentary, acknowledges the "careless shift from the plural to the singular in his mention of the bandits," as well the fact that Oedipus will "zero in on the report of 'many bandits' as the detail that ought to guarantee his own innocence."[11] But why should we ascribe the latter to policy, but the former to "carelessness"? How, we might ask, could the sharp-witted Oedipus ever be careless about so crucial a detail? His reference to a single murderer is understandable enough as a "slip of the tongue," as a manifestation of unconscious guilt. Although it is true that Oedipus has no reason to think that he is the murderer of Laius, he is well aware that he killed a man of Laius' age, at the time of Laius' death and on the road from Thebes.

Oedipus has already shown his ability to repress facts from consciousness, and he does so again now: he does not suspect that he may be the murderer of Laius. But he betrays his guilt of just such a crime by persisting in the one detail which links him to the killing of Laius; he knows that *his* crime he committed alone. He refers to the guilt of a single man many times and then recovers his repression at precisely the moment at which he might be expected to do so, the moment when the need for repression was greatest, in colloquy with the dangerous seer Teiresias, who might know or divine his guilt. We are faced once again with the significance of a chosen ignorance on the part of Oedipus. His continued reference to a single murderer contradicts the report as given and gives us a glimpse into the guilt which has survived for so many years. His manipulation of the singular and plural reference is a first indication, too, that he is more governed by the force of guilt than by his conscious search for the means to cure his city. To say that Oedipus confuses such a vital matter through inadvertance is to find him mentally defective, something he unquestionably is not. The Freudian view, which holds that such slips are motivated as are all other mental events, helps us to a more tenable explanation.

The ensuing scene with Teiresias must also seem to be singularly inexplicable on any basis but that Oedipus is repressing knowledge of parricidal and incestuous wishes (enacted against Laius and Jocasta, but acquired in childhood with Polybus and Merope). At first Oedipus greets Teiresias as a great prophet, "a master of all omens—public and secret, in the sky and on the earth." Teiresias refuses to divulge the information he possesses but obliquely implies that Oedipus is responsible for the plague: "If you will listen to me you will endure your troubles better." "I see your understanding comes to you inopportunely." "I'll never bring my grief to light—I will not speak of yours." "I will grieve neither of us."[12] Of course this kind of talk is ambiguous. But a less clever man than Oedipus could feel an accusation being made. Teiresias, in fact, uses a *double entendre,* and implies that Oedipus is unaware of the identity of the woman he lives with. As Gould translates it, Oedipus, though he has eyes, cannot "see.her who lives with him."[13] Yet Oedipus ignores the riddling hints, and shifts into a resistance against them; he suddenly accuses the blind prophet of having engineered the murder of Laius himself.

Gould finds the accusation a "shrewd," if incorrect, guess. But if Teiresias were guilty, why ever would he confess knowledge of the crime and refuse to speak further? Such self-incriminatory practices are avoided by guilty men. And what motive could Teiresias have had for the killing in the first place? It is as though Oedipus has intuitively understood that he must either discredit the prophet or stand accused of the murder himself. Such an interpretation is, at this point in the play, admittedly conjecture. But what follows gives it overwhelming support. Teiresias, now taunted with the murder, specifically names Oedipus the "vile polluter of this land." Oedipus first pretends he has not heard, and then refuses to consider what is said:

Oedipus: Who taught you this? Not your prophetic craft!
Teiresias: You did. You made me say it. I didn't want to.
Oedipus: Say what? Repeat it so I'll understand.
Teiresias: I made no sense? Or are you trying me?
Oedipus: No sense I understood. Say it again!
Teiresias: I say you are the murderer you seek.
Oedipus: Again that horror! You'll wish you hadn't said that.
Teiresias: Shall I say more, and raise your anger higher?
Oedipus: Anything you like! Your words are powerless.[14]

Oedipus heard well the first time, and it is not like an innocent man, falsely accused, to pretend he has not heard an accusation. Oedipus' charge that Teiresias' words are powerless is simply resistance to the truth. He might easily reflect that he has in fact slain a man of Laius' age, at about the time the murder was committed, and on the very road from Thebes. But that is the point. He cannot take the natural recourse of every innocent man, a calm consideration of his own whereabouts at the time of the crime. He has too much to hide.

Teiresias now refers to the heart of Oedipus' predicament, his ignorance of the identity of his parents, and his knowledge of the Delphic oracles: "You live, unknowing, with those nearest to you in the greatest shame. You do not see the evil."[15] And again: "Do you know your parents? Not knowing, you are their enemy, in the underworld and here. A mother's and a father's double-lashing terrible-footed curse will soon drive you out."[16] Oedipus' reply is a scream of pain at what he is being constrained to face: "Am I to listen to such things from him? May you be damned! Get out of here at once! Go! Leave my palace! Turn around and go!"[17] Once again Teiresias turns the screw: "Stupid I seem to you, yet to your parents who gave you natural birth I seemed quite shrewd."[18]

It has been pointed out before that Oedipus has always doubted the identity of his parents, and inferences were drawn from this fact. Oedipus now, for one instant, reveals again those doubts. This time he hears Teiresias and replies to his words directly: "Who? Wait! *Who is the one who gave me birth?*"[19] Teiresias again exclaims that "this day will give you birth, and ruin too." Notice that his comments, taken all together, say plainly enough to Oedipus, given his knowledge of the past: "Polybus and Merope were not your parents. You have fulfilled the prophecies, since you have murdered your father Laius, and have wedded your natural mother." Yet even now, with his doubts freshly awakened, Oedipus replies: "What murky, riddling things you always say!"[20]

How perfectly ignorance serves Oedipus, the solver of riddles *par excellence.* He is like the neurotic who resists truth in analysis. One is reminded of Freud's description of this kind of neurotic strategy:

Whenever we are on the point of bringing to [the patients'] consciousness some piece of unconscious material which is particularly painful to him, then he is critical in the extreme; even though he may have previously understood and accepted a great deal, yet now all these gains seem to be obliterated; in his struggles to oppose at all costs he can behave just as though he were mentally deficient, a form of "emotional stupidity." . . . His critical faculty is not functioning independently, and therefore is not to be respected as if it were; it is merely a maid-of-all-work for his affective attitudes and is directed by his resistance.[21]

In his need to resist the truth, Oedipus' critical faculties are so compromised that he concludes that his old and trusted brother-in-law Creon, as well as Teiresias, are guilty of the murder and of a plot to obtain his crown. It is a vivid example of how, under the press of inner necessity (a need to defend against admitting into consciousness painful feelings of guilt, shame, and fear), perceptions of reality must be progressively distorted. Facts were forgotten. Accusations were not heard. And finally, when guilt can no longer be kept from discussion, it is inappropriately projected onto the most unlikely men in the state. Although he has no evidence of any kind, Oedipus exclaims:

"My loyal Creon, colleague from the start, longs to sneak up in secret and dethrone me. So he's suborned this fortuneteller—schemer! deceitful beggar-priest!" "What? You [Creon] here? And can you really have the face and daring to approach my house when you're exposed as its master's murderer and caught, too, as the robber of my kingship?"[22]

This is egregious slander. Nothing has been exposed. Only the baldest surmise, the most tenuous of assumptions, can make both Teiresias and Creon the proven murderers of Laius so many years before as well as the plotters against Oedipus' rule. Not only is such an assumption unsubstantiated, it is illogical. If they were capable of murdering Laius to obtain the crown, why should they have done nothing for so many years to take it from the equally vulnerable Oedipus?

Insisting that he has "caught" Creon plotting against him, Oedipus sentences him to death. Gould's explanation for the rightousness with which this penalty is called for begs the question: "Oedipus obviously believes very firmly in his 'discovery' that it was Creon who had put Tiresias up to this. Given Oedipus' honest belief that he was not the regicide, and the fact that the seer's accusation would be utterly baffling to him if he had not hit on the reasons for connecting Creon and Tiresias, we can accept this confidence as natural."[23] But why should we accept either his belief in innocence as "honest," or his failure to understand the seer's accusation? We must remind ourselves again that Oedipus murdered a man of Laius' age at the time the murder of Laius was committed, and on the same road to Delphi. And provocative comments about the identity of his natural parents, or about living in shame with those nearest him, he has encountered before and can understand well enough now. Oedipus is faced with horrors, and to close his eyes he will, to use Freud's phrase, submit to any degree of emotional stupidity. It is part of the artistry of Sophocles that this chosen stupidity increases to the very end. Always in opposition to the gradual disclosure of facts, his tenacious will to believe in his own innocence generates the central conflict of the play.

Jocasta reveals to Oedipus (1) that ministers of Phoebus had once prophesied that her child by Laius would one day murder his father, (2) that to resist the prophecy they had abandoned their child, and (3) that, "contrary to Apollo," Laius was murdered by robbers in Phocis (where "a two-forked road comes in from Delphi and Daulia"), as were the five men travelling with him. This is not information which can be ignored for being a riddle, or turned aside with accusations. Oedipus is specifically told, moreover, that the scene of the murder was the same as the locale of his own crime, that the times of the two murders were the same, that Laius was a white-headed man like the one he killed, that in both cases the same number of travelling companions were also slain, and that the one witness to the crimes, now a herdsman, begged to leave Thebes when he found Oedipus ruling in place of Laius. One detail alone differs: Laius was reported to have been slain by many men. Oedipus grasps at this one straw. It should be apparent to him by now how unsubstantial that straw is. Holding in suspense any conclusion regarding his own guilt until the witness has been searched out, despite the preponderant weight of the other evidence against him, cannot be seen as a search for the truth, but rather as another desperate refusal to face guilt. Oedipus is not battling for the welfare of his city, nor is he catching at fresh evidence regarding the secrets of his past and of his identity: He is reaching frantically for the single detail at odds with the array of evidence against him.

Notice that with all his protestations of having to get at the truth, Oedipus has dismissed Jocasta's startling revelation that the prophecy concerning her child by Laius matches Oedipus' prophecy revealed to him at Delphi. Recall too that Teiresias has already revealed that Oedipus is not only the murderer of Laius, but also a native-born Theban, an "enemy" to his natural parents, one who "will be shown a father who is also a brother; to the one who bore him, son and husband; to his father his seed-fellow and killer."[24] Oedipus is prepared, indeed eager, to doubt the veracity of the Delphic oracle, of the respected seer, of his trusted brother-in-law, and to stake all on the veracity of a single poor herdsman. One does not, of course, imagine that he consciously decides which facts he will dismiss from his mind, and how he can best resist the truth while seeming to pursue it. But this is the way he behaves, and he must be held accountable. It is a good example in fiction of what constitutes the unconscious: thought too painful to acknowledge, but too powerful to control.

Gould, in his commentary, continues to ascribe only conscious motives to Oedipus with an argument which grows increasingly tenuous. For instance, Jocasta comments to Oedipus that Laius "had a figure not unlike your own," another hint they are father and son. Gould writes:

This description of Laius is, of course, very pointed for the modern audience. However, Oedipus still has no reason to conclude that they are related. Homer sometimes gives the impression that the hereditary kings were all huge compared to the common men; it may be that Sophocles and his audience would have this in mind in picturing the heroic age. Laius, like yourself, Jocasta says, had the spendid figure of a nobleman.[25]

This may be. But if the remark is "very pointed" for a modern audience, so can it be for Oedipus. And he not only fails to *conclude* that Laius is his father, but refuses even to entertain a suspicion of it. He now declares to Jocasta that he may have "stained the dead man's bed with these my hands, by which he died," but that if he is driven into exile as punishment, he must not return to Polybus and Merope" or else be yoked in marriage to my mother, and kill my father."[26] In short, he has contrived to learn as little as possible from all that has been revealed.

When a messenger from Corinth arrives, Oedipus hears that Polybus has died, and once again he acts as though he had not the slightest doubts whether Polybus and Merope were his true parents. His heart surges with cheer. He now has to fear only incest, he says, since the death of Polybus makes it impossible for him to be guilty of parricide. But at this point the last piece of the puzzle is put into words. The messenger reports that Oedipus was not the son of Polybus and Merope—rather, that he was found with his ankles bound, just as Jocasta had bound the ankles of her abandoned son, and that he was in the possession of a shepherd of the house of Laius. Jocasta is now the perfect foil, swift in her apprehension of an incontrovertible truth. In anguish she pleads with Oedipus not to question further about the

shepherd: "What? The man he spoke of? Pay no attention! For the love
of the gods, and if you love your life, give up this search! My sickness is
enough."[27] She possesses no more of the facts than does Oedipus, yet
she easily puts them together and realizes he is her own son and the
murderer of his father. She will, within the space of the next few
minutes, return to her house to destroy herself in shame, needing no
further information, having to question no one else.

But the refusal of Oedipus to examine his guilt continues. He takes it
into his head that Jocasta is distraught at the possibility he will be
found to be "lowborn," as though anyone has accused him of it. He has
now become a theatrical magician who ostentatiously exhibits one
innocent hand while the other covertly conceals the trick. With every
insistence that he will have the truth of his birth, he denies the truth
already exposed. He asserts: "Let it burst forth! However low this seed
of mine may be, yet I desire to see it." Well might he desire it! If he is
low-born, he cannot be the son of the royal Jocasta and Laius. He
declaims that he is "the child of Chance," and she his mother; dissem-
bling too transparent to be taken seriously. Jocasta, of course, will have
none of such futile posturing. She tells him: "Man of misery! No other
name shall I address you by, ever again," and returns to her house and
to her death.

Her son-and-husband carries on as he has throughout, acting to the
last possible moment his pretense of searching for knowledge. The old
shepherd is brought before him, and Oedipus seems to stop at nothing
to get the truth. He even threatens him with death if information is
withheld. The old man finally tells Oedipus that he was son to Laius
and Jocasta, taken from his mother and finally given to the house of
Polybus and Merope. We might think that this at last is information
enough, but it is not. Although he is consciously sincere in his quest as
he always has been, his emotional stupidity still rules his thinking. To
repeat Freud's description of the neurotic in treatment, his "critical
faculty is not functioning independently, and . . . is merely a maid-of-
all-work for his affective attitudes and is directed by his resistance."
And so he continues to ask new questions which are irrelevant, or to
which he knows the answers. Told that Jocasta gave up her son for him
to be killed, he asks again if the child were her own son. Told that she
dreaded prophecies, he wants to know what they were, as though
Jocasta has not just revealed it. He asks the shepherd why he gave the
child to the house of Polybus and Merope, as though this matters now

that his guilt is proven. It is a last tactic of defense, however hopeless of success. The old man finally breaks into this line of meaningless questions with the charge: "Know your evil birth and fate!"—and feigned innocence must come to an end.

It is true that Oedipus' "complex" is never directly in evidence, since his flight from Corinth, his murder of Laius, and his marriage to Jocasta are all past history when the play begins. But these events are of his own doing, a mastery of events he would not have allowed himself had he been determined above all else to oppose his predicted fate. Had he not repressed doubts about his parentage, vented murderous anger against an old man, and married a woman old enough to be his mother, he could have allowed himself to see the truth (as did Jocasta) without confusion or delay, without berating the world with endless questions, without denials, and without hurling slanderous accusations at everybody else. Even putting out his own eyes at the end symbolically expresses the ambivalence that has ruled his life. He accepts punishment, but in a way that seems to say symbolically that he still will not see the extent of his intolerable guilt.

Notes

1. Lord Raglan, *The Hero: A Study in Tradition, Myth and Drama* (New York: Vintage Books, 1956), pp. 174-85.
2. Otto Rank, *The Myth of the Birth of the Hero* (New York: Robert Brunner, 1952).
3. Sigmund Freud, "Introductory Lectures on Psycho-analysis," In *The Standard Edition of the Complete Psychological Works of Sigmund Freud,* XV (London: Hogarth Press, 1963), p. 207. Future references are to this edition. For his first use of this term, see "Contributions to the Psychology of Love," I, *Standard Edition,* XI, p. 171.
4. "An Outline of Psycho-analysis," *Standard Edition,* XXIII, p. 205.
5. "Dostoevsky and Parricide," *Standard Edition,* XXI, p. 188.
6. "Introductory Lectures on Psycho-analysis," *Standard Edition,* XV, p. 331.
7. The Complete Plays of Sophocles, edited with an Introduction by Moses Hadas (New York: Bantam Books, 1967), p. 76.
8. *Oedipus the King,* edited with commentary by Thomas Gould (Englewood Cliffs: Prentice-Hall, 1970), p. 9.
9. Gould, *Oedipus,* lines 788-97. Emphasis added.
10. See also Gould, *Oedipus,* lines 236-37, and 266.
11. Gould, *Oedipus,* Commentary to line 124.
12. Gould, *Oedipus,* lines 320-32.

13. Gould, *Oedipus,* Commentary to line 337.
14. Gould, *Oedipus,* lines 357-65.
15. Gould, *Oedipus,* lines 336-67.
16. Gould, *Oedipus,* lines 415-18.
17. Gould, *Oedipus,* lines 429-31.
18. Gould, *Oedipus,* lines 435-36.
19. Gould, *Oedipus,* line 437. Emphasis added.
20. Gould, *Oedipus,* line 438.
21. Sigmund Freud, *A General Introduction to Psychoanalysis,* trans., Joan Riviere (New York: Pocket Books, 1969), p. 303.
22. Gould, *Oedipus* lines 385-88, 532-35.
23. Gould, *Oedipus,* Commentary to line 703.
24. Gould, *Oedipus,* lines 457-60.
25. Gould, *Oedipus,* Commentary to line 743.
26. Gould, *Oedipus,* lines 825-26.
27. Gould, *Oedipus,* lines 1056-57, 1060-61.

Fantasy of Paternity
and the Doppelgänger:
Mary Shelley's *Frankenstein*

i The Riddle of Birth

Of the hundreds of Gothic novels written during the late eighteenth and early nineteenth centuries, few have taken hold of the modern imagination as has Mary Shelley's *Frankenstein.* The novel was written, Mrs. Shelley tells us, "to awaken thrilling horror," "to make the reader dread to look around, to curdle the blood, and quicken the beatings of the heart." Horror, indeed, is invoked. But *Frankenstein* has survived as a horror story long after other works, equally well-written and more ghastly in their effects, have been forgotten. Classics of the Gothic period now hardly remembered, such as Lewis' *The Monk,* or Walpole's *The Castle of Otranto,* depict murder, rape, sadistic punishments, incest, pacts with the devil, and inhumanly cruel protagonists. *Frankenstein* is tame by comparison. It makes no use of sensational Gothic devices, such as the gloomy castle, imprisoning convent, secret vault, cruel inquisition, or the tyrant's pursuit of the heroine. And the Frankenstein monster is not the fiend one might imagine without having read the book, but a creature of intelligence and compassion driven to murder only by a world which utterly denies him love. What is it, then, that can account for the survival of *Frankenstein* as one of the world's great stories of horror?

Part of the explanation concerns the difference between the devices a Gothic writer uses to produce terror and what does in fact terrify the reader. The mere addition of frightening events often will destroy credibility and seem ridiculous. It is not the quotient of enacted violence which grips the reader, but rather the extent of his own identification with those impulses which underlie the action. The crimes we fear most are those we are moved to vicariously share, and which we carefully guard against in life. *Frankenstein* has survived because of the horror we feel at the thought of a man destroyed by his own creation. Even the name itself, "Frankenstein monster," has gone into the language as a synonym for the murderous recoil of the things we make. It is not the magnificent achievement of Frankenstein, whom Mary Shelley likened to a modern Prometheus, which so fascinates and repels us; nor is it the blasphemy of his usurpation of God's life-giving powers, as she also suggested. Rather, we react to the Gothic character of the transgression in which a creature given life destroys his maker. The peculiar horror of such an event has to do with its symbolic meaning which attracts our vicarious participation, and then repels us. This meaning is as rich, and yet highly condensed into the fewest symbols, as we might experience in our dreams—or our nightmares.

The connection between *Frankenstein* and the dream process is superbly indicated by the manner in which the novel was first conceived. During a rainy summer in 1818, Lord Byron proposed that he, Shelley, and Mary each write a story to rival the Gothic tales they had been reading. Byron and Shelley immediately began, while Mary, feeling a "blank incapability of invention," was unable to write. But one night she listened "long past the witching hour" to Byron and Shelley talk about the principles of life, the experiments of Darwin, and the effects of Galvanism. She went to bed and, unable to sleep, saw a frightening vision: "When I placed my head on my pillow I did not sleep, nor could I be said to think. My imagination, unbidden, possessed and guided me, gifting the successive images that arose in my mind with a vividness far beyond the usual bounds of reverie. I saw—with shut eyes, but acute mental vision—I saw the pale student of unhallowed arts kneeling beside the thing he had put together."[1] So horrified was Mrs. Shelley that she opened her eyes in terror. A thrill of fear ran through her, and she struggled both to dispel the vision, and to recall herself to reality. On the following morning, the "hideous fantom" still persisted, and she began her novel, "making only a transcript of the grim terrors of my waking dream."

Mrs. Shelley attributes her experience of terror to a moral sense that the creation of life, by the "pale student of unhallowed arts," is sacrilegious. She writes that "supremely frightful would be the effect of any human endeavour to mock the stupendous mechanism of the Creator of the world." This well may be, but it seems doubtful that it is the entire explanation. A conscious judgment about what is blasphemous could hardly produce a terror so profound that she momentarily cannot distinguish between what is real and what is imagined. Nor does it explain what causes her imagination to be possessed by unbidden thoughts in the first place. And, too, she tells us that it is her very effort to be rid of the vision which prompts her to transcribe it into a novel. It is hard to miss the suggestion in all of this that her relation to the vision is more complex, more deeply and unconsciously motivated than would be the case with the simple conception of a modern Prometheus. If the novel is a transcript of her dream-vision, it is in the work itself, in the dramatization of those images which sprang unbidden from beyond "the usual bounds of reverie," that the reasons for her terror will be found. And we can expect that they will be the reasons for the fearful fascination of readers as well, who have no interest in the many bloodier tales of the Gothic period.

Mary Shelley's *Frankenstein* is more complex than the early movie version which starred (who could forget?) Bela Lugosi, Basil Rathbone, and Boris Karloff—and, in many respects, the tale is surprisingly different. The narration is divided into three parts. In the first, there is an account of Victor Frankenstein's childhood, his early interest in the occult, his university studies in chemistry and anatomy, the experiments which culminate in his creation of a living creature which resembles a man, his fearful flight and long nervous collapse, his eventual realization that the creature has murdered his brother, and the climactic confrontation of the two at the top of a glacial mountain. In the second part, the creature tells his creator about his own life from the time he first received life, through his efforts to understand the world and his bitterness for being abandoned by his creator, to his eventual, revengeful murder of Frankenstein's younger brother. The last part recounts Frankenstein's initial efforts to placate the lonely creature by creating a mate for him, his reversal of this decision, and the bitter and murderous consequences of this decision for Frankenstein and his entire family.

Until the moment Frankenstein creates his man-like creature, there is nothing to strongly suggest a psychoanalytic reading of the story. His interest in the occult and in the secrets of life seem formed in his mind at an unusually early age, but these interests find scientific application with maturity. His zeal for creating life is comparable to any other passionate quest for discovery, and his determination to bring the light of knowledge into the world is understandable on its own terms. There seems to be nothing sinister about him. He does not sell his soul for the ability to create life, nor does he exercise magic powers. His achievement is based on hard work and exacting scientific experimentation. If his creative achievement violates the limits imposed by God, that fact is never reflected in Victor's mind. And so, in the apparent absence of internal conflict and without discord in his life, he seems simply an imaginative, gifted scientist who, by extraordinary application, achieves extraordinary results.

But this ambitious dedication that shapes his life leaves us all the more unprepared for what follows. In the magic moment when Victor succeeds in creating his living creature—when he sees it open its eyes, breathe, and convulsively move its limbs—he conceives a lasting horror which not only drives all other thoughts from his mind, but which also leads to his nervous disorder and possesses him to the day of his death.

The importance of this horror cannot be overestimated, since it is the force which transforms the being he has created from what it is when its life begins—a creature not only helpless and lonely, but also disposed to sensitivity, virtue, and love—into the killer it later becomes. Why should Frankenstein react in this astounding way? He has labored many years, as he tells us, to "pour a torrent of light into our dark world." And now the knowledge and skill are his to impart. Yet we are expected to believe that, in one instant, he is overcome with loathing for his work solely because the creature is ugly in appearance! At least this is the only explanation Frankenstein gives us. He writes that "the different accidents of life are not so changeable as the feelings of human nature. I had worked hard for nearly two years for the sole purpose of infusing life into an inanimate body. For this I had deprived myself of rest and health. I had desired it with an ardour that far exceeded moderation, but now that I had finished, the beauty of the dream vanished, and breathless horror and disgust filled my heart. Unable to endure the aspect of the being I had created, I rushed out of the room. . . . "[2]

And how ugly is this being? We are told it has "watery eyes, that seemed almost of the same colour as the dun white sockets," "straight black lips," and a shrivelled yellow skin which "scarcely covered the work of muscles and arteries beneath." This is its ugliness—perhaps a disappointment after the beauty he may have sought to give it. But what an achievement is here. Ugly or not, it moves, breathes, lives! He has, we can recall, been familiar with the creature's appearance for a long time—throughout its construction. And to achieve success, he robbed graves by night, collected bones from charnel-houses, and kept in his workshop materials from slaughter-houses and dissecting rooms. Surely this is a long association with ugliness. Even the most extreme ugliness—which his description does not portray—is essentially beside the point. He has done well enough for man's first creation of artificial life. Is this, for which he worked so hard, to be negated because its color is wrong? It does not seem credible. With the description he gives, he might just as easily, and more realistically, have marvelled that the resemblance to a man was so close.

One does not doubt his sincerity, however. His terror is real. But if we are to understand him, and the novel as well, we must presume that this terror, having its origin in other causes, is transferred to a convenient pretext. A likely explanation, one which Mrs. Shelley herself suggested, is that Frankenstein recoils from the realization that he has transgressed the limits imposed by God. He suddenly perceives that his creature is unnatural, and so he is overcome by superstitious dread of his own work. But aside from the fact that, in his efforts to justify his terror, Frankenstein never refers to his achievement as sacrilege, he specifically tells us how removed his is from any view but the scientific. For instance, he writes, "In my education my father had taken the greatest precautions that my mind should be impressed with no supernatural horrors. I do not remember to have trembled at a tale of superstition, or to have feared the apparition of a spirit. Darkness had no effect upon my fancy; and a churchyard was to me merely the receptacle of bodies deprived of life. . . . "[3]

We have come full circle to Mary Shelley's waking dream. In explanation of her terror, she, too, stressed the "hideous" appearance of the creature, with its "yellow, watery" eyes. And she attributed this ugliness to the hideousness of the creative act, which "mocks the stupendous mechanism of the Creator of the world." But such a moral judgment, after the fact, was not enough, we felt, to explain why, with eyes shut, and head on the pillow, she produced her waking vision in the first place. She does, however, offer an illuminating hint in a second explanation of the terror felt by the creator in her vision. She said that "success would terrify the artist." The most interesting thing about this comment is its illogicality. If the artist is not horrified by his attempts to create life, why should success be intolerable? But this is, in fact, exactly the way it also happens in the novel. Frankenstein's overwhelming disgust and terror begin only when the creature is suddenly possessed of life. Of this moment, we may recall, Frankenstein writes, "How can I describe my emotions at this catastrophe?"—as though the "catastrophe" is not precisely what he worked so hard to achieve. And he writes, "Now that I had finished, the beauty of the dream vanished, and breathless horror and disgust filled my heart." It is as though the motive to create is allowable only so long as it is not successfully implemented in reality. We can recall now that Mrs. Shelley, too, was particularly frightened by the thought that her vision was real, and was able to master her fright only by dispelling this confusion.

In all of this, there is the suggestion that such a motive to create life is part of an infantile fantasy. There are many fantasies of childhood—narcissistic, grandiose, aggressive, and sexual—which we may keep in our thoughts, but refuse to gratify directly in reality. We preserve the "beauty of the dream," even as we set against it disgust at the thought of translating the dream into an accomplished fact. We do know that Frankenstein's desire to bring the light of knowledge into the world, his expressed motive, was not the dominant one, or he would not have found success intolerable. We must look for another motive, one infinitely more personal, infantile, and unconscious. Fortunately, Mrs. Shelley gives us an account of his early life; and it is there the motive can be found, as well as an explanation of his terror.

What we do know about Victor Frankenstein's childhood has the greatest value for an interpretation of future events. In the first place, he tells us that his quest for hidden knowledge dominated his thoughts throughout his earliest years. He writes that "my temper was sometimes violent, and my passions vehement; but by some law in my temperature they were turned, not towards childish pursuits, but to an eager desire to learn, and not to learn all things indiscriminately. . . . It was the secrets of heaven and earth that I desired to learn; . . . the physical secrets of the world."[4] This curiosity cannot be the metaphysical preoccupation of a philosophical mind, or the scientist's interest in knowledge for its own sake. Children do not search for knowledge that has no immediate and practical value in their own lives. We must also remember that his quest is not merely curiosity, but an obsession which rules his life.

The possibility that such an obsession is rooted in infantile sexuality cannot be overlooked. Psychoanalysis has long since shown that obsessions characteristically have their origin in sexual conflict. As Victor himself describes the infantile beginning of his quest for the facts of life, his language invariably conveys a sexual *double entendre*. The comment that his desire for knowledge was not a childish pursuit hints that his curiosity is sexual, as does his expression for the object of that curiosity—the "physical secrets" of the world. He writes that, at seventeen, when he begins his studies at the University of Ingolstadt, he is dominated by the wish to "unfold to the world the deepest mysteries of creation." "Whence," he often asks himself, "did the principle of life proceed? It was a bold question, and one which has ever been considered as a mystery." And at last, when his researches are successful, he tells us that he discovered the "cause of generation and life." We do not need psychoanalysis to tell us that, for the child, the "deepest mysteries of creation" is the sexual act. Sex and pregnancy are the "cause of generation and life," the mystery which, for children, can be resolved by "bold questions only." It is true that at seventeen he presumably has the facts of life. But obsessions out of childhood can retain an independant force; voyeurism, exhibitionism, fetishism, for instance, are all sexual interests arising in childhood that survive into adulthood in spite of the opportunities for mature sexuality. Once an obsession is formed, and then divorced from a conscious recognition of its underlying sexual character, no amount of later sexual information will cancel its existence.

Sexual curiosity in children is, of course, quite common, if not universal. Freud has given us an accurate picture of how a quest for knowledge in children can represent a sublimated search for knowledge of where babies originate. So crucial is Freud's analysis to an understanding of Frankenstein that a long quotation is given here:

At about the same time as the sexual life of children reaches its first peak, between the ages of three and five, they also begin to show signs of the activity which may be ascribed to the instinct for knowledge or research. . . . Its relation to sexual life, however, is of particular importance, since we have learnt from psychoanalysis that the instinct for knowledge in children is attracted unexpectedly early and intensively to sexual problems and is in fact possibly first aroused by them. It is not by theoretical interests but by practical ones that activities of research are set going in children. The threat to the bases of a child's existence offered by the discovery or the suspicion of the arrival of a new baby and the fear that he may, as a result of it, cease to be cared for and loved, make him thoughtful and clear-sighted. And this history of the instinct's origin is in line with the fact that the first problem with which it deals is not the question of the distinction between the sexes but the riddle of where babies come from.[5]

In this light, the scientist interested in only the question of where life comes from, and the child preoccupied by the riddle of how babies come to exist, are psychologically joined. The equation may sound surprising, even improbable, but nothing else explains the equally improbable obsession from childhood. In support of Freud's explanation of the child's quest for knowledge, one also finds that the only other childhood event Frankenstein vividly describes, besides his own quest for knowledge, is the wonderful way his mother brings home a baby girl as a gift. The child, Elizabeth, is a foundling taken by Frankenstein's mother from poor foster parents who could not keep her and she is brought home looking, we are told, like a "radiant apparition." One can take this improbable event as the child's naive and romantic explanation of the sexual act and its consequences, neither of which he understands.

One thinks of the tales told to children about infants magically obtained or received from the stork. In this view, the gift of Elizabeth is in reality her birth, distorted, as are so many other events in the novel, according to the child's conception of events. But even accepting it on its own terms, as an actual occurrence, what could be more perplexing, more anxiety-provoking, than having a mother who brings such gifts home for the family? Given the extent to which, as Freud puts it, the child's love and security in the family are jeopardized, what could be more of a riddle needing to be understood? It is important to note that this event has no consequence in the plot which follows. There is no later discovery scene of the true parents, or of situations which depend upon this girl having been a foundling. True, Victor eventually marries Elizabeth, something he could not do were she his "real" sister. But given how little she appears in the story, she might just as easily be the girl next door. As a result, there is the implication that her appearance, listed as one of two great events in his childhood, is related to the other—his childish quest for knowledge. His curiosity about the origins of life are begun, it would appear, by the appearance of this radiant apparition, a baby sister. We have not yet accounted for Frankenstein's disgust and horror at his success in creating a "man." But there is one more piece to the puzzle which, in place, gives us the explanation. Elizabeth is not brought home as a gift for the family, but rather brought home, in the father's absence, as a gift for Victor himself. Frankenstein tells us that, "on the evening previous to her being brought to my home, my mother had said playfully, 'I have a pretty present for my Victor—tomorrow he shall have it.' And when, on the morrow, she presented Elizabeth to me as her promised gift, I, with childish seriousness, interpreted her words literally, and looked upon Elizabeth as mine—mine to protect, love, and cherish. All praises bestowed on her, I received as made to a possession of my own."[6]

We do not know why Victor's mother should choose to be playful in this way, but it is not difficult to interpret the young boy's seriousness. It is for the father to protect, love, and cherish; for the father to accept the praises bestowed on the child as his own possession. Victor has adopted the fantasy that he is himself the parent. Since his own father is away, the fantasy is so much the easier to enjoy. The conception of a "gift," as mentioned before, charmingly preserves the child's ignorance of sexual information. But, in addition, as is so often the case with symbolism, a simple reversal of one element can unlock key information. In his fantasy of paternity, Victor may imagine the little girl is his own gift to his mother. There are, indeed, less logical ways of imagining why the father takes credit for the infant's appearance, after having done nothing observable to earn the credit. Paternity is always the gift of life. A non-psychoanalytic critic might take exception at this point, and maintain that the oedipal motif has been arrived at in only a speculative way, and that if we are free to reverse details of the plot, then nothing restrains any critic from imposing any interpretation he likes. Our reply is not simply that psychoanalysis has long since established both the sexual meaning of obsessional curiosity, and the use of reversal to disguise guilt-laden ideas, but that the novel dramatizes highly puzzling events comprehensible in no other light.

We can begin to see, then, that Victor Frankenstein's life is governed by a particular oedipal obsession—the question of where babies originate. He wishes to know how Elizabeth was produced, so that he can present his mother with another baby. Such a wish is common enough in children. It is part of a possessiveness toward their mothers which first finds expression, not in a desire to perform the sexual act, of which children cannot conceive and biologically do not require, but rather in the more subtle sexual wish to undertake the observable features of the father's pleasurable role with the mother. The child is well aware that the love his father receives from the mother is partly a result of the father's stature as provider—in some obscure fashion—of new children. Just as the young girl fantasizes "having" a baby of her own, the boy can imagine that he is the provider of one. But the girl can hold her doll, while the boy has no such easy, tangible solution. He is faced with what must be for him the first metaphysical problem of his life: what it is that constitutes paternity? How complex and obsessive that problem can be, the novel dramatizes for us.

This is the context in which to understand Frankenstein's disgust and horror at his success in putting together a "man." It is true that there is, in the creation, no obvious indication of an infantile fantasy of paternity. In the first place, the creation is sexless; no woman is involved. In the second, the being is a gigantic creature who is immensely strong, not a baby. And, finally, Frankenstein's horrified recoil seems to deny that his success is the fulfillment of a childhood wish. The first objection is the simplest to answer. Without a conception of sexuality and pregnancy, the child can more easily imagine that babies are made in a laboratory than in the body of a woman. And the novel, which describes so much else in detail, gives scant attention to how the creature is put together. We are told little more than that one day Victor learns the secret, and after a lapse of time that does not seem real, the creature is made. Such vagueness regarding details and facile success has just the quality of a child's wish-fulfilling fantasy.

In its theory of symbol formation, psychoanalysis provides the means to answer the second objection. In the language of symbolism, a gigantic man is an ideal way to represent an infant. The principle of the association has to do with the logic which equates opposites. Gigantic size is the reverse of the infant's very small size and, in consequence, can represent it. One is reminded of the ludicrous, and yet spellbinding, film of King Kong, and of the gigantic gorilla holding in his hand a lovely and helpless young woman. The question of what a creature that size should want with a miniature female and what he can do with this treasured but tiny object seems never to have disturbed anyone in the audience. The logic of the attraction is unaffected by the dissimilarity in size because we reverse the relationship unconsciously. The possessive desire belongs to the small vulnerable child who wishes the love of the adult woman. In similar fashion, the hugely strong, gigantic man represents, in *Frankenstein,* the small and helpless baby. Such an equation between giant and baby must seem improbable. But one of the fascinating aspects of the novel is the way Mary Shelley makes this symbolic meaning increasingly clear.

The third objection, that Frankenstein's horror does not suggest wish fulfillment, can be further resolved psychoanalytically. We pointed out that the distinction between Frankenstein's desire to create life and his eventual success was comparable to fantasies we permit ourselves in thought, but which we would not translate into action. The guilt connected with such fantasies is controlled by the realization that fulfillment is only imagined. The pleasures we obtain from films, fiction, and drama, for example, are guilt-free because we know we are not actually engaged in the actions we vicariously enjoy. But when, as with Frankenstein, the fantasy becomes fact, guilt is suddenly and overwhelmingly felt. It is true that he is not conscious of guilt. But even when we admit guilt into consciousness, we have the means to deny it. Like the dreamer who arranges in his dreams to have "other people" do his killing, or like the paranoid who imagines it is other people who cannot be trusted, Frankenstein projects onto his innocent and helpless creature his own feelings of criminal guilt. The infantile fantasy of replacing his father necessarily implies the idea of having him killed. The fantasy of giving his mother the gift of a baby cannot be kept from the eventual knowledge of how incestuous that idea really is. Parricide and incest are ugly crimes. And so Frankenstein runs from his creature, conscious of a frightful ugliness, but attributing it, however inappropriately, to the life he has brought into the world. Never will he be able to perceive that he has created a compassionate, virtuous, and loving being, because his need to deny his own criminality over what this creation has meant to him will outweigh all other considerations. Because he thinks himself guilty, however unconsciously, of parricidal and incestuous motives, he now falls into a nervous fit, destroys his scientific career, and, as we shall see, never recaptures the sense of reality he needs to save himself and his family. Now we can understand why he chose to create a human, rather than, as a scientist would for his first effort, a simpler form of life, and why he kept his project a secret from his family, notwithstanding the professed altruism of his motives. It is not the watery eyes and yellow skin of the creature which brings disaster, but the disgusting transformation of a "beautiful dream" into reality.

It remains surprising and difficult to accept, no doubt—this equation between the Frankenstein "monster" and the new-born infant. But in support of this interpretation, Mrs. Shelley continues to describe the creature precisely in this fashion, as a new-born infant and then as a growing child. Her first description of him, in his earliest moments of life, subtly gives this impression: "his jaws opened, and he muttered some inarticulate sound, while a grin wrinkled his cheeks." And the creature himself gives us a description of his early life which exactly matches the first consciousness of an infant. He tells us that:

It is with considerable difficulty that I remember the original era of my being: all the events of that period appear confused and indistinct. A strange multiplicity of sensations seized me, and I saw, felt, heard, and smelt, at the same time; and it was, indeed, a long time before I learned to distinguish between the operations of my various senses.[7]

I was a poor, helpless, miserable wretch; I knew, and could distinguish, nothing; but feeling pain invade me on all sides, I sat down and wept.[8]

Sometimes I wished to express my sensations in my own mode, but the uncouth and inarticulate sounds which broke from me frightened me into silence again.[9]

His crying helplessness, the confusion of his senses, his vulnerability to pain, his inability to communicate, portray the human child at birth as accurately as we could wish.

Immediately after his "birth," the creature is abandoned by Frankenstein. During this time, he must survive as best he can. His predicament and the means he finds to solve it continue to provide a superb portrait of the infant achieving growth and maturity. He hides in a small hovel which adjoins a cottage, and thereafter spends his time observing the family who lives there. Like the infant, he passively watches and then imitates an adult family. And after a period of time, he learns to speak, then to read, and finally to understand much about the world. And most to the point, all that he does is motivated by the wish to be accepted and loved by this family. As is the case so frequently in this romance, the plot is unconvincing in the extreme.

How could a gigantic creature observe a family at home for months without once being detected? The persuasive quality of the episode is derived from its metaphoric meaning: the monster is equated with the infant who learns by observing a family and who wishes above all to be accepted and loved by them.

ii Theme of the Doppelgänger

Freud, Kris, and others have pointed out that there is a class of fiction which is "egoistic"–fiction in which all events are designed solely to serve the desires of the protagonist. In the broadest sense, it is the genre we term melodrama. Chance, accident, and the actions of other characters, may seem to direct events, but the outcome is always in accord with the wishes of the central figure. Easy success, poetic justice to family, friends, and enemies, the defeat of competitors, glory, wealth, and the perfect love match are all the regular features of melodrama. It is a genre particularly close to fantasy and daydreaming, since considerations of reality are, as in dreams, never a barrier to the fulfillment of wishes. Frustrations, defeats, and delays are designed to make the hero's eventual triumphs the more sweet, and seemingly true to life. Hanns Sachs gives this description of the daydream—one which serves equally well to describe melodramatic fiction:

The daydream is fully and unashamedly egocentric. . . . Other persons, when they appear in the daydream, are there for the hero's sake, so that he can lead them or defeat them, exalt them or humble them, be good and noble, or proud and disdainful towards them, can be admired and loved, hated and persecuted by them. They can be withdrawn or exchanged at any time at the whim of the author or because of changes in his emotional attitude to their prototypes. But the hero is always the same; when he is for a time absent from the stage, it is but an artifice to make his entrance more melodramatic.[10]

The Gothic genre, to which *Frankenstein* belongs, is a class of melodrama characterized by the subordination of events to the production of terror. The various conventions used in this genre, such as the gloomy castle, the dungeon, the supernatural, are always a means to achieve this end. From the psychoanalytic point of view, such terror is the counterpart of the particular nature of the gratification which this

melodrama affords. As the leading critics of this fiction—Varma, Summers, Railo, and Praz—have acknowledged, the oedipal emotions of
incestuous love and murderous anger toward parents are a staple of the
genre. Given the guilt-provoking effects of oedipal wishes, an atmosphere of terror is needed in part to disguise that very gratification. If
too plainly dramatized, such wishes would repel the reader by evoking
condemnation and displeasure. In this regard, Gothic fiction is comparable to the nightmare, in which the experience of fright disguises the
guilt-provoking gratification that produces the dream and gives it its
nightmarish cast. The constant dramatization of terror in Gothic fiction
enables the reader to believe that crimes are committed *against* the
wishes of the seemingly innocent protagonist. The reader can lose sight
of the essential fact in melodrama: the hero's desires, however shocking
they may be, must be gratified by a fixed convention of the genre. The
crimes may be frightening, but they are desired.

Critics of the Gothic genre acknowledge the importance of the incest
motif, although they detect its literal representation only, and ignore its
far more frequent expression in symbols. And since none of them
analyze the motif in any given work, the peculiar connection between
terror and incest is unexplored. Devendra Varma, for instance, in *The
Gothic Flame,* writes that, "in *The Castle of Otranto* there is a vague
suggestion of incest; Ambrosio ends by raping and murdering his sister
in *The Monk,* and henceforward the incest theme seems to pass into the
convention of the Gothic novel."[11] But what he calls a vague suggestion is, it could be shown, the dramatic focus of both works.[12]
Montague Summers, in *The Gothic Quest,* lists nineteen novels of the
period by name in which, as he puts it, "the main plots or at any rate
the climax and most striking scenes turn upon consanguinity in some
kind."[13] He indicates that the motif is to be found "in a great number"
of works besides. But he, too, declines to examine the motif as it is
dramatized in particular works. Mario Praz in *The Romantic Agony,*
extends the point, and attributes incest to Romanticism in general. He
writes that,

the old recognition-scene of the Greek romances became one of the
mainstays of the "tale of terror," as it was to be of Romanticism in
general. Parents who rediscover their children in the most dramatic
circumstances—this was the mainspring of the plays and novels of about
1830 . . . a formula which also found favour in the eyes of the Roman-
tics on account of the flavour of incest which could be extracted from
it.[14]

But Praz is interested only in "sado-masochism," and not in whether a destruction-self-destruction theme can itself be an expression of oedipal dynamics. The "mainspring" he leaves unanalyzed. The most searching statement is given by Railo, who makes a point of the connection between Gothic horror and the incest motif: "as the motive offers good opportunities of evoking that terror and suspense-filled atmosphere of mystery which is one of the chief aims of the terror-romanticism, it is to be expected that wherever literature turns into romantic channels, the subject of incest will sooner or later emerge."[15] But to say that incest is chosen simply as a means to terror is rather like saying that anger is assumed as a pretext to dramatize murder. The priority is wrong. There is no murder except as an expression of the anger which underlies it. Incest is not chosen as one means to evoke terror, but rather the reverse. It is the atmosphere of terror which conveys the incest motif. Indeed, at a later point Railo gives this support for an assumption that the incest motif implies something more than a means to suspense and mystery: "proof that romantic eroticism, when it is truly romantic, displays symptoms of abnormality is provided, in my opinion, by the incest motif. . . . " And he finds in *The Monk,* one of the most characteristic and popular works of the genre, the "fruits of inflamed, neurasthenical, sexual visions, of a pathological character. . . . "[16] This states the case more accurately. Abnormal eroticism—the incest motif—is more fundamental a part of the genre than the atmosphere of terror and suspense in which it is enacted.

To sum up, then, our own view of the Gothic genre, it depicts in varying degrees of explicitness the passions of the oedipal child. Parents or parental figures are the objects of overwhelming desire and hate. In this Gothic world, in which crimes are regularly committed, the mother is as subject to murder as she is coveted, since the oedipal child hates her for her rejection of him as much as he loves her. And fathers may be tenderly loved, even as forces within the story destroy them. The oedipal mentality is filled with emotional contradictions, and this ambivalence is fully dramatized in the Gothic novel. The disguises used to conceal the character of the crimes committed are equally complex and varied. On the simplest levels, parents may die of "natural" causes, an illness, for instance; but other elements in the story reveal what gratification that death may have brought. Similarly, a parent may be murdered or a sister raped while the villain is in ignorance of their true identities, but mistaken identity is no more than a fictional contrivance to make these desired crimes representable. And the atmosphere of terror partly expresses the revulsion which must accompany these crimes. But, more essentially, such an atmosphere effectively masks the fact that what happens is more wished for than feared.

A good example of this disguise in *Frankenstein* is the fairy tale formula in which a father lives alone with his daughter, or with his wife who is young enough to be his daughter. The first situation is doubly incestuous because it not only fulfills the daughter's wish to replace the mother, but it also constrains the young suitor for the daughter's hand to win from the father the only woman of the house—hence, symbolically, the mother. The incestuous element is particularly pronounced if this extreme difference in age or absence of one parent has no relevance to the larger plot. In *Frankenstein*, we find no fewer than six relationships in which these arrangements occur for no apparent purpose. First, Frankenstein's father is "in the decline of life" when he marries, and his wife is much younger than himself. Second, his wife, prior to their marraige, had been living alone with her aged father. Third, Elizabeth, Frankenstein's "sister," had first lived alone with her father, her mother having died in childbirth. Fourth, the family which the monster observes from his hovel consists of an aged father, living with his daughter and son, but not with his wife. Fifth, the son of this family falls in love with a young lady who lives alone with her father. The cumulative effect of this obsessively repeated design is to reinforce the incestuous character of the central events in the novel. This is a world in which beautiful women are taken from older men—a desired achievement underlying Frankenstein's actions and fears from the beginning.

Another example of how the motif affects every aspect of the story is the "frame tale," the narrative device by which the story is actually communicated. Frankenstein's account of his life is not given directly to the reader, but to an explorer, Richard Walton. When the novel begins, Walton relates the story by letter to his sister, and thus to the reader. For no apparent dramatic purpose, this narrator's life recapitulates the most important details of Frankenstein's life. We learn that, as with Frankenstein, Walton is dominated by a quest for knowledge which began in his childhood. At that time, his father opposed his quest, just as Mr. Frankenstein rejected his son's quest for knowledge as an interest in "sad trash." Both fathers then die "prematurely." And the sons, as a result of their respective quests, journey to the North Pole where their lives are endangered. Most to the point, both men direct their deepest affections to a sister. Although there remains to be examined the incestuous quality of Frankenstein's love for his sister, it is apparent that Walton's story duplicates in miniature the larger dramatization of the incest motif in Frankenstein's life. The parallel features are too numerous to be ascribed to pointless coincidence. We must conclude that the design of the narrator's life, like everything else in this melodramatic story, "belongs" to the egoistic interests of the central figure.

Frankenstein offers, above all, as good an example of the connection between terror and the oedipal motif as any work of the genre. We have already seen how the fantasy of paternity, itself a part of the oedipal motif, betrayed its presence in Victor Frankenstein's "gothic horror" over the success of his efforts to create life. If the reader accepts that horror without questioning it, and if he tells himself the whole thing is simply a horror story, he will never understand it as part of Victor's childish obsession with the "facts of life." Similarly, the reader can choose to accept the subsequent murders of Frankenstein's childhood friends, his brother, his sister-wife, and, indirectly, his father as merely horrid doings of a horror novel. But that is to overlook the particular pattern of deaths. This story is not about a monster set loose in the world who kills indiscriminately. No one dies except the family of the man who makes the monster, and the friends of his childhood. The world destroyed is the one which belongs to Frankenstein and, directly or indirectly, it is because of him that it happens. We must not overlook too quickly the possibility that he intends it this way, and that the monster becomes no more than an agent of his wishes—the embodiment of his own monstrous passions, sexual and murderous.

It is one of the standard devices used in melodrama, the dramatization of conflicting motives which specifically belong to one individual by distributing them among a number of fictional characters. There are numerous advantages obtained by this dramatic strategy. It becomes possible to expose not only the face which a character presents to the world, but also his potentialities, his hidden passions, his concealed remorse, all simultaneously in action. These "partial figures" who serve to compose one dramatic identity are doubles of each other: the theme of the *Doppelgänger*. And the reader—who identifies with the nobler, or more acceptable, half—can ignore the fact that he is psychologically tied to the second figure. He can experience Gothic horror at the doings of the second figure without recognizing how implicated is the one with whom he has identified. This device is used, of course, by Stevenson in *Dr. Jekyll and Mr. Hyde,* by Poe in *William Wilson,* more subtly by Melville in *Bartleby the Scrivener,* and by Conrad in *The Secret Sharer.* Mary Shelley also makes extensive use of the *Doppelgänger.* As astonishing as it may seem at first, the life of the "monster" eventually recapitulates in vivid fashion all the important features of Frankenstein's own existence. Parts of the oedipal motif which are subtly revealed in Frankenstein's thoughts, and which find only symbolic expression in his behavior, are made more explicit in his creature. This use of the *Doppelgänger* enables Mrs. Shelley to bring into dramatic focus aspects of Frankenstein's psychology which would not have been directly represented in a censored (and pre-Freudian) age. The creature is artificial, non-human; and within the "inhuman" breast there could be dramatized the sexual and violent passions which Freud would find widespread in the fantasies of the most civilized men.

An early indication of this *Doppelgänger* is the way the creature's thoughts turn to questioning how his life began. His puzzlement is understandable enough, since he was artificially created by means of which he knows nothing. But how striking it is that his young mind should turn obsessively to the preoccupation of Frankenstein's youth. The creature asks, "And what was I? Of my creation and creator I was absolutely ignorant"; and again, "Who was I? What was I? Whence did I come? What was my destination? These questions continually recurred, but I was unable to solve them." Victor accidentally comes upon occult literature in which he searches for "the secrets of nature." In similar fashion, the creature finds Frankenstein's secret journal, which he then "studies in diligence," obtaining at last, as Frankenstein did in his studies at Ingolstadt, the answer to the puzzle. This quest for the riddle of his life re-enacts the symbolic search for sexual facts which dominated so much of Frankenstein's life.

The most important and revealing aspect of the *Doppelgänger,* however, is the series of murders committed. It is here that their sharing the same passions—the incestuous and murderous passions of the oedipal motif—is dramatized. Frankenstein is, of course, never a direct party to the crimes. He tells himself that he wishes to prevent them, and that he grieves for the dead. But his complicity is unmistakable. Indeed, toward the end of the novel, he comes to recognize his own guilt. When his brother William and his childhood friends, Justine and Clerval, are dead, he cries out: "I am the cause of this—I murdered her

[Justine]. William, Justine, and Henry—they all died by my hands." And on another occasion he says, "I am the assassin of those most innocent victims; they died by my machinations." He means to say that he created the monster who destroyed them, and that, therefore, his own guilt is manifest. But, in fact, he is saying a good deal more. "I am the assassin"; "I murdered her"; these confessions are not appropriate self-accusations from a scientist who created life to benefit mankind and who never expected that death would be the consequence of his work. They are the confessions we would expect from the monster. And that is the point. Frankenstein may cry out that "a thousand times would I have shed my own blood, drop by drop, to have saved their lives," but as the novel unfolds, we see that he does not act that way. He and the monster are one.

The first murder committed is a complex episode. When the monster has been abandoned by Frankenstein and then rejected by the family he has grown to love in secret, he finally identifies with the Biblical Adam, and tells us they are both creatures "united by no link to any other being in existence." Lamenting that "no Eve soothed my sorrows, nor shared my thoughts," he feels the "bitter gall of envy." He curses his creator and journeying to Frankenstein's home for revenge, he murders his young brother. He looks down and sees, on the breast of the dead boy, a miniature portrait of Frankenstein's mother. "In spite of my malignity," he tells us, "it softened and attracted me." He "gazes with delight on her dark eyes, fringed by deep lashes, and her lovely lips." And then with the sudden thought that "she whose resemblance I contemplated would, in regarding me, have changed that air of divine benignity to one expressive of disgust and affright," his murderous rage returns. Seeking to hide, he enters a barn and finds asleep another beautiful woman, Justine. His sexual longing now overwhelms him and bending over her, he whispers to this unknown person: "Awake, fairest, thy lover is near—he who would give his life but to obtain one look of affection from thine eyes: my beloved, awake!" Imagining once more how he would be rejected, his rage increases and quite irrationally he blames this woman for the murder he has already committed. He cries out, "The murder I have committed because I am for ever robbed of all that she could give me, she shall atone. The crime had its source in her: be hers the punishment!" And he revengefully places in this unknown woman's pocket the portrait taken from the dead boy, so that she will be blamed for the murder.

This is as puzzling a scene as one can find in fiction. Out of the whole world in which to focus his sexual longing, it is astonishing, to say the least, that he should gaze with desire first on the face of Frankenstein's mother. And what follows seems incomprehensible. Why should the imagined rejection of this woman make him exclaim, "Can you wonder that such thought transported me with rage? I only wonder that at that moment, instead of venting my sensations in exclamations and agony, I did not rush among mankind and perish in the attempt to destroy them." We must remind ourselves that he sees only the portrait of an unknown woman on a locket, and the locket he has seen only an instant before. And how can he call himself the lover of Justine, the woman in the barn whom he has never met before? Above all, how can he punish her as the one responsible for a crime he commits before he even knows of her existence? It is a riddle, but one which we can understand if we see that the action belongs to another time and place, and to the protagonist whose wishes govern the story.

If gazing on the lovely face of Frankenstein's mother moves the monster to love for the first time, we have a powerful suggestion of Frankenstein himself as a child. We have already seen expressions of that love in the obsessions of his youth and in the ambitions of his adulthood. Now there is not only a more directly sexual expression of love, but also a great deal else: the murder of a sibling, and rage against the rejecting mother. It is precisely at this point, where the violent passions of the oedipal motif go undisguised that the identities themselves are masked; in consequence, the motif itself remains hidden. The monster becomes the disguised agent of the passions of Frankenstein's childhood. The mother becomes no more than a portrait. And even that attenuated version is replaced by a second beautiful woman. But the language tells the story as the child would imagine it in fantasy. He offers to "give his life to obtain one look of affection" from the mother he loves. He postures and calls her his "beloved" and himself her "lover" although she does not hear. Imagining, not without reason, that she would answer his declaration with "disgust," he wishes grandiosely to "rush among mankind and perish in the attempt to destroy them." But his rage finds a more exact expression in the destruction of his rival brother and against his mother with the revengeful accusation that since the crime is done for her, she should be punished. This is, no doubt, a highly interpretive reading of the text. But the scene makes no sense otherwise. And everything which follows does support this shared identity between the infantile passions of Frankenstein and the monster he creates.

How, for instance, are we to explain the fact that when Frankenstein learns of his brother's death and comes rushing to the scene, he can be certain of the monster's guilt? Consider what the action of the story has been to this point. Frankenstein succeeds in creating his creature. At that instant, he runs from him, falls into a long nervous collapse, and slowly recovers. During all this time, he hears nothing of the creature, never sees him, and is completely ignorant of the character of the being he has made. It might be argued that he knows the creature is ugly, and that anything unnaturally put together in violation of God's order can be expected to be ugly in character and to violate the laws of God's morality. The argument is a good one, and one we would have to accept were it not that the story itself is eloquent in its representation of the reverse. The irony of this novel is that the general impression of it, perhaps based on the movie version, should be so far from the truth. In fact, it is the monster who is given the far more sympathetic treatment by Mrs. Shelley. He begins life in innocence, wants only affection, systematically suffers rejection by his creator and the family he loves, and becomes murderous only in the pain of isolation and despair. In perhaps the most moving passages of the book, the creature describes the love he feels for the family from whom he learns about life by observing them in secret, and the hope that one day they might accept him in affection. He tells us that he imagined "that they would be disgusted, until, by my gentle demeanour and conciliating words, I should first win their favour, and afterwards their love." It is not putting it too strongly to say that this monster's moral sensibilities develop to a degree not attained by anyone else in the story! For instance, he asks—as a Hamlet or a Houyhnhnm might:

Was man, indeed, at once so powerful, so virtuous and magnificent, yet so vicious and base? He appeared at one time a mere scion of the evil principle, and at another as all that can be conceived of noble and godlike. To be a great and virtuous man appeared the highest honour that can befall a sensitive being; to be base and vicious, as many on record have been, appeared the lowest degradation, a condition more abject than that of the blind mole or harmless worm. For a long time I could not conceive how one man could go forth to murder his fellow, or even why there were laws and governments; but when I heard detail of vice and bloodshed, my wonder ceased, and I turned away with disgust and loathing.[17]

This is not a creature whose guilt can be intuitively known without reference to any facts and solely because Frankenstein momentarily glimpses him in the distance when he returns to his home. How is it possible for Frankenstein, knowing nothing of the creature or of the life he has led, to be so certain of his guilt that he can exclaim: "No sooner did the idea cross my imagination than I became convinced of its truth. . . . I could not doubt it. The mere presence of the idea was an irresistible proof of the fact." This is strange language indeed. No one can know guilt in such a fashion, unless it is a guilt which he shares, and which he can therefore detect within himself. Creator and his creature thus complement one another in more intricate a fashion than any simple separation between vice and virtue, or passions and conscience, as in the tales of Poe and Stevenson. The creature retains the essential innocence of every child who, for all his "monstrous" passions, needs only kindness and love to become a virtuous figure. Frankenstein, on the other hand, is portrayed as the grown Oedipus, who moves in society, venting his passions in disguised fashion, secretly allied to the monster, and destroying himself in guilt. With unusual acumen, Mrs. Shelley dramatizes how acceptance and integration of our childhood selves is essential if we are to adjust to the world. That is the ultimate point of the story. Frankenstein cannot see the monster for what he is—in effect no more than a child. He sees him only as ugly and, in terms of the *Doppelgänger*, represses that part of himself by running from his creation. But as the psychoanalyst so often points out, what is repressed, returns. When the creature reappears in his life, he is murderous. And the mature Frankenstein must suffer for the oedipal passions he might otherwise have controlled.

Frankenstein's secretly shared guilt is further manifested in the way he declines to save Justine, the woman whom the monster incriminated in the murder of Frankenstein's brother. We might expect that Frankenstein, in the knowledge of the real murderer, would acquit her without delay. But this does not happen. Justine is tried for the murder and eventually executed, and Frankenstein lets it happen. He attends her trial and tears his breast, but it no longer deceives the reader. Frankenstein writes that "it was to be decided, whether the result of my curiosity and lawless devices would cause the death of two of my fellow-beings: one a smiling babe full of innocence and joy: the other far more dreadfully murdered. . . . Justine also was a girl of merit, and possessed qualities which promised to render her life happy: now all was to be obliterated in an ignominious grave; and I the cause!" He hears her sentenced, even sees her manacled in prison, but keeps his silence until she is dead. He laments, describes the tortures of his heart, and tells us that in spite of his "passionate and indignant appeals" in her behalf and her own "heartrending eloquence," the judges were not moved from their "settled conviction in the criminality of the saintly sufferer" (as though the judges were to blame). He suffers and protests too much for a man who has only to speak out to save her. He tells us that he keeps his silence because no one would believe in his creation of a monster. There are always likely rationalizations at hand when one needs them. Well he might expect the judges' surprise at the tale he could tell. But a monstrous murder must be accounted for, and he has the explanation. In a world which allows for the creation of a monster, an acceptance of its reality is possible to more than its creator. Frankenstein should easily know this. At the least he might try to explain, in the interests of saving an innocent woman. What can we believe but that he does not wish to save her? At the end of the story, when all have died, *then* he confesses his creation—and is immediately believed by the magistrate, who says, "If it is in my power to seize the monster, be assured that he shall suffer punishment proportionate to his crimes." Why, then, does he not speak out sooner? No explanation is left, other than that he protects the guilty agent of his own criminality. To expose the monster is to expose the monstrous spirit in which it was created. And abetting that agent by allowing Justine to die, in itself gives us fresh evidence—although there is still better to come—that murderous anger is deflected from his mother onto women he has no reason to hate.

There are, we can note, three women in his life: his mother, sister, and a friend from childhood. All are remarkably alike: young, beautiful, described only in the most superficial details, and, most to the point, all die. We have, in this story, a pattern of killing which suggests the manner in which the psychopath destroys the women who remind him of his mother. The previous scene, involving the monster, Mrs. Frankenstein, and Justine, showed the pattern in a highly disguised fashion. A far clearer expression is the climax of the story—the last, stunning murder of Frankenstein's sister-bride, Elizabeth, on their wedding night. An examination of this event, and the forces which produce it, offers the last piece of the puzzle. It begins when creator and creature finally come together. The monster pleads for a mate and tells his maker in the clearest way that he will be virtuous if he possesses a female "with whom I can live in the interchange of those sympathies necessary for my being." In his situation, alone in the world, what human would not similarly say:

If I have no ties and no affections, hatred and vice must be my portion; the love of another will destroy the çause of my crimes. . . . My vices are the children of a forced solitude that I abhor; and my virtues will necessarily arise when I live in communion with an equal. I shall feel the affections of a sensitive being, and become linked to the chain of existence and events, from which I am now excluded.[18]

There is an utterly human pathos in the plea that his creator not reject him again, and that he receive compassion from Frankenstein, if from no one else. "If any being felt emotions of benevolence toward me," he says, "I should return them an hundred and an hundred fold; for that one creature's sake, I would make peace with the whole kind . . . Oh! my creator, make me happy; let me feel gratitude toward you for one benefit! Let me see that I excite the sympathy of some existing thing; do not deny me my request!" Frankenstein struggles to overcome the horror and loathing he has felt toward him from the first. He perceives the justification of the creature's request, and the compassion which is due him. He tells us that,

I was moved. I shuddered when I thought of the possible consequences of my consent; but I felt that there was some justice in his argument. His tale, and the feelings he now expressed, proved him to be a creature of fine sensations; and did I not as his maker owe him all the portion of happiness that it was in my power to bestow? . . . I thought of the promise of virtues which he had displayed on the opening of his existence, and the subsequent blight of all kindly feeling by the loathing and scorn which his protectors had manifested toward him. . . . I concluded that the justice due both to him and my fellow-creatures demanded of me that I should comply with his request.[19]

And so he agrees to create a mate for his creature. But as he does so, he is overcome with the conviction that his creature is a "fiend of unparalleled barbarity," and that another must not be made. He trembles at this idea, which the evidence contradicts, and tears to pieces the work he has begun. In a sense, the story has returned us to the point at which it began. When Frankenstein ran from his first creation and fell into his nervous collapse, his reason was no more than that the creature was ugly and possessed of watery eyes and yellow skin. The preposterous inadequacy of such an explanation, given his scientific triumph, brought us to the sexual meaning the creation had for him: there breaks into consciousness the childhood fantasy which led him obsessively to that moment—to be, with his mother, the parent of a baby. With the sudden thought that such an act is abhorrent, he finds the creature itself abhorrent; the painful idea is projected away from himself. And now, creating a second creature, his own guilt asserts itself again. The story, in effect, is functioning on many levels. On the "realistic" level (we use the word in a relative way, since the story is fantastic in its entirety), Frankenstein can rid himself of the monster by creating a mate and so return in safety to a normal life reasonably sure there will be no more killing. But on the symbolic level, in which he and the monster are linked to a shared identity, he is confronted all over again with the sexual desire which brought him to his collapse in the first place. And so he views his monster, as he views himself, as a fiend of unparalleled barbarity.

The monster now says to Frankenstein, "I shall be with you on your wedding-night." What a perfectly Delphic oracle his warning is. His words are a riddle which holds the whole meaning of the story. And Frankenstein's inability to solve the riddle is as revealing as is the ignorance of Sophocles' Oedipus, when so many others have divined the truth of his parentage. Frankenstein assumes the monster means that on the day he marries his sister, the monster will destroy him. He overlooks, in the first place, that the monster need not have waited to kill, if Frankenstein were the intended victim. In addition, Frankenstein continues to keep secret from the world the existence of the monster, even though that confession alone might enlist help in stopping the monster. He marries Elizabeth without telling her of the danger. And on the wedding night he arms himself against the struggle, sends his wife alone to bed, and walks the house wondering where the creature might be. When suddenly he hears a "shrill and dreadful scream" from Elizabeth's room, he tells us: "The whole truth rushed into my mind, my arms dropped, and motion of every muscle and fibre was suspended; I could feel the blood trickling in my veins and tingling in the extremities of my limbs. This state lasted but for an instant; the scream was repeated, and I rushed into the room." Elizabeth, of course, is dead: "Lifeless and inanimate, thrown across the bed, her head hanging down, and her pale and distorted features half covered by her hair." This is the essence of the Gothic: a tale of horror, of gruesome detail and sensational fright. But the *point* of what happens is that it need not have happened. It was easily avoidable in any number of ways. It should be obvious that the monster who kills Victor's brother, his best friend, and indirectly Justine, might just possibly intend to kill Elizabeth. Recall that after Elizabeth's death, the world believes Frankenstein's story of the monster; why, then, does he wait to tell until it is too late? Why does he not at least let Elizabeth know of the danger, so that she need not have been so defenseless? How can he send her to bed alone, at that crucial moment, although he has no idea where the creature might be? No answer is tenable other than that he wishes her death, that the monster is his agent-double, and that his ignorance, secretiveness, and folly are all feigned. Even the manner in which we are told, "The whole truth rushed into my mind," suggests how the thought is kept from consciousness only until it is too late. Behind the facade of Gothic horror, we have the desired event: the wedding-night destruction of his sister-bride. With the economy of a dream, all motifs are fused in a single apocalyptic event. The incestuous love and rejected rage of his childhood combine in the single fantasy in which a woman hardly distinguishable from his mother is both married and murdered.

In conclusion, we can see that Mary Shelley's Gothic novel conforms to the genre: Terror is used as the outward manifestation of a disguised oedipal motif. The continued popularity of the work is attributable to a symbol peculiarly well-suited to the dramatization of childhood fantasies--the monster who destroys his creator. We may recall how this monster began his existence as a vision in the mind of Mrs. Shelley. She wrote of the event: "My imagination, unbidden, possessed and guided me, gifting the successive images that arose in my mind with a vividness far beyond the usual bounds of reverie." There could be no better description of how fiction can find its origins in the unconscious; of how frightening passions that have been repressed since childhood can return unbidden, no less frightening and still seeming real. Perhaps her own rejection of oedipal passions was the stronger for not abandoning those images to the night, but giving them dramatic life of their own in fiction. If the world can share her fearful vision, she can feel that she has disowned it.[20]

Notes

1. Mary Wollstonecraft Shelley, *Frankenstein* (London: J. M. Dent & Sons, 1945), pp. x-xi.
2. Shelley, *Frankenstein,* pp. 51-52.
3. Shelley, *Frankenstein,* p. 45.
4. Shelley, *Frankenstein,* p. 28.
5. Sigmund Freud, "Three Essays on the Theory of Sexuality," in *The Standard Edition of the Complete Psychological Works of Sigmund Freud,* VII (London: Hogarth Press, 1962), pp. 194-95.
6. Shelley, *Frankenstein,* p. 26.
7. Shelley, *Frankenstein,* p. 104.
8. Shelley, *Frankenstein,* p. 105.
9. Shelley, *Frankenstein,* p. 105.
10. Hanns Sachs, *The Creative Unconscious* (Framingham, Mass.: Sci-Art Publishers, 1951), p. 14.
11. Devendra Varma, *The Gothic Flame* (New York: Russell & Russell, 1964), p. 224.
12. See Morton Kaplan, *Iris Murdoch and the Gothic Tradition,* Columbia University dissertation, 1969.
13. Montague Summers, *The Gothic Quest* (New York: Russell & Russell, 1964), p. 391.
14. Mario Praz, *The Romantic Agony* (Cleveland and New York: Meridian Books, 1967), p. 113.
15. Elino Railo, *The Haunted Castle* (New York: Humanities Press, 1964), p. 271.
16. Railo, *Castle,* p. 281.
17. Shelley, *Frankenstein,* p. 124.
18. Shelley, *Frankenstein,* p. 156.
19. Shelley, *Frankenstein,* pp. 154-55, 157.
20. It is true, of course, that this vision of Mary Shelley's is interpreted in the light of the male psychology. But then it is equally true that the work itself has a male protagonist. This psychological flexibility has always been one the features of the artist's psyche. Consider, for example, Joyce Carey's tale of the same story through the eyes of both a man and a woman in *The Horse's Mouth* and *Herself Surprised.*

The Development of
Psychoanalytic Criticism

"The word has come down from the Dean/That with the aid of the teaching machine/King Oedipus Rex/Could have learned about sex/ Without ever touching the Queen." As the words of this anonymous graffitist make clear, the best alternative to learning by doing is learning through example. Consequently, to help the student of psychoanalytic criticism develop his own acumen, in Part III we briefly survey the major work in the field, including examples both good and bad. And, as the latent content of the graffito also indicates, the word that comes down ought to be authoritative, whether from the Dean or from some other father-surrogate. In keeping with this, we feel that our years of independent study, professional psychoanalytic training, and experience in co-editing *Literature and Psychology* enable us to speak of psychoanalytic criticism authoritatively and to provide reliable evaluations for the guidance of the student.

At the outset, however, we would like to indicate one major flaw in Part III (others will doubtless become apparent). Our critique is not definitive. We have attempted to provide for the layman a critical survey of only the important work done by both psychoanalysts and literary critics from Freud to the present—a period spanning three-quarters of a century. Because of this time span, because of the "Gutenberg Galaxy," because of the ever-increasing interest in matters psychological, Part III, as projected, suffers from an embarrassment of riches. The sheer volume of psychological and psychoanalytic criticism published during the last twenty years alone has made comprehensiveness both impractical and impossible and has enforced selectivity. This part is, then, in perfect keeping with its relation to psychoanalysis, a compromise formation.

We have had to choose, and we believe our choices will familiarize the reader with most of the important literary theories, major critics, and valuable works he is likely to come in contact with during his apprenticeship. Feeling that he could profit from both positive and negative examples, we have taken pains to include both, trying to restrict our considerations to those which have had some strong influence on psychoanalytic criticism. Accordingly, we have discussed, in addition to superior seminal works like Ernest Kris's *Psychoanalytic Explorations in Art,* poor pioneering efforts like Albert Mordell's *The Erotic Motive in Literature.* And, mingled with the names of Simon Lesser and Frederick C. Crews, both fine psychoanalytic critics, are those of Joseph Campbell and Leslie Fiedler, both best termed quasi- or pseudo-psychological critics. Many others, however, are missing, either by choice or by necessity. For example, not a word appears about Norman O. Brown, whom we consider both showman and shaman, having made a reputation solely by speaking loudly and carrying a big *shtick*. On the other hand, only lack of space prevented consideration of several score of other critics in the field; these we have credited at the end of the section in a summary.

The space devoted to each critique in this section is, generally speaking, in relative proportion to the critic's influence. The critiques are arranged in chronological order, beginning with Freud himself, with cross-references to show the relationships among critics and their ideas. Though the critiques can be read sequentially, they yet retain a high degree of integrity and may be read individually as encapsulated evaluations of a particular critic and his work.

The standards by which we have judged the critic's contributions are those evolved over the larger part of a century by hundreds of practitioners. We have set these forth in Part I and have here employed them as criteria in our critiques. It is particularly important that we, as psychoanalytic critics, maintain high standards for our discipline and set our own house in order lest we be accused of thinking ourselves beyond criticism, practitioners of an occult science, dismissing peremptorily any disapproval as merely the grumblings of the uninitiate. Like the practitioners of psychoanalysis itself, we must make every effort to evaluate and re-evaluate our own productions and keep our system open so we can change theory to fit facts as they are brought to the fore by continual research. To fail to do so is to condemn psychoanalytic criticism to become a rather interesting art form, a kind of entertaining fiction to help pass the time but not to be taken seriously.

These are tumultuous times, when people everywhere turn to psychology to help themselves understand the causes and effects of the revolutionary events which crowd our days. This inspection is often followed by introspection. Renewed interest in astrology, Oriental religions, occultism, and mysticism has led thousands into communing with the dead, congregating with witches, consulting *I Ching,* or casting themselves into Jungian psychology to try to comprehend the forces that impinge upon their lives. Psychology, if not King, is at least Prince, and its use—and abuse—is everywhere: encounter groups, sensitivity training, Institutes of Growth, parlor games that foster anxiety and super-sincerity, leaving Bob and Carol and Ted and Alice and innumerable nameless others in their wake.

These phenomena, however, do not concern us here. The application of psychology to literature does. In an age when Everyman believes himself a certified amateur psychologist, much abuse is bound to arise, in literary criticism as elsewhere. Consequently, the largest amount of psychoanalytic criticism being done today is being done poorly, and the reason is obvious: one cannot be an amateur; one must be a master, of two faculties—literature and psychology—and be able to effectively interrelate them. Louis Fraiberg has tersely delineated what is expected of the psychoanalytic critic:

... The effective use of psychoanalytic ideas in literary criticism depends first of all upon a working knowledge of psychoanalysis. This does not mean that the critic must become a psychoanalyst or that he must himself be psychoanalyzed but that he ought to know what psychoanalysis tries to do, how it functions, what its successes and failures have been, what it has firmly established as fact and what it can account for only hypothetically, the limits beyond which it cannot go, the conditions under which it may have validity for fields of knowledge outside its own and finally, the degree of its applicability to a given literary situation. These goals ought, ideally, to be reached by a combination of study and experience. Among the many things which should be studied are the fundamental scientific assumptions of psychoanalysis, its clinical methods, its historical and scientific development under the influence of Freud, his followers and those who differed with them, its findings, its interpretations of these in the light of psychoanalytic principles, and its possible directions in the future.[1]

Given these stringent demands it is no wonder that the majority of psychoanalytic criticism being done is flawed in some way. In the Appendix, we detail the flaws of the three major psychologies—Jungian, Rankian, and Adlerian—and their allied literary criticism, and we refer the reader there for our objections and conclusions. Here, we examine, regardless of psychological orientation, the major work of critics from Freud to the present, praising where deserved, damning where necessary. The unexamined criticism, we feel, is not worth practicing.

Though it is difficult to generalize with any degree of safety, research and experience have shown that abuses appear most often in writings that do not consider the literary work as a unified art object for critical study, but rather as a subject for clinical study; that is, generally speaking, in the work of psychoanalysts. There are exceptions, of course, but, by and large, seventy-five years of criticism has seen analysts lead unwary students by bad example into faulty critical habits. A useful corrective to this trend has been the recent work of Drs. Jose Barchilon and Joel Kovel, particularly their study of *Huckleberry Finn.*[2] There, Barchilon and Kovel take their colleagues somewhat to task for their insensitivity to the integrity of the literary work and present an approach to literary study designed to prevent as many abuses as possible. They urge the critic to rely, for his interpretation, *solely* upon the text and not to venture into the life of the author or into other of his works for corroboration of their conclusions. As they make clear, this initial rule commits the critic to analysis of the text as case history of the literary character. In his clinical practice, the psychoanalyst does not consult the patient's family or friends for information but only the patient himself; so he should analyze the literary character solely from textual evidence. The results, given a competent critic, will be more gratifying as well as more valid.

We ourselves would like to recommend, in addition to these few *caveats,* a healthy dose of skepticism for both psychoanalyst and literary critic, to be taken repeatedly, but especially just before and just after writing a critical study. Untempered by skepticism, the authoritative tone too rapidly becomes the authoritarian. This healthy dose we ourselves have taken. We have probably erred, most likely in some evaluations, most certainly in some omissions. We can only attribute this to our sheer ignorance which is, in the words of Santayana, still "wide and varied." Despite this, we have urgently felt the need to commit ourselves, and we have tried to do so with integrity, fairness, and a modicum of discretion. For we believe, too, with Ernest Jones that "discretion is ... incompatible with a good presentation of psychoanalysis. One has to become a bad fellow, transcend the rules, sacrifice oneself, betray, and behave like the artist who buys paint with his wife's household money, or burns the furniture to warm the room for his model. Without some such criminality there is no real achievement."[3] We have hoped in this way to direct both the reader and the future course of events in psychoanalytic literary criticism.

Notes

1. Louis Fraiberg, *Psychoanalysis and American Literary Criticism* (Detroit: Wayne State University Press, 1960), pp. 238-39.
2. José Barchilon and Joel S. Kovel, *"Huckleberry Finn:* A Psychoanalytic Study," *Journal of the American Psychoanalytic Association,* 14, No. 4 (1966), pp. 775-814.
3. Ernest Jones, *The Life and Work of Sigmund Freud* (New York: Basic Books, 1955), II, p. 139.

Sigmund Freud

In solving the riddle of the Sphinx, Sigmund Freud unknowingly laid the foundations for a new school of literary criticism, for it was he who solved, as well, the riddle of *Hamlet* and the riddle of Rebecca Gamvik of *Rosmersholm*. And, by showing the relationship between the poet and daydreaming, he provided a basis for a psychoanalytic theory of creativity. As others have made detailed studies of Freud's complete writings on art and creativity,[1] we shall concern ourselves only with his contributions to the study of literature itself.

For Freud to involve himself in literature was most natural. He was extremely well-read—as his letters, works, and library attest—and, clinical evidence being scarce when psychoanalysis was in its infancy, he sought corroboration for his discoveries in his reading. From within the isolation in which he found himself after his promulgation of the sexual origin of the psychoneuroses, the first (and for many years the only) psychoanalyst reached out most naturally for additional validation to art, sanctioned by long tradition and familiar to both Freud and his readers.

Freud's initial venture into the interpretation of literature he himself never published, but instead included in a letter to his close friend Wilhelm Fliess in 1898. In the previous year, Fliess had introduced

Freud to the works of the Swiss writer, Conrad Ferdinand Meyer. By June 20, 1898, Freud had completed and sent to his friend an essay entitled "Die Richterin,"[2] analyzing a short story of the same name. Meyer's tale is set in the mountains of Switzerland during the reign of Charlemagne, soon after his coronation by Pope Leo. Stemma, the ruler of the canton of Graubünden, has poisoned her husband fifteen years earlier and reigns in his stead. Her stepson, who fled after his father's murder, returns with a unit of Charlemagne's army to claim his rightful place and has a love-affair with his half-sister, Palma. Die Richterin is eventually revealed as a murderous usurper and commits suicide. It is a gloomy tale of tragedy, full of violence, incest, suicide, and murder.

Freud was thoroughly dogmatic in his interpretation, asserting rather than proving. He had no doubts that the short story was Meyer's defense against the memory of an affair with his sister. Adducing as evidence the obvious family romance in the tale and the incestuous desires on the part of the young woman, he noted a parallel confirmation, from case histories, of the common fantasy of female servants that they will somehow displace the mistress of the house and take her place in the master's eyes. This fantasy becomes extremely important as well in Freud's later interpretation of "Rosmersholm."

The existence of "Die Richterin," however, remained unknown for several decades. Freud's first literary analysis set before the public at large was that of *Hamlet,* an analysis that continues to provoke critical arguments, both pro and con. Originally a one-paragraph footnote in the first edition of *The Interpretation of Dreams* (1900), it has, since 1914, been included in the text.[3] In this lengthy paragraph, Freud explains that *Oedipus Rex* and *Hamlet* have the same well-spring—the Oedipus complex. The major difference is that, in the former, the incestuous impulses are openly expressed, and, in the latter, they are repressed. As a consequence, Hamlet is inhibited by the nature of his task, by having to kill the man who has done in reality what he himself wished to do in fantasy. As Sir Ernest Jones has observed,[4] the consequences of this interpretation were momentous, for it was the first instance in which the manifest motives of a literary character were correlated with the latent motives they presupposed, and it well demonstrated the psychological integrity of a literary work throughout its many levels. Jones himself developed Freud's ideas into an entire book (see p. 169).

Freud's next foray into literary analysis was made in 1906 in "Psychopathic Characters on the Stage" (*SE*, VII, 305-10). This is a highly-compressed essay that studies the ways in which certain arts, particularly drama, affect their audiences. Freud indicates that although we view tragedy in order to suffer vicariously, we will not abide drama that shows physical suffering, which would remove our mental enjoyment; rather, we insist upon *mental* suffering being depicted. Considering first the various other types of drama—religious, social, and character—Freud focusses finally upon psychological drama, in which the conflict causing the suffering is within the hero's mind and ends not with his death, but with the renunciation of one of the conflicting impulses. He then distinguishes psychological drama from *psychopathological* drama, drama in which the suffering stems not from the conflict between two conscious impulses, but between a conscious impulse and a repressed one. Citing *Hamlet,* he asserts that the play is successful because of three constituents: first, the hero is not psychopathic at the outset, but only becomes so in the course of the drama; second, the repressed impulse is one present in all spectators; and third, the impulse is never named, so that the spectator, caught up in his emotions, does not resist what he is viewing. Any drama that uses psychopathic characters and fails to meet these conditions will be ineffective, says Freud; for, if we meet the character in the grips of his illness at the rise of the curtain, we can gain no insight into him and if we recognize his conflict, we forget that he is ill. The most important of the three conditions is the diversion of attention from the nature of the conflict. "Psychopathic Characters" is a rich essay, one in which many of the insights have yet to be elaborated upon in psychoanalytic literature.

In 1907, Freud completed the longest of his literary explorations, the famous and charming "Delusions and Dreams in Jensen's *Gradiva*" (*SE*, IX, 3-95). Jung had called Freud's attention to this novel of Wilhelm Jensen, the Danish author, published four years earlier, and Freud produced his study during his summer vacation in 1906. Jensen had subtitled his novel *A Pompeian Phantasy* and the appearance of delusions and dreams in the novel gave the first psychoanalyst an opportunity to apply his dream theories to literature.

Gradiva is the tale of a young archaeologist, Norbert Hanold, who falls in love with a Grecian maiden of striking gait depicted on a bas-relief in a Roman museum (this bas-relief can still be seen in the

Vatican Museum). He indulges in many fantasies about her and dreams of the manner and place in which she perished—burial in the destruction of Pompeii in A.D. 79. Hanold journeys to the excavated site of that city and, indeed, finds the maiden there, though it is unclear whether she is spirit or living being. She, however, recognizes his delusion and enters into it in order to cure him, eventually doing so. She is then revealed as a childhood friend of Hanold, still living in the same town but completely forgotten by him. Freud's analysis of this novel praises Jensen for his intuitive grasp of psychological process, for, as Freud shows, the workings of Hanold's mind substantiated his own findings. The archaeologist had constructed his fantasies around the childhood playmate, turning her into a Grecian maid with a distinctive manner of walking. Her first name was, in reality, Zoe (Greek for "life"); her last, Bertgang (German for "one who steps brightly," equivalent to Latin *gradiva*). The two-thousand-year-old life in Pompeii of which he had dreamed was in actuality the time of childhood when they had played together; the burial under the volcanic ashes, the repression of these memories. These and other points served to corroborate Freud's theories of repression, the unconscious, and compromise formations, all still under attack by contemporary medical authorities.

In "Creative Writers and Daydreaming" (*SE*, IX, 143-53), an essay written the year after the study of "Gradiva," Freud introduced numerous ideas which are found in the writings of Hanns Sachs and later in those of Simon Lesser and Norman Holland. Although this essay is not concerned with a specific literary work, we examine these ideas so we can recognize them when they eventually appear. As with the "Gradiva" essay, Freud is here concerned with fantasy. He proposes that, like the child at play, the writer creates a world of fantasy, full of emotion but sharply separated from reality. Further, in the same way that the child's play is determined by his wishes (really just one, the wish to be grown up), the writer's fantasies, too, fulfill wishes and improve an unsatisfactory reality. Says Freud, the fantasy arises from a strong feeling occasioned by a current impression which awakens a desire. This fantasy then wanders back to a memory of an infantile experience in which the wish was fulfilled, after which it creates a daydream relating to the future and representing fulfillment of the desire. "Thus past, present, and future are strung together, as it were, on the thread of the wish that runs through them." (*SE*, IX, 148) Freud adds that although we usually hide our daydreams or fantasies from others because we are ashamed of them, the writer has apparently found a means of sharing his without guilt and without arousing repulsion in his audience. More than likely he does this by two means: first, he changes and disguises the fantasy, softening its egotistical character in the process; second, he "bribes" the reader with purely formal or aesthetic pleasure in order to entice him into sharing his fantasy. At this point, Freud, feeling that he is on the threshold of very complicated problems, rather abruptly ends his study, but we shall discover many of the ideas he set forth here recurring again and again in the course of the development of psychoanalytic criticism, greatly elaborated by those writers especially concerned with the origins of literature in the unconscious.

Freud did not produce any more literary analyses until 1913 when he wrote "The Theme of the Three Caskets," which is discussed at length in relation to the theories of Alfred Adler (see p. 302). In 1915 in "Some Character-Types Met with in Psycho-Analytic Work" (*SE*, XIV, 309-33) he used examples from drama to illustrate the psychodynamics of the character-types of "The Exceptions" and "Those Wrecked by Success." Freud noted that in practice he frequently came across individuals who refused to renounce satisfactions that would ultimately have detrimental consequences, who insisted that they had been called upon to suffer enough in the past and that they ought now be *exceptions* to this rule. As an example, Freud pointed to Richard III, whose motivation apparently stemmed from his congenital deficiency. He observed that Gloucester's opening soliloquy reveals this cast of mind, for being "rudely stamp'd," he will see that he gets reparation from life for his deformities and he need not have the scruples of other people because, wrong having been done him, he will simply repay in kind.

Freud devoted the second section of his essay to those wrecked by success, people who insisted on snatching defeat out of the jaws of victory. Such individuals are well and happy until they arrive within reach of a very important goal in their lives; at this point, they may unconsciously frustrate their own efforts to achieve or, having achieved, fall sick as a result. In explanation, Freud differentiated between *internal* and *external* frustrations and posited that the illness arose from an internal frustration, the external one having been replaced by a wish-fulfillment. The ego apparently tolerates the wish as long as it remains a fantasy, but once it becomes reality or threatens to do so, the ego responds with threats and defenses of its own. As illustrations of this type of person, Freud cited both Lady Macbeth and Rebecca Gamvik of Ibsen's *Rosmersholm*. Lady Macbeth, before our eyes, changes from an unscrupulous, unhesitating woman, little given to introspection, to a thoroughly guilt-ridden, conscience-tormented individual, borne down inexorably by remorse to total collapse and ultimate death. Freud believes it impossible to come to any firm conclusion about the causes of this deterioration, but he theorizes that the theme of the play is childlessness (an idea later elaborated upon by Jekels) and that Lady Macbeth's illness is a reaction to her failure to produce a male heir to the throne. Finding it impossible to reconcile this proposition with the time span of the play—one week—he then speculates, following a suggestion from Jekels, that both Macbeth and his Lady are really "splits" of the same character, noting that their psychological reactions complement each other and that together they exhaust the possibilities of reaction. Realizing, however, that like Macbeth himself, he has stepped in quicksand which pulls him relentlessly downward, Freud completely abandons his exploration at this point, leaving the mystery unsolved.

He was, though, eminently more successful in his analysis of Rebecca Gamvik, so much so that the study remains today as the best literary criticism he ever produced and a model of the type. Rebecca, the adopted daughter of a certain Dr. West, has been raised to be a free thinker, shunning the prevailing morality and religious ethic which deprive life of its joys. After her foster father's death, she takes a position at Rosmersholm and soon discovers herself passionately in love with her employer, Johannes Rosmer, a former pastor. Resolving to have him at all costs, she contrives to estrange his wife, Beata, from him and finally manages to drive her to suicide. For a year following the death, Rebecca and Rosmer live together platonically until gossip arises. To stem this talk, Rosmer proposes to Rebecca who, though momentarily elated, suddenly and surprisingly rejects him, saying that such can never be and adding, ominously, that should he persist in his desires, she too might take her own life.

Sometime later, Rector Kroll, brother of the late Beata, arrives at Rosmersholm with the explicit intention of humiliating Rebecca, whom he suspects to have had some hand in his sister's death. He reveals to her that she is illegitimate, that her foster father, Dr. West, was indeed her real father, she being adopted after her mother's death. Rebecca's reaction is adverse, intense, and disproportionate to the secret revealed. She refuses to believe it, denies its possibility, accuses Kroll of lying, cries out that never in the world could it conceivably be the truth. Kroll himself is dumbfounded by the intensity of the emotion, but upon inquiring is met only by the reply that she does not want to be illegitimate. Still later, Rebecca confesses her part in Beata's death to both Kroll and Rosmer. The latter forgives her the crime of passion and asks her once more to be his wife. But Rebecca, adamant, refuses for the last time in the play, reaffirming the impossibility of the union and darkly hinting of a "past" preventing it.

The virtues of Freud's analysis of the play are many. To begin with, Freud starts with neither psychoanalytic theory nor clinical data; instead, he notes only at the outset that the *text* of *Rosmersholm* presents the reader with several problems: how is it that Rebecca rejects what she desired most, the marriage to Rosmer? Why her overwrought reaction to Kroll's revelation of her illegitimacy, emotion far beyond that called for by the facts? Freud answers these in a careful textual analysis, disposing of objections to his conclusions, commenting on the necessity of Ibsen's keeping Rebecca's motives partially hidden, and only at the end citing analogous clinical support for his assertions.

Briefly, he notes that there can be but one possible solution to the textual problems. The "past" Rebecca speaks of can mean only that she has had sexual relations with another man and her overreaction to Kroll's revelation can mean only that that man was Dr. West, her own father, as it horrifyingly turns out. The early guilt over pre-marital intercourse—the reason for her initial refusal of Rosmer—is thus exacerbated by the revelation of actual incest, finally leading to her confession and decision to bear her terrible secret alone. Freud, in closing, cites again the common fantasy, derived from the oedipal situation, of female servants that they will take the mistress's place in the home, adding that the tragedy of *Rosmersholm* proceeds from one added element: that Rebecca's fantasy of such had been preceded earlier by an exactly corresponding reality. All of this is in his lucid, authoritative style, totally free from jargon or even scientific terminology. The study thus derives its excellence from many of those qualities which make for any sterling psychoanalytic study: first, it is meant to explain the literature and not to substantiate prior theory; second, it relies exclusively upon the text; third, it considers and disposes of possible objections; fourth, it discusses parallels to analytical literature point by point; and fifth, it carefully distinguishes between inference and direct textual evidence. The reader will discover all of these qualities for himself when he looks at the essay.

No further literary analyses appear until 1919, when Freud produced two writings on E. T. A. Hoffman's tales. The first was but a brief note appearing under the initials *S.F.* in the *Internationale Zeitschrift für Psychoanalyse* (5, 308). Both Strachey and Jones attribute to Freud this short comment on the censorship which separates conscious from unconscious as illustrated in Hoffman's *Die Elixer des Teufels*.[5] In addition, Freud analyzed another of Hoffman's tales, "The Sandman," from *Nachtstücken* in The *"Uncanny"* (*SE*, XVII, 227-33). This famous tale is the story of Nathanael, who as a child was terrified and terrorized by an old lawyer friend of his father's, Coppelius, whom he believed to be the Sandman, a sort of boogeyman who steals children's eyes as food for his own children. Nathanael's father is killed by an explosion during an obscure black magic experiment he is conducting with Coppelius, and the latter vanishes soon afterwards. Years later, he seems to appear again in the form of an Italian eye-glass peddler, Coppola, in the town where Nathanael is now a student. Nathanael, though frightened of what seems to be a revenant, buys a telescope from the merchant and looking across to the house of Spalanzani, one of his professors, spies his beautiful daughter Olympia and falls in love with her, forgetting Clara, his beloved at home. After a frenzied courtship during which Olympia says hardly a word, Nathanael discovers to his horror that she is only an automaton, constructed by the professor and Coppola, who, after a fight with Spalanzani, carries Olympia off. Nathanael falls mad and attacks Spalanzani but is prevented from strangling him by fellow students. After a long delirious illness, he appears to have recovered his senses and is preparing to marry Clara and settle down in his home town. One day, while walking with Clara and her brother Lothair, Nathanael passes the high tower of the town hall which Clara suggests they all climb. Lothair prefers to remain below, and the couple make it to the top, from which Nathanael, through his telescope, spies Coppola on the street below and once more becomes insane. He tries to throw Clara over the parapet, but Lothair saves her, and the frenzied youth, with a last look at Coppola, casts himself off the tower and dies crushed on the cobblestones below. Coppola once again vanishes into the crowd and the tale ends.

Initially, in his analysis, Freud disputes the previous assertion of a medical doctor that the sense of the uncanny in the story came from the discovery that Olympia was an automaton. Rather, he said, the central theme was that of the Sandman, the one who steals children's eyes. Freud shows that this fear of having one's eyes stolen or damaged is a substitute for fears of castration (compare Oedipus), and he points out that in the tale the fear is closely linked with the father's death and that the Sandman, Coppelius/Coppola, is always the disturber of love. The Sandman, then, represents the father himself, from whom one expects and fears castration. Freud, at this point, seeking not to diverge too far from his discussion of the "uncanny," interprets the psychodynamics in a lengthy, dense footnote. He suggests that the father always appears in the tale split into his good and bad images, first as the original father/Coppelius pair, then as Spalanzani/Coppola; that Olympia's lifelessness symbolizes Nathanael's feminine attitude toward his father in infancy; that as a result of this attitude he remains fixated upon his father and incapable of loving a woman. All of these suggestions are plausible and doubtless had Freud not been more interested in the "uncanny" than the story as an illustration of it, he would have detailed his study more thoroughly. That he had not exhausted the richness of the tale is well demonstrated by Theodor Reik's "The Three Women in a Man's Life" (see p. 206), a study of the opera *The Tales of Hoffman* based partially on this story. There Reik, too, posits the splitting of the father, but arrives at a different, complementary meaning.

Almost an entire decade passed before the appearance in 1928 of Freud's next, and last, contribution to the psychoanalysis of literature, "Dostoevsky and Parricide" (*SE,* XXI, 175-96). The study of Dostoevsky falls into two distinct parts. In the first, Freud deals with the author's character in general, noting his masochism, his powerful guilt feelings, his epilepsy, and his bisexual disposition in the Oedipal situation. Freud sees the sense of guilt as arising from parricidal impulses and Dostoevsky's epileptic fits as probably a neurotic symptom, a falling into a death-like state to identify with the father who was murdered when the author was eighteen. The fits were thus self-punishment for death wishes against a hated father. Dostoevsky's unjustified and unprotested exile to Siberia as a political prisoner consequently becomes comprehensible as submission to punishment from a father figure, The Czar. Freud cites as evidence of these parricidal desires common to all men the three literary masterpieces, *Oedipus Rex, Hamlet,* and *The Brothers Karamazov,* which he believed the greatest novel ever written. After briefly discussing the parricide committed out of sexual rivalry in each one, Freud passes on to the second section of the essay, an attempt to determine the sources of Dostoevsky's compulsive gambling. He attributes this, too, to self-punishment and shows how Stefan Zweig's short story "Four-and-Twenty Hours in a Woman's Life" illustrated his points. By means of this tale he demonstrates that compulsive gambling is a substitute for masturbation, the "primal addiction," which is only later replaced by other addictions. Dostoevsky's gambling then becomes understandable in the light of the relationship between the fear of the father and the attempts of the individual to suppress his primal addiction. Freud's analysis greatly illuminates Zweig's story, but his glance at *The Brothers Karamazov* goes little beyond the obvious. This is comprehensible, however, in view of the fact that he completed the essay quite reluctantly, being busy with other matters[6] and that all of his ideas had been anticipated by Jolan Neufeld, whom he credits, in a book written in 1923.

To attempt to estimate Freud's influence on psychoanalytic criticism would, of course, be futile. In one way or another he influenced all of it. His analyses, like that of "The Sandman" or *Macbeth,* have been used as the basis for others or, like that of *Rosmersholm,* are the last word on the subject. Literary allusions and hints at explanations of literary problems throughout the large body of his work have been seized upon and have formed the nucleus of countless other essays. And, of course, his theories, early and late, original or revised, are those which inform most modern psychoanalytic critics. By determining the significance of the father to each of us, and the father in each of us, he became the father to all of us.

Notes

1. See, for example, Louis Fraiberg, *Psychoanalysis and American Literary Criticism* (Detroit: Wayne State University Press, 1960), pp. 1-46; Norman Holland, *Psychoanalysis and Shakespeare* (New York: McGraw-Hill, 1966), pp. 1-44; and Ernest Jones, *The Life and Work of Sigmund Freud* (New York: Basic Books, 1957), III, pp. 408-16.
2. This letter may be found in Sigmund Freud, *The Origins of Psychoanalysis: Letters, Drafts and Notes to Wilhelm Fliess, 1877-1902,* eds., Marie Bonaparte, Anna Freud, Ernst Kris; trans.,

Eric Mosbacher and James Strachey (New York: Doubleday, 1957), pp. 259-60. See also William G. Niederland's thorough discussion of this analysis in "The First Application of Psychoanalysis to a Literary Work," in *The Psychoanalytic Quarterly*, 29, No. 2 (1960), pp. 228-35.

3. *The Standard Edition of the Complete Psychological Works of Sigmund Freud*, trans., James Strachey, Anna Freud, Alix Strachey, and Alan Tyson, 24 volumes (London: Hogarth Press, 1953-00), IV, pp. 264-66. Future references read *Standard Edition*.

4. Jones, *Life and Work*, III, p. 428.

5. *Standard Edition*, XVII, p. 233n.; Jones, *Life and Work*, III, p. 426

6. *Standard Edition*, XXI, pp. 175-76.

Otto Rank

Otto Rank's early search for the ideal man (see p. 308) led him to become deeply interested in the psychology of art, of the artist, and of creativity in general. This in turn led to his first book, *The Artist*, published in 1907 when Rank was but twenty-three years old. The work was prepared before he was introduced to Freud, but he made use of the latter's criticisms in the revision of the manuscript. The artist to Rank, as we already know from his psychological theories, is the non-neurotic, the ideal man of society, harmonious, integrated, unified. He has been able to achieve this degree of unity only because, unlike the normal individual who expresses unconscious psychic conflicts solely through dreams or other psychic manifestations, the artist channels his conflicted fantasies into more tangible creative works. In doing so, he not only works out his own psychic difficulties, but also provides aesthetic pleasure to an audience eager to receive his gifts as aids in relieving their own conflicts through identification and "abreaction." Twenty-five years later, in *Art and Artist,* Rank returned to this subject, elaborating upon it in the light of his maturer thought and post-Freudian psychological theory.

His greatest contribution to applied psychoanalysis, however, came the year after *The Artist,* with the publication of *The Myth of the Birth of the Hero.* This detailed examination of fifteen mythical heroes, among them Gilgamesh, Oedipus, Jesus, Hercules, and Tristan, demonstrated the parallel structure of the myths and their origin in the very human motives of men. Proceeding inductively from the myths, Rank outlines their common underlying structure: the hero is of distinguished lineage, generally the son of a king. Difficulties begin even before his birth; there is usually barrenness, continence, or furtive intercourse on the part of the parents because of some prohibition or obstacle. Prior to conception or during pregnancy a prophecy (oracle or dream) warns that the child, when born, will be a threat to his father. As a result he is abandoned, only to be found and nurtured by animals or people of low caste. When of age, he finds his original parents, venges himself on his father in some manner, winning rank and accolades.

Rank rightly interprets this pattern as a projective fantasy, stemming from the pregenital infantile complexes:

> The myths are certainly not constructed by the hero, least of all by the child hero, but they have long been known to be the product of a people of adults . . . constructed from the consciousness of their own infancy. In investing the hero with their own infantile history, they identify themselves with him, as it were, claiming to have been similar heroes in their own personality. The true hero of the romance is, therefore, the ego, which finds itself in the hero, by reverting to the time when the ego was itself a hero, through its first heroic act, i.e., the revolt against the father.[1]

In addition Rank concludes that, since in reality the son wishes to depose the father and the myth reverses this to show the father hostile to the son, this particular myth must be, in essence, a paranoid structure. The two parent-couples of the myth are in reality the real and imaginary parent-couples of the "family romance" and, in accordance with the overvaluation of the parents in infancy, the deposition of the real father by a better, worthier one is simply an expression of the child's desire to return to a better, happier time when his father was the wisest and strongest of men and his mother the kindest and most beautiful of women. To those early readers who might have been disturbed by his discovery and explanation of the common elements of parricide and incest in these myths, Rank proposed a simple solution, that "one must either become reconciled to these indecencies, provided they are felt to be such, or one must abandon the study of psychological phenomena."[2] The thoroughness of this early work and the cogency of his argument showed fully the brilliance of Rank's early career in psychoanalysis.

His prolificacy continued unabated in the following year, 1912, during which he both received his Ph.D. from the University of Vienna and published his third book, *Das Inzest-Motiv in Dichtung und Sage.* This gigantic volume testifies to the continuing fascination which the incest theme has had for story tellers through the ages and the many and various ways in which they have modified it to make it artistically and morally acceptable. The book contains a number of essays on the plays of Shakespeare, one of which is the first psychoanalytic elaboration of the Freud-Jones theory of *Hamlet.*[3]

Several other works by Rank are of interest to the student of applied psychoanalysis. *The Significance of Psychoanalysis for the Mental Sciences,* co-authored with Hanns Sachs, appeared in 1913. This slim volume is a series of essays describing the mutual contributions of psychoanalysis and other disciplines, among which are several dealing with literature and linguistics.[4] Finally, an essay, "The Double," published in 1914 and expanded in 1932, contains provocative suggestions about this motif in literature, particularly in the writings of E. T. A. Hoffman, R. L. Stevenson, Adelbert Chamisso, and Fyodor Dostoevsky. Of the latter, for example, Rank asserts that:

Originally, the double was an identical self (shadow, reflection), promising personal survival in the *future;* later, the double retained together with the individual's life his personal *past;* ultimately, he became an opposing self, appearing in the form of evil which represents the perishable and mortal part of the personality repudiated by the social self. Those three essential stages in the development of the ideas on the double we find epitomized in the successive treatment of this theme in three of Dostoevsky's masterpieces: his early story, "The Double," his most fascinating study, *The Possessed,* and his last and the maturest work, *The Brothers Karamazov.*[5]

One never ceases to regret, in reviewing the genius and productivity of Rank's early career that he became caught up in the *idée fixe* of the birth trauma and ultimately never fulfilled his early promise as Freud's favorite and one of his most brilliant pupils.

Notes

1. Otto Rank, *The Myth of the Birth of the Hero and Other Writings,* ed., Philip Freund (New York: Vintage Books, 1964), p. 84.
2. Rank, *Myth,* p. 12.
3. Otto Rank, *Das Inzest-Motiv in Dichtung und Sage,* 2nd ed. (1912; reprinted Leipzig: Franz Deuticke, 1926). A French translation of this work appeared in 1934, but as yet the book has not been rendered into English. For a discussion of Rank's views on *Hamlet,* see Norman N. Holland, *Psychoanalysis and Shakespeare* (New York: Oxford University Press, 1966), pp. 166-69.
4. This study was recently reprinted in Harry Slochower, ed., *Psychoanalysis as an Art and a Science* (Detroit: Wayne State University Press, 1968), pp. 7-133.
5. Otto Rank, *Beyond Psychology* (New York: Dover, 1958), pp. 81-82. For an excellent full-length consideration of the doppelgänger motif, see Robert Rogers, *A Psychoanalytic Study of the Double in Literature* (Detroit: Wayne State University Press, 1970).

Ernest Jones

In one of the innumerable displays of his inimitable wit and self-confidence, Freud once remarked, "After all, the conflict in *Hamlet* is so effectively concealed that it was left to me to unearth it." (*SE,* VII, 310) He was referring, of course, to his incidental solution of the three-hundred-year-old riddle of Hamlet embedded in *The Interpretation of Dreams:*

What is it, then, that inhibits him in fulfilling the task set him by his father's ghost? The answer, once again, is that it is the peculiar nature of the task. Hamlet is able to do anything—except take vengeance on the man who did away with his father and took that father's place with his mother, the man who shows him the repressed wishes of his own childhood realized. Thus the loathing which should drive him on to revenge is replaced in him by self-reproaches, by scruples of conscience, which remind him that he himself is literally no better than the sinner whom he is to punish. (*SE,* IV, 265)

From this interpretation, which extends little beyond a page and a half of text, came one of the earliest and most influential extended applications of psychoanalysis to literature. Little more than a decade later, Sir Ernest Jones, Freud's biographer and the first British psychoanalyst, published "The Oedipus Complex as an Explanation of Hamlet's Mystery: A Study in Motive," precipitating a controversy which yet rages. Dr. Jones later revised his work, publishing it in 1923 in *Essays in Applied Psychoanalysis*; this version was still further revised and extended, appearing finally in book form in 1949 as *Hamlet and Oedipus.*[1] It is this final study to which we now turn our attention.

After brief prefatory remarks in which he raises and meets the more common objections of non-analytic critics, that is, the definitions of "normal" and "abnormal" and the attribution of an unconscious to a fictional character, Jones turns to the problem of Hamlet and surveys the explanations offered by scholars for his hesitancy in revenging the murder of his father. He divides these explanations into three categories: (a) the "subjective," those which trace his inhibitions to "some vicious mole of nature" in Hamlet himself, (b) the "objective," those which trace it to the nature of the task to be performed, and (c) those which trace it to some feature of the task which makes it repugnant to the Prince. The disposition of the arguments of the adherents of the subjective and objective views follows the same pattern used by Freud in his artistic investigations, one which the student would be advised to follow; that is, having thoroughly researched previous explanations, Jones refutes them on the basis of internal evidence.

The subjective view, he says, is indefensible since, to begin with, it is apparent that with the exception of the present task, Hamlet is perfectly capable of decisive action and has little compunction about killing. His murder of Polonius, his deliberate arrangement of the deaths of Rosenkrantz and Guildenstern, his scornful treatment of Ophelia and Gertrude, none of these are signs of a gentle, weak nature. Nor is there any hesitation in his confronting the ghost, his boarding the pirates' ship, his leaping into the grave with Laertes, or his accepting the challenge of the duel. Where, then, is the paralysis of doubt which critics have believed afflicts him? In addition, Hamlet never acts as if he is unequal to the task, but rather as if, for some reason, he simply cannot bring himself to perform his duty.

On the other hand, Jones continues, the objective critics have complicated the definition of "revenge" and greatly exaggerated the importance of the external obstacles. The strongest refutation of their contention is Hamlet's own attitude toward the task. "He never makes any serious attempt to deal with the external situation, and indeed throughout the play makes no concrete reference to it as such, even in the significant prayer scene when he had every opportunity to disclose to us the real reason for his continued non-action. There is therefore no escape from the conclusion that so far as the external situation is concerned the task was a possible one, and was regarded as such by Hamlet."[2]

But, if Jones finds fault with the objective critics for exaggerating the external obstacles, we must find fault with him for minimizing them. He says earlier that not for an instant did Hamlet doubt he was the legitimately appointed instrument of punishment, an assertion which completely ignores the Prince's serious doubts about the reality of the ghost and the veracity of its revelations and charges. Hamlet consequently arranged *The Mousetrap,* because "The spirit that I have seen may be the Devil, and the Devil hath power to assume a pleasing shape." (II, ii, 627-29) Any member of an Elizabethan audience would accept these precautions on his part, just as they would assent to his reason for not killing Claudius in the prayer scene: "And am I then revenged, To take him in the purging of his soul, When he is fit and seasoned, for his passage? No." (III, iii, 84-87) Therefore, when Jones states that Hamlet had every opportunity to disclose to us the real reason for his continued non-action, he fails to see that *at this point* in the unfolding events of his life, these reasons are to Hamlet the "real reasons," discover though we may ultimately that they are only the best possible rationalizations.[3] Hamlet, like the analysand, does not admit to his not knowing why he is doing what he is doing until all his rationalizations have been cut away from under him. This occurs only later, when on the plain, ready to take ship for England, he witnesses the march of Fortinbras—a Prince fully capable of doing honor to his father—and admits, doubtless in great anguish,

I do not know
Why yet I live to say "This thing's to do,"
Sith I have cause, and will, and strength, and means
To do 't. (IV, iv, 43-46)

Now and only now have the external obstacles been brought into perspective. Hamlet has finally admitted his total ignorance of the reasons for his inability to act. The reader must now admit that Hamlet's motives were overdetermined. And, as William Griffin has pointed out in another context, "For if we ask why Hamlet delayed his revenge, we must be prepared to include among our answers the admission that Shakespeare arranged matters so."[4] Jones' failure to consider Hamlet's "reasons" is a serious flaw in his analysis.

If indeed the inhibition lies not in the nature of Hamlet's task, we must then turn to Jones' third category, that it lies in some special feature of the task which makes it repugnant. Jones, the critic, at this point, must proceed like Jones the psychoanalyst: refuse to accept what the analysand *says* and look beyond to what he *does,* to understand the nature of his problem, that is, to his actions and the *unspoken* motives behind them. The psychoanalytic critic must resist the strong tendency to believe that the certain way to find out why someone does something is to ask him, with assurance that his answer will prove reliable. Man's conception of himself as wholly conscious, possessed of self-knowledge, is his final exertion in the frantic effort to maintain an anthropocentric universe, Copernicus, Darwin, and Freud to the contrary notwithstanding. No character in the play understands the motive's for Hamlet's actions, least of all Hamlet himself. Though chronically complaining of the difficulty of his task, in none of the many soliloquies does he give even the slightest hint of the nature of his mental conflict; he seems incapable of even that. As Jones so aptly puts it, "Hamlet's advocates say he cannot do his duty, his detractors say he will not, whereas the truth is that he cannot will." (59) Yet conceal his conflict as he may, it will out, expressing itself in externals which can be interpreted by the trained observer. Thus the necessity of, at this point, the analysis of the psyche.

Jones begins this analysis by observing that none of the reasons Hamlet gives for his hesitancy ultimately stand up under close inspection; he is engaged only in self-deception, in obscuring his unspoken motive. Nothing assures us so much of this as his constant and frantic changing of his spoken motive. (One is reminded immediately of Raskolnikov, much given to the same frenzied search for a plausible reason for his action.[5]) "In short, the whole picture presented by Hamlet, his deep depression, the hopeless note in his attitude towards the world and towards the value of life, his dread of death, his repeated references to bad dreams, his self-accusations, his desperate efforts to get away from the thoughts of his duty, and his vain attempts to find an excuse for his procrastination: all this unequivocally points to a *tortured conscience,* to some hidden ground for shirking his task, a ground which he dare not or cannot avow to himself." (64)

This assumption leads Jones to the methods by which one can hide psychic material from oneself, most specifically to the psychoanalytic concept of *repression*. After a general discussion of this defense mechanism, Jones examines closely the function of repression in Hamlet's attitude toward the object of his vengeance, Claudius, and the exact nature of Claudius' crime:

> The uncle has not merely committed each crime, he has committed *both* crimes [murder and incest], a distinction of considerable importance, since the *combination* of crimes allows the admittance of a new factor, produced by the possible inter-relation of the two, which may prevent the result from being simply one of summation. In addition, it has to be borne in mind that the perpetrator of the crimes is a relative, and an exceedingly near relative. The possible inter-relationship of the crimes, and the fact that the author of them is an actual member of the family, give scope for a confusion in their influence on Hamlet's mind which may be the cause of the very obscurity we are seeking to clarify. (69)

Thus, concludes Jones a là Freud, Claudius' murder of Hamlet's father and marriage to his mother have mobilized in Hamlet the repressed memories of his childhood Oedipal wishes, bringing to light again intolerable thoughts, creating an insoluble psychic conflict with its consequent frustration and inhibition of action. Jones tempers this conclusion with the remark that, at any rate, this is the mechanism actually found in the real-life Hamlets investigated psychoanalytically. He then offers clinical evidence of "real Hamlets" in two chapters entitled "Tragedy and the Mind of the Infant" and "The Theme of Matricide." Here he explores the psychodynamics of the family, its rivalries, jealousies, hatreds, discussing generally the Oedipus complex, but applying the clinical observations to the inter-relationships of Hamlet, Claudius, Ophelia, and Gertrude. (These sections are commendable for their clarity and lack of analytic jargon.) Jones sees Hamlet's misogyny and sexual revulsion as an outgrowth of the Oedipal situation and its memories reactivated by recent events, with Ophelia and Gertrude as "splits" of the mother-image into contrasting figures, the virgin and the whore. And, "when sexual repression is highly pronounced, as with Hamlet, then both types of women are felt to be hostile: the pure one out of resentment at her repulses, the sensual one out of the temptation she offers to plunge into guiltiness. Misogyny, as in the play, is the inevitable result." (97-98)

Hamlet's feelings toward his uncle-father, however, are much more complex. Though he despises him, it is the jealous hatred of a less-successful evil-doer toward a more-successful one. Hamlet can never denounce him vehemently, for that would only stir up his own unconscious feelings. He thus remains impaled on the horns of a dilemma: if he transforms his feelings into action, he stimulates his own horrifying wishes; if he does not, he ignores his duty—the vengeance commanded by his spectral father. "His own 'evil' prevents him from completely denouncing his uncle's, and in continuing to 'repress' the former he must strive to ignore, to condone, and if possible even to forget the latter; *his moral fate is bound up with his uncle's for good or ill.* In reality his uncle incorporates the deepest and most buried part of his own personality, so that he cannot kill him without also killing himself." (99-100)

Though the critic would do well to emulate Jones' extensive research, his continual revision and amplification of previous statements, and his general methodology (refutation and proof from textual evidence), he would be wise to shun psychoanalysis of the author, a procedure Jones begins in the sixth chapter of his book. Perhaps, "is led into" would be more exact, for he is obviously following Freud's suggestion that the death of Shakespeare's father is of great importance to this drama. This abuse is so common that the strictures against it bear repeating, with specific reference to Jones' analysis. Griffin gives us one of these strictures when he queries, "Now, if the author under analysis has created more than one character, it seems reasonable to ask on what grounds it may be supposed that in one rather than another he has expressed 'the core of his psychical personality.' "[6] This objection may be carried one step further. By what criterion is one element [of a character] biographical and another simply the intuitive perceptions of the creative artist?"[7] Both of these questions are likely to produce embarrassment but no answers. Or, if answers come, they will be subjective and nebulous. There is, of course, no objective answer possible, and however interesting biographical speculation may be, it is ultimately futile and not the proper province of the psychoanalytic literary critic.

The twenty-odd pages which Jones spends trying to find "The Hamlet in Shakespeare" are at times a curious mixture of guardedness and dogmatism; thus the words "surmise" and "hypothetical" alternate with statements like "The intrinsic evidence from the play decisively shows that Shakespeare projected into it his inmost soul; the plot, whether he made it or found it, became his own, inasmuch as it obviously corresponded with the deepest part of his own nature." (122-23) After extensive "evidence" adduced from history and Shakespearean biography, dogmatism wins out, and we learn that the play arose from Shakespeare's feelings toward two recent events: the death of his father and the unhappy resolution of the love triangle depicted in the sonnet sequence. By composing a tragedy which took as its theme the suffering of a tortured soul unable to avenge his injured feelings, says Jones, Shakespeare alleviated his own suffering and saved his sanity. In addition, the jealousy portrayed in all the great tragedies and the Sonnets is most probably "that of a bisexual man suffering from deep inner conflicts." (135)

Those who accept the underlying Freudian principles will accept most of Jones' conclusions about the drama itself; others, however, will doubtless be tempted to ask with Oscar Wilde, "Are the commentators on Hamlet mad or only pretending to be?" Neither group can deny, though, the importance of this exploration of the Oedipal conflict in the play. Jones's interpretation was widely accepted by scholars and critics at the time, as it is now, and has remained one of the most provocative, influential commentaries on *Hamlet* ever written.

Jones continued his pursuit of the Oedipal conflict in two other literary essays, "The Death of Hamlet's Father" and a study of *Julius Caesar,* incorporated in the final version of *Hamlet and Oedipus.*[8] In the first of these, unfortunately with no textual evidence whatsoever to give credibility to his suppositions, he asserts that the poison which Claudius uses to kill the elder Hamlet would signify to the unconscious "any bodily fluid charged with evil intent" and the ear, a displacement for the anus. The murder, consequently, must be seen as a homosexual assault. Further, the younger brother attacking the older is merely a repetition of the father-son conflict and represents the castration of the former by the latter. To the previous view, then, that Hamlet's delay stems from his repressed hatred of his father, Jones adds one more— that Hamlet has a feminine attitude toward his father, fears this feeling, and is unable to face it.

The father-son conflict, too, was at the core of *Julius Caesar.* Following Otto Rank's interpretation of the play closely, Jones contends that, whereas in *Hamlet* the father was split in three—Hamlet the Elder, Claudius, and Polonius—in *Julius Caesar* the father remains one, Caesar, while the son is split into three: Brutus, the rebellious aspect;

Cassius, the remorseful; and Antony, the pious. And though the sexual element seems absent from the play, it is in evidence, says Jones, in Brutus' "Not that I loved Caesar less, but that I loved Rome more." Because cities and countries are unconscious symbols of the mother, he interprets this statement to mean that Brutus killed the father whom he considered to be ill-treating and tyrannizing the mother.

Jones wrote no other literary essays and though each of the previous short studies contains interesting observations, each is deficient in textual support for its conclusions. Thus his major contribution to applied psychoanalysis remains his work on *Hamlet,* a seminal study that was the single most important psychoanalytic treatise on literature done in the first quarter of this century.[9]

Notes

1. A detailed summary of the similarities and differences in these three versions is available in Claudia C. Morrison, *Freud and the Critic: The Early Use of Depth Psychology in Literary Criticism* (Chapel Hill: University of North Carolina Press, 1968), pp. 161-62.

2. Ernest Jones, *Hamlet and Oedipus* (New York: Anchor Books, 1954), p. 45. All subsequent references are to this edition.

3. In *Shakespearean Tragedy* (New York: World, 1965). A. C. Bradley examined these reasons closely and reached the same conclusion, determining that they are finally inadmissible: the arrangement of *The Mouse Trap* "an unconscious fiction, and excuse for his delay" (112); the prayer scene excuse "again is an unconscious excuse for delay. . . . " (114) He believes, however, that the cause of Hamlet's delay is a morbid state of melancholy induced by a "violent shock to his moral being" (100).

4. William Griffin, "The Uses and Abuses of Psychoanalysis in the Study of Literature," *Literature and Psychology: Reprint of Leading Articles and Bibliographies from Volumes I and II* (September, 1953), p. 14.

5. For a provocative analysis of the over-determination of motives in this particular case, see Edna C. Florance, "The Neurosis of Raskolnikov: A Study in Incest and Murder," *Archives of Criminal Psychodynamics,* 1 (1955), pp. 344-96.

6. Griffin, "Uses and Abuses," p. 14.

7. Morton Kaplan, *"The American Imago* in Retrospect," *Literature and Psychology,* 13, No. 4 (1963), pp. 112-16.

8. "The Death of Hamlet's Father," *International Journal of Psychoanalysis,* 29 (1948), pp. 174-76; *Essays in Applied Psychoanalysis* (London: Hogarth Press, 1951), I, pp. 325-28; William Phillips, ed.,

Art and Psychoanalysis (New York: Criterion Books, 1957), pp. 146-50. The study of Caesar appears in *Hamlet and Oedipus,* pp. 137-43, and in M. D. Faber, ed., *The Design Within: Psychoanalytic Approaches to Shakespeare* (New York: Science House, 1970), pp. 57-61.

9. For interesting studies which deviate from this basic approach of Jones, see Frederic Wertham, "The Matricidal Impulse: Critique of Freud's Interpretation of *Hamlet," Journal of Criminology and Psychopathology,* 2 (1941), pp. 455-64 (reprinted in *The Design Within,* pp. 111-12); and Neil Friedman and Richard M. Jones, "On the Mutuality of the Oedipus Complex: Notes on the Hamlet Case," *American Imago,* 20 (1963), pp. 107-31 (reprinted in *The Design Within,* pp. 123-46).

Albert Mordell

Looking at the table of contents in Albert Mordell's *The Erotic Motive in Literature,* one sees a well-organized, comprehensive outline of one theory of psychoanalytic literary criticism. Unfortunately, one reads the book and spoils that impression. For it rapidly becomes evident that Mordell is not so much interested in explicating and enriching the literature as he is in "analyzing" the author. A few sentences into the introduction and one finds the thesis: "In studying literature thus, I aim to trace a writer's books back to the outward and inner events of his life and to reveal his unconscious, or that part of his psychic life of which he is unaware."[1]

The handwriting is on the wall and it reads very clearly *caveat lector.* The impossibility of analyzing the author has been discussed earlier; its dangers are particularly evident here in the egregious assumptions Mordell soon makes, as when he tells us that "with a man's literary work before us and with a few clues, we are able to reconstruct his emotional and intellectual life, and guess with reasonable certainty at many of the events in his career" (2). And conversely, "I do not think it would be difficult for us to deduce from the facts we have of Dante's life that he naturally would have given us a work of the nature of the *Divine Comedy*" (2). The absurdity of these statements is *prima facie* evidence of the author's ineptitude in psychoanalytic criticism and should warn the reader not to take seriously either the task Mordell sets for himself or the conclusions he reaches in his wide-ranging examination.

This is the more regrettable since Mordell was courageously pioneering in a new mode of criticism at a time when psychoanalysis itself was still regarded by the American public as a sort of voodoo ritual of exorcism. His decision to analyze the author instead of the text was one of the first faltering steps of the new criticism. Exactly *why* we should be concerned with the unconscious of an author Mordell does not make clear from the start. Only later does he supply us with the rationale. "Psychoanalysis is always interested in learning exactly how literary masterpieces are born. Just as it seeks to know through dreams some of the hidden secrets in the unconscious, so it tries to discover what unconscious life made the writer project his vision" (85). He then adds later that "it is our contention that a literary work is better appreciated after the facts about an author's life are revealed to us, and this does not usually happen for years after his death" (187).

The biographical fallacy aside, it is obvious that Mordell commits the first of the Deadly Critical Sins: he works *away* from the text. Psychoanalytic literary criticism is first literary and only secondly psychoanalytic; if one is not concerned with explication, one has no business pretending to be a critic. Mordell's ineptitude throughout is of such high quality that his study is a virtual primer of *don't*s for the neophyte. His conclusions are dogmatic, his style atrocious, his familiarity with basic psychoanalytic principles superficial. Thus he is capable of attributing *reaction-formation* to an entire country or era and of mishandling dreams in literature. Needless to say, he errs by attributing the dreams to the authors instead of to the characters who have them. Though he is able to detect the mechanism of *condensation* at work in a dream of R. L. Stevenson, he totally ignores the dream-work in dreams of Homer's Achilles and Miss Brontë's Jane Eyre. Apparently one can choose either manifest or latent content as best representative of reality, according to one's purpose in writing a book.

His analysis of imagery in literature is equally as deficient. One is reminded of the Yiddish woman, suffering from senile dementia, being questioned by a psychiatrist: "What is this?" asked the doctor, holding up a fork. "Dass iss ein gopl." "And this?" holding up a teaspoon. "Dass iss ein teylefl." "And this?" holding up a banana. "Dass iss ein phallic symbol." For Mordell, this punchline becomes a thesis. Everything from Wordsworth's skylark to Kipling's interest in machinery becomes phallically charged, and we are offered such "literary criticism" as the following: "A colloquial designation for a woman's pubic hair is 'the bushes.' May Turgenev, who has given us so many landscapes, not have been unconsciously thinking of his first love disappointment when he described them?" (121). We do not deny, of course, that phallic imagery may be present in literature, but we do caution that it should not be read in where it does not exist but read out where it does and where it functions integrally in the work. We concur with Theodor Reik that "the concept that an airplane is in the first place a penis symbol and that beyond that it can be used as a flying machine is distorted."[2]

Mordell was led into this distortion, of course, by his over-emphasis on the id to the neglect of the ego, perhaps as a result of Freud's concentration on the id in his earliest writings. This same stress probably caused him to see the artist as neurotic and to conclude that "a book is not an accident. The nature of its contents depends not only on hereditary influences, nor, as Taine, thought, on climate, country and environment, alone, but on the nature of the repressions the author's emotions have experienced. The impulses that created it are largely unconscious, and the only conscious traces in it are those in the art of composition." (2).

It is not our task to criticize at length the ignorance and misapprehension in this passage. Kubie has amply and ably demonstrated the distinctions between the artist and the neurotic and the role of the unconscious, preconscious, and conscious in creativity,[3] as has Ernst Kris in his work (see p. 220).

Given the preceding catalogue of critical and psychoanalytic sins, one might be amazed to discover that Mordell was highly praised by Freud himself in a personal letter to the former.[4] Perhaps Freud, in his tremendous struggle against the resistance to psychoanalysis, attempted to enlist as many allies as possible. Less to his credit, it might be said that Freud himself believed, at that time, some of these ideas about art and the artist. The Master, however, revised many of his theories; the pupil did not. Successive editions of *The Erotic Motive in Literature* even contained elaborate prefatory defenses of his position. We must agree, however, with a few early critics (among them Hanns Sachs[5]), that the study exemplifies all that is bad in psychoanalytic literary criticism. With the discipline still in its infancy in 1919, Albert Mordell did little to ably guide its first faltering steps.

Notes

1. Albert Mordell, *The Erotic Motive in Literature,* rev. ed. (1919; reprinted, New York: Collier Books, 1962), p. 1. All subsequent references are to this edition.
2. Theodor Reik, *The Psychology of Sex Relations* (New York: Grove Press, 1961), p. 77.
3. Lawrence S. Kubie, *Neurotic Distortion of the Creative Process* (1958; reprinted, New York: Noonday Press, 1968).
4. Quoted in full in Jones, III, p. 442.
5. Hanns Sachs, *International Journal of Psychoanalysis,* 1 (1920), pp. 477-78.

Maud Bodkin

"Let it be said to the credit of this all but unknown woman and her book that in one sense she performed as essential a job for literary criticism as Sigmund Freud did. He turned the blinding light of science on the depths of the human unconscious; she showed that in the fierce glare even the most delicate poem need not wither away."[1] With this poetic opinion, Stanley Edgar Hyman closes his critique of Maud Bodkin's *Archetypal Patterns in Poetry,* a work he considered the best use of psychoanalysis in literary criticism to that time. Miss Bodkin's ideas, as set forth in that work, have indeed been influential in the history of psychological criticism, even to the present day. Simon Lesser notes her copious insights and his indebtedness to her in his *Fiction and the Unconscious,* and Norman N. Holland's *The Dynamics of Literary Response* owes much to her concept of meaning itself lying in the reader's feeling-response to the work of art. Disciples of Holland, whose number grows daily as his influence extends throughout Academia, deviate little from this approach. Because of this influence and because *Archetypal Patterns* well exemplifies the Jungian critical mode, we examine it in detail, repeating as little as possible what we say of that mode elsewhere.

Moving comfortably in the shade of Frazer's *Golden Bough,* Miss Bodkin elaborates theories she had set forth in embryo several years earlier in two significant articles.[2] Her aim, stated at the outset, is to examine a single hypothesis of Jung:

> The special emotional significance possessed by certain poems—a significance going beyond any definite meaning conveyed—he attributes to the stirring in the reader's mind, within or beneath his conscious response, of unconscious forces which he terms "primordial images," or archetypes. These archetypes he describes as "psychic residua of numberless experiences of the same type," experiences which have happened not to the individual but to his ancestors, and of which the results are inherited in the structure of the brain, *a priori* determinants of individual experience.[3]

It follows, then, that an "archetypal pattern" will be "that within us which . . . leaps in response to the effective presentation in poetry of an ancient theme. The hypothesis to be examined is that in poetry . . . we may identify themes having a particular form or pattern which persists amid variation from age to age, and which corresponds to a pattern or configuration of emotional tendencies in the minds of those who are stirred by the theme" (4). In her study, Miss Bodkin examines these archetypal patterns in detail by two means: discussion of an archetype in a single work, for example, that of rebirth in *The Ancient Mariner*; and discussion of the variations of archetypes in several works, for example, those of Heaven and Hell as they appear in "Kubla Khan," *Paradise Lost, The Aeneid,* and so on. The analyses are greatly detailed and display a far-reaching knowledge of philosophy, anthropology, religion, and sociology. Miss Bodkin's work, though not the first to apply Jungian principles to literature,[4] was nevertheless the most influential.

We should, however, at this point, pause and cast the "fierce glare" of the critic's eye upon this work and let the withering come if need be. What, for example, is the perceptive reader to make of such statements as the following, in which she is laying the groundwork for her study?:

> In Jung's formulation of the hypothesis [of archetypes] . . . it is asserted that these patterns are "stamped upon the physical organism," "inherited in the structure of the brain"; *but of this no evidence can be considered here.* Jung believes himself to have evidence of the spontaneous production of ancient patterns in the dreams and fantasies of individuals who had no discoverable access to cultural material in which the patterns were embodied. *This evidence is, however, hard to evaluate;* especially in view of the way in which certain surprising reproduc-

tions, in trance states, of old material, *have been subsequently traced to forgotten impressions of sense in the lifetime of the individual* (4).

The concept of racial experience enters the present essay in two ways: (1) all those systems of tendencies which appear to be inherited in the constitution of mind and brain may be said to be due to racial experience in the past. *It is not necessary for our purpose to determine exactly the method of this "biological inheritance" from our ancestors* (24).

We have italicized portions of the preceding passages to call especial attention to the methods by which Miss Bodkin deals with objections the reader or critic might have to the existence of racial archetypes in the first place; she ignores them. This neglect, of course, calls into question the validity of the premise upon which her entire work rests, and although her exploration reveals the persistence of certain patterns throughout the history of literature, these are not of necessity "archetypes" in the Jungian sense. Ultimately, one must say of archetypal criticism that everything which it explains mystically in terms of racial inheritance, psychoanalysis can explain empirically in terms of individual learning and adaptation. Some of Freud's weakest writings are those in which his speculative flights take a phylogenetic rather than an ontogenetic course, as in parts of *Totem and Taboo*. One need not posit a "primal father" for the tribe to depose when one's own father has existed and has had to be dealt with on a personal basis. Thus, that Dante's Beatrice resembles Vergil's Dido who resembles Milton's Eve in certain respects means not necessarily, as Miss Bodkin avers, that this image of woman was somehow inherited by all three men, but more probably that these three men had, in those certain respects, a particular image of woman, patterned on their original woman—the first and most important one they knew—their mother.

If, however, for the sake of literary criticism, one is to grant the existence of the "racial archetype," one is still left with the fact that Jungian criticism at its best is reductive, mere labeling. All women become the *Magna Mater;* elderly males become the figure of the *Wise Old Man; animi* and *animae* proliferate; *individuation* either takes place or does not; meanwhile the text is left to fend for itself and the dynamics of the psychological process are left untouched. Like the primitive, the Jungian critic believes that he comprehends and controls something if only he is able to call it by name. Exchanging one label for another does nothing for the literary work except obscure it further, expecially when the labels are as jargonistic as Jungian terminology.

It must be said to Miss Bodkin's credit, however, that she is not guilty of this labeling game, beyond the basic appellations of "archetype" and "collective unconscious." She is, though, guilty of moving *sideways,* a direction one commits oneself to in choosing the archetypal approach. Let us examine critically for a moment the conclusion she reaches in her discussion of *Othello.* After establishing that Iago is an archetype of the devil, she explains that:

If we attempt to define the devil in psychological terms, regarding him as an archetype, a persistent or recurrent mode of apprehension, we may say that the devil is our tendency to represent in personal form the forces within and without us that threaten our supreme values. . . . We also, watching or reading the play, experience the archetype. Intellectually aware, as we reflect, of natural forces, within a man himself as well as in society around, that betray or shatter his ideals, we yet feel these forces aptly symbolized for the imagination by such a figure as Iago . . . (223-24).

The astute reader will note here that Miss Bodkin is talking in non-psychological terms about the defense mechanisms of projection and displacement. But, if he is especially astute, he will find himself asking a most important question, *"What* is being projected and displaced and *why?"* In other words, what are these "natural forces" "within and without us that threaten"? To stop where Miss Bodkin does is to be satisfied with synonyms; to explore further is to engage in depth psychology. Compare, for example, the definition of the devil above with that given by Freud a decade earlier:

We have here an example of the process, with which we are familiar, by which an idea that has a contradictory—an ambivalent—content becomes divided into two sharply contrasted opposites. The contradictions in the original nature of God are, however, a reflection of the ambivalence which governs the relation of the individual to his personal father. If the benevolent and righteous God is a substitute for his father, it is not to be wondered at that his hostile attitude to this father, too, which is one of hating and fearing him and of making complaints against him, should have come to expression in the creation of Satan. Thus, the father, it seems, is the individual prototype of both God and the Devil (*SE,* XIX, 86).

Though Freud in the very next sentence begins, perhaps, to compromise this insight by lapsing briefly into his concept of the "primal father," the important contrast to note here is that between Miss Bodkin's vague "forces" accreting somehow around an inherent devil archetype and Freud's clear concept of the projection of acquired familial hostilities extant in the mind of each and every individual.

In moving to the second charge leveled here against Jungian criticism—that of consistent reductiveness—it is necessary to return to Hyman's encomium and examine a few of his statements more closely, starting with his censure of the Freudian approach and its alleged reductiveness. Though he is obviously reacting to much of the bad early Freudian criticism, he goes to the opposite extreme, asserting that "the collective and affirmative nature of Jung's psychology is its greatest advantage for literary criticism . . . ," sensing that it had its dangers (" . . . a tendency to turn into a glorification of irrationality, mysticism, and 'racial memory . . . ' "[5]), yet failing to see that in its own way Jungian criticism is *always* reductive, whereas only bad Freudian criticism is. It is not, as Hyman believes, that:

> . . . only one study can be written, since every additional one would turn out to say the same thing. Ernest Jones could do a beautiful job finding the underlying Oedipus complex in *Hamlet*, but had he gone on to analyze *Lear* or *A Midsummer Night's Dream* or the *Sonnets* he would have found to his surprise that they reflected Shakespeare's Oedipus complex too, and, in fact, granting his theories, he would have made the same discovery about any other work of art. A criticism that can only say, however ingeniously, that this work is a result of the author's repressed Oedipal desires, and that everybody has repressed Oedipal desires, turns out not to be saying much.[6]

In considering Hyman's remarks, we might first note that, given his prejudices, it is a wonder that he does not accept the Oedipus complex as an archetypal pattern, since, like the pattern of rebirth, for example, it appears in work after work. Doubtless Hyman's anti-Freudian bias prevents him from seeing this, just as it causes him to forget that Jones' objective in his study was not to find an Oedipal pattern in *Hamlet*, but rather to explain Hamlet's inaction, a riddle three-hundred years old. Competent Freudian critics do not proceed deductively, as Hyman seems to believe, with mold in hand, seeking a tale to force into it, but, rather, inductively, as does psychoanalysis itself. They analyze only when the text requires it, to explain an otherwise inexplicable action, inaction, or reaction, often to explain entire works like those of Franz Kafka, which might otherwise be dismissed as the products of a deranged mind.

In addition, Hyman's contention that Jones would have reduced all of the other works of art to the Oedipus complex is, of course, absurd. Perhaps his acrimony is a reaction to the excesses in which Jones occasionally indulges, excesses which we ourselves have condemned. Whatever the reason, he is most lavish in his praise of Miss Bodkin as he reaches the end of this review: "By focusing, not on the neurosis of the artist, not on the complexes concealed beneath the work, not on the art as a disguised fulfillment of repressed wishes, but on *how* a work of art is emotionally satisfying, what relationship its formal structure bears to the basic patterns and symbols of our psyches, she has furnished psychological criticism with endless vistas."[7]

And, though he had stated earlier that "I am not competent to discuss the ideas of Dr. Jung (or any psychologist) technically,"[8] this disavowal of expertise does not prevent Hyman from delivering *ipse dixits* on the relative merits of the two psychological systems under discussion and ultimately blundering into the belief that one of Miss Bodkin's prime virtues is her eclecticism, her blending of the best of the two schools as she tries to mediate between Freud and Jung. However, as Edward Glover has so clearly shown in *Freud or Jung?*, one cannot be an eclectic. It is an either/or situation, and one *must* choose. In his argument, Glover cites the words of John Morley from "On Compromise": "At the bottom of the advocacy of a dual doctrine slumbers the idea that there is no harm in men being mistaken, or at least so little harm as is more than compensated for by the marked tranquility in which their mistake may wrap them. Men leave error undisturbed, because they accept in a loose way the proposition that a belief may be 'morally useful without being intellectually sustainable.' "[9]

We are tempted to substitute the word "critically" for "morally" immediately above and thus simply dismiss the practicability of Miss Bodkin's criticism. As well, we would like to think that compromises of this sort, made in the face of facts revealed by advancing scientific knowledge, eventually come to a deserved end: Tycho Brahe, the Renaissance astronomer, attempted to compromise the teachings of

Copernicus by theorizing that though the earth's orbit was indeed heliocentric, that of the other planets was geocentric. He was burned at the stake anyway.

We urge neither witch-burning nor book-burning; we urge only that the reader mark well that the eclecticism of Miss Bodkin is ultimately untenable, that the basis of her approach—the archetype—is unverifiable, and that the trend in modern psychoanalysis is now and has been for the past several decades counter to her work, ego-oriented rather than id-oriented. If, after noting all this, the reader still prefers her critical mode, godspeed. But we fear he will produce explications that explain nothing: nothing about a particular text and, worse still, nothing about man himself as he is reflected in the vast panorama of the world's literature.

Notes

1. Stanley Edgar Hyman, *The Armed Vision,* rev. ed. (New York: Vintage Books, 1955), p. 160. All subsequent references are to this edition.
2. "The Relevance of Psychoanalysis to Art Criticism," *The British Journal of Psychology,* 15 (1924), pp. 174-83; "Literary Criticism and the Study of the Unconscious," *The Monist,* 37 (1927), pp. 445-69.
3. *Archetypal Patterns in Poetry* (1934; reprinted, London: Oxford University Press, 1963), p. 1. All subsequent references are to this edition.
4. James M. Thorburn had slightly preceded her. In 1921, he published "Art and the Unconscious," *The Monist,* 31 (1921), p. 589f.; and four years later, a book by the same name (London: Kegan Paul, 1925). For an account of his work, see Morrison, pp. 86-92.
5. Hyman, *Armed Vision,* p. 136.
6. Hyman, *Armed Vision,* pp. 159-60.
7. Hyman, *Armed Vision,* p. 160.
8. Hyman, *Armed Vision,* p. 133.
9. Edward Glover, *Freud or Jung?* (Cleveland: World, 1965), p. 187.

Marie Bonaparte

Probably the earliest psychoanalytic interpretation of the entire canon of an author was Princess Marie Bonaparte's *Edgar Poe, Étude Psychoanalytique*.[1] Later translated into English, this classic study by a pupil of Freud's, one who ransomed him from the Nazis with her own personal fortune, has continued to provide rich insights to critics who wish to approach Poe psychoanalytically. Her examination of the famed American author is divided into four books, the first, a biography with interpretations of the poems interwoven; the second two, interpretations of the tales categorized into those dealing with the mother and those with the father; the fourth, a lengthy consideration of the psychic processes which govern the production of literature and enable us to understand its deepest level of meaning.

Mme. Bonaparte's two-hundred page biography follows, for the most part, Hervey Allen's life of Poe, *Israfel*. She builds upon it, however, by continuous extrapolation, by concern at every moment with demonstrating in Poe's early life those experiences which became the psychic determinants of the contents of his works. Such analysis, of course, must be highly speculative—at times even imaginative—and rather often we find extraordinary passages like these:

We must also remember the part played by the surrounding negroes in those slave-owning days in the South. Doubtless, he would often have visited the slaves' quarters on his guardian's estate with his black nurse and, possibly, even the negro part of the town. The strange songs and legends he would have heard! Dread tales of spectres and of the dead brought to life! The primitive imaginings of these negroes would awake an instant response in the child's mind, a mind already unconsciously, ineradicably, haunted by its unassuageable longing for a mother left dead, long ago, in a small room. Thus, that which already dwells in us, seeks out and absorbs, from the outer world, whatever will give it sustenance and power.[2]

Speculation of this sort makes for lively reading, but we cannot consider it fact or accept it as evidence for psychoanalytical inference. Such flights of fancy aside, Poe's life provides enough fact for Mme. Bonaparte to "analyze" him, insofar as it is possible for a dead man to be analyzed, and she blends all the separate elements of his life into a whole: a detailed picture of a talented writer, traumatized in infancy, emerging eventually as a tormented psychopathic necrophiliac, destroying himself with alcohol and opium.

Her analyses of the tales themselves follow the same pattern as does the biography, but where in the biography an event is related to a characteristic analytically inferred or later revealed in the writings, in the analyses a textual word or deed is related back to its psychic determinant in Poe's infancy. The analysis of "The Gold Bug" well illustrates this method.

After a recapitulation of the plot, interwoven with the drawing of parallels between Legrand and Poe (for example, both are intelligent manic-depressives, fond of solving cryptograms), Mme. Bonaparte concludes that, because Poe was two years old in his early anal erotic phase, when he first visited the very shores on which the treasure is discovered, " . . . the story of Legrand is an epic search for the mother's *faeces,* inside her body, symbolized here by the earth, since solids are the dominant substance in the child's anal erotic phase" (366).

Regrettably the text provides no problem that necessitates such an explanation, nor does it provide much evidence in support of this analysis. Mme. Bonaparte herself points out that the key to the tale came from a remark of Freud's that buried treasure stories possibly take their origin from a phylogenetic event in human history, the period of human sacrifice, and that treasure which is discovered might possibly be an embryo in the abdomen of the victim, but,

At the time, this seemed to me too far-fetched, and I could not see its connection with Captain Kidd's treasure. And yet, even the name of the pirate hero (Kidd=kid=child) hints at the latent content of this tale. But, in particular, it is Poe's choice of the South Carolina coast wherein to place the discovered treasure, this very coast where, in infancy, he had doubtless pondered the riddles of birth, that proves that this story could not be due to chance, since chance no more exists in the psychic than in the physical world (363).

The story is thus revealed as an infantile fantasy of anal birth, the gold being equated with faeces and the faeces with child.

Mme. Bonaparte reveals infantile fantasies in all the other tales, of course, but more often with sufficient textual evidence as support, as in, for example, "Never Bet the Devil Your Head." Its protagonist, Toby Dammit, once more equated with Poe (". . . precocious and given to anger, drink, gambling and rebellion against authority!" [526]), while walking one day with the narrator, makes the bet of the title that he can leap the turnstile at the end of a covered bridge they have traversed. During the leap, however, his head is cut off by an unseen bridge strut and falls into the apron of the devil, in the shape of a black-clad, lame, old man, who immediately races away. Dammit's body, though interred, is eventually dug up and sold as dog's meat.

Mme. Bonaparte begins her analysis with a discussion of the general symbolism of bridges, citing primarily Ferenczi's investigations in this area, and noting his conclusions that the bridge usually represents the father's penis connecting two bodies, that of himself and that of the mother:

Thus, the two stretches of country linked by a bridge would symbolise the parents connected by an immense penis-bridge, their colossal dimensions in this picture deriving from the fact that the parents appear as giants to the child. The river, or water which the bridge spans, according to the general symbolism of water, once again represents the mother from whose amniotic waters all humanity emerged. Thus the mother is twice displayed: in the country to be reached and in the water to be crossed (530).

Mme. Bonaparte believes, that in this instance, however, the bridge represents not the penis, but the vagina:

The bridge Mr. Dammit enters would seem to represent the similarly extroverted mother-vagina, a representation especially in accord with Poe's characteristic fear, apparent in all he wrote, of the *vagina dentata.* The story, "Never Bet the Devil Your Head," would thus admirably illustrate the way each parent, in Poe's unconscious, behaves as castrator. Mr. Dammit enters the bridge-vagina in a manner "excessively lively"; then, as naturally happens when the penis enters the vagina, we see him "wriggling and skipping about" and exulting. When nearly over the bridge, just when we might say he is actually within reach of the further bank by the leap he is contemplating—this leap which perhaps is symbolic of the terminal ejaculation of coitus—the Devil appears. Mr. Dammit has taken the plunge, so to speak, his endless bets, doubtless, representing the risks he ran in daring to approach the mother in spite of the father. This time, however, the father has taken his bet and, if he fails, will claim his head, i.e., penis. And it so happens that the son fails and drops, decapitated, before he can overleap the stile. Thus, the mother *vagina dentata*—for the fatal bar is but one of many that brace the structure—becomes the organ which, enforcing the father's Oedipal bans, effects castration (534).

Like most of Mme. Bonaparte's other analyses, this is lucid, detailed, most likely analytically correct, and yet somewhat deficient as literary explication.

For, as Freud himself points out in his foreword to this study, however, "investigations such as this do not claim to explain creative genius, but they do reveal the factors which awaken it and the sort of subject matter it is destined to choose" (xi). The final three words are not paradoxical, of course, to the psychoanalytically informed reader, and Mme. Bonaparte's study emphasizes the first of these words, rather than the last. Writing at a time when the ego was believed to be not only impelled by the id, but compelled as well, she herself is compelled to conclude that:

As for consciousness, its part is limited, although psychology once included every psychic function in this category. It would appear to be merely our capacity for apperception but, here, turned inwards to happenings in the psyche. And, just as our capacity for external perception, via the senses, can only perceive phenomena without probing their essence, so our faculty of inner perception can only observe surface movements and gleams of happenings in the inaccessible depths of our unconscious. Thus our conscious ego is never but the more or less watchful spectator of ourselves (641-42).

Advances in ego psychology in the past decades have rendered this last statement false, for we know today that the ego is not only seer but doer as well, not only spectator but vital and vigorous participant in psychodynamic processes. Emphasis in psychoanalytic literary criticism has, consequently, shifted in accordance with our new knowledge. That "all ladders start, in the foul rag-and-bone shop of the heart," in infantile emotions and fantasy, is no longer contested or denied, but we now recognize that merely determining the infantile fantasy upon which the ladder rests tells us little about the author, less about textual problems, and nothing about the nature of artistic creation.

Despite the multitude of valid and valuable insights Mme. Bonaparte provides, despite her excellent chapter on the psychic mechanisms governing the elaboration of literary works,[3] despite her success in the monumental task of integrating the life and the works, she has still produced, not a literary explication, but rather a clinically detailed case study of a highly-neurotic man who *happened* to be a writer.

The impossibility of analyzing a writer through his works aside, what Mme. Bonaparte ultimately succeeds in doing is equating Poe with his id: "Nevertheless, the supreme, forbidden, instinctual urges thus sung by Poe; urges which he himself hardly comprehended and which exceed those our love instinct is permitted to gratify, cast such a spell on mankind that even in his life there rose a chorus of adulation" (668). But the man himself—as in any man—was more than a mask which hid his id. And the adulation quite possibly, we submit, was in response to other qualities in Poe's fiction. As Frederick Crews has phrased it, in another context,

The crucial difference between literary creation and symptom-formation resides in the extra demand that we make of literature that it confirm and extend our sense of truth. Whereas symptoms are rigidly stereotyped, are usually accompanied by guilt, and subtract from an individual's rapport with his surroundings, in the highest literary enjoyment we feel that our pleasure is being sanctioned by reality itself, whose principles have been set before us. This is an illusion, but the illusion can be practiced only by artists whose perceptiveness has not been obliterated by ego-needs. A work that flouts our conscious intelligence, as symptoms do, may have an "escape" interest but will soon be rejected for its crudeness or empty conventionality.[4]

Mme. Bonaparte's study, which sees Poe's tales and poems as symptoms rather than as literary creations, thus places the author in the wrong perspective. That his works have not only "escape interest" is attested to by their survival; that we have the strength of Poe's negotiating ego to thank is an insight brought to us by ego psychology. The definitive explication of the work of Poe the neurotic has been written by Marie Bonaparte. The definitive explication of the work of Poe the artist has yet to be done.

Notes

1. Princess Marie Bonaparte, *Edgar Poe, Étude Psychoanalytique* (Paris: Denoël et Steel, 1933).
2. *The Life and Works of Edgar Allan Poe: A Psychoanalytic Interpretation* (London: Imago, 1949), p. 12. All subsequent references are to this edition.
3. This entire chapter is reprinted in William Phillips, ed., *Art and Psychoanalysis* (Cleveland: World, 1957), pp. 54-88.
4. "Anaesthetic Criticism," *Psychoanalysis and Literary Process* (Cambridge, Mass.: Winthrop, 1970), p. 21.

Hanns Sachs

The one creative act shared by all people is the dream. As indisputable as this statement now is, it is significant that it could not have been made with any validity prior to 1900. For in that year, of course, Freud published his *magnum opus, The Interpretation of Dreams,* disclosing the causes, mechanisms, and significance of dreams, and indirectly providing the foundation for a study of human creativity in general and, more specifically, for a study of the causes and effects of literature and literary response. Less than a decade later, Freud himself, in his boundless curiosity, began to explore the relationship between the creative writer and dreaming. Utilizing the insights of Freud in these writings and contributing his own vast knowledge and experience of psychoanalysis, Hanns Sachs, one of the original members of the Vienna Psychoanalytic Society, carried the exploration further still and collected his studies in a volume published in 1942 entitled *The Creative Unconscious.*

The one creative act shared by all people is the dream. With this as his foundation and the proposition that "every creative possibility is contained in the 'stuff dreams are made of,' "[1] as his thesis, Sachs builds Freud's early statements and suggestions into a theory of aesthetics, providing the substructure to be built on later by such critics as Simon O. Lesser in *Fiction and the Unconscious* and, more recently,

Norman N. Holland in *The Dynamics of Literary Response*. Taking the daydream as his starting point—since it is the fantasy counterpart of its nocturnal equivalent, hence the name—Sachs moves from it to poetic creation by first comparing and contrasting the two and then demonstrating the complexities of the mechanism by which daydreams become poetry.

The daydream, he first notes, is completely, shamelessly egocentric. And why not? Since its purpose is to fulfill through fantasy the wishes of the dreamer, it is he who occupies stage center; it is he who defeats the villain or subordinates all others, aggrandizing his power, wealth, or sexual prowess. Since he is both author and audience, the writing of a pleasure-giving script is an easy matter. Furthermore, as is the case with its nocturnal counterpart, the daydream will usually contain a high degree of aggressive and erotic content since it functions to compensate for the frustrations suffered by the individual in reality. It follows then that the daydream will be at base asocial: few members of society would be willing to play the parts relegated to them in another individual's fantasy and few would approve of the aggression and eroticism displayed therein. Poetry, on the other hand, is a social phenomenon; the poet writes to touch and move the minds and sensibilities of others.

Secondly, the daydream, though it may have an unchanging nucleus of material, is essentially formless. Details or large segments are neglected; order, coherence, and continuity are minimally present or entirely absent. As long as the dream accomplishes its goal of fulfilling the dreamer's wishes, it need not be a well-wrought, highly polished, artistic piece. Poetry, on the other hand, cannot exist without form. Third, words do not occupy the position of importance in the daydream as they do in the poem. Since the audience and author are one in the daydream, there is little danger of its becoming incomprehensible, so little regard is given to words. Further, there is in daydreaming a tendency to regress to a more primitive level of expression, where words become less important and can be replaced by pictures with symbolic rather than referential meaning. However, "to the poet, words are the life element, the only possible material for his creative urge; he forms and moulds them till he feels that they express truly and faithfully all that he desired to express" (16).

Finally, notes Sachs, the daydream is a direct, open gratification of the dreamer's wishes, whereas immediate wish-fulfillment is apparent only in the popular but low-class literature formulated of stereotyped people and events and characterized by the presence of the "happy ending." "The more obvious the tendency to serve as 'entertainment'— i.e., momentary wish-fulfillment—becomes, the greater the resemblance to a typical daydream" (20). This step in his argument, however, has brought Sachs to a seeming contradiction: we would expect that those literary works most closely allied with the unconscious would be, in accordance with the foregoing theory, more distant from true art. Yet this is not so. "Happy ending" stories are forgotten before the book is replaced on the coffee table, while those tales which admit the unconscious as collaborator endure, extending their social impact through time and space. To put it more simply, Why is it that we would be repelled by material in a daydream, and yet when the same material is presented to us in literature, we not only accept but also embrace it?

. . . The essential *ars poetica* lies in the technique of overcoming the feeling of repulsion in us which is undoubtedly connected with the barriers that rise between each single ego and the others. We can guess two of the methods used by this technique. The writer softens the character of his egoistic daydreams by altering and disguising it, and he bribes us by the purely formal—that is, aesthetic—yield of pleasure which he offers us in the presentation of his phantasies. . . . It may even be that not a little of this effect is due to the writer's enabling us thenceforward to enjoy own own daydreams without self-reproach or shame (*SE*, IX, 153).

Thus Freud. Sachs, following him, now provides the transition which diminishes self-reproach and shame: the "mutual daydream," that is, a wish-fulfilling fantasy shared by at least two people, thus being no longer asocial, but not yet being art. Sachs elaborates two clinical examples of this fantasy-sharing, concluding that

The advantage of the "mutual daydream" lies . . . [in one's] having found a collaborator who, by his readiness to share one's own daydream, demonstrates that he too is in the same psychic situation, driven by the same urges, and threatened by the same guilt-feeling. This gift of fortune makes it possible for both to get out of their isolation and to join hands. What neither would have done for himself, each does for both. This getting rid of the isolation means a greater alleviation of their guilt-feeling. To be the only sinner, excluded from the community, is unbearable, especially when the sin is an unconscious wish, so that the daydreamer does not know what sin he has committed and cannot defend himself against the indictment (36).

But the mutually-shared fantasy, says Sachs, is also a mutually-shared guilt: "Our wishes are identical, your sin is my sin." It is but a small step from this to an extension of the mutuality and "Everybody's sin is nobody's fault," and it is in that direction that Sachs' inquiry now moves. To get there, however, he must first dispose of a slightly thorny problem. All of this is fine if one can find an uncritical partner to share the daydream openly, but what happens if the right partner does not show up, as is most likely the case with the majority of people? Fortunately, Freud himself has already answered this question, stating that the writer must, in this situation, induce as many people as possible to indulge in his fantasy by disguising its nature and by presenting it with such formal attributes that we are incapable of immediately and consciously being repelled by it. The wisdom of the ages once again comes to the fore: art lies in concealing art. "Anything which would threaten to uncover the screts of the Unconscious would produce the strongest revulsion in the creator and violent repugnance in his audience. The aim must be to reproduce as much of the unconscious fantasies as can be reconciled with ignoring their existence. The disguise must be as complete as it is in a dream, but it must be constructed with much more diligence" (39-40).

It is exactly here, in the study of that diligent construction, that Sachs makes his lasting contribution to psychoanalytic literary criticism. Form is not simply the container for the contents; it is not imposed upon content from the outside, but to be effective must grow organically, disguising the inherent dangers while simultaneously alluring the reader.

We understand by *form* everything that makes the poem (or story or play) pleasing and attractive to the audience. This is done by different techniques; some of them are what we may call "external," i.e., symmetry, rhythm, rhyme, alliteration, the euphony and clarity of language, the prosody of a poem, the manner of presentation on the stage, or the progression of an epic. Other form-elements are woven into the texture of the composition and less easily traced. Among these belong the atmosphere in which the whole or each separate part is steeped, the style in which it moves, the structure of the plot and its relation to the characters, the retardations and accelerations, the subsequent grades of intensity and expectation; and most of all, the way in which all these various techniques are concealed from the conscious attention. *Ars est celare artem*—the audience should feel their effect without being aware of them and should be surprised by what it was unwittingly led to expect (44-45).

"The need for form and beauty," concludes Sachs, "is a consequence of the social function of art" (45). If the audience has liked and accepted the poet's construction and has felt the same emotions which caused him to create it, his fantasy has become the daydream of every individual member of the audience, a "mutual daydream" with a limitless number of partners. The achievement of this large-scale mutuality, though, raises another problem, which Sachs is able to dispose of through the use of psychoanalysis. If the daydreamer uses his fantasy to narcissistically gratify himself, what happens to this narcissism when the dreamer must surrender it in order to induce a mutual sharing of the fantasy? We know it cannot simply be thrown out, but must be accounted for in any system of dynamic psychology. Sachs sees it as being transferred during the creation of the work of art; though temporarily sacrificed, it is "reborn as the poet's desire for the beauty of his work. In other words, the form or facade which originally was but a means to an end becomes, after the transformation, a part of the end in itself; the narcissism has been replaced and shifted from the creator to his creation. In this way the poet's work becomes the essential part of his personality; since his narcissism has been transferred to it, it is generally more important than friendship or love or all the rest of life" (49).

With this final insight demonstrating the inseparability of the two primary unconscious aims of the writer—relief of guilt and replacement of narcissistic gratification—Sachs concludes his basic discussion of the dynamics of literary creativity. The remainder of *The Creative Unconscious* consists of essays which examine, among other matters, Shakespeare's *Measure for Measure* and *The Tempest* and the psychoanalysis of movies and the machine age. We leave these for the reader to pursue on his own.

Of more importance, we feel, are the ideas of Sachs presented above. As we have noted, his lasting contribution lies in them, for it is they which Ernest Kris will use and elaborate in terms of ego psychology, and it is they which Simon Lesser and Norman Holland will extend to

their logical conclusions in their detailed theories of form as defense
and disguise. In this way and through these men, the innovative concepts of *The Creative Unconscious* have maintained their powerful
influence, even to the present day.

Notes

1. Hanns Sachs, *The Creative Unconscious,* ed., A. A. Roback, 2nd
   ed. (1942; reprinted, Framingham, Mass.: Sci-Art, 1951), p. 11. All
   subsequent references are to this edition.

Frederick J. Hoffman

The first significant examination of the relationship between Freud's psychoanalytic theories and modern literature was made by Frederick J. Hoffman in his *Freudianism and the Literary Mind.*[1] In this study, Hoffman moves from an opening primer of Freudian theory, through a close examination of the spread and influence of that theory, into a discussion of the specific ways in which the theory entered into the works of a dozen writers—primarily British and American.

As Ernst Kris has rightly pointed out, "the greatest merit in Hoffman's approach lies in the attempt sharply to distinguish between the scientific function of Freud's hypotheses and the use which writers make of them."[2] Hoffman traces in great detail those theories of Freud adopted or adapted, used or abused, by both the masses and the literati during the initial era of psychological ferment, the twenties and thirties of this century.

The average man, says Hoffman, could not possibly escape exposure to the new psychology, though his ability to grasp its principles was made doubly difficult by the misinterpretations and misapplications of both advocates and opponents. The intellectual, on the other hand, eagerly embraced psychoanalysis, for, having rejected traditional social and moral values, not being ready yet for a highly developed system like Marxism, he sought most of all "a *method,* a psychological approach to and justification for his own soul-searching; he welcomed psychoanalysis because it did not legislate against his desires or restrict them with the mores of his (for the present) hateful society. Psychoanalysis was made to order for his personal revolt against tradition" (72).

Hoffman shows us the home of these alienated intellectuals— Greenwich Village of the new century—and we circulate freely in the drawing room of Mabel Dodge Sterne among Walter Lippman, who early paid homage to Freud in *The New Republic* and his *Preface to Politics;* A. A. Brill, practicing psychoanalyst and first English translator of *Die Traumdeutung* and *Drei Abhandlungen Zur Sexual-Theorie,* and thus in his way an extremely important influence; and such other notables as Floyd Dell and Margaret Sanger. Hoffman details the reception afforded psychoanalysis by the press and the little magazines of the time, notes the contamination of Jungian psychology, and concludes that "if psychoanalysis contributed anything worth preserving or even studying in the literature of this period, it is not to be found in extravagant demonstrations of sensuality or adolescent attacks upon the mores, but rather in its sponsorship of, or at least its concessions to, introspection" (75). A passion for intricate mental analysis in literature was rampant, and "no single motive explained any single act; rather, any one act presupposed a variety of motives, intricately bound up with the 'hidden life' of the character" (73).

Tracing Freud's influence is no mean task, as Hoffman demonstrates, for example, in his consideration of the transformations the concept of *repression* suffered:

. . . *Repression* as Freud defined it lost much of its original meaning in a discussion; but it gained new cultural ingredients from the particular area in which it found an audience. The single term repression, therefore, suffered a variety of changes, which may be formulated as follows: Freud's definition of the term: *Repression, minus* what has been lost through hasty generalization or inadequate knowledge of its source-meaning, *plus* cultural ingredients which have been attached to the already altered concept, *equals* repression as American convention imposed upon free sex expression, or *neo-Puritanism.*
The factor of metaphor must also be considered. Hence the *mechanism* of repression was often replaced by the picture of a *repressed person,* or a repressed people. In the matter of an amateur or aesthetic usage of a

term, the example is more important than the term it is designed to illustrate; and the term acquires the qualities of its illustration, and loses its original accuracy or "abstract purity" (88-89).

In concluding this view of the turbulent twenties and thirties, Hoffman contends that Freud's primary contribution to literature lay in two works, and both of those very early: *The Interpretation of Dreams,* especially the section on "Dream-Work," and the *Three Contributions to a Theory of Sex.* The former demonstrated the existence of a complex unconscious life; it raised the dream to greater importance; it opened the way for a new language which utilized such phenomena as condensation, multiple determination, splitting, displacement, and manifest and latent content; it provided innovators with impetus for experimenting with the absurd, and "surreal." The latter made *oedipus complex* and *electra complex* the stock in trade of writers who explored domestic relationships and provided a host of possibilities for further exploration of the "eternal triangle," despite the sex or age of its members.

It is indeed unfortunate that the individual essays on Joyce, Lawrence, Kafka, and others, which follow this extensive groundwork, though of interest in themselves, are of little use to the psychoanalytic literary critic. Completely nondynamic, the studies deal with those manifestations of Freud's theories in the individual writers and center mainly on stylistic and thematic matters. The essay on Joyce, for example, examines the influence of psychoanalysis on the writer, contains a brief historical section on the development of the "stream-of-consciousness" novel, from Dujardin to Faulkner, and demonstrates how the style and content of both *Ulysses* and *Finnegans Wake* resulted from psychoanalysis' influence on Joyce when he was "yung and easily freudened," as he himself put it. Hoffman sums up the influence thus:

(1) He regarded the dream work, and especially the suggestive ambiguity of words as a factor of much importance in the development of experimental writing. (2) More than any other writer of his time, he was aware of the several stages by which the individual recedes from consciousness, and of the aesthetic problem involved in each case. (3) He thought that much of character motivation could be more adequately developed by recourse to the psychoanalytic explanation of familial relationships than by any other method. (149)

Hoffman's final chapter, "Precursors of Freud," is interesting in that it demonstrates in brief how the thinking of other important figures such as Schopenhauer, Nietzsche, and Bergson, for example, influenced twentieth-century attitudes and in a sense made ready the way for Freud's great impact. As a chronicle of this impact on the literary world, *Freudianism and the Literary Mind* is an especially absorbing book, one which remained the standard work of its type until the recent publication of Claudia Morrison's *Freud and the Critic*.[3] We recommend them both to the reader for their wealth of background material, the latter particularly for the depth and additional breadth it adds to Hoffman's general survey of this exciting era in literary history.

Notes

1. Frederick J. Hoffman, *Freudianism and the Literary Mind*, 2nd ed. (1945; reprinted, Baton Rouge: Louisiana State University Press, 1967). All subsequent references are to this edition.
2. Ernst Kris, *Psychoanalytic Explorations in Art* (1952; reprinted, New York: Schocken, 1964), p. 271.
3. Claudia Morrison, *Freud and the Critic* (Chapel Hill: University of North Carolina Press, 1968).

Theodor Reik

As difficult as it is to evaluate Theodor Reik's multitude of contributions to psychoanalysis, it is perhaps more so with his contributions to psychoanalytic literary criticism. It is not that he has done none; it is rather that he has done almost too much. His psychological writings, like Freud's, overflow with literary allusions, references, interpretations. Primarily a clinician, however, Reik rarely devoted himself to a systematic analysis of a single literary work, carefully worked out with sufficient textual support. He was content, rather, to generalize, to interpret as soundly as possible with minimal textual evidence; to suggest psychoanalytic interpretations; to furnish a brilliant insight into a work in a sentence or a phrase, then move on, leaving the proof to the reader or critic of literature. All of his admirable interpretations suffer considerably from this lack of textual support. But his recent death has left us with almost a hundred volumes of remarkable perceptions, literary and otherwise, with which the critic can work.

What critic could fail to make use of, for example, Reik's suggestion in *Masochism in Sex and Society* that major portions of *A Tale of Two Cities, The Brothers Karamazov,* and *Don Quixote* spring from the masochistic fantasies of their authors? Or his suggestions that what his students have called *Reik's Law* (the degree of hostility of a person toward the opposite sex is in direct proportion to his homosexual attraction to the same sex) is at work in Hamlet's hostility toward Gertrude and Ophelia?[1] That *Great Expectations, The Magic Flute,* Goethe's *Wilhelm Meister,* and Schiller's *Geisterseher* are all informed by "paranoid fantasies of grandeur and of persecution as well as the unconscious homosexual tendencies with regard to father representative figures . . . ."?[2] That even if Hamlet's father had died a natural death and his mother remained single afterward, Hamlet still would have been hostile toward her?[3] That Shylock, as shown by his character, his speech, and the imagery used in reference to him, "seems to be a personification of that second sadistic, cannibal phase of orality as it is sketched in Karl Abraham's psychoanalytic theory?"[4] And so on. One cannot begin to enumerate Reik's many observations.

Twenty of his more specifically literary essays were collected in a work entitled *The Secret Self,* containing analyses of Schnitzler's *Reigen, The Merry Wives of Windsor, Faust,* France's *Our Lady's Juggler,* Ibsen's *The Master Builder,* and others. One can greatly profit from the reading of any of these. To make such an abstract recommendation more concrete, let us look more closely at Reik's work in detail. A fine essay is at hand in his "The Three Women in a Man's Life."

Beginning with free association, as is his wont, Reik speaks of being haunted for a while by a melody which, when finally tracked down, turns out to be Antonia's aria from *The Tales of Hoffman.* This leads him to recall his initial exposure to the opera as a child in 1901 at the Vienna Opera House. In recreating the past he briefly summarizes the plot: young Hoffman recounts for his drinking companions his past foolish loves, three in number. First was Olympia, the daughter of the famed scientist Spalanzani, who turns out to be not a woman at all but rather a skillfully-fashioned automatic doll, ultimately destroyed by Coppelius, a vengeful citizen swindled by her "father." Second was Giulietta, a beautiful siren bribed by the demonic figure Dapertutto to solicit Hoffman's love. Hoffman, after fighting and killing one of her many suitors, finds he has been jilted and last sees his beloved in the arms of another. Third was old Crespel's daughter, Antonia, who had inherited the beautiful singing voice and dread disease of her mother, dead from consumption. Though both her father and lover beseech her not to sing and to conserve her life, the evil physician Dr. Mirakel counsels her otherwise; she yields, sings, and dies as a result. After recounting his three lost loves, Hoffman is left drowning his sorrows in drink.

Reik calls attention to the emergent pattern in each of these encounters: "the easily inflamed passion of the young man meets an antagonistic power, self-deceiving, and self-harming, which causes him to fail."[5] Though represented outwardly by the sinister figures of Coppelius, Dapertutto, and Dr. Mirakel, the source is most probably inward, an unconscious part of Hoffman working successfully to frustrate his achievement. Reik notes this force operative already in his choice of love object. "As if led by a malicious destiny, as if thwarted by a demon, he falls in love each time with a woman who is unsuitable: Olympia, a lifeless automaton, Giulietta, a vixen, and Antonia, doomed from the beginning" (155). Reik tentatively proposes that the women represent the three typical figures playing a part in a young man's life; they are the child-woman, the mature, sexually desirable woman, and the woman who vacillates between wanting to be a wife and following a career of her own. He then begins the psychoanalytic exploration with the figure easiest to understand, Giulietta, whose sensuality and middle position in the sequence suggests she represents the figure governing the mature years of a man's life. But how understand her predecessor, Olympia, the automaton, and her successor, Antonia, the self-destructive singer?

At this point, Reik makes the astute suggestion that one interpret these women and their roles by means of *reversal*. Since the manifest content remains impenetrable otherwise, one must get at the latent content by standard methods of psychoanalytic dream interpretation. Consequently, though Olympia the marionette seems to be made to walk and talk and sing and dance by being led and manipulated, reversal shows that it is rather she who is leading and manipulating Hoffman as if he were incapable of it without her, as if, indeed, he were an infant. Reversal reveals, as well, that it is Hoffman, not Antonia, who vacillates between love and art and dies as a consequence. "The three female figures appear to us now in a new light: Olympia is the representative of the mother, object of the love of the helpless and dependent little boy; Giulietta as the desired mistress of the grown man; Antonia as the personification of death which the old man is approaching" (159-60).

The method is, of course, almost identical to that used by Freud in his famous *The Theme of the Three Caskets,* yet no less productive, for as both Freud and Reik observe, the pattern commonly recurs in innumerable myths and tales, ancient and modern. The Master discovered in *The Merchant of Venice* and the Disciple in *The Tales of Hoffman* that

> Behind all these figures is originally a single one, just as in the triads of goddesses whom modern comparative history of religion has succeeded in tracing back to their prototype of one goddess. For all of us the mother is the woman of destiny. She is the *femme fatale* in its most literal sense, because she brought us into the world, she taught us to love, and it is she upon whom we call in our last hour. The mother as a death-dealing figure becomes alien to our conscious thinking. But she may become comprehensible in this function when death appears as the only release from suffering, as the one aim desired, the final peace (163).

Equally as astute is Reik's consideration of *Othello* in *The Psychology of Sex Relations.* Stimulated by a recent reading of a paper on the drama, Reik speculates that the author's thesis is incorrect—that *Othello* is not a tragedy of jealousy—and offers the play as corroboration of his own lifetime observation of the dynamics of jealousy. He proposes first his "provisional psychological results": that the individual's feelings of insecurity are perhaps the psychic origin of jealousy:

> Originally love is motivated by the dissatisfaction of a person with himself, conditioned by a sense of inner insecurity and awareness of failure in the attempt to fulfill certain demands arising from within. Love seems to fulfill these demands by the extension of a person's ego and by incorporating another ego, the love-object. Dissatisfaction disappears. The person is not only content with himself and others, but is definitely happy. . . . The certainty of loving and being loved sweeps away all personal insecurity. . . . Jealousy, [then,] marks the return of the original self-distrust after one has first attained security through love.[6]

These self-doubts, which usually remain unconscious, are expressed initially, says Reik, in "suspicions of one's own worth as evaluated by the love-object," and "can only become conscious in the form of doubt about the real love of one's object" (176). Reik underscores several points.

The suspicion is there before the rival appears on the scene. It is as if the person who wants to be jealous were in search of the man of whom to be jealous. His research is always successful. If no such rival exists, the doubter will create one in fantasy, and all his imaginings will point to the fact that the rival is preferred by the love-object. He then becomes a phantom-figure, so to speak, the personification of a thought-possibility, and a substitute for a better self. Disappointment in the love situation is unconsciously prepared for and a hundred times anticipated.

A real rival is missing, as is also proof of the love-object's infidelity. The existence of both, however, can be easily established by the doubter, either by misinterpretation of real facts or by the distorting power of imagination. The mind of the jealous person never tires of finding circumstantial evidence to confirm his suspicions. At all events, he seizes every opportunity to make certainties and convictions of doubts and suspicions. The second trait, belief in the object's unfaithfulness, cannot be easily shaken because its deepest roots are in self-doubt and in the lingering thought of one's own unworthiness transferred to the loved one (177).

That the foregoing describes almost exactly the psychological development of Othello is so obvious that Reik need not even prove it to the reader and he does not. He begins rather by demonstrating that Othello is indeed insecure, "a homeless foreigner of a despised race, without riches, no longer young, unlike and racially not considered the equal of the proud lords of [the] city" (176). Iago, then, as others have noticed, represents these unconscious thoughts and emotions and serves to give them voice, though "it is fairer to say that they made use of Iago than that Iago made use of Othello" (179). Othello's psychic problem is almost completely encapsulated in ten words of the drama: "and when I love thee not, Chaos is come again" (III, iii, 91-92).

Unfortunately, this is the only line of text which Reik cites in support of his interpretation. That others could be found goes without saying; in seeking the exact citation for the line, we came across this speech: "'Tis not to make me jealous To say my wife is fair, feeds well, loves company, Is free of speech, sings, plays, and dances well. Where virtue is, these are more virtuous. *Nor from mine own weak merits will I draw The smallest fear or doubt of her revolt, For she had eyes and chose me*" (III, iii, 183-89; italics ours). This deficiency of textual support, as has been noted, is endemic throughout Reik's literary analyses and is easily understood. A clinician first, Reik was not concerned with literary explication (though he is credited with the first psychoanalytic-literary doctoral dissertation, a study of Flaubert's *Temptation of Saint Anthony*); he was interested instead in demonstrating the universality of psychoanalytic principles as reflected in literature and their anticipation by the poets. It is significant, then, that he ends the Othello study by observing that La Rochefoucauld, as well as Shakespeare, knew the psychology of jealousy well, for he wrote in his *Maximes* that there is more self-love than love in jealousy. The often meagre textual support in Theodor Reik's literary studies is a small price to pay in exchange for the treasure of his thought.

Notes

1. Theodor Reik, *Sex in Man and Woman* (New York: Farrar, 1961), p. 34.
2. Reik, *Sex,* p. 122.
3. Theodor Reik, *The Search Within* (New York: Grove Press, 1956), pp. 331-49. Also available in *The Secret Self: Psychoanalytic Experiences in Life and Literature* (1952; reprinted, New York: Grove Press, 1960), pp. 11-32.
4. Reik, *The Search Within,* p. 433.
5. Theodor Reik, "The Three Women in a Man's Life," in William Phillips, ed., *Art and Psychoanalysis* (Cleveland: World, 1957), pp. 151-64.
6. Theodor Reik, *The Psychology of Sex Relations* (New York: Grove Press, 1961), p. 175. All subsequent references are to this edition.

Joseph Campbell

Joseph Campbell is, without a doubt, one of the foremost mythologists of our time, and his tetralogy, *The Masks of God,* stands a monument to his own scholarship and to the mythopoeic mind of man. There, in over 2500 pages, Professor Campbell exhaustively explores the dominant motifs of primitive, oriental, and occidental mythology—those myths by which man has made his experience intelligible to himself for thousands of years, and discusses in a final volume the "disintegration" of mythic tradition in this century.

Campbell's work is significant for the mythologist and the anthropologist and, in a certain sense, for the psychologist. Yet since it is at base an archetypal approach, it functions as a terminal point for the mythologist, but only as a starting point for the psychologist. Though Mark Schorer believes that all human activity has myth as its essential substructure, the psychologist realizes that myth does not exist apart from mind and thus seeks to determine the structure and dynamics of the mind that expresses the myth. It is unnecessary here to belabor the point beyond examining a few of Professor Campbell's conclusions to determine their validity and usefulness to the psychoanalytic critic. Consider, to begin with, his explanation of the source of creativity in artists:

. . . The shared secret of all the really great creative artists of the West
has been that of letting themselves be wakened by—and then recipro-
cally reawakening—the inexhaustibly suggestive mythological symbols
of our richly compound European heritage of intermixed traditions.
Avoiding, on the one hand, the popular mistake of reading mythology
as a reference to hard historic fact and, on the other hand, the puerility
of rejecting the guidance of the centuries and so drowning like a puppy
in the shallows of one's own first depth, they have passed, one and all,
beyond this general wrecking point of Scylla and Charybdis to that sun
door of which the knowers have sung through all ages, each in the
language of his own world. Having let their imaginations be roused by
the waking power of the symbols, they have followed the echoes of
their eloquence within—each opening thus a way of his own to the
world and its companionship, having learned from their own depths the
grammar of symbolic speech, they are competent to touch to new life
the museum of the past as well as the myths and dreams of their
present—in that way to bring (as in the closing chorus of Wagner's
Parsifal) "redemption to the Redeemer," causing the petrified, histori-
cized blood of the Savior to flow again as a fountain of spiritual life.[1]

Plangent prose, indeed, but like the Song of the Sirens, it lures with
its superficial beauty the unwary reader, inviting him to founder on the
reefs. One need not be lashed to the mast to prevent this however; one
need only examine the song more closely to see that, while the melody
is captivating, the lyrics are meaningless. The sentimental simile of the
drowning puppy aside, what is one to make of such unmoored abstractions as "letting themselves be wakened by," "sun door of which the
knowers have sung," "imaginations," "eloquence within," and "learned
from their own depths the grammar of symbolic speech"? As seman-
tically empty as they are psychologically irrelevant, they seem to be
useful only to prepare the reader for the flight into mysticism in the
final sentence, resulting in—to coin a phrase—"epiphany as criticism."
Shorn of its abstractions and value-judgment words, the passage says
simply that the artist, informed by archetypes, re-expresses them in his
own way, insuring their continuity through revivification. We are thus
merely returned to the archetype as prime source, the most tenuous of
all propositions with which to begin.

The superficiality of Campbell's archetypal criticism becomes all too
apparent when it is compared (odium intended) with a closely-reasoned
psychoanalytic interpretation of the same subject. For example, at one
point in his lengthy consideration of the tradition of courtly love which

arose in Europe in the middle of the twelfth century, Campbell clarifies what he believes the significance of this love to be, declaring that "the whole meaning of [the troubadours'] stanzas lay in the celebration of a love the aim of which was neither marriage nor the dissolution of the world. Nor was it even carnal intercourse; nor, again—as among the Sufis—the enjoyment, by analogy, of the 'wine' of a divine love and the quenching of the soul in God. The aim, rather, was life directly in the experience of love as a refining, sublimating, mystagogic force, of itself opening the pierced heart to the sad, sweet, bittersweet, poignant melody of being, through love's own anguish and love's joy" (178).

Not only do I defy the reader to understand that final sentence, I direct him to the interpretation of the same concept offered by Maurice Valency in one of several engrossing chapters of *In Praise of Love:* "The high degree of perfection projected by the lover upon the lady is the very condition of this love. . . . The lady, while he loves her, is for him really the loveliest and best of women, for it is in terms of his own self-love that he sees her, and we know what power to transfigure is in that. . . . The narcissistic nature of love is a commonplace of medieval literature."[2] The key words, of course, illuminating the dynamics of the situation, are *narcissistic* and *projected.* Campbell's interpretation lacks even the simple power of clear prose and uses the word *sublimating* without explaining it; Valency explains the concept without using the word:

. . . It is in the shifting of emphasis to these minute and delicate contacts that the troubadours may be said to have invented something new in the way of love-making. By the concentration of erotic attention upon tiny areas of behavior they were able to transform the forthright joy of physical union, quickly attained and soon forgotten, into a love affair of great duration adorned with a wealth of highly charged poetic detail. . . . The consequence was to transform the sexual pursuit from an athletic activity into a work of art requiring the greatest sensitivity and taste. Concomitantly, the hero became an artist and a gentleman. The art which he professed was called, appropriately, *cortesia* (28-29).

The difference between these two explications can not be simply attributed to Campbell's lack of knowledge of psychoanalysis, for he knows it and knows it well. It is rather that, when faced with the choice between Freud and Jung early in his career, he unfortunately opted for the latter. His earlier book-length study, *The Hero with a Thousand Faces,* shows his familiarity with Freudian concepts and his recognition of the family romance as the central motif of the heroic myth, an idea obviously derived from Otto Rank. He sets forth this recognition in prose equally as lucid and equally as psychoanalytically-informed as Valency's, but soon his propensity for Jung's ideas—and regrettably, Jung's prose style—becomes obvious and the reader soon flounders in a welter of abstract, mystical concepts: "In a word: the first work of the hero is to retreat from the world scene of secondary effects to those causal zones of the psyche where the difficulties really reside, and there to clarify the difficulties, eradicate them in his own case (i.e., give battle to the nursery demons of his local culture) and break through to the undistorted, direct experience and assimilation of what C. G. Jung has called 'the archetypal images!' "[3] In the remainder of the book, Campbell now and then pays lip service to Freudian tenets to lend a verisimilitude of scientific psychology to his statements, but soon passes over them, plunging again into Jungian spiritualism.

The Masks of God, to which we now return, shows the continuation of this descent into the mystical maelstrom, with Freud mentioned perhaps a dozen times, the name of Jung invoked repeatedly. In the final volume of this tetralogy, *Creative Mythology,* Campbell summarizes the socializing purpose of myth:

One of the chief concerns of the ritual lore of primitive and developed human groups, therefore, has always been that of guiding the child to the adult state. The infantile response system of dependency must be transformed to responsibility, and specifically in terms of the requirements of the local social order. The son has to become father, and the daughter, mother, passing from the sphere of childhood, which is everywhere essentially the same, to that of the variously offered social roles, which radically differ according to the modes of human life. The instincts have to be governed and matured in the interests both of the group and of the individual, and traditionally it has been the prime function of mythology to serve this social-psychological end. The individual is adapted to his group and the group to its environment, with a sense thereby of gratitude for the miracle of life" (674).

Though the prose is for once clear, the ideas it expresses are still superficial, no specific, concrete examples being supplied to illustrate them. In sharp contrast to this generalizing, others have been very specific in their study of the psychology of myth. Most recently, Jacob

Arlow's "Ego Psychology and the Study of Mythology"[4] provided a sturdy frame of reference for a psychoanalytic approach to myth. Arlow sees myth as a form of shared fantasy, communally acceptable, expressing wishes previously expressed only in guilt-laden privacy. The myth thus functions defensively, to ward off guilt and anxiety and adaptationally, to bring the individual into relationship with reality and the social group. In doing so, myth further helps to crystallize his identity and to form his superego. This concept of the myth as a special category of fantasy allows us to apply psychoanalytic insight about fantasies to the myth itself. Campbell, despite his awesome erudition, has been unable to supply an equally productive framework for the study of myth. We must be grateful to him for the resources he has provided by the breadth of his study, but it is certain that the depth study of myth will have as its bases not the Jungian theories of Joseph Campbell but rather those espoused by ego psychologists and elucidated so well by Jacob Arlow.

Notes

1. Joseph Campbell, *Creative Mythology* (New York: Viking, 1968), p. 94. All subsequent references are to this edition. This is the fourth volume of the tetralogy *The Masks of God;* the other three are *Primitive Mythology* (1959), *Oriental Mythology* (1962), and *Occidental Mythology* (1964).
2. Maurice Valency, *In Praise of Love* (New York: Macmillan, 1961), p. 26. All subsequent references are to this edition.
3. Joseph Campbell, *The Hero with a Thousand Faces* (1949; reprinted, Princeton: Princeton University Press, 1968), Bollingen Series XVII, pp. 17-18.
4. Jacob Arlow, "Ego Psychology and the Study of Mythology," *Journal of the American Psychoanalytic Association*, 9 (1961), pp. 371-93. See also, Martin S. Bergmann, "The Impact of Ego Psychology on the Study of Myth," *American Imago*, 23, No. 3 (1966), pp. 257-63; a detailed summary of a panel on this subject held in 1962.

F. L. Lucas

Probably the most scholarly and urbane book written on the relationship between literature and psychology is F. L. Lucas' *Literature and Psychology*.[1] Originally a series of lectures given at Cambridge University in the half dozen years after World War II, the essays have been rewritten, expanded, and integrated into a beautifully readable book meant to demonstrate how a knowledge of Freudian psychology can help the critic in his dual role of interpreter and judge. Professor Lucas, therefore divides his study into two parts, each of which deals with one of these functions of the critic.

He devotes his initial section to a large number of literary interpretations in which the use of psychoanalysis is almost entirely restricted to showing that indeed fact is stranger than fiction. For example, after calling attention to Lady Macbeth's sleepwalking scene in which she is obsessively concerned with the imagined blood on her hands, Lucas announces that such is not merely poetic fiction but actual human behavior as well. He then quotes an extensive autobiographical description of a compulsive handwasher from the case studies of Wilhelm Stekel, concluding that Shakespeare's work in its entirety gains from such verisimilitude to life.

He points out, too, that it is quite possible that Pentheus' moral suspicions in Euripides' *Bacchae* may have been justified, because a similar convulsive ecstasy among a Methodist sect in Kentucky and Pennsylvania in the nineteenth century had its natural consequences; "for three nights of such devotional exercises are said to have produced eighty illegitimate children within a radius of four miles" (127). The value of such analogues is obvious in that they strongly support arguments for the use of psychoanalysis in the understanding of literary characters. In addition, they may serve simply but powerfully to verify, to hold up the mirror to art, as it were; I myself had for years remained unconvinced of the ability of Richard III to woo and win Anne Glenville even as she walked in the funeral train of her murdered husband, until Lucas cited from Stekel a young man whose sole object of passion was recent widows and he prized most highly those he had won on the very day of the funeral! Most of Lucas' considerations of specific literary genres, figures, or periods—for example, legends, King Lear, Romanticism—consist of similar comparisons. He cites the opinions of previous critics and analogous clinical cases, then states his own position.

And his own position is sometimes different from Freud's: feeling that the crumbling of an ideal mother image has crushed Hamlet equally as much as, if not more than, the death of his father, he disagrees with the Freud-Jones interpretation and takes a position close to that of Frederic Wertham; he contends that Freud's interpretation of Lear in *The Theme of the Three Caskets* does not explain the contention between father and daughter (Freud never claimed it did) and cites copious instances of real life conflict; he disputes Freud's definition of wit and propounds one of his own, that wit always deals with the challenge of a riddle.

Although he never directly cites Freud and takes all of his clinical examples from Stekel, it is clear from these disagreements and from his oblique references to psychoanalytic principles throughout that Professor Lucas is well acquainted with a great many of Freud's writings. On occasion, but very rarely, he will employ this knowledge of tenets in original criticism, as when he asserts that Realism is related to dominance of the ego; Classicism, to dominance of the super-ego; and Romanticism, to dominance of the id, as demonstrated by its concern with the primitive, incest, the figure of the original rebel against the father-Satan, and by its narcissism and aggression (100-11). These strike us as sound and useful insights.

There is less overt application of psychoanalysis in the second section of the book which opens with a discussion that establishes the relativity of taste and then defines the "good" literary work—one which endures:

(1) Every work of art is different for every percipient, since the percipient's own faculties and associations must collaborate with the artist's work to produce the artistic impression.

(2) Therefore every percipient, cultivated and intelligent enough to give a work a fair trial, is his own—and only—judge how far it is artistically satisfying to him.

(3) The rank of writers can only be assigned on the basis of their power to go on pleasing intelligent readers in general (212).

This, of course, leads naturally to the qualities which make a literary work endure; Lucas believes that these are two, the ability to please, "its power to give us valued states of mind," and its ability to influence, "its power to induce future states of mind that are sometimes valuable, sometimes lamentably the reverse" (216).

Believing the latter power the more important, he discusses it in detail and contends finally that the ability to inculcate values is the ultimate criterion of good literature but, "all values are vain, unless we can feel, as well as see, their value. Knowledge without feeling is like an electric motor without current" (261).

Literature must thus move us, constrain us to *feel* that X is of value and Y is not. It must, as Sir Philip Sydney believed, improve men by adding emotional appeal to the finest of human qualities. Feeling at this point a little too didactic, Lucas asks what, then, should those values be? In reply to his own question he cites the results of several polls he took of his students who answered the query "What are your four chief desires?" Highest on the list was health, both physical and mental. This wish can be, and ought be, fulfilled by literature, he says, and in order to clarify the concept of mental health, he offers his own definition:

"To face reality, yet accept it; to learn from the past without repining; to use the present, without growing unnerved by its transience; to prepare the future, without being dismayed by its inscrutability; to get the best from the people, the experiences, the work that comes one's way; to be content to be forgotten when those who once loved one shall vanish in their turn . . . " (312).

Thus, if the writer is mentally healthy—and one might add, talented—he will conduct that health to the reader. Lucas' view of literature is thus a moral one, an ethical one, since one's mental health affects one's relations with oneself and to others. To criticize this theory in detail would take another book in itself. We wish only to point out its one major fault—oversimplification—and comment briefly upon certain aspects of the conclusion.

We do not agree, to begin with, that the meaning of a literary work lies in the reader; whatever meaning there is, is in the text and in it alone. To reach backward into the author's mind or forward into the reader's for meaning is to become enmeshed in a jungle of hypotheses, speculations, projections, and difficulties the likes and horrors of which Kurtz never conceived. But more importantly, it is to move, purely and simply, from literary criticism to psychology.

Further, Professor Lucas' contention that great literary works provide healthy values for absorption cannot possibly explain the appeal of Raskolnikov or Richard III. Closer to the truth, we suspect, is that a great deal of lasting literature provides us—in the words of one of the present writers—"respite from the burdens of our health," allows us, for example, to rid ourselves of hostility by murdering in fantasy a filthy old pawnbroker in St. Petersburg or by drowning a competitor in a tun of malmsey. Early in his book Professor Lucas called attention to the bad literary criticism done by psychoanalysts, adding that it would have been better had it been tempered by a bit of healthy skepticism. We feel a bit of that same skepticism would have helped Professor Lucas in his aesthetic theorizing. Yet the overall value of his book is not seriously impaired by its absence. He has written a learned, useful book. By phrasing psychoanalytic principles in layman's language, skillfully utilizing it in his criticism, and lending the weight of his august name to the result, Professor Lucas has made his contribution a signal one.

Notes

1. F. L. Lucas, *Literature and Psychology,* revised edition (1951; reprinted, Ann Arbor: University of Michigan Press, 1957). All subsequent references are to this edition.

Ernst Kris

"Earlier studies of creativity had in common a recognition of the fact that, although conscious processes played an important role in the final shaping of the form of the creative product, the roots of creativity lie in deeper and more obscure processes which work with a speed far greater than can be achieved by that fragment of our psychological processes of which we are conscious. In early days the importance of the unconscious derivation and shaping of the neurotic process was still a fresh and astonishing discovery. Therefore it was natural to assume that it must also be the source of the creative drive and of the great creative inspiration in human life."[1]

The first tentative steps away from this excessive concern with the role of the unconscious in creativity were taken by Hanns Sachs in *The Creative Unconscious*. Greater strides were made in the next decade as a result of the publications of Ernst Kris, one of the earliest ego psychoanalysts, especially in his most important contribution, *Psychoanalytic Explorations in Art*. Kris's meticulous studies of the preconscious processes—which range widely through literature, painting, and sculpture, considering not only literary criticism but also the art of the insane and the psychology of the comic—made it impossible ever afterward to seriously attribute creativity to the power of the unconscious or to equate the artist with the neurotic.

Kris surveys first the contributions of psychoanalysis to art and its limitations in discussing art, then briefly considers the desirability of utilizing the psychologies of Jung and Rank to analyze artistic processes and products. These systems he dismisses as useless for this purpose because they are both simplistic and closed. In contrast to them, Freudian psychology provides the best method for validating the theories he is about to set forth since, he maintains, it alone offers the best opportunity to understand and predict human behavior. An open system, it has been constructed by synchronizing hypotheses formulated over the entire span of the development of psychoanalysis and has been constantly amplified and emended.

At this point, Kris takes up the more recent development of ego psychology and its application to art. He traces its origin back to several early works of Freud devoted to the interaction of the ego and the id and then shows how it forms the basis of his own theories:

The relationship of the ego to the id encompasses not only the question of the extent to which id strivings are being satisfied or warded off or the compromises that are achieved. It also encompasses the relationship of primary to secondary processes; but the relationship familiar in dream work is reversed: We are justified in speaking of the ego's control of the primary process as a particular extension of its functions. What in the dream appears as compromise and is explained in terms of overdetermination appears in the work of art as multiplicity of meaning, which stimulates differentiated types of response in the audience. The fruitfulness of these points of view in the progress of modern criticism and the theory of art has been considerable. . . . At the same time it offers an access to that complex field which we mean when we speak of the psychology of *the* artist.[2]

Kris's starting point in the understanding of the psychology of the artist is, like that of Sachs, the daydream. Virtually restating Sachs's concept of the socialization of the daydream (the transformation of the individual's fantasy to one shared by the community), he likewise concludes that unconscious self-criticism, the force of the superego, is kept in abeyance by the approval of an audience. The illicit becomes licit by sharing it with others. He goes beyond Sachs, however, in positing that the shared fantasy may have in addition other motivations and functions; it may well be part of the repetition-compulsion. As a means of gaining control over repressed traumatic influences, it provides enjoyment through the reproduction, with variations, of the

pleasant experience of victory. This serves as a way of making contact
with others through sharing of the experience. The socialization of the
daydream, consequently, places the artist in an unique position:

> At this stage the artist assumes a position of leadership. His message,
> the work of art, is not a call to common action—which is the nature of
> propaganda—nor a call to common spiritual experience, linking com-
> municator and audience to an ideal to which both submit—which is the
> function of the priest; nor does the artist teach his public in order to
> widen its insight. All this he may do. At any given time all or some of
> the arts may be more or less closely linked to the call to action or be
> part of religious or secular teaching. While some such links exist of
> necessity at all times, the specific meaning in which the word "art" is
> used in our civilization refers to another function: The message is an
> invitation to common experience in the mind, to an experience of a
> specific nature (39).

It is important to note that throughout his study, Kris continually
emphasizes the function of the ego, in accordance with the advances
made in ego analysis. Thus Aristotle's catharsis is no longer seen as
release of id impulses, pure and simple, purgative and curative, but
rather as a more complex phenomenon when viewed in the light of new
knowledge of the ego functions:

> . . . We are no longer satisfied with the notion that repressed emotions
> lose their hold over our mental life when an outlet for them has been
> found. We believe rather that what Aristotle describes as the purging
> enables the ego to re-establish the control which is threatened by
> dammed-up instinctual demands. The search for outlets acts as an aid to
> assuring or re-establishing this control, and the pleasure is a double one,
> in both discharge and control. The maintenance of the aesthetic illusion
> promises the safety to which we were aspiring and guarantees freedom
> from guilt, since it is not our own fantasy we follow. It stimulates the
> rise of feelings which we might otherwise be hesitant to permit our-
> selves, since they lead to our own reaction which, without this protec-
> tion, many individuals are unwilling to admit to themselves; with many,
> we know, this is due to educational pressures, which under certain
> cultural conditions have generally devalued high intensity of emotional
> display except in regulated and institutionalized channels: Art offers
> such socially approved occasions (46).

Further, inspiration is not, says Kris, Plato's "divine madness," but,
since the ego is controlling and utilizing the primary process, is rather

to be contrasted with madness or psychosis, where the ego is overwhelmed by the primary process. Kris insists repeatedly upon the
importance of the idea of the public in artistic creation, believing that
the former must precede the latter. He sees the response as essential to
confirm the artist's own belief in his work and to restore the balance
which the process of creativity may have disturbed.

Continuing to elaborate on the functions of the ego, Kris shows how
its control explains the fascination which the artistic process often has
for the creator:

The shifts in cathexis of mental energy which the work of art elicits or
facilitates are, we believe, pleasurable in themselves. From the release of
passion under the protection of the aesthetic illusion to the highly
complex process of re-creation under the artist's guidance, a series of
processes of psychic discharge take place, which could be differentiated
from each other by the varieties and degrees of neutralization of the
energy discharged. All these processes, however, are controlled by the
ego, and the degree of completeness of neutralization indicates the
degree of ego autonomy.

In assuming that the control of the ego over the discharge of energy
is pleasurable in itself, we adopted one of the earliest, and frequently
neglected, thoughts of Freud in this area: the suggestion that under
certain conditions man may attempt to gain pleasure from the very
activity of the psychic apparatus (63).

In developing his theses, Kris devotes a major portion of his study to
the artistic creations of—perhaps surprising to the layman—the mentally
ill. As Kubie was to point out in later years, however, "we learn most
from that which is furthest from the norm. We learn from the autopsy
table the lessons that ultimately make it possible to prevent the disease
which produced the death. So we learn from the extremes of illness the
lessons which illuminate and ultimately safeguard the normal. This has
been true in physiology; and it is proving to be true in psychology."[3] In
addition to three lengthy chapters on the art of the insane and four on
the psychology of the comic, *Psychoanalytic Explorations* contains one
essay in literary criticism and it is to that which we now turn, leaving
the reader to pursue further Kris's work in the book itself or in Louis
Fraiberg's excellent critique of them.[4]

Kris opens "Prince Hal's Conflict" by enumerating the three inconsistencies in the character of Hal: his possible hypocrisy in announcing

beforehand his intention to reform, yet continuing to act truant from the court; his protracted, repeated reformation; and his merciless severity in dealing with his former companions, particularly Falstaff. After discussing the historical justifications for each of these, Kris turns for a solution to psychoanalysis. Citing previous studies, particularly Alexander's "Note on Falstaff," he builds on the latter's concept of Hotspur as Hal's double, an open rebel representing Hal's unconscious parricidal impulses. He sees Hal as sharing his impulse with his own father who had gained the throne by regicide. "The Prince," Kris says, "tries to dissociate himself from the crime his father had committed; he avoids contamination with regicide because the impulse to regicide (parricide) is alive in his unconscious. When the King's life is threatened, he saves the King and kills the adversary who is his alter ego. In shunning the court for the tavern he expresses his hostility to his father and escapes the temptation to parricide. He can permit himself to share Falstaff's vices because he does not condone the King's crime; but hostility to the father is only temporarily repressed. When finally he is in possession of the crown, he turns against the father substitute; hence the pointed cruelty of Falstaff's rejection" (282). Thus in one fell swoop are the three inconsistencies seen to be perfectly consistent, psychologically. And the reader should note that Kris here emphasizes the ego functions—for example, the defense mechanism of Hal's displacement of hostility onto Falstaff—and not the id impulses in his explication of Hal's character.

Kris matches the perceptions of this essay again and again throughout the many essays which comprise this volume. And each essay is built around the central idea of ego strength. For ego psychology, in exploring the creative mental processes, has shown over and over that the artist is not a man being driven, but rather a man driving. Utilizing his "flexibility of repression," he successfully courts dangerous unconscious material, controls it, and exploits it to fullest advantage. In *Psychoanalytic Explorations in Art,* Ernst Kris amply proves this, further substantiating Freud's dictum "Where Id is, there shall Ego be," and contributing to literature the most important book on the psychoanalytic approach to aesthetics since Freud himself.

Notes

1. Lawrence S. Kubie, *Neurotic Distortion of the Creative Process* (1958; reprinted, New York: Noonday Press, 1968), p. 47.

2. Ernst Kris, *Psychoanalytic Explorations in Art* (1952; reprinted, New York: Schocken, 1964), p. 25. All subsequent references are to this edition.
3. Kubie, *Distortion*, p. 65.
4. Louis Fraiberg, *Psychoanalysis and American Literary Criticism* (Detroit: Wayne State University Press, 1960), pp. 90-119.

Simon O. Lesser

The purpose of Simon O. Lesser's *Fiction and the Unconscious* is, in his own words, "to identify the more or less pandemic and immutable needs which lead men to read fiction and the more or less universal attributes of fiction which enable it to satisfy those needs."[1] The degree to which he succeeds in this enormous task is admirable, so much so that the book has become a minor classic in psychoanalytic literary criticism. Professor Lesser begins by analyzing the needs impelling us to read fiction, then considers some of the subject matter and formal characteristics of fiction that enable us to satisfy these needs, follows this with an examination of the conscious and unconscious processes involved in the response to fiction, analyzes two short stories to demonstrate unconscious response and, finally, considers that which we call the esthetic response. He does all of this in lucid prose, free from what Theodor Reik has dubbed "Psychoanalese," and rewards the layman as well as the psychoanalytically-informed reader.

Using as his starting point Freud's observation that the little satisfaction man can squeeze from reality still leaves him starving, Lesser considers at length the desperate condition of being human. In prose so moving as to be poetic, he itemizes the innumerable conflicts, frustrations, inhibitions, and disappointments attendant upon merely being a man in society, concluding that "that list is endless. Culture in general

seems indifferent if not hostile to the goal of individual happiness"
(31). Accordingly,

> It is to make good some of the deficiencies of experience that people
> read fiction. A perfectly satisfied person, Freud declares, would not
> daydream. Nor would a perfectly satisfied person feel any compelling
> need to read stories. We read because we are beset by anxieties, guilt
> feeling and ungratified needs. The reading of fiction permits us, in
> indirect fashion, to satisfy those needs, relieve our anxieties and assuage
> our guilt. It transports us to a realm more comprehensible and co-
> herent, more passionate and more plastic, and at the same time more
> compatible with our ideals, than the world of our daily routine, thus
> providing a kind of experience which is qualitatively superior to that
> which we can ordinarily obtain from life (39).

Because many of these·needs are repressed, says Lesser, the reader
would not be able to satisfy them simply through fiction since their
being repressed in the first place indicates that they are repugnant or
dangerous to the reader, who would react with distaste to their expression in fiction. Consequently, "repressed tendencies can only secure
expression when they are sufficiently disguised so that their connection
with a repudiated impulse is not perceived by the censorious ego and
when they do not threaten to lead to action. Great fiction can easily
satisfy these conditions" (42). The reader might recognize here Freud's
ideas as he elaborated them in *Creative Writers and Day-Dreaming.*

After pointing out that disguise alone is not a guarantee of pleasure
since a concomitant of disguise must be relative freedom from anxiety
or instinctual impulse which insures relaxation of the ego, Lesser
examines the characteristics of fiction, the most essential of which is
conflict. He believes we take pleasure in our own conflicts as reflected
in fiction because in it they are aired more thoroughly and because
fiction "strives for resolutions based upon maximum fulfillment, rather
than the illusory kind achieved by denying or slighting certain
claims . . . " (79). This is the core of our response to fiction. Expressed
psychoanalytically, the dynamics of the resolution are simple. " . . . We
can readily reconstruct the nature of the intra-psychic interchange
which the attitude of fiction stimulates: it is a kind of confession based
upon acceptance and love. The ego withholds nothing and it asks for
nothing, neither for extenuation of punishment nor even for forgiveness. The superego voluntarily gives the ego something it evidently

values even more than these, understanding and the assurance of continued love" (92).

Exploring wish-fulfillment as it is reflected in fiction, Lesser demonstrates that we often overlook its presence since the wishes that are fulfilled are themselves disguised and rightly so, for "the truth is that we regard as great only that fiction which provides us with a lavish amount of emotional gratification, which satisfies our deepest and most primitive longings. The greatest narrative works deal with what might be called sacred crimes, transgressions of the tabus on which human society is founded; they deal with incest and parricide, cruelty of parents to children and children to parents, ruthless ambition and murder, betrayals and lust" (107). Given such repugnant subject matter then, it is obvious that disguises or defenses provided by form and language are necessary if fiction is to be read with pleasure. Consequently, Lesser details in several chapters the functions of form and language in fiction, the most important of which is control of response, allowing maximal satisfaction with minimal mobilization of anxiety. (We ourselves might point out here how, in the most famous work of literature in which the interdicted crimes of incest and parricide are most evident, *Oedipus Rex,* form works to conceal the horror, revealing through "flashbacks" only as much of it at a time as Oedipus is able to cope with.)

Lesser caps his lengthy discussion of fiction and the unconscious with analyses of Sherwood Anderson's "I Want to Know Why" and Nathaniel Hawthorne's "My Kinsman, Major Molineux," both of which are exemplary psychoanalytic interpretations. He begins his analysis of "My Kinsman," for example, by showing that the tale generally resists analysis. Few critics can explain Robin's untoward response to his kinsman's plight and, more importantly, none can explain why the tale should continue to interest generation after generation. Lesser's explanation is that the tale says one thing to the conscious mind and another, quite different thing, to the unconscious mind.

To begin with, says Lesser, Robin is never really as intent as he seems to be on finding his kinsman: he forgets to ask the ferryman where his uncle lives (the psychopathology of everyday colonial life), he wanders about town instead of proceeding directly, he strays into the meanest part of town and has an encounter with the prostitute immediately after resolving to search more diligently for the illustrious Major Molineux. Citing this and other evidence throughout the text, Lesser asserts that Robin does not want to find his kinsman (and doesn't know he doesn't) because the Major, a father figure, represents restraint and unwelcome authority to the adolescent, and that the crowd at the end acts out Robin's repressed impulses toward such figures and successfully invites him to join them in open derision, freeing him to begin life as an adult.

This brief critique, of course, cannot do justice to Professor Lesser's argument—one of the classics of psychoanalytic criticism as its continued appearance in anthologies clearly shows.[2] His analysis lucidly explains Robin's actions and simultaneously explains the appeal of the tale. We like it because we are Robin, or have been, having at one time had to leave our kinsmen and strike out on our own to mature. We identify with Robin, or as Lesser would say, "analogize." Analogizing is "the creation of stories parallel to the ones we read in which we play a part" (200). For example, as he tells us in a different essay and a different context, when reading Kafka's *The Trial* we find that "the causes of K.'s guilt are only faintly indicated, [and] we tend to supply the explanation for it out of our own knowledge and experience. We fill in the blank spaces with reminiscences of the things which cause us guilt; we evoke our own conflicts, our own 'trial.' "[3] We leave the choice between "identify" and "analogize" to the reader.

Lesser's analysis of *The Trial* is another fine piece of criticism. We urge the reader to seek it out as well as other of his shorter pieces such as that on *The Idiot*.[4] All of his essays are exemplary; moreso the regret we feel that he has never devoted himself to a full-length study of, for example, one particular author's work.

Regrettable as well is that the reputation of one of the essays he is best-known for, is not so deserving as it may seem. *"Oedipus the King: The Two Dramas, the Two Conflicts,"* written in his matchless prose, reached a wide readership when it appeared in *College English* in 1967.[5] In addition to reaching scholars, it apparently affected them, if one is to judge from the continuous references to it in psychoanalytic literary criticism. And yet it is possibly the least original of all his excellent essays, for most of the major insights in it were detailed carefully by one of the present writers in "Dream at Thebes" six years earlier.[6]

"The Two Dramas" proposes that, in addition to the foreground drama of *Oedipus Rex* there is one in the background which is "composed of what is repressed and wins its way to the light despite and against resistance" (175). "Dream" has as its thesis Oedipus' repressed knowledge of his own incestuous desires and parricidal motives which, against his own resistance, come to light with terrifying consequences. "The Two Dramas" provides as evidence (a) Oedipus' resistance being shown by his shifting his intention from discovering the murderer to determining if he is base-born (178), (b) slips of the tongue by which Oedipus betrays that he "knows" there is one murderer and not many (180-81), (c) Oedipus' seeming resistance to Teiresias' accusations, which turn out to have been perfectly understood "unconsciously" (181-82), (d) Oedipus' accusations against Teiresias and Creon as projections of his own guilty feelings (182), and (e) Oedipus' resistance exemplified by his inability to see the obvious connection between the two fateful prophecies (184-85).

These insights, evidence of the repressed finally emerging, form the core of Lesser's essay. Derived from close textual analysis, they are significant and brilliant, but appeared for the first time in "Dream at Thebes," on, respectively, pages 18, 14, 15, 16, and 17. Other parallels we need not detail. It is true that Lesser adds much original textual evidence himself and equally as true that in a footnote he credits "Dream" in a general way for "groundbreaking," but only after he has presented three-fourths of his essay. Justice might have been better served if he had been more specific in citing the origin of some of the ideas which form the largest and most vital portion of his now-famous paper.

Professor Lesser's overall accomplishments are significant, but they must be placed in proper perspective. Few of the basic ideas in *Fiction and the Unconscious* originated with him. From Freud's *Creative Writers and Day-Dreaming*, Hanns Sachs's *The Creative Unconscious*, and Ernst Kris's *Psychoanalytic Explorations in Art*, the concepts of the shared wish-fulfilling fantasy, the necessity of disguise through form and language, for example, have long been familiar to the student and practitioner of psychoanalytic criticism. Lesser's contributions in this volume lie in his lucid elaborations of these basic concepts, the additional examples he provides, and the many astute, original observations he makes, all in nontechnical language. Through this admirable popularization, Lesser has disseminated many of the fundamental ideas of psychoanalytic criticism and immensely influenced countless students of literature.

In addition to this, *Fiction and the Unconscious* contributed greatly to shifting the emphasis in psychoanalytic criticism from the text to the reader, a shift which one of the most prolific of the critics, Norman Holland, has carried to its utmost in his latest attempts to construct a theory of literary response.

Notes

1. Simon O. Lesser, *Fiction and the Unconscious* (1957; reprinted, New York: Vintage Books, 1962), p. 12. All subsequent references are to this edition.
2. This interpretation has survived both the test of time and the onslaught of Roy Harvey Pearce's "Robin Molineux on the Couch: A Note on the Limits of Psychoanalytic Criticism," *Criticism*, 1, No. 2 (1959), pp. 83-90. This essay is reprinted in Irving Malin, ed., *Psychoanalysis and American Fiction* (New York: Dutton, 1965), pp. 309-16. Pearce, while criticizing Lesser for ignoring the conscious determinants in the tale, curiously proceeds to ignore the unconscious determinants; Lesser says *both* are there; Pearce seems to say *either-or.* Interpretations in accord with Lesser's are Hyatt H. Waggoner, *Hawthorne: A Critical Study,* revised edition (1955; Cambridge, Mass., 1963), pp. 56-64; Franklin B. Newman," 'My Kinsman, Major Molineux': An Interpretation," *University of Kansas City Review,* 21 (1955), pp. 203-12; Louis Paul, "A Psychoanalytic Reading of Hawthorne's 'Major Molineux': The Father Manqué and the Protégé Manqué," *American Imago,* 18 (1961), pp. 279-88; Frederick C. Crews, *The Sins of the Fathers: Hawthorne's Psychological Themes* (New York: Oxford University Press, 1966), pp. 72-79.
3. "The Source of Guilt and the Sense of Guilt," in Hendrik Ruitenbeek, ed., *Psychoanalysis and Literature* (New York: Dutton, 1964), p. 190.
4. "Saint and Sinner—Dostoevsky's *Idiot,*" in Leonard and Eleanor Manheim, eds., *Hidden Patterns* (New York: Macmillan, 1966), pp. 132-50.
5. Simon O. Lesser, "*Oedipus the King*: The Two Dramas, The Two Conflicts," *College English,* 29, No. 3 (December, 1967), pp. 175-97. All subsequent references are to this article.
6. Morton Kaplan, "Dream at Thebes," *Literature and Psychology,* 11, No. 1 (1961), pp. 12-19. All subsequent references are to this article.

Leon Edel

Often a major critic will utilize psychoanalysis competently and fruit-fully without being totally committed to it. Such is the case with Leon Edel. Probably his best and best-known essay demonstrating this is "Willa Cather and *The Professor's House.*"[1] Originally an address, the essay was later printed in *Literature and Psychology* and finally in greatly expanded form became a chapter entitled "Psychoanalysis" in Professor Edel's *Literary Biography.*[2] The chapter is beautifully orga-nized. In the first two of its seven sections, it explains, criticizes, and justifies the use of psychoanalysis. The third part summarizes the plot of Miss Cather's novel, the fourth and fifth parts analyze it, the sixth explains specifically how one's understanding and appreciation have been enriched by the use of psychoanalysis, and the final section relates events in Miss Cather's life to her tale, discussing particularly the symbol of the house, and explaining why the novel is, in a sense, incomplete.

Professor Edel proves that the novel does not consist, as is usually believed, of two inconclusive fragments, one telling us of an aging university teacher who clings desperately to his old attic study in a house he has rented for thirty years; the other relating the adventures of Tom Outland, one of the teacher's former students who discovers a cliff dwellers' village in New Mexico. Rather, says Edel, both men have

in common the desire to cling to a womb-like existence, to possess the
mother totally once more, to recreate the narcissistic-infantile paradise.
Professor Edel's analysis, of course, is much more complex than this
and extends into Miss Cather's life itself, relating the novel to her
sojourn in Pittsburgh and her relationship with her closest friend,
Isabelle McClung Hombourg.

Edel writes with such clarity, such authority, and such perspective
on both literature and psychology that one is aware at every moment
that indeed psychoanalysis has a great deal to contribute to the understanding of both the lives and literature of writers and at every moment
Edel shows exactly how. In addition to this essay, we recommend
others of his as well: "Hawthorne's Symbolism and Psychoanalysis,"
"The Biographer and Psychoanalysis," "Notes on the Use of Psychological Tools in Literary Analysis," and "Literature and Biography."[3]

Notes

1. Leon Edel, "Willa Cather and *The Professor's House*," in Irving
   Malin, ed., *Psychoanalysis and American Fiction* (New York:
   E. P. Dutton, 1965), pp. 199-221.
2. Leon Edel, *Literature and Psychology*, 8, No. 4 (1958), p. 54f;
   Literary Biography (Toronto: The University of Toronto Press,
   1957), pp. 56-80.
3. Leon Edel, "Hawthorne's Symbolism and Psychoanalysis," in
   Leonard and Eleanor Manheim, eds., *Hidden Patterns* (New York:
   Macmillan, 1966), pp. 93-111; "The Biographer and Psycho-
   analysis," in *International Journal of Psychoanalysis*, 42, (1961),
   pp. 458-66; "Literature and Biography," in James Thorpe, ed.,
   *Relations of Literary Study: Essays on Interdisciplinary Contribu-
   tions* (New York: Modern Language Association, 1967), pp. 57-72.
   See especially pp. 60-65.

Leslie Fiedler

It is time to lay to rest the illusion that Leslie Fiedler is a psycho-analytic critic. He is not. It is difficult, even, to call him a psychological critic, for psychologists, as behavioral scientists, are more careful about theorizing from observed data than is Fiedler in his explorations. A curious admixture of acute perceptiveness, Jungian concepts, and mis-understood and misapplied Freudian principles and terminology, a number of his major essays and larger critical works have entranced the reading public for several decades. It is past time to separate the dross from the precious stuff.

"Archetype and Signature," an early essay which encourages the use of psychology in literary criticism, provides a convenient point of embarkation. Fiedler there declares that the key to analyzing the poem is "symbolics" and that the poem itself is a combination of what he calls *archetype* and *signature:*

> The word Archetype is the more familiar of my terms; I use it instead of the word "myth," which I have employed in the past but which becomes increasingly ambiguous, to mean any of the immemorial patterns of response to the human situation in its most permanent aspects: death, love, the biological family, the relationship with the Unknown, etc., whether those patterns be considered to reside in the Jungian Collective Unconscious or the Platonic world of Ideas. The

archetypal belongs to the infra- or meta-personal, to what Freudians
call the Id or the Unconscious; that is, it belongs to the Community at
its deepest, preconscious levels of acceptance.

I use Signature to mean the sum total of individuating factors in a
work, the sign of the Persona or Personality, through which an Archetype is rendered, and which itself tends to become a subject as well as a
means of the poem. Literature, properly speaking, can be said to come
into existence at the moment a Signature is imposed upon the Archetype.[1]

The dangers of reification aside, one would have to go a long way to
find a paragraph more misleading in its use of psychological terminology than the above. Even were we to grant the existence of the
highly-dubious entities called archetypes (since they are not subject to
empirical verification, they are certainly a safe basis for a critical
theory), Carl G. Jung himself would balk at their being equated with
Plato's Ideas.[2] Infinitely worse, however, is the final sentence of the
first paragraph, with its implications and its total confusion of fundamental Freudian terminology and concepts. The implications are that
Freudians accept this outré concept of the Jungian archetype (they do
not), that they believe, like Jungians, in a Communal Unconscious
(they do not), and that structural and topographical concepts are
interchangeable (they are not). The id, though it is primarily unconscious, is not equivalent to the Unconscious (portions of the ego and
the superego as well are unconscious), and that which is unconscious
cannot also be preconscious, as Fiedler states. Such abuse of basics
obviously indicates that we are not dealing with a psychological critic,
while preference for concepts such as "archetype" and "persona" reveal
a Jungian.

Indeed, Fiedler's preference for Jung is announced at the end of the
essay when he enjoins that "to understand the Archetypes of Athenian
drama, [the critic] needs (above and beyond semantics) anthropology;
to understand those of recent poetry, he needs (beyond 'close analysis')
depth analysis, as defined by Freud and, particularly, by Jung" (472).
Since we have elsewhere criticized the Jungian approach in general, we
shall turn here to specific objections to Fiedler's work. "Come Back to
the Raft Ag'in, Huck Honey!" offers ample opportunity. As is now
well-known, using *Huckleberry Finn* as his focus and adducing the
additional evidence of several other early American novels, Fiedler
contends that these works "Proffer a chaste male love as the ultimate

emotional experience. . . . "[3] Citing the relationships between Ishmael and Queequeq, Huck and Nigger Jim, Natty Bumppo and numerous Indians, he concludes that these works celebrate an undeniable archetype, "the mutual love of *a white man and a colored*": "So buried at a level of acceptance which does not touch reason, so desperately repressed from overt recognition, so contrary to what is usually thought of as our ultimate level of taboo—the sense of that love can survive only in the obliquity of symbol, persistent, obsessive, in short, an archetype: the boy's homoerotic crush, the love of the black fused at this level into a single thing" (125).

Fiedler's generalities do not merely glitter; they bedazzle. To discern a pattern is one thing; to deduce an archetype from it quite another. He himself states, "I do not recall ever having seen in the commentaries of the social anthropologist or psychologist an awareness of the role of this profound child's dream of love in our relation to the Negro" (126). That the reason might be that there is no such archetype does not seem to occur to him. But since archetypes provide a convenient means by which to avoid explaining the psychodynamic origins of observed behavior, such an omission may be understandable.

Fiedler avoids, in addition, other matters: is this homoerotism definitely present (he offers scant textual evidence in each instance)? What, if anything, is its significance? What is its origin? How does this help us to understand the text? We are not told. We hear, finally, only that "behind the white American's nightmare that someday, no longer tourist, inheritor, or liberator, he will be rejected, refused, he dreams of his acceptance at the breast he has most utterly offended. It is a dream so sentimental, so outrageous, so desperate, that it redeems our concept of boyhood from nostalgia to tragedy" (129). Nice sentiments, but no longer either psychology or literary criticism. This is armchair philosophy, capable of being practiced by anyone. One can, after all, feel racial guilt without the aid of archetypes and without having to read a 700-page novel about whales to induce it.

Love and Death in the American Novel[4] is this same *schtick* expanded until it has become *kitsch*. To the thesis of "Come Back to the Raft," Fiedler has added the element of incest and once again concocted a heady mixture of brilliant insight, reification by Capital Letters (or, as we should like to call it, *Archetypewriting*), and abuse of psychoanalytic concepts. One of Professor Fiedler's problems is that he cannot leave well enough alone. For instance, after reaching the probably valid conclusion that incest is the key to gothic horror,[5] Fiedler exclaims

... Incest of brother and sister—daughter bred out of an original incest of mother and son—the breach of the primal taboo and the offense against the father! In more general terms, the guilt which underlies the gothic and motivates its plots is the guilt of the revolutionary haunted by the (paternal) past which he has been striving to destroy; and the fear that possesses the gothic and motivates its tone is the fear that in destroying the old ego-ideals of Church and State, the West has opened a way for the irruption of darkness: for insanity and the disintegration of the self (115).

From the reasonably concrete conclusion about a dynamic of the gothic novel, we are rushed off into clouds of cultural history so abstract as to almost defy interpretation. Among the absurdities that we are asked to believe, seemingly, are that all revolutionaries are driven by infantile fears of incest and that fear motivated an entire hemisphere in its actions.

Grandiose conclusions, often expressed in Jung's prose style, abound in this work: in his consideration of James Fenimore Cooper's use of the Indian, Fiedler at one point calls the Noble Savage a symbol for the "offended id" (188). Earlier, however, he had noted that "the Indian represents to Cooper whatever in the American psyche has been starved to death, whatever genteel Anglo-Saxondom has most ferociously repressed, whatever he himself had stifled to be worthy of his wife and daughter; but the Indian also stands for himself . . . " (185). Apparently, as with a Chinese menu, a person can choose one from Column A and two from Column B, filling up on whatever in this scholarly Chow Mein happens to please him most. Indeed, we are sure that Fiedler considers this a virtue of his work; any reader offered so many conclusions—and their number is overwhelming—expressed in such sweeping abstract terms, is bound to be pleased with something somewhere or at the very least be awed by the magnitude on all sides.

The worst criticism to be made, of course, is that such pretentiousness masquerading as psychological criticism is destructive of valid psychological criticism itself. Professor Fiedler's disservice to the discipline in this respect cannot be overemphasized. This is not to say that there is not virtue in his criticism in general. The precious metal is there, but it has to be separated from the fool's gold.

Despite his acknowledgement in the preface that he has treated his psychological borrowings "cavalierly," Fiedler seems surprised and not a little unhappy about the way in which people have misunderstood him, as in his protestation that " 'homoerotic' is a word of which I was never fond, and which I like even less now. But I wanted it to be quite clear that I was not attributing sodomy to certain literary characters or their authors, and so I avoided when I could the more disturbing word 'homosexual.' All my care has done little good, however, since what I have to say on this score has been at one the best remembered and most grossly misunderstood section of my book. *Ubi morbus, ibi digitus*" (349 n.). If Professor Fiedler has been misunderstood, he has nobody to blame but himself. Less dense prose, more precise use of psychological concepts and terminology, and more specific examples would have greatly increased the clarity. Never has so little been so misunderstood by so many.

Notes

1. Leslie Fiedler, "Archetype and Signature," in William Phillips, ed., *Art and Psychoanalysis* (New York: Criterion Books, 1957), p. 462. All subsequent references are to this article.
2. See Jolande Jacobi, *The Psychology of C. G. Jung* (New Haven: Yale University Press, 1962), p. 42.
3. Leslie Fiedler, "Come Back to the Raft Ag'in, Huck Honey!," in Irving Malin, ed., *Psychoanalysis and American Fiction*, p. 123. All subsequent references are to this article.
4. Leslie Fiedler, *Love and Death in the American Novel*, revised edition (1960; reprinted, New York: Dell, 1969). All subsequent references are to this edition.
5. For a more thorough exploration of the element of incest in the gothic novel, see Morton Kaplan, "Iris Murdoch and the Gothic Tradition," Columbia University dissertation, 1969.

Louis Fraiberg

Louis Fraiberg's intention in *Psychoanalysis and American Literary Criticism* is to trace the adventures of psychoanalytic ideas during the two phases of psychoanalysis of which the public was aware—those of the id and the ego, summarize the results, and consider the contributions the disciplines of literature and psychology can make each to the other.

Professor Fraiberg, consequently, divides his book into two equal parts. In the first, he offers precis of the contributions of Freud, Jones, Sachs, and Kris to the understanding of art. In the second, he examines closely the work of six major American critics who have used psychoanalysis in their writings—Brooks, Krutch, Lewisohn, Wilson, Burke, and Trilling. The first part provides the apparatus by which the critics of the second part are judged.

Fraiberg's discussion of the four analysts' contributions is not very deep, depth being neither necessary nor desirable for the scope and purpose of his study. His examination and evaluation of the critics and their works, however, is thorough and incisive. He knows well both his literature and his psychoanalysis and he knows well when the latter is being used to abuse the former. Because it provides reliable evaluations of major American criticism informed by depth psychology, Fraiberg's study is a most valuable contribution.

He is eminently fair in his assessments of the critics and sets down their virtues as well as their deficiencies. From his vantage point, he ultimately finds each of them guilty, in some way, to some degree, of faulty application of psychoanalysis, for "each fell victim, at least part of the time, to similar misconceptions and encountered similar difficulties, difficulties which grew not out of the idiosyncracies of their critical positions but out of their simple human reactions to psychoanalysis."[1]

These difficulties had three causes which distorted the critics' view of psychoanalysis. First, says Fraiberg, they appeared unaware of the vast body of psychoanalytic literature produced by Freud and his adherents and, as a result, they placed most emphasis on the few principles which they felt most sure of, thus overemphasizing them while neglecting others equally as or more important. Second, their assumption that psychoanalysis was a closed system rather than a process constantly undergoing re-examination and redefinition led them to see the psychoanalytic literature they did know as definitive rather than temporary. Third, in many instances, they were unable to comprehend the meaning of the psychoanalytic material with which they were familiar, for example, sometimes believing it to mean the opposite of what Freud had said, combining incompatible systems (Freudian and Jungian), or attributing to Freud ideas outside of, or incompatible with, psychoanalytic principles.

Fraiberg reaches these conclusions only after individually assessing each critic's comprehension of psychoanalytic principles, application of them, and the resultant benefit to both psychoanalysis and literature. It would have been difficult for him to conclude other than that the criticism was deficient overall, after finding again and again such egregious errors as misunderstanding or misuse of concepts or terminology (Burke's "psychosis" and Brooks' "repression"); reductiveness (both Wilson and Krutch in their equation of art with neurosis); overextended concepts (Lewisohn); and deductive rather than inductive analysis (Krutch's tendency to impose the pattern on the work rather than to allow it to emerge, if it exists at all).

Because his perception is so acute and his assessments so just (Kenneth Burke's glossolalia finally receives the *coup de grâce*), it is indeed curious that Fraiberg thinks most highly of Lionel Trilling, ranking him first among the critics. When Trilling does use psychoanalysis his interpretations are superlative,[2] but he is consistent neither within nor between his critical writings in his use of it. Professor Fraiberg nowhere notes this and sees Trilling apparently only in the perspective of the other critics discussed.

Fraiberg closes his study with a useful discussion of the minimal credentials which should be held by any literary critic who chooses to make psychoanalysis one of his tools. He emphasizes that, by that choice, "the critic has an intellectual obligation to master it—just as he does any other non-literary technique or body of knowledge which he wishes to use—for it, like his criticism, deserves to be judged on its own merits. If he elects to use more than one non-literary discipline, then I do not see how he can escape the obligation to become competent in each of them."[3] Especially important in this context is Fraiberg's penultimate paragraph:

An understanding of the help which psychoanalysis is capable of giving for the evaluation of literature and the development of critical theory can probably best be acquired by studying its concepts of the ego. Its functions are many and complex, but the ones that have most concerned us here are its regulation of the psychic equilibrium and its role in bringing the individual and his environment into a satisfactory relationship. Since each writer is a unique human being, a knowledge of his personality from this standpoint is bound to illuminate his artistic achievement. His works, in turn, as demonstrations of his way of contemplating and meeting certain aspects of his world, afford insights into his personality. The increasing scope of ego psychology permits greater penetration than ever before into the mysteries of art.[4]

Professor Fraiberg has delineated the ways in which ego psychology helps to penetrate the mysteries of art in two essays which, along with *Psychoanalysis and American Literary Criticism,* we recommend to the reader: "Psychology and the Writer: The Creative Process" and "New Views of Art and the Creative Process in Psychoanalytic Ego Psychology."[5]

Notes

1. Louis Fraiberg, *Psychoanalysis and American Literary Criticism* (Detroit: Wayne State University Press, 1960), p. 236.
2. See, for example, Lionel Trilling's brilliant insights into Keats in

Louis Kronenberger, ed., *The Selected Letters of John Keats* (New York: Farrar, 1951), pp. 3-49. Also reprinted in Lionel Trilling, *The Opposing Self* (New York: Viking, 1955), pp. 3-49.
3. Louis Fraiberg, *Psychoanalysis,* p. 238.
4. Louis Fraiberg, *Psychoanalysis,* p. 240.
5. Louis Fraiberg, "Psychology and the Writer: The Creative Process," *Literature and Psychology,* 5 (1955), pp. 72-77; "New Views of Art and the Creative Process in Psychoanalytic Ego Psychology," *Literature and Psychology,* 11 (1961), pp. 45-55.

Mark Kanzer

A prominent psychoanalyst who has made significant contributions to literary study is Dr. Mark Kanzer. Over the past several decades, Dr. Kanzer has written a number of essays which would greatly profit the student of criticism. His writings are models of clarity and organization and while we may not agree with some of his conclusions, they are based upon the soundest analytical theories and procedures. We shall consider here, as examples, four of his studies, two each on works of Shakespeare and Sophocles.

In "The 'Passing of the Oedipus Complex' in Greek Drama,"[1] Dr. Kanzer demonstrates that just as the *Oedipus Rex* showed the disastrous results of unconscious forces, the *Oedipus at Colonus* shows application of the same forces in a restorative, socially adaptive way which anticipates Freud's own theories of the passing of the Oedipus complex through development of the superego. As with every neurosis, Oedipus' basic drives constantly repeat themselves, says Kanzer, in an attempt to master the original trauma. Hence, once more we see him horrifying the people by entering with his mother-daughter, Antigone, into a sacred region, the grove of the Eumenides, which symbolizes the mother's genitals. The Eumenides represent the unconscious drives which must be appeased by reason; Creon is a father-figure who threatens castration (death) to Oedipus; Theseus, another father-figure,

who forgives Oedipus' rebellion and thereby undoes the crime of
parricide. The passing of the Oedipus complex through formation of
the superego is ultimately evident in Oedipus' identification with the
Father as he curses his own undutiful son, Polyneices.

Dr. Kanzer elaborated upon these ideas several years later in "The
Oedipus Trilogy,"[2] a more detailed view of the psychological development outlined above. To his earlier insights he adds a new hypothesis
which, unfortunately, is probably the most egregious error he makes in
his many literary analyses. He postulates that the cause of Oedipus'
undoing in the *Tyrannus* is the renewal of his oedipal conflicts as a
result of Jocasta's being pregnant with a son, a possible rival to himself.
Thus, the cycle is complete: as Laius attempted to avert parricide, so
does Oedipus, bringing calamity. Kanzer tries to prove Jocasta's pregnancy through negative evidence—the lack of fruitfulness in the land,
barren women, "sterile blossoms," and so on—which he believes neurotically deny the actuality. This is so unlikely as to be fantastic; not a
single line of text exists in reference to Jocasta's pregnancy and this is
one time that Dr. Kanzer's habitual use of minimal textual evidence lets
him down flat. This is not to say that this entire essay is invalid, any
more than its predecessor is. Both are full of highly original ideas and
provocative suggestions as to the meaning of, for example, the Riddle,
the symbol of the Sphinx, and the interrelationships of the main
characters.

Much the same can be said for Dr. Kanzer's explorations of Shakespeare. In "The Central Theme of Shakespeare's Works,"[3] for example,
he perceives patterns of great importance. Shifting the usual focus from
the masculine characters to the feminine, he contends that the central
theme is the fidelity of the heroine of the drama, with the hero always
suffering anxiety that she will prefer a rival. He sees the works as
classifiable into three periods: the first, "romantic-comic," in which the
heroines are virginal; the second, tragic, in which they are mature,
voluptuous, and treacherous; and the third, in which there is a return to
maidens, with emphasis on the father-daughter relationship. Dr. Kanzer
argues cogently for his thesis and is quite convincing. Regrettably,
about halfway through, he begins to read back into the Bard's life in an
effort to seek the source of the anxiety pattern and surmises that with
the birth of Shakespeare's brother Edmund, the poet had to compete

for his mother's love with not only his father, but with a new rival as
well. This infantile conflict is reflected in the heroine's (mother's)
constantly vacillating between characters which represent the poet's
own "split" selves, Shakespeare himself deriving satisfaction by
omnipotently controlling all.

Such speculative analysis of the long dead author does not appear in
one of Dr. Kanzer's more recent essays, "Imagery in *King Lear*,"[4] an
apparent outgrowth of his previous "Autobiographical Aspects of the
Writer's Imagery."[5] In the earlier essay, he had argued for close attention to imagery in order to understand the ways in which literary and
psychological factors are interrelated and to discern the essential unity
and meaning in an author's many and varied productions; in the later
essay, he applies to *Lear* the propositions he had set forth. He begins by
asserting that all the major characters of the play are really splits of
single personalities and can be grouped as follows: Lear-Gloucester,
Edgar-Edmund, and Cordelia-Goneril-Regan. In actuality, then, we
really have but three persons: father, son, and daughter. Kanzer then
goes on to show how the central image of the drama, the male body
moving violently in excruciating pain, expresses the sexual crimes and
punishments of the central characters. He sees the theme of the play as
that of the "son as successor," and contends that Edgar, through his
actions, loses his innocence and becomes capable of ruling. Thus all
this—"birth" of the son; the animal, nakedness, and tortured body
images—is unified in the dominant fantasy, that of childbirth, and on a
deeper level, in a sadistic primal scene. Mastery of the conflict is
represented by Edgar, a symbol of the finally-unified ego joined with
the superego and emerging triumphant.

In addition to these essays, the reader will find informative most of
Dr. Kanzer's literary studies, among which are "The Figure in the
Carpet," a study of Henry James's story of the same name, and the
"The Self-Analytic Literature of Robert Louis Stevenson," an essay in
which he shows how careful study of self-analytic writers' notebooks
and writings on dreams can enrich the authors' works immeasurably.[6]
In general, all of Dr. Kanzer's studies have this enriching virtue, and we
wish only that more analysts would bring literary sensitivity and
breadth of knowledge comparable to Dr. Kanzer's to their own literary
criticism.

Notes

1. Mark Kanzer, "The 'Passing of the Oedipus Complex' in Greek Drama," *International Journal of Psychoanalysis,* 29 (1948), pp. 131-34; reprinted in Hendrik Ruitenbeek, ed., *Psychoanalysis and Literature* (New York: Dutton, 1964), pp. 243-50.
2. Mark Kanzer, "The Oedipus Trilogy," *Psychoanalytic Quarterly,* 19 (1950), pp. 561-72; reprinted in Leonard and Eleanor Manheim, eds., *Hidden Patterns* (New York: Macmillan, 1966), pp. 66-78.
3. Mark Kanzer, "The Central Theme in Shakespeare's Works," *Psychoanalytic Review,* 38 (1951), pp. 1-16.
4. Mark Kanzer, "Imagery in *King Lear,*" *American Imago,* 22 (1965), pp. 3-13. Reprinted in M. D. Faber, ed., *The Design Within: Psychoanalytic Approaches to Shakespeare* (New York: Science House, 1970), pp. 219-31.
5. Mark Kanzer, "Autobiographical Aspects of the Writer's Imagery," *International Journal of Psychoanalysis,* 40 (1959), pp. 52-58.
6. Mark Kanzer, "The Figure in the Carpet," *American Imago,* 17 (1960), pp. 339-48; "The Self-Analytic Literature of Robert Louis Stevenson," in George B. Wilbur and Warner Muensterberger, eds., *Psychoanalysis and Culture: Essays in Honor of Geza Roheim* (New York: Wiley, 1951), pp. 425-35.

Maurice Valency

In the nature of things, all children in our culture grow up under the absolute dominion of the mother, and the need, the rule, and the love of the mother underlie all other considerations in the infantile mind. . . . Genetically the mother comes first, and it is to her that men look first of all for shelter, for nourishment, and for love. It is in her also that they find their first frustrations and disappointments. Toward her they direct their first hostility. The father is, for all his magnificence, a secondary figure in the psychic system. The initial equipment of aspirations, disappointments, aggressions, and fears with which we enter upon life's career is developed with relation to the mother and the mother alone.

It is evidently to this fundamental complex of love, fear, and hostility that we must in the first place refer the ambivalent attitude toward women which characterizes our cultural pattern.[1]

So lucid is the prose, so profound the implications, that these might be the words of Freud in Victorian Vienna preparing still another essay to furrow the brows of men; yet they are not. They are rather those of Maurice Valency laying the foundation for his treatise *In Praise of Love,* an absorbing examination of the poetic tradition of the Troubadours which reached its zenith in Petrarch and Dante. Written with wit, grace, and charm and completely lacking in jargon, the book is an

insufficiently well-known but masterful example of the application of
psychoanalysis to literature and a literary tradition.[2]

By contrasting the heroic lover with the romantic lover, Valency
shows that it is not the concept of love *per se* that changes from the
classic to the courtly love tradition but rather the proper object of the
love expressed: while the ancients considered love of woman a vice and
transmitted this concept to the church fathers, the troubadours made it
a virtue, indeed the most ennobling one. Scrutinizing the courtly
tradition for the psychodynamics of this reversal, Valency concludes
that it results from—although he does not use the word—the family
romance. "... The characters in this elementary drama are easily
recognized. The situation is, from the genetic viewpoint, if not the first
of the fantasies of childhood, at least the most readily available for
literary purposes" (76).
The family romance, he says, was the sole plot relied upon.

The troubadour love-song involved, generally speaking, a single situation. The background was the loveless marriage. The *dramatis personae*
consisted of the discontented wife, the jealous husband, the desirable
lover—a trio with predictable interrelations. ... The little drama, invariable in concept and structure, must be considered one of the prime
literary creations of Western culture. It was endlessly reproduced and
elaborated not only in the various forms of the love-lyric, but in every
literary genre which came under the influence of the love-lyric. ...
After serving for centuries as a source of poetry, both lyric and
narrative, [it] furnished the novelist with stories and the dramatist with
comedies, tragedies, and farces without number, and afterward with
melodramas, problem plays, social comedies, and every other form
which the stage supports. (75-76)

By implication, therefore, all the plots of Western literary tradition
are variations on one basic theme, the original eternal triangle—mother,
father, and child. Valency reaches this conclusion, however, only after
carefully considering the individual elements of the psychic process
being expressed in the situation. He astutely observes that the love of
the medieval lover for his lady is at base narcissistic and, projected upon
the lady, transforms her virtues to perfection; that the desire to be
accepted rather than to possess makes the sexual reward superfluous;
that, as a result, greater sensuality comes to be attached to casual acts,
transmuting the coarseness of normal sexual pursuit into an artistic
endeavor necessitating taste and sensitivity: thus arose *cortesia*.

Further, since the situation is in reality the recreation of an infantile fantasy, what could be more normal than for the stricken lover to assume the pose of the helpless, weak, pitiable child, dependent upon the mother to alleviate his suffering? But, notes Valency, since desire does not normally produce such adverse effects, it must be fear so afflicting the lover, and understandably, because in petitioning for love in the role of the son, he is subject to the revenge of the father. This situation, like the family romance itself, is full of conflict; indeed, conflict is a necessity. Fear-ridden, the couple attempted—rarely successfully—to consummate their love despite the jealous husband, the prying eyes, the whispering tongues (doubtless the ubiquitous lying tale-bearer himself represents a form of institutionalized guilt, if you would, the superego).

The eventually total desexualization of love, then, came about not only as a result of the foregoing psychodynamics, but also as a need to distance the woman, unconsciously identified with the mother, thus preventing incest and allowing her to remain pure, even virginal in the infantile fantasy of the lover. As Valency demonstrates, this desexualization reached its logical conclusion in the work of the *stilnovisti* in which the lady was utterly transformed into an ideal.

Valency's entire argument is detailed, scholarly, and rich and helps us better understand one of the most important of Western literary traditions, one which seemed to arise from nowhere, but started, like so very much else, in the emotional relationships between mother, father, and child.

Notes

1. Maurice Valency, *In Praise of Love* (New York: Macmillan, 1961), p. 14. All subsequent references are to this edition.
2. So little-known is it that Valency's observations are still being duplicated by other students of the courtly love tradition. See, particularly, Melvin W. Askew, "Courtly Love: Neurosis as Institution," *The Psychoanalytic Review,* 52 (1965), p. 21f; and Richard A. Koenigsberg, "Culture, Fantasy and Courtly Love," *The Psychoanalytic Review,* 54, No. 1 (1967), pp. 36-50. Since Askew and Koenigsberg independently reach the same conclusions as Valency, we may consider them corroborative.

Daniel Weiss

Though Daniel Weiss thanks Professor Richard Ellmann, in the preface of his *Oedipus in Nottingham: D. H. Lawrence,* for helping him limit the scope of his study, one wishes the latter were not so parsimonious in his judgment and the former so grateful for the thrift. For this slim volume of just over a hundred pages is so rich in insight that one can only lament that the study is not longer than it is.

Professor Weiss concentrates his efforts on one principal novel, *Sons and Lovers,* dealing with the images of the parents in two chapters aptly titled "The Father in the Blood" and "The Mother in the Mind," and in a final chapter "The Great Circle" briefly considers the recurrent themes in other Lawrence works, for example, *Women In Love,* "The Prussian Officer," and *The Man Who Died.* His thesis is that, "In short, *Sons and Lovers* is a coin whose reverse is the remainder of Lawrence's works,"[1] and that *Lady Chatterly's Lover* represents the final stage in the reversal.

The shift from the parricidal Paul Morel running to his mother's arms while the father whines in the kitchen, to the "great blond child-man," Clifford Chatterly, fondling the housekeeper's breasts while the game-keeper waits in the Park, represents the total dilapidation of Lawrence's Oedipal longings and the perfection of his reactive anti-Oedipal vision of life. Along with the heroic contempt for the mother image in

absolute decay comes the full identification with the once despised
father (109).

Weiss notes that this despised father-image is the only one present in
Sons and Lovers, Lawrence having eliminated from a first draft the
idealized image, in the person of a minister whose sermons Gertrude
Morel helped compose, and in a second draft having had him die a
murderer in jail. As with *Hamlet,* the good father has been killed and
the protagonist has only the bad, base-born, inferior father with which
to deal. Weiss details, through close analysis of the abundant sexual
imagery, the picture Lawrence creates of the sexually aggressive (therefore violent) father and the pure virginal mother, the "victim" of his
desires; and the incestual inclinations of young Paul and his mother and
Walter Morel's helpless recognition of this bond.

He then demonstrates the function of the other characters as parental surrogates. Baxter Dawes is the recipient of feelings Paul has
displaced from his father, not pure hatred but a seemingly inexplicable
tenderness tempering it. Yet, as Weiss explains, following Freud in
Dostoevsky and Parricide, this is a reaction-formation, partly out of
castration fear, partly out of submission of the ego to the super-ego as
punishment for the guilt of incestuous desires. Clara Dawes and Miriam
Leivers are, of course, maternal surrogates; the former, the sexual
mother, the latter, the virginal. Drawing from Freud's "Three Essays on
Sexuality," Weiss shows that "Clara fulfills all the conditions Freud
describes as proper to her being chosen by Paul. She is the possession of
another man, the 'injured third party,' Baxter Dawes, from whom it
seems desirable that Paul 'rescue' her. . . . There is implicit the further
desire by Paul that Clara be a fallen woman, Magdalen, the 'harlot' "
(59). Miriam, though attractive in many ways, cannot produce the
"injured third party" Paul needs and finally, "Paul's relationship with
Miriam fails because his repressed image of the beloved is fundamentally denied him. Like Ophelia she is sexually desirable, or should be,
but her virginity is a supreme article of her desirability. With her as with
his mother, Paul cannot act out the desired incest" (ibid.).

Following the death of his mother, Paul's walk out under the starry
night sky at the novel's close and his turning toward town is, contends
Weiss, a rejection of the mother and an acceptance of the father's
values, as is progressively shown in the later works. In his discussion of
Gertrude Morel's death, Weiss displays the excellence of his psychoanalytic ability by clarifying the overdetermination the event has for

Paul: it renders the consummation of an unnatural relationship impossible; it preserves the mother uncorrupted and virginal; it stirs in him thoughts of his death as a union with her (he rejects, however, his brother William's way) and his hastening of it with an overdose of morphine is one final attempt to interpose himself between his father and his mother (44-46).

Weiss' treatment of the remainder of Lawrence's work, compressed as it is into the final third of the book, must of necessity be more superficial and less successful than the extended analysis of *Sons and Lovers,* yet the reader can come away from it, too, with new insights:

> The sexual descriptions in Lawrence's novels contain always the imagery of what is recognizable as coitus anxiety, which implies a neurotic regression to some prior state, before the genitals have assumed primacy as the sexual organ par excellence, when for the child the pleasurable organ is the mouth, which does not give but receives through sucking. The orally dependent infant, for whom all orifices in phantasy satisfy oral (sucking) needs, fears the giving of himself in an orgasm. His own hunger, which he attributes as well to the object of his desire, the nursing mother, threatens to devour him. The neurotic Oedipal man, for whom the nursing situation was the paradisal one, equates orgasm with loss and withdraws in horror from a mother image that is more predator than nurse. The clinical descriptions are consistently those of death; violent, explosive annihilation; and mutilation (100-1).

This is a book that could have gone wrong in many ways: faulty use of psychoanalysis, analysis of the author through the work, utilization of biography to substantiate textual readings. Happily, in none of these ways does Professor Weiss err. Instead, he follows Lawrence's own injunction, "Trust the tale and not the teller," and produces required reading for any Laurentian and exemplary analysis for any fledgling critic.

Notes

1. Daniel Weiss, *Oedipus in Nottingham: D. H. Lawrence* (Seattle: University of Washington Press, 1962), p. 14. All subsequent references are to this edition.

Jose Barchilon and Joel Kovel

"Huckleberry Finn: A Psychoanalytic Study," by Jose Barchilon and Joel S. Kovel, is a model essay which we urge more psychoanalysts to study before embarking on literary explorations of their own. As Drs. Barchilon and Kovel make clear from the start, the technique they use was evolved over many years of trial-and-error in a seminar on "Great Novels" which they gave in the Department of Psychiatry, Albert Einstein College of Medicine. In their essay they first explain the method generally, apply it to the novel, and afterwards recapitulate the steps in the method more specifically, showing exactly how and why a certain thing was done, and, in addition, what benefits were gained by the action.

Drs. Barchilon and Kovel take their most important step at the very beginning when they emphatically state that any formulation they make is based *solely* on what is explicitly stated in the text and that they have not considered any other material, either from the life of Twain or his numerous works. (A stand like this we have consistently argued for throughout this volume, believing that the best foundation for psychoanalytic analyses is to respect the integrity of the text.) They draw the simple analogy to the analytic situation in which the analyst is loath to admit into his considerations any material coming from sources outside the patient. Not making any change in procedure should then be a simple matter for an analyst interested in literary analysis. Drs. Barchilon and Kovel insist, however, that they did not use this method as a result of their analytic practice, but rather that it imposed itself upon them over the years as the most beneficial, meaningful way of approaching literature.

Analyzing the novel as if it were the life history of a real person—psychologically consistent with events which are derivative of unconscious nuclear substrates of the characters and with a constant relationship between manifest and latent content—they examine first Huck himself. Through close textual analysis, they conclude that Huck is basically passive, longs to be dead to be reunited with his mother, is in a rage against her for abandoning him—a rage which reaction-formation converts to the passivity initially mentioned. Drs. Barchilon and Kovel next take up a theme which they feel dominates the novel: Huck as Moses (with the concomitant, Mississippi as Nile), undergoing rebirth into a new identity by abandoning archaic modes of regaining his mother and adapting to a reality of substitute objects. There follow shorter considerations of sexuality in the novel, Tom Sawyer's character, Jim's character, and a longer section on the way Huck matures through his relationship with Jim. The authors make it perfectly clear that Jim is the key to Huck's potential success, for it is almost solely in interaction with him that Huck's ego gains the necessary strength to combat the forces of his id and superego.

They then detail the significance of the sibling-like relationship of Huck, Jim, and Tom and in a final section strengthen their analysis by integrating their psychoanalytic insights with the geographical-social setting of the novel. In a postscript, as previously mentioned, they recapitulate their technique step-by-step, persuasively justifying each step as having maximum benefits relative to other possible procedures. Finally, they suggest how this technique can best serve literary biography, education, aesthetics, and psychoanalysis itself.

The many virtues of this essay should now be manifest to practitioners of psychoanalytic criticism. It is without a doubt the best short model-primer of critical procedure available. We know that Drs. Barchilon and Kovel have analyzed as many as fifty novels during the course of their teaching. Perhaps someday they will make these analyses available in a collection to benefit the community of critics at large.

Notes

1. José Barchilon and Joel S. Kovel, "*Huckleberry Finn:* A Psychoanalytic Study," *Journal of the American Psychoanalytic Association*, 14, No. 4 (1966), pp. 775-814.

Frederick C. Crews

Ernst Kris's *Psychoanalytic Explorations in Art* deals throughout with the artist's "flexibility of repression" (the term is Freud's), his ability to utilize in his creativity a certain amount of material from the id without his ego's being overwhelmed by it. The loss of this flexibility of repression in a writer and his work has never been better chronicled than in Frederick C. Crews's *The Sins of the Fathers: Hawthorne's Psychological Themes.* Crews's thesis is that Hawthorne was not, as most of his modern critics would have us believe, a calm, didactic moralist, but instead a writer full of tension, full of conflict, full of moral uncertainty. His work thus demonstrates what Freud believed to be the essence of the psychological novel, the author's personification of "the conflicting currents of his own mental life in several heroes" (*SE,* IX, 150).

Hawthorne's ambiguity—always acknowledged, but seldom skillfully explored—is not a conscious strategem, Crews maintains, but rather reflects an ambivalence, is a symptom, "a sign of powerful tension between his attraction to and his fear of his deepest themes. For behind his moralism, and often directly contradicting it, lies a sure insight into everything that is terrible, uncontrollable, and therefore *demoralizing* in human nature. Hawthorne himself, like his latest admirers, wanted to be spared this insight, but beneath layers of rationalization and euphemism it asserts its right to expression."[1]

It is this assertion of its right to expression, the return of the repressed, which Professor Crews systematically and forcefully demonstrates in his consideration of Hawthorne. His evidence is carefully organized and meticulously presented in order to show clearly the devolution of the author's art. Crews calls upon the reader to accept credible assumptions in successive detailed explications of the works in chronological sequence; by the final chapter, the accumulated evidence is overwhelming and the reader is forced to agree with Crews. Crews contends that guilt, whether real or fantasied, returns continuously from its repressed state and dominates, in one way or another, Hawthorne's fiction. His formal diction, poise, sentiments, all are defenses against the repressed; his imagery reflects it; his language suggests unconscious obsession with it. "And, in fact, one of the abiding themes of Hawthorne's work is the fruitless effort of people to deny the existence of their 'lower' motives. The form of his plots often constitutes a return of the repressed—a vengeance of the denied element against an impossible ideal of purity or spirituality. Thus it is not enough, in order to speak of Hawthorne's power as a psychologist, merely to look at his characters' stated motives. We must take into account the total, always intricate dialogue between statement and implication, observing how Hawthorne—whether or not he consciously means to—invariably measures the displacements and sublimations that have left his characters two-dimensional" (17).

Professor Crews begins his examination of the unspoken motives of Hawthorne's characters with "The Maypole of Marymount" and ends with the four unfinished works the author toiled over until his death in 1864. His analyses of these works and those in between reveal not only the recurrent themes of incest and parricide, but also a struggle against the emergence of such fantasies, a struggle ending with Hawthorne in a paralytic state, producing only chaotic plot fragments. As Crews points out, these fragments "follow the psychoanalytic pattern of symptom-formation with astonishing exactitude; they offer an unceasing flow of repressed fantasy which is counteracted by increasing denial and distortion" (257). Since the identical situations, images, repressions, and expressions are present as well in the earliest works of his career and in the polished works of his maturity, the conclusion that he was obsessed from the beginning and lost control only later is inescapable.

Professor Crews is no mere debunker, no iconoclast, no medium raising the ghost of Freud to analyze the ghost of Hawthorne. His is a sympathetic attempt to understand, step by step and story by story, the blurring of Hawthorne's artistic vision and his fall from integrity to fragmentation. And he does it admirably well. His analyses throughout are thorough and stay firmly within the text, with no adducing of external biographical details to support a point. Let us glance briefly, for instance, at his discussion of "My Kinsman, Major Molineux."

Crews's interpretation of this tale is close to that of Simon O. Lesser, previously discussed. Crews further enriches our understanding, however, by noting, additionally, that the episode with the prostitute probably represents a fantasy of parental sexuality; that Robin is constantly hindered by father figures, powerful men who threaten him in one way or another; that each and every one of these encounters is accompanied by phallic imagery; and that the entire series of events in the tale may possibly be an unconscious fantasy of Robin's. The tension between Robin's stated desire to find his kinsman and his own continuous thwarting of that desire illustrates well, of course, Crews' argument that the motive will out, whether Hawthorne will have it so or not. And, after *The Scarlet Letter,* he is less capable of controlling the matter. "Like his own monomaniac heroes, Hawthorne finds himself unable to suppress the fantasies he no longer cares to recognize as belonging to 'our common nature.' The fantasies return in symbolism—just as they did for his heroes—with such heightened urgency that Hawthorne becomes anxious to disown his whole fictional world. His recourse is to ironic self-criticism, comic digression, and finally an unwillingness to bring his blatantly incestuous plots to any conclusion at all" (154).

Nowhere throughout the study is the reader confronted with and inhibited by psychoanalytic jargon to heighten his resistance; everywhere is he treated to clarity, wit, and close textual analysis in support of the thesis. *The Sins of the Fathers* is a model for full-length psychoanalytic critiques of a single author's work.

We must mention, in addition, two essays by Professor Crews, obligatory reading for the critic. The first is "Literature and Psychology," written for the MLA publication *Relations of Literary Study,*[2] a collection of seven essays demonstrating interdisciplinary contributions. An excellent introduction to the relationship between the two disciplines, Professor Crews's piece briefly recapitulates the birth of psychoanalytic literary criticism with Freud, who provided the critic with a revolutionary method of interpreting literature. Crews then recognizes the objections of others to the use of this method, and admirably rebuts seven major of these objections at length before concluding that the critic who does not utilize the well-formulated and time-tested tenets of psychoanalysis will usually end up concocting his own "homebrew" psychology. It is thus not a question of whether to use psychology, but of which psychology to use. The footnotes to this essay contain a multitude of extremely useful references for the reader.

The other mandatory reading is Professor Crews's "Anaesthetic Criticism," the initial chapter of his recent *Psychoanalysis and Literary Process.*[3] A virtual flinging down of the gauntlet to all other types of literary criticism, this chapter takes to task those "anaesthetic" criticisms which, while objecting to psychoanalytic criticism, fearing that it goes too far, themselves go nowhere and thus arrive nowhere.

A criticism that explicitly or implicitly reduces art to some combination of moral content and abstract form and genre conventions is literally an anaesthetic criticism. It insulates the critic and his readers from a threat of affective disturbance—a threat that is perfectly real, for there is no reason to suppose that a reader's ego will prove more flexible and capacious than the artist's was. All literary criticism aims to make the reading experience more possible for us, but anesthetic criticism assumes that this requires keeping caged the anxieties that the artist set free and then recaptured. The effect is often to transform the artist from a struggling fellow mortal into an authority figure, a dispenser of advice about virtue and harmony" (14).

Following this, Professor Crews begins his cogent argument for the use of psychoanalysis, a body of theory which alone provides a coherent system for the study and appreciation of "the renunciation and risks" literary production entails. He shows that psychoanalysis can do this and can be validated, because in performing this service it simultaneously makes fuller sense of texts than rival criticism can. Yet it is not without its perils, as Crews is quick to point out with specific examples. Wielded well, however, it can supply inestimable benefits, for "the real value of literary psychoanalysis is that it can embolden us to be alone with books, to recognize our own image in them, and from that recognition to begin comprehending their hold over us" (20).

Though speaking strongly in this essay, Crews has been careful to set

his own house in order at the same time he tells other critics that theirs
are uninhabited. Such caution, always a healthy buffer, should be an
example to the reader, who, we hope, will seek out this essay to follow
Professor Crews' careful argument for himself.

From his riotous satire of psychoanalytic criticism in *The Pooh
Perplex,* through his meticulous exploration of Hawthorne, to his
cogent argument for psychological criticism of the Freudian school,
Professor Crews is always competent, witty, and provocative of further
thought. One eagerly awaits the next products of his fertile mind, for,
almost always controversial in some respect, they put one in mind of
Oscar Wilde's *bon mot,* "An idea that is not dangerous is hardly worth
having at all."

Notes

1. Frederick C. Crews, *The Sins of the Fathers: Hawthorne's Psychological Themes* (New York: Oxford University Press, 1966),
   p. 8. All subsequent references are to this edition.
2. Frederick C. Crews, "Literature and Psychology," in James
   Thorpe, ed., *Relations of Literary Study: Essays on Interdisciplinary Contributions* (New York: Modern Language Association,
   1967), pp. 73-88.
3. Frederick C. Crews, *Psychoanalysis and Literary Process* (Cambridge, Mass.: Winthrop, 1970), p. 21. All subsequent references
   are to this edition. "Anaesthetic Criticism" previously appeared
   serially in *The New York Review,* Part I (February 26, 1970), pp.
   31-35; Part II (March 12, 1970), pp. 49-52.

M. D. Faber

Another young critic, whose impact on the discipline is being more increasingly felt year by year, is M. D. Faber. No matter how exhaustively a literary work might seem to have been treated from a psychoanalytic point of view, Professor Faber is still capable of looking at it afresh and calling our attention to something it had been diverted from or had resisted seeing. His recent and intense interest in his two specializations, Shakespeare and suicide, provides cases in point.

Though two highly skilled analysts, Ernst Kris and Franz Alexander, looked carefully at *Henry IV* and discussed the Oedipal situations therein, Professor Faber was bold enough to take a third glance and enrich psychoanalytic criticism thereby. In his "Oedipal Patterns in *Henry IV,*"[1] he begins by crediting those analysts with the elucidation of the father-son conflict acted out by Falstaff, Bolingbroke, Hotspur, and Hal and goes on to maintain that Hotspur is Hal's double, really as well as symbolically, that we see "a smoldering, largely unconscious oedipal rivalry . . . which explain[s] the fantastically developed aggressions of Hotspur and his irrational, fathomless abhorrence of Bolingbroke . . . " (432).

Initially, in support of his thesis, Faber points to somewhat obvious evidence: that Hotspur and his father Northumberland never give us the feeling of a friendly father-son relationship; indeed they never exchange one friendly word. Then he begins to examine the text more closely, principally in conjunction with Northumberland's failure to join the rest of the rebel forces when so badly needed. Faber points out that Northumberland, knowing that the rebellion has little chance of succeeding without him, strongly urges (gives "bold advertisement") that his son plunge to the fray, though the father lie sick. Worse still, the Induction to *Henry IV, Part 2* tells us that Northumberland was feigning illness ("lies crafty-sick")! Though other critics have questioned his motive for his duplicity and found it to be cowardice, Faber contends that such an explanation cannot account for the curious manner in which Northumberland receives the various rumours of his son's death. He is reluctant to accept the good ones and seems to insist upon and relish the bad ones. Demonstrating this with copious textual evidence, Faber concludes that "Northumberland, far from being a father to his son, has resented and hated him, and that Hotspur has not known the fatherly affection so crucial to the development of a normal personality. Thus the Earl has produced a kind of 'monster,' a fiercely destructive, fiercely independent sort of person more interested in war than in women, and driven continually by an enormous appetite for slaughter" (436-37). Bolingbroke, the King-Father, is thus close enough to this psychic conflict to receive Percy's open rage and distant enough to allow Percy's superego to accept such overt acts of aggression.

One of Professor Faber's best critical traits, however, is his ability to give us just one more thing—one added significance, one more facet to a character, one more implication. In this case, the bonus is his added comment that the Histories as a whole take on deeper significance because Shakespeare shows us in this relationship that "the failure of the rebellion is rooted not only in material considerations but in the very fabric of the rebels' lives, and that those who would disrupt society, who would, through murderous aggression and hatred, split a nation and sow the seeds of civil war, are themselves disrupted and split and at war" (437).

Professor Faber has often combined his two major interests by writing on the subject of suicide in Shakespeare, as in, for example, "Two Studies in Self-Aggression in Shakespearean Tragedy," "Ophelia's Doubtful Death," "Lady Macbeth's Suicide," and "Some Remarks on the Suicide of King Lear's Eldest Daughter."[2]

This interest in self-destruction as depicted in literature has culminated in his recent *Suicide and Greek Tragedy,*[3] a study of the plays of

Sophocles and Euripides which have suicidal heroes or heroines. Relying on close textual readings and his vast knowledge of self-destructive behavior, Faber has contributed numerous valuable insights to the rapidly growing body of psychoanalytic criticism and has given us a fresh look at the complex motives of suicidal behavior.

In his examination of *Oedipus Rex*, for example, he brings to light hitherto unnoticed significance in the minutest actions of Oedipus and Jocasta. He directs our attention to Oedipus' venting his aggressive impulses upon himself in the form of symbolic self-castration *only* after he has been thwarted in his attempt to discharge them upon someone else, specifically Jocasta. "And indeed, as one examines self-mutilating and self-killing actions in Sophocles' work as a whole, he discovers that this tendency to turn onto the self aggressions which were originally meant for others is the one clear constant in Sophocles' depiction of self-destruction" (26).

Oedipus' first impulse, contends Faber, is to *murder*, not to commit suicide. His frantic search for Jocasta, sword in hand, reflects his hatred for the source of all his troubles, for his betrayer.

The murderous impulse toward Jocasta which surges up in Oedipus when he discovers the truth is, then, an irrational impulse rooted primarily in the unconscious where the hero's *basic trust*, or *primal trust*, the trust which originates in the infant's relationship with the parent, has been violated. Not only has wife turned out to be mother, but *mother has turned out to be wife*. The original creator of trust has, in an instant, become something other than it seemed, for an instant, to be (28).

His sensitivity to this abandonment, of course, is heightened by his already having been once abandoned by the mother when he was a child. "What is of special interest here is that Sophocles in *Oedipus Rex* departs from the usual rendition of the source-myth by emphasizing that it is the mother, Jocasta, and not the father, Laius, who gives Oedipus to the herdsman. *Her role in the separation is stressed" (Ibid.)*.

Faber adduces as well the third significant violation of trust Oedipus has suffered, that of the drunken Corinthian's disclosure that he is not, in truth, the son of Polybus and Merope. Such violations, as Faber shows with ample evidence from clinical studies, are conspicuous in the developmental history of matricides; Oedipus' new wound is, in actuality, an old one which has reopened under psychic stress.

Jocasta, however, by committing suicide, has prevented Oedipus from fulfilling his wish to kill her and, in doing so, added fuel to his rage: for the psychic reality is that

> . . .*Oedipus' wish has come true:* Jocasta is dead, and in terms of the hero's "frenzied," unconscious inclinations, *he has murdered her.* Thus the aggression which Oedipus turns onto himself derives not only from the rage he felt toward Jocasta having betrayed him, but also from the superego where he has become, of a sudden, guilty of the mother's murder. Jocasta has abandoned Oedipus for a final time in death, but by her death she has awakened in him a measure of guilt related to the very same murderous impulses which he felt toward her upon discovering that she had betrayed him as mother by becoming wife. (31-33)

Professor Faber then tops this brilliant insight with one further—that Oedipus' lack of self-knowledge is *still* present, that his actions toward his mother are determining the course his fate is to take *within the next few minutes:* "With regard to the effectiveness of the play *as a play,* the implications of this view are obvious: Sophocles, through the Messenger's report, is presenting us with a fully dramatic, *developing* character whose behavior is predicated by what he is actually *doing* in the *now* of the tragedy, rather than by what he has done before the tragedy has gotten underway" (32).

Before turning to Jocasta's suicide, Professor Faber notes one additional significance of Oedipus' self-blinding, one beyond that of the symbolism of which numerous commentators have spoken. Quoting Oedipus' own words to the gathered multitude before his exile— " . . . Had I sight, I know not with what eyes I could e'en have looked on my father, when I came to the place of the dead, aye, or on my miserable mother."—Faber demonstrates that this "magical possibility of reunion with the lost love object" is a frequent factor in cases of "real" suicide and cites case and instance. Thus in his self-blinding, Oedipus expresses

> . . . not only his patricidal guilt, his unconscious need for castration, his regressive anger at the mother for having betrayed him, and his rage at himself for "blindly" undoing and destroying the mother; he is also expressing his *fear of reunion.* . . . When Oedipus blinds himself he ensures the indefinite future that lies "in darkness" before him by 1) punishing and making impotent the incestuous husband-son and 2) punishing and making powerless the "blind," impulsive parent-killer. If

he is to meet Jocasta and Laius in "another world" (the world of his
future thoughts), he will meet them in a "safe" condition, a condition
which not only calls to mind the helpless, groping child at the time of
its emergence from the mother's womb, but which announces an
inchoate, belated recognition of the unconscious forces that drove him
to his unmentionable crimes. (33-34)

    Jocasta's self-destructive behavior, too, contains elements of dis-
placed aggression. Her rage, which ultimately she turns against herself in
suicide, was originally directed against Laius, as Sophocles tells us in the
Messenger's description: " . . . Once within the chamber, she dashed the
doors together at her back; then called on the name of Laius, long since
a corpse, mindful of that son, begotten long ago, by whom the sire was
slain, leaving the mother to breed accursed offspring with his own."
    Faber sees in this emphasis on abandonment the same violation of
trust previously witnessed in the suicidal motivation of Oedipus:
"Jocasta's suicide, then, is not charged simply with guilt, with the
feeling that the self, because of what it has done, has grown hateful and
deserves to be killed; it is also charged with a helpless, frustrated anger
towards the dead husband, an anger which wants to be discharged *now*
and which ultimately finds an outlet in an inwardly-directed aggressive
action" (36).
    Perceptions like these, based on close textual analysis and present
knowledge of self-destructive behavior, abound in Faber's study. Antigone, Ajax, Phaedra, Alcestis, among others, undergo scrutiny and
emerge more fully realized as a result. Patterns emerge, as well, from
the entire corpus of extant works of Sophocles and Euripides, for, as
Faber concludes,

In contrast to Sophocles, where suicide is a savagely aggressive act
provoked by the need to expiate failure, to attack the significant other,
to resurrect the good self by punishing the bad self,—in short, an act
that announces the terrible toll human beings are prone to exact from
themselves for what they have *done,* or for what they believe others
have *done,* Euripides is preoccupied with suicide as a phenomenon
intimately bound up with the problem of choice, with the problem of
allowing oneself to become a person who is unlike the person one
imagines oneself to be by *doing* something "bad" or unacceptable,
something that forces one to "face up to" the truth of one's character.
As far as suicide is concerned, Sophocles is a playwright of guilt,
Euripides of anxiety. (205)

Suicide and Greek Tragedy, Professor Faber's initial book-length
study, is, we hope, just the first of many we can expect from him.

Notes

1. M. D. Faber, "Oedipal Patterns in *Henry IV,*" in *The Design Within: Psychoanalytic Approaches to Shakespeare* (New York: Science House, 1970), pp. 429-38. All subsequent references are to this article. The essay first appeared in *The Psychoanalytic Quarterly,* 36 (1967), pp. 426-34.
2. M. D. Faber, "Two Studies in Self-Aggression in Shakespearean Tragedy," *Literature and Psychology,* 14 (1964), pp. 80-96; "Ophelia's Doubtful Death," *Literature and Psychology,* 16 (1966), pp. 103-9; "Lady Macbeth's Suicide," *American Notes and Queries,* 5 (1966), p. 19; "Some Remarks on the Suicide of King Lear's Eldest Daughter," *University Review* (Kansas City), 33 (1967), pp. 313-17.
3. M. D. Faber, *Suicide and Greek Tragedy* (New York: Sphinx Press, 1970). All subsequent references are to this edition.

Norman N. Holland

One of the most prominent and certainly the most prolific of the modern psychoanalytic critics is Norman N. Holland. Professor Holland has been on the scene for a number of years and his career has shown a shifting of critical stances which it will be our purpose to describe.

Professor Holland's early expertise is well-illustrated by his superb explication of a three-line dream from one of Shakespeare's early dramas. He opens "Romeo's Dream and the Paradox of Literary Realism"[1] with Freud's assertion that "Invented dreams can be interpreted in the same way as real ones," and cites Freud's proof of such by his foray, at Jung's challenge, the study of Jensen's *Gradiva*. Adhering to Freud's procedural method, Holland observes that if we are to interpret Romeo's dream properly, we must first establish the context in which it was dreamed and the chronology of the day-residue which may occur in it. That chronology is as follows: on Sunday morning Romeo was in love with Rosaline; that same evening he fell in love with Juliet. On Monday morning he married her, only to kill her cousin that same afternoon. After remaining to consummate the marriage Monday night, Romeo escapes to Mantua on Tuesday morning and has a dream that same night:

I dreamt my lady came and found me dead
(Strange dream that gives a dead man leave to think!)
And breathed such life with kisses in my lips
That I revived and was an emperor. (V, i, 6-9)

Anticipating, as did Freud, the arguments of the opposition, Holland
now notes that although we do not have the dreamer's free associations
to his own dream—the only valid way to analyze—we can still provide,
independent of him, interpretation of symbols and associations of the
analyst which the dreamer himself for some reason might not have been
able to make. He then begins his analysis by interpreting the symbol of
the life-giving kiss as a representation of the opposite. In subsequent
reality, it will be Romeo who, after drinking the poison, *dies* "with a
kiss," and Juliet who does not breathe life into her lover, but instead
attempts to kiss some poison from his lips that she too might perish.
Reversal enters also into the wish-fulfilling and sleep-preserving elements of the dream. The dream fulfills Romeo's wish to be with Juliet
rather than separated as they are and turns him from an outcast into an
exalted ruler, "an emperor." It preserves his sleep by creating within
itself a substitute awakening—"I revived."

Taking next the symbol of the emperor, Professor Holland examines
its overdetermination. For one thing, he says, citing Reik, it represents
the chief characteristic of an adolescent romantic affair, the desire to
change the old self for a new one built up out of the beloved. For
another, it is a common symbol for the father and probably represents
Romeo's identification with or replacement of the father; he has, after
all, on the night before consummated his marriage, done what fathers
do. But since fathers do that only to mothers, the women in Romeo's
life must come under scrutiny.

He appears on the basis of the play's evidence to be drawn to
mother-figures, women forbidden him for one reason or another—
Rosaline by choice, Juliet by birth. His death in the dream, then,
represents his punishment for becoming the emperor-father and possess-
ing the forbidden woman-mother (though in the dream the sequence is
reversed). Holland notes further Romeo's submissive relationship to
two other fathers in the drama, the friar, "the holy father" and the
apothecary, "an unholy father."

Moving next into the dream-work, he suggests that Romeo's ridicul-
ing himself in recounting the dream represents a reversal of his being

ridiculed by others for his own romantic, dreamy propensities and that the thinness of the dream—its abstract quality, the lack of supporting detail—hints at a reluctance on Romeo's part to dream. Romeo's wish that he were not a dreamy type is last substantiated by his making himself wake up in the dream. The latent content may contain, given the recent honeymoon, wish for continual sexual potency, expressed through the symbol of the dying and being reborn as an emperor. Here a possible body-as-penis identification may be represented in the change from a limp to an erect, potent state. Holland proposes further that there is a great deal of orality in the latent content. An obvious person to give life (that is, milk) into the lips is the mother, as Romeo's use of the phrase "My lady" implies. Thus, by reversal, Romeo is at first the emperor (the omnipotent child), then his mother gives him life, then he lapses into the sleep of contentment, "death."

Though it may seem at this point that the dream should "be called Bottom's dream, because it hath no bottom," Professor Holland brings his analysis to a close by momentarily becoming his own devil's advocate. He concedes that all of these associations and explanations come to naught if they provide no understanding of the work as a whole. Thus to change them from mere "psychological curios" to valid critical insights, he proposes "a more exact and convenient test [:] to see whether the psychological description of the character (or event) can be phrased in words that can apply to the total work, be they ordinary critical language or the technical terms of psychoanalysis" (102). He then capably demonstrates that the entirety of *Romeo and Juliet* is deeply concerned with dreams, from Mercutio's poetic lesson on Queen Mab to the dream quality of the couple's love itself and that the role of dreams, as any Elizabethan would know, is to provide "the flattering truth of sleep." The dream operates throughout the drama by the process of reversal, everywhere reversing the reality of situations and events. The play itself is, says Holland, "a most exquisite expression of the child's inverted wish for love, 'Wait till I'm gone. *Then* they'll be sorry'" (103). Finally, the action of the tragedy itself is a reversal, through the deaths of the lovers, of their families' old hate; the strife and contention with which the play opened is at an end with the end of the play. Love sprung from hate: in the beginning Romeo and Juliet's; in the end, the Montagues' and Capulets'.

The key to this analysis has been, of course, Holland's very careful insistence that the dream be placed *in the context* of Romeo's life, for only in this way, as with a "real" dream, can a literary dream be analyzed. He is thus able to explore the condensation of the dream exhaustively. As Freud tells us,[2] every dream is, in a sense, bottomless, never really exhausted to its content. Consequently, Holland is able to extract a wealth of useful material from this one, more than the innocent observer might believe to lie in a hitherto neglected three-line dream. Such are the virtues of psychoanalysis.

As psychoanalytic criticism, Professor Holland's essay is exemplary. Anticipating opposition, he builds his argument carefully, grounds it in accepted theory, never uses jargon, and relies solely upon textual evidence. Further, he considers overdetermination and respects the integrity of the work by showing how the one element he has analyzed fits in perfectly with the whole. The reader can do no better than attempt to emulate the excellence of his early criticism. Despite the excellence of the essay, however, it contains a credo of Professor Holland's— "... I still feel that the proper place to apply psycho-analytic techniques is to the real minds of the audience. ... " (102)—with which we must take sharp issue when the opportunity presents itself.

Holland's tireless research in Shakespearean lore resulted in 1964 in the publication of his *Psychoanalysis and Shakespeare.*[3] This volume, a tour de force of scholarship, is useful to the reader both as a standard reference book and as an introduction to the relationship between psychoanalysis and literature. Comprised of two parts, the book first develops an argument for a psychoanalytic theory of literature and relates Shakespeare to it, and then, in the second half, surveys, sum-marizes, and evaluates everything written about the Bard from a psychoanalytic point of view from Freud to the time of publication. As might be expected, this latter half is somewhat tedious reading, as would be any encyclopedia; but it provides at the least invaluable sources, reference, notes, and bibliographies for the student.

In the theoretic section, Holland lays the groundwork for a psycho-analytic theory of literature by surveying and expounding upon the contributions of Freud himself to the study of the artist, the work, and the response of the audience, spectator, or reader to the work. A brief chapter then considers the contributions of others like Jekels, Brill, Sachs, and, most importantly, Ernst Kris. Holland approaches Shake-speare himself with a chapter on Freud's many comments, references, and studies of the Bard's characters and works. After surveying the first psychoanalyst's contributions, he summarizes Freud's methodology, concluding that he would

... take a pattern of mental life (which had been established scientifically) and hold it up, as it were, against the play to discover a congruous pattern. He would then go on to draw conclusions either about psychoanalysis or about the author, the play's effect, the probability of some or all of the plot, the structure, or the language. If about the author, Freud would point to two things: first, an infantile wish common to all men embodied in the play; then some event in the author's biography that would reactivate the wish at the time of writing the play. ... If Freud's conclusion was about the play's effect on an audience, he would speak in terms of an unconscious factor, explaining, for example, that a villain like Richard III appeals to us because he plays on our own wish to be an "exception." ... Thus, in Freud's writings at the very beginning of psychoanalytic criticism we find the basic schism in method that has persisted ever since: psychoanalysis used on the one hand to justify the realism of the events; on the other, to find in unreal events a psychological truth. (73-74).

There follow then the three lengthy chapters which survey all existing psychoanalytic Shakespearean criticism, classified according to its primary concern with the man, the artist, or the works. Finally come two chapters of conclusions both "logical" and "not so logical," explorations of the role, obligations, and types of psychoanalytic criticism. Here Professor Holland examines the three main ways of critical reading: toward the author's mind, toward the character's mind, and toward the audience's mind. After considering the virtues and defects of each, he plumps—not unsurprisingly in view of his statement in the essay on Romeo's dream—for the last direction as *the one way.* "Thus, deviously, we have arrived at a way of understanding the psychology of Shakespeare's works: namely, to consider the play or poem as a configuration, a multiple projection or symbolization or stimulus of unconscious impulses of the audience, interacting through such primary thought processes as identification, condensation, displacement, and the like" (312-13).

An astute reader might have noticed Professor Holland moving in this particular direction early in his study (15), a movement which we have watched with rising apprehension over the years. In his discussion of Freud's investigations of art, Holland emphasizes Freud's interest in the artist's method of disguising the infantile fantasy and wish-fulfillment latent in his creation. He discourses here on the mechanisms of defense or disguise, noting two especially—condensation and displacement—and noting as well that Freud's literary analyses were almost always expressed in terms of one or another kind of displacement. As we shall soon see, in Holland's most recent work, these elements, infantile fantasy and defense in terms of displacement, become the foundation upon which he takes his latest critical stance.

This stance is encapsulated in *Psychoanalysis and Shakespeare* in a discussion of response to a particular joke he has used as an illustration:

> In short, although Freud has spoken only of certain special types, he has, between the lines, as it were, set out a general theory of literature in terms of form and content, impulse and defense. And with the theory goes a method of analyzing the audience reaction to a work of literature. . . . First, one should consider the nature of the pleasure provided by the outstanding features of the genre: What unconscious impulses does this genre gratify? . . . Second, we would consider form and ask what combination. of sense and nonsense, what intellectual "play," loosens the psychic bonds, for example, the displacements and condensation. . . . Third, we would go on to the unconscious significance of the broad patterns of the action in the particular work in question. . . . Finally, one would consider the individual details of the work, particular little events, specific images. . . . One could, I suppose, go even further and consider the separate reactions of individual spectators. (36)

It is this "general theory of literature in terms of form and content, impulse and defense" which occupies the entirety of Professor Holland's *The Dynamics of Literary Response,* to which we now turn.

He opens this theoretical study with the disclaimer, "This not a book of literary criticism."[4] We agree. We feel also that Holland is less than frank in this statement in that, ultimately, he concludes with a consideration of critical do's and don't's. But conclusions follow propositions, and we do not want to get ahead of ourselves.

Holland proposes, to begin with, that his study is an attempt to answer the basic question of the textual critic: "What is the relation between the patterns he finds objectively in the text and a reader's subjective experience of the text?" (xiii). To this end, he hypothesizes that at the core of every literary work is an unconscious infantile fantasy and that "the story 'means' in that it transforms its unconscious fantasy into social, moral, intellectual, and even mythic terms. Meaning is not a static set of relevancies, but a dynamic process of transforming one kind of relevancy, unconscious, to another, conscious" (27-28).

The transformation of our unconscious wishes and fears into significance and coherence provides the pleasure we receive from the literature. These infantile fantasies stem directly from factors in the seven phases of the individual's development: the anal, oral, urethral, phallic, oedipal, latent, and genital. Holland provides, as an aid to the layman, a dictionary in which he discusses at length the fantasies attendant upon each phase and illustrates their presence in literature with numerous examples. Halfway through his discussion, however, he observes that the pleasure derived from literature comes not only from the gratification of the unconscious wish, but also from the fantasy's having been properly "managed" or defended against. That is, pleasure comes from the ego's successful use of one of its many unconscious strategies, or defense mechanisms, in warding off the anxiety which might be aroused by some aspect of the fantasy, as when gratification of the wish to replace the father is accompanied by fear of retribution from the father. The dictionary of fantasy becomes at this point a dictionary of defense mechanisms, all translated into one or another kind of displacement. The sketch of Freud's concern with infantile fantasy and its disguise by variations of displacement which we saw earlier in *Psychoanalysis and Shakespeare* has thus become a highly-detailed mindscape; it lacks but the finishing touches.

These Holland supplies in his examination of our "willing suspension of disbelief." We bring to literature, he says, two expectations which allow us this suspension: "we do not expect to act on the external world; we expect pleasure. Even if the work makes us feel pain or guilt or anxiety, we expect it to manage those feelings so as to transform them into satisfying experiences" (75). Literature, then, ' acts out a psychological process which we introject. That process is the transformation of a central fantasy toward a central meaning" (101). Having formulated his general theory, Holland makes it more concrete by discussion in three lengthy chapters of form, language, and meaning as defenses in literary response, utilizing, as well as excerpts from poetry and prose, an occasional movie. The last third of the book he devotes to applying his model to problems of literary evaluation, style, and so on; again he uses copious examples to illustrate his points.

As ambitious as is Professor Holland's undertaking and as complex as are the results, we must take serious exception to them, as we do to any literary criticism that leads us away from, rather than toward, the text. We believe it to be, as well as extra-literary, reductive in its broad generalizations made from tenuous premises, and seriously flawed at base by solipsistic thinking. Finally, we regret that his theory attempts to move psychoanalytic literary criticism in the opposite direction from that in which psychoanalysis itself is moving—toward the ego instead of toward the id.

To illustrate this movement away from the text, let us glance for a moment back to his essay on Romeo's dream. Just as we praised him for his insistence that the dream be placed *in context* in order that its meaning be validated, so we must now blame him for failing to insist on the same unity and continuity in his explications in *Dynamics.* Illustrations of this failure are plentiful, but we can take as an example Holland's interpretation of the "Tomorrow, and tomorrow, and tomorrow" speech from *Macbeth.* Through free association, analysis of symbols and images (and later, sound symbolism), he concludes that these ten lines have as their nuclear infantile fantasy a primal scene, the child's witnessing his parents at night in the midst of sexual intercourse. If we grant the validity of this interpretation, we must then ask, as literary critics, the only question ultimately important: *cui bono?* Of what use is it to us? It is not meant, apparently, to enrich our knowledge of the play, for Holland makes no attempt to integrate it—as he did with Romeo's dream—though he does assert elsewhere that *Macbeth* is a virtual treasury of primal scene imagery (46). It is not meant, apparently, to have us believe that Macbeth himself has come to his pretty pass as a result of having witnessed a primal scene, for Holland nowhere says that or even implies it. And if he asserts—and he does—that the lines fascinate us because of this primal scene nucleus, I can simply reply that, though I was forced to memorize them by my high-school English teacher, I never really cared much for them one way or another. Which brings us back to the reductiveness and solipsism.

When he validated his interpretation of Romeo's dream by integrating it with the rest of the drama, Holland was observing one of the fundamental principles of Freudian psychology—*continuity of behavior,* which can be summarized as follows: "Any single item of experience can be fully understood only in the light of the total experience of a person. The past, present, and future are tied together in a unified whole. Whatever happens to a person in the present is related to causes in his past and to the motivational goals he hopes to achieve in the future."[5] Holland knows full well that a dream *can* mean *anything* (whether literary or real) but actually *does* mean only "one" particular thing when placed in the total context of a person's mental and physical life; he thus guards himself against an idiosyncratic interpretation by putting Romeo's dream in context. But he takes no such care with Macbeth's speech, and such carelessness places in grave doubt his contention that his interpretations derive from the nature of the stimulus rather than from an idiosyncratic response.

Holland attempts to guard against this in his preface with the statement that "at ... times you may feel that my response is idiosyncratic—so be it. The important thing is that we be as candid as we can, I in my assertions, you in your disagreements" (xiv-xv). But "so be it" is hardly enough. There are, after all, appropriate and inappropriate responses (one thinks immediately of Charles Addams' famous cartoon of a movie audience in its entirety bathed in tears except for his creepy little man in black laughing his head off). And a man spends a great deal of time on a couch in psychoanalysis because his responses are inappropriate. All the candor in the world—though it is the first and only rule—will not make him healthy enough to eventually leave the couch. He needs, in addition, the appropriate responses of the rest of the world at large, concentrated for a time in the psychoanalyst, compared and contrasted with his own, to bring him to that. This is not to imply, emphatically, that Professor Holland's response is inappropriate or unhealthy; only that it is his and not necessarily yours or mine.[6] To imply that it is, as he does, is to be reductive. Three persons shown the same ink-blot might give three different responses; which of these is the "correct" one? The nature of the stimulus in each case is, of course, the same, but the response obviously tells us more about the person than about the ink-blot.

Thus, Professor Holland's procedure has nothing in it *per se* to guard against one of the most common of critical errors, what we might call the *projective fallacy*. Just as the analyst must undergo psychoanalysis himself in order to minimize projection of his own problems into his patient, the critic too must be sufficiently aware of himself so as to not project his into the literary text (we have all met the student who felt Raskolnikov justified in his deeds). Twenty years ago, in one of the first issues of *Literature and Psychology,* Leon Edel pointed out this danger in his "Notes on the Use of Psychological Tools in Literary Scholarship."[7] It is unfortunate that we here and now must be speaking of the same matter. We grant that the projective fallacy might be guarded against by the use of corroborative tests, Rorschach and word association, for example, but once again this is extra-literary involvement moving us towards therapy and away from the text. This movement away from the text is, of course, our prime quarrel with Professor Holland. We had hoped that he would remain a New Critic (as psychoanalytic criticism is but a branch of New Criticism), committed to the autonomy of the text, bound to finding meaning within it. Such has not been the case. We regret as well that this movement away from the text has been counter to the movement of psychoanalysis as a whole; Holland's general tendency is to say "Where Ego is, there shall Id be." Five years prior to *The Dynamics of Literary Response,* Pitcher and Prelinger in their study of the fantasy element in children's tales emphasized the organizing, integrative, and differentiating ego functions, pointing out that movement toward id-interpretations of tales was both retrograde and sterile in itself:

Drive contents are rarely expressed directly in the stories; if they are, this in itself would have to be understood in terms of particular and perhaps exceptional ego states. There are various circumstances under which such relatively rare expressions of drives could occur: there might be actual failures of ego control, or the ego might be using regressive material for a particular adaptive purpose, such as coping with the investigator whom the child might perceive in some special way. The actual conditions of such phenomena, however, can never be fully ascertained from the stories alone. Meaningful individual analysis and interpretation of stories would require a good deal of additional material such as, for instance, clinical situations provide.[8]

Frederick C. Crews—in what amounts to a virtual Declaration of Independents for psychoanalytic critics—deplored the anaesthetic quality in Holland's theory when he asserted that

A criticism that cheerfully catalogues the unconscious tricks we play on ourselves and equates literary power with a judicious recipe of wishes and tactics, introjection and intellection, cannot avoid becoming a new version of anaesthesia—a version using Freud's terminology but lacking Freud's sympathy for the way great artists court unconscious engulfment in order to recreate the conditions of a human order.

Criticism starting from an infantile fantasy rather than from this task of reconciliation [of the competing claims of the ego, superego, and id] will not be able to do justice to the cognitive aspect of literature, which is just as "psychoanalytic" as fantasy itself. The crucial difference between literary creation and symptom formation resides in the extra demand we make of literature that it confirm and extend our sense of truth.[9]

We must, therefore, caution the aspiring critic against following Holland's lead; it can only take him away from his prime commitment to literature. Indeed the lure is strong. Professor Holland writes with a flair, great wit, and high intelligence and interprets with facility. But we must not, like Polonius, affirm "'Tis very like a camel indeed," and then with the next interpretation say "Very like a whale," when in reality we are looking at what is still, despite all our wishes, a cloud.

Notes

1. Norman N. Holland, "Romeo's Dream and the Paradox of Literary Realism," *Literature and Psychology*, 13, No. 4 (1963), pp. 97-103. All subsequent references are to this article.
2. Sigmund Freud, *The Standard Edition of the Complete Psychological Works of Sigmund Freud* (London: Hogarth Press, 1953), IV, p. 279.
3. Norman N. Holland, *Psychoanalysis and Shakespeare* (New York: McGraw-Hill, 1966). All subsequent references are to this edition.
4. Norman N. Holland, *The Dynamics of Literary Response* (New York: Oxford University Press, 1968), p. vii. All subsequent references are to this edition.
5. Abram Kardiner *et al.*, "A Methodological Study of Freudian Theory," *International Journal of Psychiatry*, 2, No. 5 (1966), p. 497.
6. When he first published this interpretation in *Literature and Psychology*, 15 (1965), pp. 79-91, under the title "Toward a Psychoanalysis of Poetic Form: Some Mixed Metaphors Unmixed," Professor Holland attempted to guard against such idiosyncrasy by including a paragraph on the difficulties of generalizing from his "conclusions." Since this paragraph appears nowhere in the present study, we can only assume that he feels more strongly confirmed now in the rightness of his interpretation.
7. Leon Edel, "Notes on the Use of Psychological Tools in Literary Scholarship," *Literature and Psychology*, 1, No. 4 (1950); available in *Literature and Psychology: Reprint of Leading Articles and Bibliographies from Volumes I and II* (September, 1953), pp. 6-8.
8. Evelyn Pitcher and Ernst Prelinger, *Children Tell Stories* (New York: International Universities Press, 1963), pp. 20-21.
9. Frederick C. Crews, *Psychoanalysis and Literary Process* (Cambridge, Mass.: Winthrop, 1970), pp. 19-21.

Additional Critics

We now recommend other critics whom we have been unable to consider at length, along with at least one of their studies which we feel adequately reflects the individual critic's competence. Worth the reader's consideration, then, are Franz Alexander's "A Note on Falstaff," *Psychoanalytic Quarterly*, 2 (1933), pp. 592-606; Wayne Burns's "Freudianism, Criticism, and *Jane Eyre*," *Literature and Psychology*, 2, No. 5 (1952), 4-13; Richard Chase's analysis of "Billy Budd" in *Herman Melville* (New York: The Macmillan Co., 1949); Kurt Eissler's *Goethe: A Psychoanalytic Study, 1775-1786* (Detroit: 1963) and *Discourse on Hamlet and "Hamlet"* (New York: International Universities Press, 1970); Angus Fletcher's *Allegory: The Theory of a Symbolic Mode* (Ithaca: Cornell University, 1964); Selma Fraiberg's "Tales of the Discovery of the Secret Treasure," *Psychoanalytic Study of the Child*, 9 (1954), pp. 218-241 and "Kafka and the Dream," *Partisan Review*, 23 (1956), pp. 47-69; Phyllis Greenacre's *Swift and Carroll: A Psychoanalytic Study of Two Lives* (New York: International Universities Press, 1955); William J. Griffin's "The Uses and Abuses of Psychoanalysis in the Study of Literature," *Literature and Psychology: Reprint of Leading Articles and Bibliographies from Volumes I and II*

(September, 1953), pp. 9-18; James G. Hepburn's "Disarming and
Uncanny Visions: Freud's " 'The Uncanny' with Regard to Form and
Content in Stories by Sherwood Anderson and D. H. Lawrence," *Literature and Psychology,* 9 (1959), pp. 9-12; Richard Hovey's *Heming-
way: The Inward Terrain* (Seattle: University of Washington Press,
1968); Ludwig Jekels' "The Problem of the Duplicated Expression of
Psychic Themes," *International Journal of Psycho-analysis,* 14 (1933),
pp. 300-309, and "The Riddle of Shakespeare's *Macbeth,*" *Selected
Papers* (New York: International Universities Press, 1952); F. L. Lucas'
Literature and Psychology (Ann Arbor, Michigan: University of Michigan Press, 1957); Leonard F. Manheim's *"A Tale of Two Cities* (1859):
A Study in Psychoanalytic Criticism," *English Review* (1959), pp.
13-28, and "Thanatos: The Death Instinct in Dickens' Later Novels,"
Psychoanalysis and the Psychoanalytic Review, 47, No. 4 (1960), pp.
17-31, reprinted in his *Hidden Patterns* (New York: Macmillan, 1966),
pp. 113-31; Charles Mauron's *Introduction to the Psychoanalysis of
Mallarmé,* translated by Archibald Henderson, Jr. and Will L. Mc-
Lendon (1950; rpt. Berkeley: University of California Press, 1963);
Henry Murray's *"In Nomine Diaboli,"* *Psychology Today,* 2, No. 4
(1968), p. 64 ff. and his introduction to Herman Melville's *Pierre, or
the Ambiguities* (New York: Farrar, 1949); Clarence P. Oberndorf's
The Psychiatric Novels of Oliver Wendell Holmes (New York: Columbia
University Press, 1946); Robert Rogers' "The Beast in Henry James,"
American Imago, 13 (1956), pp. 427-54, and "Prometheus as Scape-
goat," *Literature and Psychology,* 11, No. 1 (1961), pp. 6-11; Claire
Rosenfield's "Men of a Smaller Growth: A Psychological Analysis of
William Golding's *Lord of the Flies,*" *Literature and Psychology,* 11
(1961), pp. 93-96, 99-101, and "The Shadow Within: the Conscious
and Unconscious Use of the Double,' " *Daedalus,* 92 (1963), pp.
326-44; Ella Freeman Sharpe's comparison of poetic devices and dream
mechanisms in the initial chapter of her *Dream Analysis* (London:
Hogarth Press, 1961); Harry Slochower's "Incest in *The Brothers
Karamazov,*" *American Imago,* 16 (1959), pp. 127-45, and *Mythopoesis*
(Detroit: Wayne State University Press, 1970); Gordon Ross Smith's
"The Credibility of Shakespeare's Aaron," *Literature and Psychology,*
10 (1960), pp. 11-13, and "Iago the Paranoic," *American Imago,* 16
(1959), pp. 155-67; Alfred von Winterstein's *Der Ursprung der Tragödie*
(Leipzig; Internationaler Psychoanalytischer Verlag, 1925); William

Wasserstrom's *Heiress of All the Ages: Sex and Sentiment in the Genteel Tradition* (Minneapolis: University of Minnesota Press, 1959), and "Cooper, Freud, and the Origins of Culture," *American Imago,* 17 (1960), pp. 423-37; and Frederick Wyatt's "Analysis of a Popular Novel (Case-study of a Collective Day-dream)," *American Psychologist,* 2 (1947), pp. 280-81.

Selected References

I. Bibliographies, Dictionaries, and Encyclopedias

American Handbook of Psychiatry. 3 vols. Silvano Arieti, ed. New
York: Basic Books, 1959-66.

The Annual Survey of Psychoanalysis: A Comprehensive Survey of Current Theory and Practice. John Frosch *et al.*, eds. New York:
International Universities Press, 1950-.

Encyclopedia of Psychoanalysis. Ludwig Eidelberg, ed. New York: The
Free Press, 1968.

A Glossary of Psychoanalytic Terms and Concepts. Burness E. Moore
and Bernard D. Fine, eds. New York: The New York Psychoanalytic Association, 1967.

The Index of Psychoanalytic Writings. 10 vols. Alexander Grinstein, ed.
New York: International Universities Press, 1956-60.

Psychiatric Dictionary. 3rd ed. Leland E. Hinsie and Robert J. Campbell, eds. New York: Oxford University Press, 1960.

II. Serial Publications

International Psychoanalytical Library. Ernest Jones, ed. London: The
Hogarth Press and the Institute of Psycho-analysis.

The Psychoanalytic Study of the Child. Ruth S. Eissler, Anna Freud,
Heinz Hartmann, and Ernst Kris, eds. New York: International
Universities Press, 1945-.

Psychoanalysis and the Social Sciences. Géza Róheim, Warner Muen-
    sterberger, and Sidney Axelrad, eds. New York: International
    Universities Press, 1947-.
Yearbook of Psychoanalysis. Sandor Lorand, ed. New York: Inter-
    national Universities Press, 1945-.

III. Journals

The American Imago.
Imago (Vienna).
International Journal of Psycho-analysis (London).
Journal of American Psychoanalytic Association.
Literature and Psychology. Morton Kaplan, ed.
Psychoanalytic Quarterly.
Psychoanalytic Review.

IV. Freud's Writings

The Basic Writings of Sigmund Freud. A. A. Brill, ed. New York:
    Modern Library, 1938.
Collected Papers. 5 vols. Translated and edited by Joan Riviere. Lon-
    don: The Hogarth Press, 1924-50.
Gesammelte Schriften. 12 vols. Vienna: Internationaler Psycho-
    analytischer Verlag, 1925-34.
Gesammelte Werke. 18 vols. London: International Psychoanalytic
    Press, 1940-52.
*The Standard Edition of the Complete Psychological Works of Sigmund
    Freud.* 24 vols. Translated and edited by James Strachey, Anna
    Freud, Alix Strachey, and Alan Tyson. London: The Hogarth
    Press and the Institute of Psychoanalysis, 1953-.

V. Freud's Life and the Psychoanalytic Movement

Alexander, Franz G. and Sheldon T. Selesnick. *The History of Psy-
    chiatry.* New York: Harper and Row, 1966.
Arlow, Jacob. *The Legacy of Freud.* New York: International Universi-
    ties Press, 1956.
Binswanger, Ludwig. *Sigmund Freud: Reminiscences of a Friendship.*
    New York: Grune and Stratton, 1957.
Freud, Ernst, ed. *Letters of Sigmund Freud.* New York: McGraw-Hill,
    1964.
Glover, Edward. *Freud or Jung?* Cleveland: The World Publishing Co.,
    1965.
Hoffman, Frederick J. *Freudianism and the Literary Mind.* 2nd ed.
    Baton Rouge: Louisiana University Press, 1967.

Jones, Ernest. *The Life and Works of Sigmund Freud.* 3 vols. New York: Basic Books, 1953-57.
Monroe, Ruth. *Schools of Psychoanalytic Thought.* New York: Holt, 1955.
Mullahy, Patrick. *Oedipus: Myth and Complex.* New York: Grove Press, 1955.
Oberndorf, Clarence. *A History of Psychoanalysis in America.* New York: Grune and Stratton, 1953.
The Origins of Psychoanalysis: Letters, Drafts, and Notes to Wilhelm Fliess, 1887-1902. Marie Bonaparte, Anna Freud, Ernst Kris, eds. New York: Anchor Books, 1957.
Psychoanalytic Pioneers. Franz Alexander, Samuel Eisenstein, Martin Grotjahn, eds. New York: Basic Books, 1966.
Rieff, Phillip. *Freud: The Mind of the Moralist.* New York: Anchor Books, 1961.
Roazen, Paul. *Freud: Political and Social Thought.* New York: Knopf, 1968.

VI. The Dissenting Schools

Adler, Alfred. *The Individual Psychology of Alfred Adler: A Systematic Presentation in Selctions from His Writings.* Heinz L. and Rowena Ansbacher, eds. New York: Basic Books, 1956.
_____. *The Science of Living.* Heinz L. Ansbacher, ed. New York: Anchor Books, 1969.
Horney, Karen. *New Ways in Psychoanalysis.* New York: Norton, 1939.
_____. *Neurosis and Human Growth.* New York: Norton, 1950.
Jung, C. G. *The Basic Writings of C. G. Jung.* Violet S. DeLaszlo, ed. New York: The Modern Library, 1959.
_____. *Collected Works.* 18 vols. Herbert Read, Michael Fordham, and Gerhard Adler, eds. New York: Pantheon, 1953.
Rank, Otto. *The Myth of the Birth of the Hero and Other Writings.* Phillip Freund, ed. New York: Vintage Books, 1964.

VII. Psychoanalytic Theory

Brenner, Charles. *An Elementary Textbook of Psychoanalysis.* New York: Anchor Books, 1955.
Erikson, Erik. *Childhood and Society.* 2nd ed. New York: Norton, 1963.
Fenichel, Otto. *The Psychoanalytic Theory of Neurosis.* New York: Norton, 1955.
Freud, Anna. *The Ego and the Mechanisms of Defense.* Rev. ed. Vol. II. *The Writings of Anna Freud.* New York: International Universities Press, 1966.

Gill, Merton. *Topography and Systems in Psychoanalytic Thought.* New York: International Universities Press, 1963.

Hartmann, Heinz. *Ego Psychology and the Problem of Adaptation.* New York: International Universities Press, 1958.

――――. *Essays on Ego Psychology.* New York: International Universities Press, 1964.

Hendrick, Ives. *Facts and Theories of Psychoanalysis.* 3rd ed. New York: Knopf, 1958.

Kardiner, Abram, Aaron Karush, and Lionel Ovesey. "A Methodological Study of Freudian Theory." *International Journal of Psychiatry.* Vol. 2 (1966), pp. 489-542.

Madison, Peter. *Freud's Concept of Repression and Defense.* Minneapolis: University of Minnesota Press, 1961.

Psychoanalysis and Current Biological Thought. Norman S. Greenfield and William C. Lewis, eds. Madison: University of Wisconsin Press, 1965.

Psychoanalysis as an Art and a Science. Harry Slochower, ed. Detroit: Wayne State University Press, 1968.

Psychoanalysis as Science. E. Pumpian-Mindlin, ed. Stanford: Stanford University Press, 1952.

Psychoanalysis, Scientific Method, and Philosophy. Sidney Hook, ed. New York: New York University Press, 1964.

Psychoanalytic Psychiatry and Psychology. Robert Knight and Cyrus Friedman, eds. New York: International Universities Press, 1970.

The Psychoanalytic Reader. Robert Fliess, ed. New York: International Universities Press, 1967.

Rapaport, David. *The Structure of Psychoanalytic Theory.* New York: International Universities Press, 1960.

Sherwood, Michael. *The Logic of Explanation in Psychoanalysis.* New York: Academic Press, 1969.

Waelder, Robert. *Basic Theory of Psychoanalysis.* New York: Schocken, 1960.

VIII. Applied Psychoanalysis

Arlow, Jacob. "Ego Psychology and the Study of Mythology." *Journal of the American Psychoanalytic Association.* Vol. 9 (1961), pp. 371-93.

Contemporary Educational Psychology: Selected Essays. Richard M. Jones, ed. New York: Harper and Row, 1967.

Freud and the Twentieth Century. Benjamin Nelson, ed. New York: Meridian, 1965.

Kardiner, Abram. *The Psychological Frontiers of Society.* New York: Columbia University Press, 1963.

Kris, Ernst. *Psychoanalytic Explorations in Art.* New York: International Universities Press, 1952.

Psychoanalysis and Culture. George Wilbur and Warner Muensterberger, eds. New York: Science Editions, 1967.

Psychoanalysis and History. Bruce Mazlish, ed. Englewood Cliffs, N. J.: Prentice-Hall, 1963.

Rank, Otto. *The Myth of the Birth of the Hero and Other Writings.* Phillip Freund, ed. New York: Vintage Books, 1964.

Ricoeur, Paul. *Freud and Philosophy.* Translated by Denis Savage. New Haven: Yale University Press, 1970.

Róheim, Géza. *Psychoanalysis and Anthropology.* New York: International Universities Press, 1950.

Thass-Thienemann, Theodore. *The Subconscious Language.* New York: Washington Square Press, 1967.

―――. *Symbolic Behavior.* New York: Washington Square Press, 1968.

IX. Psychoanalytic Theory of Literature

Crews, Frederick C. "Literature and Psychology." *Relations of Literary Study.* James Thorpe, ed. New York: Modern Language Association, 1967.

Edel, Leon. "The Biographer and Psychoanalysis." *International Journal of Psychoanalysis.* Vol. 42 (1961), pp. 458-66.

Fletcher, Angus. *Allegory: The Theory of a Symbolic Mode.* Ithaca: Cornell University Press, 1964.

Holland, Norman. *The Dynamics of Literary Response.* New York: Oxford University Press, 1968.

Lesser, Simon. *Fiction and the Unconscious.* Boston: Beacon, 1957.

X. Psychoanalytic Literary Criticism

Annual Bibliography of Literature and Psychology. Morton Kaplan, senior ed., and Robert J. Kloss, ed. Teaneck, N. J.: Fairleigh Dickinson University, 1964-.

Art and Psychoanalysis. William Phillips, ed. New York: Meridian, 1957.

Barchilon, Jose and Joel S. Kovel. "*Huckleberry Finn:* A Psychoanalytic Study." *Journal of the American Psychoanalytic Association.* Vol. 14 (1966), pp. 775-814.

Bodkin, Maud. *Archetypal Patterns in Poetry.* New York: Vintage Books, 1958.

Bonaparte, Marie. *The Life and Works of Edgar Allan Poe.* 2 vols. London: Imago, 1949.

Crews, Frederick. *The Sins of the Fathers: Hawthorne's Psychological Themes.* New York: Oxford University Press, 1966.

The Design Within: Psychoanalytic Approaches to Shakespeare. M. D. Faber, ed. New York: Science House, 1970.

Faber, M. D. *Suicide and Greek Tragedy.* New York: Sphinx Press, 1970.

Greenacre, Phyllis. *Swift and Carroll: A Psychoanalytic Study of Two Lives.* New York: International Universities Press, 1955.

Hidden Patterns: Studies in Psychoanalytic Literary Criticism. Leonard and Eleanor Manheim, eds. New York: Macmillan, 1966.

Holland, Norman. *Psychoanalysis and Shakespeare.* New York: McGraw-Hill, 1966.

Jones, Ernest. *Hamlet and Oedipus.* New York: Anchor Books, 1954.

Morrison, Claudia. *Freud and the Critic: The Early Use of Depth Psychology in Literary Criticism.* Chapel Hill: University of North Carolina Press, 1968.

Psychoanalysis and American Fiction. Irving Malin, ed. New York: Dutton, 1965.

Psychoanalysis and Literary Process. Frederick C. Crews, ed. Cambridge, Mass.: Winthrop, 1970.

Psychoanalysis and Literature. Hendrik Ruitenbeek, ed. New York: Dutton, 1964.

Psychoanalysis, Psychology, and Literature: A Bibliography. Norman Kiell, ed. Madison: University of Wisconsin Press, 1963.

Weiss, Daniel. *Oedipus in Nottingham: D. H. Lawrence.* Seattle: University of Washington Press, 1962.

XI. Psychobiography

Eissler, Kurt. *Goethe: A Psychoanalytic Study, 1775-1786.* 2 vols. Detroit: Wayne State University Press, 1963.

Erikson, Erik. *Gandhi's Truth.* New York: Norton, 1969.

———. *Young Man Luther.* New York: Norton, 1958.

Myer, Bernard. *Joseph Conrad: A Psychoanalytic Biography.* Princeton: Princeton University Press, 1967.

Appendix:
The Dissenting Schools

When the eminent analyst Edward Glover, in charge of organizing the training of British psychoanalytical students, suggested to Ernest Jones, then President of the British Psychoanalytic Society, that students should be instructed in the doctrines of the important psychoanalytic schismatics, Jones tersely commented, "Why waste their time?" Though we strongly sympathize with him, we still feel it necessary, at this point, to consider briefly the revisionists, heretics, schismatics, anti-, neo-, and epi-Freudians. We have observed, for example, that Adlerian and Jungian literary explications—to mention perhaps the two most prominent—seem to be multiplying in inverse proportion to their ability to explain anything. It thus becomes incumbent upon the psychoanalytic critic to familiarize himself with these schools and others in order to be able to discuss intelligently, refute when necessary, and attack if forced to, the literary explications of non-Freudian psychological critics.

What follows, then, are brief summaries of the psychological contributions made by founders of the major schools. These are not meant to be substitutes for primary sources; there are no substitutes. They are intended only to provide an overview for the reader, who is then expected to go to the writings of the psychologists themselves. The criticisms of the schools are intended to be neither incisive nor comprehensive; they are, on the contrary, quite spare. Comprehensive criticisms have been done superlatively by others and we urge the reader, as the next step in his psychoanalytic education, to study the extensive considerations of the major schools in two noteworthy volumes, Patrick Mullahy's *Oedipus: Myth and Complex* and Ruth L. Munroe's *Schools of Psychoanalytic Thought*.[1] The former is a concise Baedeker, generally reliable though slightly colored by the author's bias toward Harry Stack Sullivan. A greater defect of this guide, however, is Mullahy's eclecticism; he leads the reader to believe that one can pick and choose among the ideas of Freud, Jung, Adler, *et al.,* selecting the more acceptable ones, in order to concoct a sort of psychological tutti-frutti to please the palate of anyone interested in the secrets of his own nature. An eclectic position is completely untenable. Worse still, eclecticism is but a placebo, a defense against the secrets of one's nature, a desire not to see the rose through world-colored glasses.

Miss Munroe, on the other hand, is consistent and committed. Her book is an excellent, lucid examination of the major schools, one which not only summarizes their theories in a beautifully organized schema, but also astutely criticizes and contributes valuable insights of the author's own.

Yet though our criticisms of the schools themselves are minimal, in accordance with the purposes of this volume, our considerations of the literary criticism utilizing their theories is more extensive and detailed. Thus, we have arranged the schools in approximate descending order of the frequency with which they generate criticism and have provided, wherever possible, specific examples of such criticism, compared and contrasted with Freudian analyses of the same work. In this way, we have attempted to demonstrate the relative weaknesses and strengths of both approaches. These comparison-contrast critiques, we feel, reveal fully the defects of the explications of the dissident schools. In general, we can level four major criticisms against the revisionists: (a) their systems have been constructed, for the most part, not inductively, but deductively, (b) as a result, they are closed systems, impervious to change, subject to destruction by empirical observation; being closed, they are as well unproductive of further hypotheses, (c) consequently, they are guiltier themselves of the charge they most often level against Freud—reductiveness, and (d) they are, in themselves, defenses against the harsh truths Freud first revealed to men. They have obviously "revised" and "improved" psychoanalysis in order to remove the most troublesome of its basic tenets—infantile sexuality and its consequent conflicts. As a result, they attempt to move too far forward in the development of the individual, as with Fromm's theory of the social formation of the ego, or too far backward, as with Rank's birth trauma theory of neurosis. Stanley Edgar Hyman, once a booster of Jungian criticism in *The Armed Vision,* much later came to recognize the defects of the revisionists and declaimed that "the result of their revisions has nevertheless, in my opinion, been not to improve or modernize psychoanalysis, but to abandon its key insights both as a science and as a philosophy. Their effect has been to re-repress whatever distasteful or tragic truths Freud dug out of his own unconscious or his patients', and to convert the familiar device of resistance into revisionist theory."[2] Thus, "the opportunity, vastly greater than Freud's, that the neo-Freudians have for acquiring some accurate information about the nature of man in society seems to have resulted only in cheerier illusions."[3]

Cheery illusion, too, is what we create if we employ any of these systems in literary criticism. Our study would be, almost of necessity, deductive, barren, reductive, and defensive. Other prominent critics have been calling the public's attention to these facts for some time. Indeed, Frederick C. Crews cogently argues not only that the criticisms of all other psychological schools are defensive, but also that all types of literary criticism except Freudian psychoanalytic criticism are both defensive and "anaesthetic."[4] The reader would do well to study Crews's arguments carefully, for there is more at stake than the winning of an academic garland. As Hyman puts it, "the trouble with the revisionist Freudians is not that they would give up art for the psychoanalytic good society, but that they pretend that it is already here, that we are well when we are in fact desperately ill, and they drive out art when it is almost the only honest doctor who will tell us the truth."[5]

C. G. Jung

Analytic Psychology was the name Carl Gustav Jung gave to the new school he founded after his split with Freud in 1914. Freud, with extreme patience, had attempted to prevent the break, for he had already suffered the defections of Adler and Stekel, and he had fully expected Jung to eventually replace him as leader of the psychoanalytic movement, going so far as to say, "When the empire I founded is orphaned, no one but Jung must inherit the whole thing."[6] Finally, however, he was forced to sever both professional and personal relations with Jung as he had with the others and would, within ten years, with Rank and Ferenczi.

Prior to his leaving the psychoanalytic circle, Jung had made significant contributions: his construction of word association tests provided the first link between experimental psychology and psychoanalysis and confirmed the existence of repression, the keystone of psychoanalytic theory; he introduced the concept and word *complex* into psychology; he constructed the first psychosomatic model for dementia praecox; and, most important of all, his contention that libido theory did not distinguish between neurosis and psychosis in the famous Schreber case forced Freud to revise the entire theory.[7]

Ernest Jones has observed that the quarrels between Freud and his disciples had their origins not, as seemed, in doctrinal divergences, but actually in unresolved infantile conflicts of the dissidents (none of them had been analyzed).[8] Aware of this, Freud took great pains to allow full exposition of the revisionists' ideas and debate and criticism of them on scientific grounds alone. Such fairness, however, could only delay, not stem, the course of the conflicts, so the breaks always came, as Freud knew and feared they would: "I am continually annoyed by the two [Adler and Stekel] . . . who are rapidly developing backwards and will soon end up by denying the existence of the unconscious."[9]

As it turned out, not only these two, but all the dissidents eventually denied the existence of the unconscious or minimized it to the point where it became simply a psychological curiosity, the vagary of an old man in Vienna. This denial in Jung's psychology is difficult to detect, for a number of reasons, but Edward Glover has shown with powerful clarity that it does exist.[10] It is hard to see, for one thing, because of the density of Jung's prose style and, for another, because Jung *seems* to place great emphasis upon the unconscious even to the extent of multiplying its number:

A more or less superficial layer of the unconscious is undoubtedly personal. I call it the *personal unconscious*. But this personal unconscious rests upon a deeper layer, which does not derive from personal experience and is not a personal acquisition but is inborn. This deeper layer I call the *collective unconscious*. I have chosen the term "collective" because this part of the unconscious is not individual but universal; in contrast to the personal psyche, it has contents and modes of behavior that are more or less the same everywhere and in all individuals. It is, in other words, identical in all men and constitutes a common psychic substrate of a suprapersonal nature which is present in every one of us. . . . The contents of the personal unconscious are chiefly the *feeling-toned complexes,* as they are called; they constitute the personal and private side of psychic life. The contents of the collective unconscious, on the other hand, are known as archetypes.[11]

Or to put it a bit more succinctly, "The collective unconscious contains the whole spiritual heritage of mankind's evolution born anew in the brain structure of every individual."[12]

This spiritual legacy, the residue of the entire ancestry of man from time immemorial, is transmitted in the form of images, "primordial images" called, as Jung has noted above, *archetypes.* These images have been created by engrams imprinted on the psyche, and they are rather "limited in number, corresponding to the relatively limited number of fundamental and typical human situations, rooted in the generalities of our existence."[13] Typical of these are the Wise Old Man, the Magna Mater, the mandala, the weeping eye of God, and the snake of the passions. Though the archetypes are the same for all people, their representation will vary from person to person, for "the term 'archetype' . . . designates only those psychic contents which have not yet been submitted to conscious elaboration and are therefore an immediate datum of psychic experience. . . . The archetype is essentially an unconscious content that is altered by becoming conscious and by being perceived, and it takes its color from the individual consciousness in which it happens to appear."[14] By way of clarification, Jung adds that "one must, for the sake of accuracy, distinguish between 'archetype' and 'archetypal ideas.' The archetype as such is a hypothetical and irrepresentable model, something like the 'pattern of behavior' in biology."[15]

Archetypes seem, then, to be not ideas, but rather inherent dispositions toward particular modes of action. They are, as well, extremely important to Analytic Psychology because, according to Jung, they "were, and still are, living psychic forces that demand to be taken seriously, and they have a strange way of making sure of their effect. Always they were the bringers of protection and salvation, and their violation has as its consequence the 'perils of the soul,' known to us from the psychology of the primitives. Moreover, they are the unfailing causes of neurotic and even psychotic disorders, behaving exactly like neglected or maltreated physical organs or organic functional systems."[16]

The archetype should not be confused with the *symbol,* another basic Jungian concept. To Jung, a symbol is a transformer of psychic energy, life-force, or *libido,* to use the term he adapted, through generalization, from Freud. "By symbol he means a representation that can supply an equivalent expression of the libido and so canalize it into a new form."[17] The symbols we experience in our dreams would exemplify this, since they represent and disclose, when interpreted, the force and direction of our psychic processes. "A conception which interprets the symbolic expression as the best possible formulation of a relatively unknown factor which cannot conceivably be more clearly or characteristically represented, is *symbolic.*"[18] *Libido,* then is not to be understood as it is in Freudian theory as *sexual* energy; for Jung it is simply a generalized energy, a life force. Sexuality has no real place in Jungian theory; it is always symbolic in the castration complex, which represents only the sacrificing of infantile wishes and in the Oedipus complex, in which the mother has no sexual significance but is merely the source of all pleasure to the child. Sex, for Jung, is basically *symbolic.*

Interpreting these symbols and archetypes to analyze the psychic forces is part of the process known, in Analytic Psychology, as *individuation* or "becoming a single homogeneous being, and in so far as 'individuality' embraces our innermost, last, and incomparable uniqueness, it also implies becoming one's own self. We could therefore translate individuation as 'coming to selfhood' or 'self-realization.' The aim of individuation is nothing less than to divest the self of the false wrappings of the persona on the one hand, and the suggestive power of the primordial images on the other."[19] To rid oneself of the *persona* is simply to unmask oneself, for "as its name shows, it is only a mask for the collective psyche, a mask that *feigns individuality,* and tries to make others and oneself believe that one is individual, whereas one is simply playing a part in which the collective psyche speaks. When we analyze the persona, we strip off the mask, and discover that what seemed to be individual is at bottom collective; in other words, that the persona was only a mask for the collective psyche. Fundamentally the persona is nothing real: it is a compromise between individual and society as to what a man should appear to be."[20]

This process of individuation, of discarding the persona, consists of several steps, the first of which is the confrontation with the archetype known as the *shadow,* "our 'other side,' our 'dark brother,' who is an invisible but inseparable part of our psychic totality. For 'the living form needs deep shadow if it is to appear plastic. Without shadow it remains a two-dimensional phantom.' 'Everyone carries a shadow,' says Jung, 'and the less it is embodied in the individual's conscious life, the blacker and denser it is. . . . If the repressed tendencies, the shadow as I call them, were obviously evil, there would be no problem whatever. But the shadow is merely somewhat inferior, primitive, unadapted, and awkward; not wholly bad. It even contains childish or primitive qualities which would in a way vitalize and embellish human existence.' "[21]

Once the shadow has been encountered and coped with, the individual is ready to embark on the next leg of the Jungian Odyssey. "The second stage of the individuation process is characterized by the encounter with the 'soul-image,' which in the man Jung calls the *anima* and in the woman, the *animus.* The archetypal figure of the soul-image always stands for the complementary, contrasexual part of the psyche, reflecting both our personal relation to it and the universal human experience of the contrasexual. It represents the image of the other sex that we carry in us as individuals and also as members of the species."[22]

Thus the soul-image represents the habitual inner attitude of a man and the persona represents his habitual outer attitude. *Attitude* itself, however, has a more specific meaning for the Jungian. As a person interacts with his world, he generally assumes one of two *attitudes:* turning toward himself or *introversion,* or turning toward the world or *extraversion.* These attitudes are apparently inherent temperamental differences and are decisive for our relationships with others and for our ideologies as well as our general disposition toward life itself. To this general disposition, the *attitude,* Jung adds four specific *functions* of the personality, methods by which one grasps and elaborates the contents of both inner and outer experience. These four are *sensation* and *intuition,* modes of apprehension, and *feeling* and *thinking,* modes of judgment. "*Sensation* concerns the present, the *now.* It tells us that a thing *is,* either in the outer world or in ourselves. *Intuition* deals with the potential—what the thing will be or has been, not what it *is. Feeling* gives a sense of values. Is the thing agreeable or disagreeable, to be accepted by the self or rejected? . . . *Thinking* tells us *what the thing is* in an abstract conceptualized manner."[23]

The task of Analytic Psychology then is to bring all these disparate elements of the personality to consciousness, integrating them in one whole, designated as the *Self*. The attitudes, functions, and aspects are balanced, the symbols and archetypes encountered—all in a struggle of heroic proportions, which, when successful, results in full harmonious development of the personality, achievement of the Self.

CRITICISM AND COMMENT

The *sine qua non* for the psychoanalytic critic—indeed for anyone interested in psychoanalysis—wanting to understand once and for all the difference between the psychologies of Freud and Jung is, of course, Edward Glover's masterful *Freud or Jung?* In this slim volume of fewer than 200 pithy pages, the eminent British analyst compares and contrasts point for point the essential tenets of both psychologies and demonstrates that the thinking man need no longer remain impaled on the horns of a dilemma, for "the truth is that no psychological theory is worth the paper it is written on unless it can give an objective account of the structure, function and dynamics of mind, can trace the stages of mental development from infancy to senescence, can indicate the main factors giving rise to mental disorder and correlate these with the mechanisms responsible for the more significant manifestations of normal mental life both individual and social."[24] Capable of satisfying these criteria is the psychology of Freud and his alone. The implications are obvious: the psychoanalytic critic should shun the psychology of Jung since, deficient at base, it can produce only deficient criticism.

It is not our purpose here to criticize Jungian psychology; Glover is the ultimate in that. He has documented and detailed full well Jung's anti-Freudian bias, destruction of the unconscious, shallowness of thought, contempt for mental illness, and other deficiencies, which include his "co-operation" with the Nazis and his anti-Semitic writings.[25] Munroe, too, has done a highly commendable job.

Our purpose is only to make clear the uselessness of the Jungian approach to literature and to stem—in Frederick Crew's fine phrase—"the Jungian Peril." That a peril exists should be evident from the number of respected critics, Frye and Fiedler among them, espousing the Jungian or quasi-Jungian method. Further, texts and handbooks are daily published containing this sort of thing: "While Dr. Jung himself wrote relatively little that could be called literary criticism, what he did write leaves no doubt that he believed literature, and art in general, to be a vital ingredient in human civilization. Most important, his theories have expanded the horizons of literary interpretation for those critics concerned to use the tools of the mythological approach and for psychological critics who have felt too tightly constricted by Freudian dogma."[26] We assume that the authors would also advocate new approaches for the astronomer who "felt too tightly constricted" by the heliocentric theory. It is indeed most probable that they do not realize that Freudian and Jungian psychology are incompatible because they understand neither.

Doubtless with good reason. Jung's ideas are not easy to comprehend. Their exposition in the previous pages was purposely written containing an inordinate number of direct quotations to illustrate the lack of clarity in Jung's prose (despite our having chosen the passages as the most lucid in his many writings). If the reader came away confused, he has company whose number is legion. Glover almost threw up his hands in despair trying to find a single clear, unqualified statement of a psychological principle,[27] and Aldous Huxley, no professional psychologist, has observed that "Jungian literature is like a vast quaking bog. At every painful step the reader sinks to the hip in jargon and generalizations, with never a patch of firm intellectual ground to rest on and only rare, in that endless expanse of jelly, the blessed relief of a hard, concrete, particular fact."[28]

Such a bog, in contrast to the firm ground of Freud's writing (the only award he ever received from his homeland was the Goethe Prize for Literature), has been noticed and analyzed by numerous people, including professional and personal friends. Viktor von Weizsaecker, in his reminiscences of Jung, concludes that "he befogged his ultimate thoughts in a certain way, but it is not certain whether those ultimate thoughts were clear. . . . His style is uneven and rather impersonal, and that seems to point to a lack of depth in his thinking and of decisive clarity at the base of his character."[29] Glover is more pungent: "It will be seen that once cleared of the transcendental spinach with which they are coated, Jung's theories contribute nothing to the understanding of art."[30] It is to that understanding of art that we now turn.

Generally, Jungian criticism is concerned with the discovery, in literary works, of archetypes, anima/animus, persona, Self, and so on, and the elucidation of what is *really* happening in the story thereby. A good example of such interpretation can be found in the handbook previously cited, *Critical Approaches to Literature*. There we are told that in Hawthorne's "Young Goodman Brown" the protagonist's persona, while appearing to be that of a "Good Man," is really false, that of a "Bad Boy" in reality. He is adolescent from start to finish, deserting his wife to be a peeping tom in the forest and failing to see, in his confrontation with Satan, his shadow or himself in all his baseness. In the same way that his persona has failed to relate him properly to the outer world, so has his anima in the projected form of his wife Faith failed to relate him to his inner world. His immaturity is expressed in his acting as if Faith, who is really the archtetype of the Magna Mater, will, like the All-forgiving Mother, accept him once again after his escapade in the forest. As a mature adult, he should act responsibly, taking the consequences for his behavior, unpleasant as they may be. Thus, the authors tell us that:

In clinical terms, young Goodman Brown suffers from a failure of personality integration. He has been stunted in his psychological growth (individuation) because he is unable to confront his shadow, recognize it as a part of his own psyche, and assimilate it to his consciousness. He persists, instead, in projecting the shadow-image: first, in the form of the Devil; then upon the members of his community (Goody Cloyse, Deacon Gookin, and others); and finally, upon Faith herself (his anima), so that ultimately, in his eyes, the whole world is one of shadow, or gloom.[31]

The astute reader at this point might say, "So what?" And with good reason, for it is the job of the critic to explain and nothing has been explained here; everything has been either labeled or described in terms which only obfuscate the underlying psychodynamics of the tale. This interpretation well demonstrates the Jungian critic's incomparable facility for turning trivia into quadrivia. One need only turn to the excellent analysis of the same story done by Frederick C. Crews in *The Sins of the Fathers* to see exactly how deficient the previous interpretation really is. There Crews demonstrates with ample textual support—Jungians are fond of asserting with little recourse to the text—that Goodman Brown is indeed immature and that the figures he meets are certainly projections, but more importantly, "Brown's fantasy-experience . . . follows the classic Oedipal pattern: resentment of paternal authority is conjoined with ambiguous sexual temptation."[32] Throughout the tale, Crews notes, fathers are transformed into devils or warlocks, mothers into witches, and the emphasis is constantly on the secret, orgiastic doings of men and women in the dark of night.

This analysis, unlike the other, has the advantages of clarity, easy integration into Hawthorne's entire canon, and validation through textual evidence. No obscurant jargon is necessary: no anima, no persona, no archetype. The very existence of such entities as the archetype and the Collective Unconscious is, in the first place, highly doubtful. No Jungian critic, however, seems to have ever taken the trouble to verify the very concepts which are his sole stock in trade; even Jung himself avoided coming to grips with the concept: "From the standpoint of the individual, the archetypes exist a priori. They are inherent in the collective unconscious, and hence unaffected by individual growth and decay. 'Whether,' says Jung, 'this psychic structure and its elements, the archetypes, ever "originated" at all is a metaphysical question and therefore unanswerable by psychology."[33] Apparently we are not expected to probe the depths of the eternal mysteries, for if we did, how could they possibly remain eternal? To question is to embarrass, as does Lawrence Kubie when he asks provcatively that if such symbols are indeed inherited, why has the airplane replaced the bird and the snake as a sexual symbol in dreams to such a great extent?[34] We might also inquire, given the overwhelming evidence of the importance of sex to man—from the cave paintings of Altamira through the graphic murals of Pompeii to the lavatory graffiti of the present day, why does Jung's list of archetypes not contain one directly and explicitly relating to sex?

Advocates of Jung, at this point, may object and cite Freud's occasionally favorable remarks on the archetypes and the Collective Unconscious in *Totem and Taboo* and *Moses and Monotheism*. However, both Glover and Selesnick[35] have amply shown that he was speaking in terms of analogy and not identity and did not dismiss the ontogenetic origin. To view archetypes phylogenetically is to be on dangerous footing at the outset, however easy the explanation which racial inheritance provides. As Norman Holland has observed, "one simple way of explaining the fact that these patterns turn up in all times, all genres, and all cultures is to say that we inherit these patterns as some kind of collective or archetypal or imprinted unconscious. But that is not the only possible explanation, and others do not require the troublesome assumption that our RNA and DNA, already so fraught with information, must carry Grimm's fairy tales as well."[36]

The other, more obvious, explanation is provided by ontogeny, the developmental history of the individual. There is no conclusion that Jungian criticism can reach through its phylogenetic approach that cannot be explained in terms of the development of the individual. We need not posit, for example, a Magna Mater archetype for Goodman Brown, which operates through his projected anima to cause him problems. We can more reasonably say that he acts toward Faith, and probably toward all other women, as he most probably acted toward his mother—emotionally dependent and fearful of her sexuality. The use of archetypes always forces Jungian critics into pseudo-explanations, that is, tautological restatements of the same phenomenon in different terms. To call Faith a Magna Mater archetype and the Devil a shadow archetype, for example, is merely to exchange one set of names for another. Things are only described thereby, not explained. Thus the Jungian, busy exchanging one label for another, rarely gets below the surface into the psychodynamics of the literature. So even if we grant the existence of the archetype—which we do not—we are still left with only pseudo-explanations.

Granting the existence of the archetype, in addition, calls attention to the reductiveness of Jungian criticism.[37] All women become the Magna Mater, all men the Wise Old Man, any evil person the Shadow; the text is left to fend for itself. A literary work, a painting, a symphony, is more than simply the spontaneous re-awakening of a long-slumbering archetype in the mind of its creator, which when caught and labeled "explains" the work in which it was elaborated. As numerous others, among them Kris, Kubie, Sachs, and Lesser, have shown, a work of art is a highly elaborate, extremely complex manifestation of mind and feeling, not to be explained simply. Glover gives us some idea of this complexity in his pithy statement of the functions of a work of art:

... The more sophisticated work of art has many other tasks [besides expression] to perform. It must not only represent the kernel phantasies giving rise to conflict in the mind of the artist, but also the expiation or negation of these same phantasies. In so doing it makes use of those infinitely complex defensive processes which affect the instinctual force at every stage of its passage from the Id, through the unconscious and preconscious ego, to the field of perceptual consciousness. In the last stages of the journey, the processes of 'secondary elaboration' and 'rationalization' take effect, cementing the compromise in such a way that the onlooker is more or less prepared to assimilate the artist's work.[38]

How, we wonder, would the Jungian critic explain these matters, armed as he is with only a quiver of archetypes? How would he cope with any non-representational work of art, with a tale by Samuel Beckett, a painting by Franz Kline, a sculpture by Henry Moore? Jungian criticism, it would appear, stands indicted. Its basic concepts lack empirical validation, its theory is circular, its analyses really pseudo-explanations. None of this should be surprising, however, since the psychology upon which it rests is deductively constructed, assuming that man is more angel than devil, then fitting the facts to the assumptions or, worse still, ignoring them. It is not really psychoanalysis, but a defense against psychoanalysis. "Indeed, Jung has proved a godsend for many critics troubled by the menace of psychoanalysis, for he spent the better part of a lifetime coping with that menace in seductive and readily adaptable ways. Even someone who applies Jung's system with unfashionable explicitness and persistence will find himself free to retain an elevated notion of literature."[39]

Frederick Crews' words are well taken. Jung, in his frantic desire to eliminate sex from psychoanalysis,[40] succeeded in reducing it from a dynamic cause of conflict to a symbolic function in his psychology. Lost from his psychology, it is lost from Jungian criticism, which now many critics, unthreatened by its relative harmlessness highly tout as the new wave. And Freud's comment on Jung's psychology rings ominously from the past: "Anyone who promises to mankind liberation from hardship of sex will be hailed as a hero, let him talk whatever nonsense he chooses."[41]

Alfred Adler

Alfred Adler became, in 1911, the first of Freud's disciples to split with him and form a school of their own. Adler at first called his little group the "Society for Free Psychoanalysis," apparently using the ambiguity to indicate both his emancipation and his pique. Since 1912, however, in deference to the uniqueness and self-consistency of the individual, Adler's school has been known as that of Individual Psychology. From the very beginning, Adler's psychology was an "ego psychology," that is, it was radically oriented toward the environment, deriving its principles primarily not from the biology of the individual, but rather from the attitude which the individual adopted toward himself, more specifically, toward the *defects* in himself. Adler's earliest psychological studies were of the effects of *organ inferiority*—bodily defects—upon personality formation. The nature of the defect, said Adler, was of no significance, only the individual's feelings and behavior toward it. One person might, for example, strive to overcome his defect, while another one with the same defect might use it as an excuse to cease striving. (Adler's interest is most probably the result of his own personal defect: because of severe rickets, he did not walk until he was four, and soon after gaining his feet he became seriously ill with pneumonia.)[42]

The only important biological fact for Adler is the helplessness of the infant, for this is the source of *all feelings of inferiority*. Here we must let Adler himself speak. "The method of Individual Psychology— we have no hesitation in confessing it—begins and ends with the problem of inferiority. Inferiority . . . is the basis for human striving and success. On the other hand the sense of inferiority is the basis for all our problems and psychological maladjustment. When the individual does not find a proper concrete goal of superiority, an inferiority complex results. The inferiority complex leads to a desire for escape, and this desire for escape is expressed in a superiority complex, which is nothing more than a goal on the useless and vain side of life offering the satisfaction of false success. This is the dynamics of psychological life."[43] Thus both organ inferiority and the environmental situation nurture inferiority feelings. The child's method of coping with these feelings and with his parents and siblings determines both the kind and pattern of his compensatory striving for superiority.

Adler calls the goal of this striving and the way in which it is achieved the *life style* of the individual. Every single thing about a person becomes understandable, that is, has an inner consistency, when once the life style becomes apparent. The concept of a life style is thus radically holistic, since every element of the personality is immediately influenced by the aim of the organism as a whole. This relentless drive of the organism toward its goal, according to Individual Psychology, is the sole precipitant of conflict. "Conflicts arise when the life style demands superiority without adequate relation to social feeling and common sense. . . . Adler considers no conflicts intrapsychic."[44] Neither does he acknowledge the importance of the unconscious, for "the use of the terms 'consciousness' and 'unconsciousness' to designate distinctive factors is incorrect in the practice of Individual Psychology.

Consciousness and unconsciousness move together in the same direction and are not contradictions, as is so often believed. What is more, there is no definite line of demarcation between them. It is merely a question of discovering the purpose of their joint movement. It is impossible to decide on what is conscious and what is not until the whole context has been obtained."[45] The Oedipal situation becomes, in this frame of reference, merely symbolic, the struggle of the boy who feels inferior and defenseless to become superior over his father and dominate his mother.

Finally, we must note for our purposes one more important concept of Adlerian psychology, that of the *masculine protest*. Because, in Western society, women are generally held in low esteem, Adler believed they developed more powerful inferiority feelings than men and, as a consequence, developed a stronger compensatory drive toward superiority. This *masculine protest,* as he called it, can also be found in men as a reaction to feminine qualities they feel they possess.

The therapeutic task in Adlerian psychology is simple: to help the patient, by warm encouragement, to come to an understanding of the devices he is using to gain superiority, to understand his own *life style.*

CRITICISM AND COMMENT

Adler made several important contributions to psychology and psychoanalysis: he called attention to inherent organ defects and the individual's formation of his image in relation to them, thus aiding psychosomatic medicine; he stressed an important human attribute, the topic of much discussion today—aggression; and, finally, with his emphasis on overcompensation, he demonstrated that the ego did indeed defend itself, and he suggested two additional defenses: the turning of aggression inward and reaction-formation.[46]

Despite this, Munroe has concluded that "in the long run his complexities have the forced quality of any radically reductionist system. The apostle of common sense tends to tie himself into quite extraordinary knots in the attempt to explain everything by the free striving of the whole personality toward superiority."[47] Freud, of course, was aware of this reductionism as he makes plain in his many and detailed objections to Adler's psychology,[48] and doubtless had it in mind when he replied to the news that Adler had been invited to lecture in America, "Presumably the object is to save the world from sexuality

and base it on aggression."[49] So once again we find the same attempt
to expunge sexuality from psychoanalysis, once again the increased
acceptance by the public resulting from the attempt, and once again we
turn to Freud for the last word: "The view of life which is reflected in
the Adlerian system is founded exclusively on the aggressive instinct;
there is no room in it for love. We might feel surprise that such a
cheerless *Weltanschauung* should have met with any attention at all; but
we must not forget that human beings, weighed down by the burden of
their sexual needs, are ready to accept any thing if only the 'overcoming of sexuality' is offered them as a bait."[50]

Adlerian criticism, like Jungian criticism, is deductive, reductive,
sterile, and defensive. Generally speaking, it is not really literary criticism so much as it is psychological ax-grinding. Adlerian critics are
almost always devoted less to interpreting the text than they are to
proving that Adler was really RIGHT and Freud, by implication if not
by direct statement, WRONG. Such direct statements are made, for
example, in an article entitled "The Casket Scenes from *The Merchant
of Venice:* Symbolism or Life Style,"[51] in which Freud is taken to task
for the wrongheadedness of his 1913 essay "The Theme of the Three
Caskets."

Freud began that essay by noting that Bassanio's speech concerning
his preference of lead to gold has a specious ring to it and, should we
hear such a speech in psychoanalytic practice, we would suspect
concealed motives and probe for them. This he does by tracing
Shakespeare's sources and noting parallels in other folk-tales and myths,
coming to the false conclusion that the caskets stand for the sun, moon,
and star suitors. Dissatisfied with this astral explanation of the myth,
Freud turns for a fresh start to psychoanalytic meanings of symbols,
theorizing that "if what we were concerned with were a dream, it
would occur to us at once that caskets are also women, symbols of
what is essential in woman, and therefore of a woman herself—like
coffers, boxes, cases, baskets, and so on."[52] The choice, then, is really
not of caskets, but of women, as was Lear's choice upon his abdication.
Freud adduces further examples of this situation from mythology—Cinderella and Aphrodite—finally showing the following pattern common
to all: a man must choose from among three women, the third of which
is the youngest and most beautiful, but characteristically silent as well.
Focussing on this silence, Freud explains that psychoanalysis tells us
that dumbness commonly represents death as, for example, in dreams.

The third sister thus becomes the Goddess of Death and, this being so, the sisters then must be the familiar figures of the Fates, or as they are variously called, the Parcae, or the Moerae.

Yet how explain Death's equation with beauty and youth? How explain the element of choice when indeed death comes, of necessity, to all? Easily enough, through another discovery of psychoanalysis: representation by the opposite. Freud proposes that in his desire to overcome death with all its unknown terror, with its terrible necessity, man denies by reversing the truth and this denial is embodied in myth and in the sub-plot of Shakespeare's work. "No greater triumph of wish-fulfillment is conceivable. A choice is made where in reality there is obedience to a compulsion; and what is chosen is not a figure of terror, but the fairest and most desirable of women."[53] Lear entering with the dead Cordelia in his arms enacts this reversal; in reality, it is the Goddess of Death bearing off the king.

In a final moving paragraph, Freud speculates that "we might argue that what is represented here are the three inevitable relations that a man has with a woman—the woman who bears him, the woman who is his mate and the woman who destroys him; or that they are the three forms taken by the figure of the mother in the course of a man's life—the mother herself, the beloved one who is chosen after her pattern, and lastly the Mother Earth who receives him once more."[54]

The reader who has found this plausible, perceptive, lucid, and informative must now be jerked back to reality by the Adlerian critic, John Lickorish, who feels that it is nothing of the sort. In his effort to set matters aright, Lickorish first offers a two-page precis of Freud's essay, detailing and deriding the argument step by step. (We shall return to this precis shortly.) He then offers a seven-page interpretation of his own, demonstrating, not surprisingly, "how the choices of the three suitors correspond to their respective life styles."[55] He successively analyzes the speeches of the three suitors almost word for word, comparing the men to types Adler noted and showing how the type would naturally make the choice he did. Thus, Morocco's life-style is aggressive, conquering, self-important. "Since he regards himself as equal to any of them, why should not the golden casket give *him* what many men desire'?"[56] Arragon, driven by Adlerian superiority and naturally expecting his superior status to be rewarded, chooses silver. Bassanio, though a spendthrift and slightly irresponsible, "is oriented toward reality rather than toward appearances. He is motivated to give, as well as to gain, or get." [57] Not deceived by appearances, he chooses lead and wins Portia.

In a brief conclusion, Lickorish charges Freud with isolating an element rather than considering the whole, failing to verify his inferences, and failing to show why the same choice (or compulsion) did not apply to the remaining suitors. He then praises Adlerian psychology for providing a means by which the inner consistency of the life styles of the suitors can be revealed.

Consistency is indeed a key word in Adlerian psychology. Even Freud, though he considered Adler's principles grossly incorrect, had to admit that they did have, in contrast to Jung's, a certain consistency. [58] Consistency marks, as well, Adlerian criticism: a consistent compulsion to derogate Freud and his theories which Adler himself showed back in 1911, and a consistent use of literature to prove Adler's ideas as if the writer found it necessary to convince himself of the validity of them.

Of the Adlerian conclusion above, we can only view it as casting pseudo-light on a non-problem. We learn nothing that we do not already know from reading the text ourselves. If Bassanio has chosen lead because appearances are deceiving, he has told us that, as have the other suitors told us their reasons. All of this delineation of life-styles is unnecessary if, as Adlerians posit, every choice is conscious. We can simply take the suitors' reasoning at face value. But since Lickorish is not primarily interested in literary criticism, these objections hardly matter. He chose his target early in his discussion when he announced that through his interpretation he hoped "to offer another illuminating example of the fundamental differences between Freudian and Adlerian literary criticism, which are due to the basic differences in the two psychologies." [59] Lickorish cannot hope to be rewarded, for proving the obvious has always been a thankless task. And why involve literature unnecessarily in an ideological battle? No competent psychoanalytic critic ever uses literature primarily to validate psychoanalysis, though his writings may indirectly serve as verification.

Lickorish himself never really refutes Freud, despite his derisive attack. He merely snipes away at him from the cover of literary interest. He never hits his target; sometimes the bullets are blanks, sometimes they misfire. He misfires, for example, with his patronizing attitude throughout his precis of Freud's essay, feigning scientific objectivity but liberally larding his comments with derogation of Freudian methods of investigation. He deprecates the interpretation of dumbness as death because "Bassanio's choice . . . was not made in a dream, but in waking life,"[60] totally ignoring the clinical evidence for such symbolism and forgetting apparently that Bassanio and his choice are indeed the "dream" of one William Shakespeare. Further, in his desire to drive sexuality from both life and literature, Lickorish is capable of making the incredibly naive statement that "regarding the caskets as sexual symbols, we may point out that in the three inscriptions only one word, 'desire,' can be interpreted as having a sexual meaning."[61] This despite the clinical evidence Freud adduces by reference to *The Interpretation of Dreams.* This despite the evidence of his own ears as he hears about him the vulgar English expression for the female genitals, "box." One should, after all, healthily ignore only so much reality.

That Lickorish does not really have a good grasp of Freudian psychology in the first place is evident in his mislabeling in several places the psychic mechanism Freud used to explain why terrible and necessary Death is represented by the choosing of a beautiful woman. He patronizingly asserts that "this contradiction is overcome by invoking the mechanism of reaction-formation."[62] Yet, as we have pointed out, Freud does not say this but says rather that the explanation lies in *reversal* or the *representation by opposites,* something quite different. *Reaction-formation,* a defense mechanism, and not part of dream work, is the development in the ego of conscious, more socially acceptable trends which are the antithesis of unconscious infantile unacceptable trends; for example, in reaction to unconscious hate for a parent, a conscious oversolicitude might form, a *reaction formation.* On the other hand, *representation by the opposite* is a mode of symbolization appearing in dreams and fantasy products. The term is self-defining and can be illustrated by Freud's example in *The Interpretation of Dreams* that being surrounded by large crowds in a dream is the dreamer's disguise for its opposite, "secrecy."[63] We noted earlier the necessity of understanding well the psychologies of other schools in order to competently refute literary criticism employing them. Lickorish's confusion of these two terms has provided us with a case in point.

But enough; his sniping has been futile and, possibly realizing it, he fires one last shot-gun blast at Freud: "A number of assumptions and simple associations are used to give a plausible connection to the quite disparate events that he links together with regard to a certain goal he apparently has in view."[64] He is not unaware, we hope, that the genius of Freud lay in just that ability to connect disparate events, to perceive analogy. He is not unaware, we hope, that Freud's long, lonely, desperate struggle was his alone for many years simply because others refused to see the relationships between seemingly disparate events. As for Freud's assumptions and associations, they are, of course, only as valid as the evidence used to support them. Three-quarters of a century of research has vindicated the vast majority of Freud's bold assumptions; the years have not been so kind to Adler's. And if associations are so "simple," we invite Lickorish to make a few which, like Freud's, lead us to the nether regions of the mind, showing us again that all men are indeed brothers under the skin.

The final accusation that Freud apparently had "a certain goal" in mind, that he proceeded deductively is belied by the entire history of Freud's methodological procedure. To the very year of his death, his body ravaged by cancer for sixteen years, Freud continued to revise his psychology as empirical evidence came to light that he had earlier erred. Adler's psychology, in contrast, stands almost intact, as it was in 1911, impervious to empirical verification. It can not be profitably used in literary criticism since, as we have demonstrated, it is deficient *per se.* That the essay discussed here is typical of Adlerian criticism we invite the reader to see for himself by perusing a few issues of *The Journal of Individual Psychology,* in which such articles regularly appear. He will find the same dreary procession of deduction, reduction, and patronizing defensiveness at the cost of literary explication.

It is certainly noteworthy that Shakespeare, while Bassanio is making his choice, has the following song sung: "Tell me where is fancy [love] bred,/Or in the heart or in the head?/How begot, how nourished?/Reply, reply." (III, ii, 63-66) Adler's reply is *the head:* that we can *will* our way to love as we can to superiority, or indeed to health itself. Freud's reply is *the heart:* that at times we *cannot will,* but we can with the greatest of courage learn to will; that will is not free, but freed. If we abandon this insight, love, compassion, and understanding become impossible, and we shall soon once again be preparing the strait-jackets for madmen and lighting the faggots for witches.

Otto Rank

The publication, in 1924, of Otto Rank's *The Trauma of Birth* brought to an end the harmony which had prevailed among Freud's early followers since Jung had followed Adler and Stekel into secession a decade before. Jones has chronicled the previous and subsequent events and observed that the book's publication "came as a great surprise to the rest of us. Freud had long thought that the painful experience of being born, when suffocation inevitably brings the infant into mortal peril, was a prototype of all later attacks of fear. Rank, now applying the word 'trauma' to this event, maintained that the rest of life consisted of complicated endeavors to surmount or undo it; incidentally, it was the failure of this endeavor that was responsible for neurosis."[65]

Rank developed his theories very gradually and, at first, remained within Freud's circle, trying to maintain personal and professional relationships. Only by 1929 was he able to separate himself formally from the group, and by this late date he had already begun to shift his emphasis from the birth trauma, the original separation, to the subsequent separations from·parental influences which the individual undergoes in his life. We must, however, examine his ideas from the beginning, so let us return to the birth trauma.

Rank felt that the change from the all-encompassing, effortless bliss of the womb to the painful hurlyburly of post-natal conditions requiring initiative from the infant—a change during which the infant experiences mortal fear—was actually determining for life: as a consequence of it, the most normal of us carry a load of *primal anxiety*. The human goal is reinstatement of embryonic bliss—and the greatest human terror is *separation*. The overwhelming trauma of the birth experience is repressed (*primal repression*). The central human conflict thus becomes the wish to return to the womb versus the terrible fear indelibly associated with the womb by virtue of the event of birth.[66]

Rank sees the excessive anxiety and fear present in childhood as attempts on the child's part to discharge the primal anxiety. A *neurotic* is anyone who fails in this task, which is made doubly difficult by the second traumatic separation, weaning, and triply so by the third, threat of castration, both of which derive additional force from the original birth trauma. That Rank attempts to explain all human emotional problems through this trauma can be seen from the following random illustrations: homosexuality is a return to a love relationship in which the original sexually undifferentiated identity of mother and child is recapitulated; sadism is the expression of rage of one who has been expelled from the womb, coupled with expression of curiosity of the nature of the inside of the body; exhibitionism is the nakedness associated with the primal condition in the womb; sexual intercourse is direct expression and partial gratification of the desire to return to the womb.

Rank refined this theory over the decade of separation from Freud, shifting its emphasis, as has already been noted, from the birth trauma to the individual's creating his own personality by a gradual freeing of himself from dependence upon others.[67] The concept of *will* comes to have great significance in his theories at this time. Will, he believed to be "that part of the personality that struggles against opposing forces that attempt to inhibit the development of separateness. It develops early with the counter-will, which is directed against parental restrictions, and continues until the uniqueness of the personality becomes realized, at which time the individual has attained independence and becomes truly 'creative.' The average man conforms to the will of others, whereas the neurotic either rebels without a goal, thus isolating himself from the mainstream of life, or becomes overly conforming."[68] This personality development proceeds in three stages. In the first, the individual wills what formerly was compulsion for him. The person who makes it at least this far Rank designates *the average man*. In the second stage, the individual becomes conflicted, that is, immersed in feelings of guilt, inferiority, or self-criticism as a result of the assertion of the *counter-will*. The person who fails to pass through this stage is *the neurotic*. In the final stage, the personality becomes harmonious, integrated, unified. The individual who achieves this Rank calls—with no reference whatsoever to talent—*the artist*.

"The 'neurotic' and the 'artist' have this fundamental point in common: they have committed themselves to the pain of separation from the herd—that is, from unreflective incorporation of the views of their society."[69] The "average man," member of the dull brute mass, wants only to be what others are. Once he has defined the latter, Rank has little truck with him, seeming to care little if anything for his type. He is concerned, then, not with the average man, who does not care at all to will, nor with the artist, who has succeeded in willing without guilt, but rather with the neurotic, who, once having begun to will, cannot win through the consequent guilt. The Rankian therapeutic task is thus to enable the neurotic to accept his will problem and, by facing it, to resolve the conflict between his *life fear*—the fear of independence—and his *death fear*—the fear of dependence.

CRITICISM AND COMMENT

Freud was much taken with Rank's birth trauma theory, initially, but the objections of the rest of the psychoanalytic circle forced him to revise his estimate of the achievement. He was quite obviously pre-disposed to such a theory (it was from him that Rank most likely got the germ of the idea), having called birth the first anxiety state as early as 1909 in the second edition of *The Interpretation of Dreams* and referring to it again in the same way in *The Ego and the Id* in 1923. Rank's extreme position of attempting to construct a new psycho-analytic theory and technique about this concept distressed Freud, however, and he criticized the ideas in a lengthy circular letter to the Committee and finally refuted them entirely in *Inhibitions, Symptoms, and Anxiety* (1926) and *Analysis, Terminable and Interminable* (1937).[70] We refer the reader to these essays for criticism of Rank's early position; for his later position, we refer him to Munroe.[71]

As Rankian analysis is now out of favor, so too with Rankian literary criticism. The few pieces that do appear occasionally cannot really be labeled "Rankian" since they are often not based on his psychological theories proper. Such is the case with one of the more recent, H. R. Wolf's "What Maisie Knew: The Rankian Hero." Wolf begins his interpretation of Henry James's work by pointing out that though most critics emphasize that James's characters have conscious control over their destinies, the unconscious is not foreign to his writings. In fact, *What Maisie Knew* exhibits a considerable number of parallel elements to Rank's *The Myth of the Birth of the Hero*: (1) the exposure of the child to the natural forces in the myth is represented in the story by Maisie's being emotionally abandoned by her parents upon their divorce, (2) the lowly couple who save the child is represented by Mrs. Wix, the servant, and Maisie's stepmother, Mrs. Beale, a former servant, (3) the eventual adoption of the child is the central motif of the tale since Maisie's parents, Ida and Beale, eventually marry again but become disenchanted, and *their* new mates, Sir Claude and Mrs. Beale, respectively, have an affair of their own; consequently there are three sets of parents—real, step-, and surrogate, the lovers, (4) the parent of high birth is represented by Maisie's idealization of Sir Claude, and (5) the biologic and protective parents are connected through Maisie's ambivalence toward the new parent couples.

Wolf sees in this erotic attraction between Maisie and Sir Claude a fusion of the myth of the birth of the hero and the family romance: "The stepfather and the idolized father of childhood fantasy are embodied in one figure who is romantically and sexually attractive to his stepchild; or to put it in another way: if the two fathers of the myth (real-noble and unreal-lowly) are fused in one figure (unreal-noble, Sir Claude), then in loving romantically and erotically her stepfather, the child also loves her real father. . . . Because the father whom the child loves is not her real father, she can more readily express her erotic responses to him"[72] (Wolf believes this attraction to be entirely "innocent," to be sure, though we ourselves might observe that Maisie does express murderous impulses toward Mrs. Beale, Sir Claude's mistress.) He concludes that what Maisie knows is her desire, but what she does not know is *why* she desires. What she renounces in giving up Sir Claude is not the forbidden wishes, for "James uses—unconsciously, to be sure—the abandoned child of the myth to protect his exploration of oedipal thought."[73]

But one of the things that strikes us first about Wolf's interpretation is the unnecessary invocation of Rank and *The Myth* and his constant willingness to call a spade a garden implement. Never once is the word "incest" mentioned though it ought to be perfectly clear that it is the dominant motif. Perfectly clear as well is Rank's conclusion in his study of myth that these stories had their origin in the incestual impulses constellated in the family romance. Why Wolf is content to compare the parallels in structure but not the more important ones in meaning, however, is not quite clear. The little dab of Rank does not help in the least, except to shift the focus away from Freudian (read: "sexual") implications abounding in the story. James did not need to disguise his exploration of oedipal material beyond splitting the real parents into fictional pairs as he did. That he used the myth of the hero "unconsciously" is insupportable; that he used the family romance unconsciously, however, is quite credible since, like you and me, he had experienced it. Had Wolf chosen to follow the implications of Rank's study to their end, he might have produced a good Freudian analysis, for *The Myth* was written when Rank was still within the fold. As it is, he chose to use only the superficial aspects of it and consequently produced a superficial analysis.

Notes

1. Patrick Mullahy, *Oedipus: Myth and Complex* (New York: Grove Press, 1955); Ruth Munroe, *Schools of Psychoanalytic Thought* (New York: Holt, 1955).

2. Stanley Edgar Hyman, "Psychoanalysis and the Climate of Tragedy," in Benjamin Nelson, ed., *Freud and the 20th Century* (Cleveland: World, 1957), p. 174.
3. Hyman, "Psychoanalysis," p. 185.
4. Frederick C. Crews, "Anaesthetic Criticism," in Crews, ed., *Psychoanalysis and Literary Process* (Cambridge, Mass.: Winthrop, 1970), pp. 1-24.
5. Hyman, "Psychoanalysis," p. 185.
6. Ludwig Binswanger, *Sigmund Freud: Reminiscences of a Friendship* (New York: Grune and Stratton, 1957), p. 31.
7. Sheldon T. Selesnick, "Carl Gustav Jung: Contributions to Psychoanalysis," in Franz Alexander *et al.*, eds., *Psychoanalytic Pioneers* (New York: Basic Books, 1966), pp. 63-77.
8. Ernest Jones, *The Life and Work of Sigmund Freud* (New York: Basic Books, 1955), II, p. 127.
9. Jones, *Life and Work*, p. 130.
10. Edward Glover, *Freud or Jung?* (Cleveland: World, 1965), pp.21-51.
11. Violet S. deLaszlo, ed., *The Basic Writings of C. G. Jung* (New York: Modern Library, 1959), p. 287.
12. Jolande Jacobi, *The Psychology of C. G. Jung* (New Haven: Yale University Press, 1962), p. 34.
13. Munroe, *Schools*, p. 553.
14. deLaszlo, *Basic Writings*, pp. 228-89.
15. deLaszlo, *Basic Writings*, p. 9n.
16. Jacobi, *Psychology*, p. 49.
17. Jacobi, *Psychology*, p. 91.
18. deLaszlo, *Basic Writings*, p. 275.
19. deLaszlo, *Basic Writings*, pp. 143-44.
20. deLaszlo, *Basic Writings*, p. 138.
21. Jacobi, *Psychology*, pp. 106-9.
22. Jacobi, *Psychology*, p. 111.
23. Munroe, *Schools*, pp. 547-48.
24. Glover, *Freud or Jung?*, p. 19.
25. Glover, *Freud or Jung?*, pp. 141-53. See also Sheldon T. Selesnick, "Jung: Contributions," pp. 75-76; and Franz Alexander and Sheldon T. Selesnick, *The History of Psychiatry* (New York: Harper, 1966), Appendix B, pp. 407-9.
26. Wilfred L. Guerin, Earle G. Labor, Lee Morgan, and John R. Willingham, *A Handbook of Critical Approaches to Literature* (New York: Harper, 1966), pp. 136-37.
27. Glover, *passim;* see especially pp. 31, 67.
28. Aldous Huxley, *Tomorrow and Tomorrow and Tomorrow and Other Essays* (New York: Harper, 1956), p. 178.
29. Viktor von Weizsaecker, "Reminiscences of Freud and Jung," in Benjamin Nelson, ed., *Freud and the 20th Century* (Cleveland: World, 1957), pp. 72-73.

30. Glover, *Freud or Jung?*, p. 173.
31. Guerin *et al.*, *Handbook*, pp. 140-41.
32. Frederick C. Crews, *The Sins of the Fathers: Hawthorne's Psychological Themes* (New York: Oxford University Press, 1966), p. 104.
33. Jacobi, *Psychology*, p. 44.
34. Lawrence S. Kubie, "Problems and Techniques of Psychoanalytic Validation and Progress," in E. Pumpian-Mindlin, ed., *Psychoanalysis as Science* (Stanford: Stanford University Press, 1952), p. 67.
35. Glover, *Freud or Jung?*, pp. 39-44; Selesnick, "Jung: Contributions," p. 69.
36. Norman N. Holland, *The Dynamics of Literary Response* (New York: Oxford University Press, 1968), p. 244.
37. Glover, *Freud or Jung?*, pp. 165-86; and Frederick G. Hoffman, *Freudianism and the Literary Mind*, 2nd ed. (Baton Rouge: Louisiana State University Press, 1945, 1967), pp. 328-30.
38. Glover, *Freud or Jung?*, p. 184.
39. Crews, "Anaesthetic Criticism," p. 8.
40. For details of Jung's attempt to expunge sex, see both Selesnick, "Jung: Contributions," p. 67, and Jones, *Life and Work*, II, p. 144.
41. Jones, *Life and Work*, p. 151.
42. Sheldon T. Selesnick "Alfred Adler: The Psychology of the Inferiority Complex," in Franz Alexander *et al.*, eds., *Psychoanalytic Pioneers* (New York: Basic Books, 1966), p. 79.
43. Alfred Adler, *The Science of Living*, ed., Heinz L. Ansbacher (1929; reprinted, New York: Anchor Books, 1969), p. 131.
44. Munroe, *Schools*, p. 435.
45. Adler, *Science of Living*, p. 15.
46. Selesnick, "Alfred Alder," pp. 85-86.
47. Munroe, *Schools*, p. 436; see also, pp. 363-64, 371-80, 436-38.
48. See especially, *The Standard Edition of the Complete Psychological Works of Sigmund Freud*, translated by James Strachey, Anna Freud, Alix Strachey, and Alan Tyson, 24 volumes (London: Hogarth Press, 1953-), XIV, pp. 50-58; XVII, p. 200f; XIX, pp. 91-92. All subsequent references are to this edition.
49. Jones, *Life and Work*, II, p. 134.
50. *Standard Edition*, XIV, p. 58.
51. John R. Lickorish, "The Casket Scenes from *The Merchant of Venice:* Symbolism or Life Style," *The Journal of Individual Psychology*, 25, No. 2 (1969), pp. 202-12.
52. *Standard Edition*, XII, p. 292.
53. *Standard Edition*, XII, p. 299.
54. *Standard Edition*, XII, p. 301.
55. Lickorish, "Casket Scenes," p. 206.
56. Lickorish, "Casket Scenes," p. 207.

57. Lickorish, "Casket Scenes," p. 210.
58. Jones, *Life and Work*, II, p. 60.
59. Lickorish, "Casket Scenes," p. 202.
60. Lickorish, "Casket Scenes," p. 205.
61. Lickorish, "Casket Scenes," p. 204.
62. Lickorish, "Casket Scenes," p. 205.
63. *Standard Edition*, IV, pp. 245-46.
64. Lickorish, "Casket Scenes," p. 205.
65. Ernest Jones, *Life and Work*, III, p. 58; for a more complete account of the schism, see III, pp. 44-77.
66. Munroe, *Schools*, p. 576.
67. An admirable, concise statement by a Rankian of Rank's later position is available in Munroe, *Schools*, pp. 579-80.
68. Franz Alexander and Sheldon T. Selesnick, *The History of Psychiatry* (New York: Harper, 1966), p. 251.
69. Munroe, *Schools*, p. 585.
70. The letter is quoted *in toto* in Jones, *Life and Work*, III, pp. 59-63. For Freud's further criticism, see *Standard Edition*, XX, pp. 135f, 150-53; *Standard Edition*, XXIII, pp. 216-17. For additional disputation of the birth trauma theory, see Abram Kardiner, Aaron Karush, and Lionel Ovesey, "A Methodological Study of Freudian Theory," *International Journal of Psychiatry*, 2, No. 5 (1966), pp. 534-35.
71. Munroe, *Schools*, pp. 594-98.
72. H. R. Wolf, "What Maisie Knew: The Rankian Hero," *American Imago*, 23, No. 3 (1966), pp. 230-31.
73. Wolfe, "What Maisie Knew," p. 234.

Index

Abraham, Karl, 206
Adler, Alfred, 158, 289, 290, 299-301
Adlerian literary criticism, 301-306
aggression as drive, 14, 15, 21
Alexander, Franz, 224
Allen, Harvey, 189
ambivalence, 8, 47, 70, 133
anality, 20-24
analogizing, 229
Analytic Psychology, 289-294
Anderson, Sherwood, 228
archetypal criticism, 182-188, 211-215, 234-238, 294-299
Archetypal Patterns in Poetry, 182-188
"Archetype and Signature," 234-235
archetypes, 183-184, 211-215, 234-236, 291-293
Arieti, Silvano
"Manic-Depressive Psychosis," 66

Aristotle, 222
Arlow, Jacob, 26, 83, 214-215
The Armed Vision, 289
Art and Artist, 165
The Artist, 165

Bacchae, 216
Barchilon, Jose, 152, 253-255
"Beauty and the Beast," 90-94 *et passim*
Beckett, Samuel
Molloy, 20, 21, 40
Bodkin, Maud, 182-188
Bonaparte, Princess Marie, 189-194
Bonime, Walter
"The Psychodynamics of Neurotic Depression," 66, 67, 71
The Brothers Karamazov, 163, 167, 205
Brooks, Van Wyck, 239, 240
Brown, Norman O., 150
Burke, Kenneth, 239, 240

Campbell, Joseph, 149, 211-215
The Castle of Otranto, 119
catharsis, 222
Cather, Willa, 232-233
Chamisso, Adelbert, 167
"Cinderella or The Little Glass
    Slipper," 19
classicism, 217
collective unconscious, 290-291
complex, 290
condensation, 179
Conrad, Joseph
    "Nigger of the Narcissus," 5, 6,
        13, 18, 37, 47-62
    "The Secret Sharer," 136
conscience (super ego), 15, 35
conversion symptom, 18
Cooper, James Fenimore, 237
Coleridge, Samuel Taylor
    "Christabel," 38
counter phobia, 18
courtly love, 212-213, 247-249
Creative Mythology, 214
The Creative Unconscious, 131,
    195-200, 220, 230
Crews, Frederick, 149, 193, 256-
    260, 276, 289, 294, 296,
    299

daydreams, 195-199, 221-222
defense mechanisms, 27-37, *see
    also* particular defenses
delusion, 49, 81
delusion of grandeur, 75
dementia praecox, 290
denial, 22, 37, 48, 49, 60
depression, 66, 67
displacement, 29, 30, 109
dissenters from Freudian Psycho-
    analytic Theory, 287-313
Don Quixote, 205
Dostoevsky, Fyodor, 162-163,
    167, 229

Doppelgänger, 135-144, 167
Dr. Jekyll and Mr. Hyde, 136
drama
    pathological, 156
    psychological, 156
dream theory and literature, 156,
    267, 270
dual instinct theory, 14, 15
Durrell, Lawrence
    Alexandria Quartet, 41, 42
    Justine, 63
    *A Key to Modern British
        Fiction*, 42
Dujardin, Eduard, 203
*The Dynamics of Literary Re-
    sponse*, 182, 196, 272-277

Edel, Leon, 232-233, 275
*Edgar Poe, Etude Psychoanaly-
    tique*, 189-194
ego, 16 *et passim*
Die Elixer des Teufels, 161
The Erotic Motive in Literature,
    149, 178-181
Euripides, 216, 265

Faber, M. D., 261-266
fairy-tale, 88 *et passim*, 134
Falstaff, 224
fantasy, 83, 127, 129, 144
    in the creative process, 157-
        158, 195-200, 221-223
Faulkner, William, 203
Faust, 206
Fenichel, Otto
    *The Psychoanalytic Theory of
        Neurosis*, 23, 50
Ferenczi, Sandor, 191
Fiction and the Unconscious, 182,
    195, 226-231
Fiedler, Leslie, 149, 234-238, 294
"The Figure in the Carpet," 245
Finnegan's Wake, 203

Flaubert, Gustave, 201
Fliess, Wilhelm, 154
Ford, Ford Madox
    The Good Soldier, 63
"Four and Twenty Hours in a
    Woman's Life," 163
Frailberg, Louis, 151, 239-242
France, Anatole, 206
free association, 74, 77
Freud, Sigmund
    *Analysis of a Phobia in a Five-
        Year-Old Boy*, 25
    *Analysis, Terminable and
        Interminable*, 309
    *Civilization and Its Discon-
        tents*, 15
    "Contribution to the Study of
        the Origin of Sexual
        Perversions," 34
    "Creative Writers and Day-
        dreaming," 157-158,
        197, 227, 230
    "Delusions and Dreams in
        Jensen's *Gradiva*," 156-
        157
    "Dostoevsky and Parricide,"
        162-163, 251
    *A General Introduction to
        Psychoanalysis*, 24, 25,
        112
    on *Hamlet*, 155, 156, 163, 169
    *Inhibitions, Symptoms, and
        Anxiety*, 309
    The Interpretation of Dreams,
        155, 169, 195, 202, 203,
        305, 309
    "Introductory Lectures, on
        Psychoanalysis," 105,
        106
    Moses and Monotheism, 297
    "An Outline of Psychoanaly-
        sis," 106
    on *Oedipus Rex*, 105, 106,

Freud, Sigmund:
    112, 155, 163
    "Psychopathic Characters on
        the Stage," 156
    on "Die Richterin," 155
    on Rosmersholm, 155, 159-
        161
    on "The Sandman," 161-162
    "Some Character-Types Met
        with in Psychoanalytic
        Work," 158-159
    "The Theme of the Three
        Caskets," 158, 208, 217,
        302-306
    "Three Contributions to a
        Theory of Sex," 202,
        203
    "Three Essays on the Theory
        of Sexuality," 125, 126
    Totem and Taboo, 297
    The "Uncanny," 161
Freud and the Critic, 204
Freud or Jung?, 187, 294
*Freudianism and the Literary
    Mind*, 201

Geisterseher, 206
Glover, Edward, 187, 287, 290,
    294, 295, 297
Goethe, J. W. V., 206
"The Gold Bug," 190-191
Gothic, 119, 120, 131-134, 237
Gould, Thomas, 106, 110, 111,
    113, 115
Gradiva, 156-157
Great Expectations, 206
Guerard, Albert, 48
guilt, 77, 83, 129, 132, 140

Hadas, Moses, 106
Hamlet, 32, 68, 155, 163, 167,
    169-175, 186, 206, 217,
    251

Hamlet and Oedipus, 170
Hawthorne, Nathaniel, 228, 233,
    256-258, 296-297
Henry IV, 261-262
Henry IV, Part 2, 223-224
The Hero with a Thousand Faces,
    214
Hoffman, E. T. A., 161, 167,
    206-208
Hoffman, Frederick J., 201-204
Holland, Norman, 157, 182, 196,
    199, 267-277, 297
Homoerotism, 33, 34, 235-238
Huckleberry Finn, 152, 235-236,
    253, 255
Huxley, Aldous, 295
Hyman, Stanley E., 182, 186-187,
    289
hypnotism, 13

Ibsen, Henrik, 159, 206
identification, 15, 120, 136
    with the aggressor, 15, 42, 72
The Idiot, 229
incorporation, 28
In Praise of Love, 213, 247-249
incest, 155, 160, 166, 173-174,
    217, 228, 230, 237, 257,
    310
incest motif, 132, 134, 135, 138,
    143
Individual Psychology, 229-301
individuation, 292-293
inhibition, 70, 72, 73, 75
irrational, 84
isolation, 36, 37
*Das Inzest Motiv in Dichtung und
    Sage,* 167
Israfel, 189
"I want to know why," 228

James, Henry, 245, 309-310

jealousy, 208-210
Jekels, Ludwig, 159
Jensen, Wilhelm, 156, 157
Jones, Ernest, 32, 155, 169-177,
    186, 287, 290, 307
Joyce, James, 203
Julius Caesar, 175-176
Jung, C. G., 289-294
Jungian literary criticism, 151,
    183-188, 211-215, 234-238,
    294-299; *see also*
    Archetypal criticism

Kafka, Franz, 203, 229
    "A Hunger Artist," 5, 6, 7, 10,
        11, 13, 14, 39, 80-87
    "In a Penal Colony," 34, 35
    "A Country Doctor," 38
Kanzer, Mark, 243-246
Kermode, Frank, 88
King Lear, 217, 245, 302-303
Kovel, Joel, 151, 253-255
Kris, Ernst, 149, 180, 199, 201,
    220-225, 230, 256
Krutch, J. W., 239, 240
Kubie, Lawrence, 23, 40, 41,
    180, 223, 297

Lady Chatterley's Lover, 250
Lady Macbeth, 159, 216
Lawrence, D. H., 203, 250-252
lex talionis, 85
libido, Jungian, 292
life style, Adlerian, 300, 301, 302,
    303-304
*Love and Death in the American
    Novel,* 236-238
Lesser, Simon, 149, 157, 182,
    195, 199, 226-231
Lewisohn, Ludwig, 239, 240
Literary Biography, 232
literary form, 198-199

"Literature and Psychology,"
258-259
Literature and Psychology, 149,
216-219, 232
Lucas, F. L., 216-219

Macbeth, 159, 274-275
manic-depressive psychosis, 65
The Man Who Died, 250
masculine protest, 301
The Masks of God, 211, 214
masochism, 33, 34, 35
Masochism in Sex and Society,
205
The Master Builder, 206
"The Maypole of Marymount,"
257
Measure for Measure, 199
Melville, Herman
"Bartleby the Scrivener," 5, 7,
10, 11, 13, 14, 30, 39,
63-79, 136
The Merchant of Venice, 206,
208, 302-306
The Merry Wives of Windsor, 206
Meyer, Conrad F., 155
The Monk, 119, 133
moral masochism, 18
Mordell, Albert, 149, 178-181
Morrison, Claudia, 204
Mullahy, Patrick, 288
Munroe, Ruth L., 288, 294, 309
Murdoch, Iris, 41
Myth
criticism, 211-215
purposes, 214-215
*The Myth of the Birth of the
Hero,* 165-167, 309-310

narcissism, 15, 19, 213
neurosis, 11, 13, 14, 35, 76, 84,
86

"Never Bet the Devil Your Head,"
191-192

obsession, 18, 52-55, 125, 127
Oedipus at Colonus, 243-244
Oedipus complex, 9, 15, 24-27,
30, 31, 32, 41, 155, 173,
203, 296, 310
Oedipus in Nottingham, 250-252
Oedipus: Myth and Complex, 288
Oedipus Rex, 5, 7, 11, 27, 28, 30,
32, 36, 39, 105-118, 155,
163, 228, 229-230, 243,
244, 263-265
omnipotence of thought, 74
oral aggression, 80 *et passim*
orality, 19 *et passim*
organ inferiority, Adlerian, 300
Othello, 208-210
Our Lady's Juggler, 206
overdetermination, 34, 35

parricide, 162, 166, 228, 230, 257
perversion, 18
phobia, 10
pleasure principle, 19, 32
Poe, Edgar Allen, 12, 189-194
The Possessed, 167
Praz, Mario, 132, 133
primal scene, 274
primary process, 16-19
The Professor's House, 232-233
projection, 35, 36, 38, 117, 129
"The Prussian Officer," 250
*Psychoanalysis and American
Literary Criticism,* 239-241
Psychoanalysis and Literary Process, 259-260
*Psychoanalytic Explorations in
Art,* 149, 220-225, 230, 256
psychoanalytic literary critic
qualifications of, 151

The Psychology of Sex Relations,
    208
psychosis, 18, 75

Railo, Elimo, 133
Rank, Otto, 105, 165-168, 214,
    306-308
Rankian literary criticism, 309-
    310
rationalization, 10, 14, 59, 72,
    141
reaction-formation, 30, 31, 69,
    70, 179, 301, 305
realism, 217
regression, 33
reification, 235-236
Reigen, 206
Reik, Theodor, 162, 180, 205-
    210
repression, 13, 29, 30, 71, 140,
    144, 173, 202-203, 290
resistance, 111, 113
reversal, 127, 128, 207
Richard III, 158, 217
romanticism, 217
Romeo and Juliet, 267-270
Rosmersholm, 159-161

Sachs, Hanns, 131, 157, 167, 180,
    195-200, 220, 221
"The Sandman," 161-162
The Scarlet Letter, 258
Schiller, Friedrich, 206
*Schools of Psychoanalytic
    Thought,* 288
Schnitzler, Arthur, 206
secondary gains, 14
The Secret Self, 206
The Seventh Seal, 52
sexuality as drive, 14, 15, 21
Shakespeare, William, 174-175,
    199, 244-245, 262, 270-

Shakespeare, William:
    272, 302, 303, 305, 306
    See also individual works
Shelley, Mary
    Frankenstein, 5, 36, 39, 119-
    145
Shorer, Mark, 63
Shylock, 206
*The Significance of Psychoanaly-
    sis for the Mental Sciences,*
    167
The Sins of the Fathers, 256- 260,
    296
slip of the tongue, 110
Sons and Lovers, 250-252
Sophocles
    See Oedipus Rex
splitting, 159, 173, 175-176;
    See also double
Stevenson, Robert L., 167, 245
sublimation, 10, 87, 125, 213
suicide, 262-266
Suicide and Greek Tragedy, 262-
    266
Summers, Montague, 132
symbol, Jungian, 292
symbolization, 17, 18, 35, 52, 60,
    61, 83, 86, 117, 127, 128

A Tale of Two Cities, 205
The Tales of Hoffman, 162, 206
The Tempest, 5, 39, 88-104, 199
*The Temptation of Saint
    Anthony,* 210
Thompson, Clara,
    *Psychoanalysis: Evolution and
    Development,* 25
"The Three Women in a Man's
    Life," 162, 206-208
transference, 15
The Trauma of Birth, 306-307
The Trial, 229

Trilling, Lionel, 239, 240-241
Twain, Mark, 253

Ulysses, 203
unconscious, 10, 13, 14, 18, 48,
    55, 58, 70, 77, 83, 86, 115,
    121, 144

Vagina Dentata, 192
Valency, Maurice, 31, 213, 247-
    249
Varma, Devendra, 132

Watt, Ian, 48
Weiss, Daniel, 250-252
Weizsaecker, Viktor von, 295
What Maisie Knew, 309-310
Wilhelm, Meister, 206
"William Wilson," 136
Wilson, Edmund, 239, 240
Women in Love, 250

Yearsley, Macleod, *The Folklore
    of Fairy-Tale,* 88, 89, 90

Zweig, Stefan, 163